BY GOD'S GRACE

CHRIS WEBBER

WPG

Webber Publishing Group

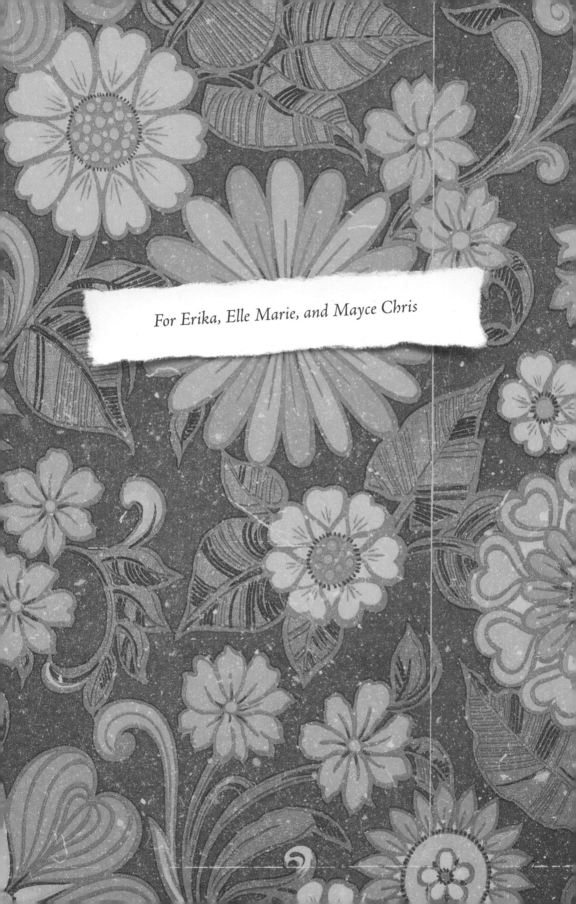

For Erika, Elle Marie, and Mayce Chris

BOOK FOUR THE FAB FIVE

BOOK FIVE THE LEAGUE

BOOK SIX THE BLESSED JOURNEY CONTINUES

I exhaled and smiled. I was in my office when I got the news. It was Wednesday, May 12th around 1 p.m. John Doleva called and welcomed me to basketball's most prestigious club: the Hall of Fame.

He said he couldn't wait to make the call and wished he could've done it sooner. He thanked me for respecting and handling the process with dignity.

I heard what he said, but I couldn't digest the enormity of the moment in a three-minute conversation.

I got off the phone…

Took in a deep breath…

Exhaled…

Laughed…

And said a prayer of thanks.

I then called my father who was absolutely beside himself. He relived stories reminding me of the time he took me to my first practice, the laughs we had in our small house in Detroit. And then midsentence, he asked, "Boy, what's wrong with you? You're supposed to be happy. You're in the Hall of Fame. You okay?" He continued, "Oooh, you ain't going to get it for a while. It didn't sink in yet. It'll probably take a few days." We laughed and then said a prayer of gratitude.

We jumped off the phone, and I popped a bottle of Ace, toasted with my wife, and told Siri to play some Earth, Wind & Fire. The twins were running around, dancing, yelling, and cheering, though they didn't have a clue as to what we were celebrating. They were just happy for Daddy.

I thought I had reconciled the news…somewhat. I mean, I was happy and grateful, but it felt like this moment wasn't about an award. It was about recognizing something bigger than myself. I needed to connect the dots in my thought pattern. Something just wasn't clicking for me. The Hall of Fame was never my dream. That was too big of a dream to dream.

I didn't have a full understanding of the honor I was being given. My brain wasn't articulating my gratefulness to my spirit. I needed a life audit. A self once-over. My heart needed a full account of the past for true reconciliation. My soul sought context for understanding and closure. I knew that I won, but I needed to know the final score.

Then four days later, at an announcement for the new class of inductees, I was in Springfield, Massachusetts, on the hallowed grounds of the Hall of Fame. Before the festivities, during the commotion of the moment, I snuck away. Alone, I walked the hall and checked out the displays and memorabilia. I paid my respect and reminisced at a new exhibit dedicated to the life and game of my man Kobe Bean Bryant. After prayers of thanks and reflection, I returned to the room where the new inductees were huddled up. My wife noticed my Kool-Aid smile and took out her camera as I sat at a table with some men of distinction...

Kevin Garnett, Ben Wallace, Chris Bosh, Paul Pierce, and I listened in awe to the G.O.A.T. Bill Russell as he blessed us with true Superman-like recounts of his life. He pulled out his phone and showed us pictures where he was competing in the high jump in high school. He set records. He was cold. He didn't jump traditionally with his back toward the target, he just jumped over, regular style. Incredible. And, he only wore one shoe. I joked and asked which foot did he jump off of—the foot with the shoe or the bare foot? And what if it rained? He laughed and continued to go on about other amazing stories from his days in high school, college, and pros with his beloved Boston Celtics.

Paul talked about his love for the Cs and how special it was to play in Boston. Ben and I chopped it up about old times as teammates. We talked about how he was undrafted and was taking a leap of faith leaving his team overseas to try out for the Bullets. He told a funny story about how I got him to start growing his famous 'fro. I had forgotten about that.

KG went on a passionate rant about his childhood that included my childhood.

His recount brought it all together for me. KG—the bad man from Chicago by way of South Carolina, the skinny kid who went straight from high school to the pros, the newly inducted Hall of Famer—added clarity and perspective to this awesome accomplishment that I was trying to grasp.

The Big Ticket told a story that only a few had been privy to. Kevin said his AAU coach made him watch a tape of me and my team, the Super

Friends, go up against Glen Robinson and his team in Chicago in a game for the ages. Kevin said he watched the game a hundred times. He said it made him step his game up. He recounted how smooth Big Dog was, how I tried to tear the hinges off of the rim, my mean mugs, handles, and passing. We put on a show. KG remembered the most distinct details of that day, and anyone who knows K knows that he paints pictures like Slick Rick. He tells stories in 5k, and he told specifics that I had forgotten.

You see, I had replayed and shared the legend of this epic game many times over the last thirty years, but I could never express the moment to my satisfaction. I could never be graphic or descriptive enough. He took me back to that time, and it was then, midreminiscing, in the midst of Bill Russell, Bosh, and Big Ben laughing at KG shouting commentary on that game, era, culture, and impact, that it hit me. Right then, my thoughts were affirmed.

We continued to talk about our childhood and the great times we had growing up, our heroes, the food, and our cities and families. We also talked about the challenges of our individual journeys. Every one of us personally marked will, fight, discipline, and perseverance as our most treasured traits. For me then, everything connected.

I believe when attempting to accomplish anything great, one must get low and stay focused. Sometimes focus—keeping blinders on to avoid distractions—can make it difficult to take a second to acknowledge great moments, to let them sink in and make sense, because you fear you're not concentrating on the battle at hand. It connected. That's what my pops was saying to me on the phone. It had connected for him.

This honor is for a lifetime of commitment. Not just for one game, one season, or championship. This honor speaks to the excellence and endurance that lies at the heart of it all: my love for the game. I knew I had a résumé that only a few could dream of when it comes to playing the game I love. I knew my journey. I knew the nights I stayed in the gym. I knew the sacrifice. I knew the incredible results. But I also knew what I had to overcome as a perceived twelve-year-old "walking lottery ticket" who'd come to know death, missteps, pain, betrayal, and jealously all too well.

I overcame in moments. I thrived in moments.

This honor would be dedicated to my village, to those who helped nurture and strengthen my gifts. Those who shared or helped me prepare as best as they could for life's moments. That's what we were discussing: the moments.

His vivid recollection triggered and set off an avalanche of memories. Moments of my life's journey flashed through my conscious in slow motion. I thought of God's Love.

I stood back and thought, *Wow, that sixteen-year-old kid made it to the Hall of Fame.* I had experienced so much by then at a young age. That game in Chicago was just the beginning of it all. I thought about God's Grace. The journey was between us.

I think that a song should be something more
Than a beautiful melody
To tell the story of truth and reality
I think that a song should be sung
By a man who knows the meaning of sorrow
And the meaning of true love
I think that a song should be shared among friends,
Then when friends are gone
The melody and meaning still lingers on
Tales of the good times
Telling of the bad
Tales of when we're happy and when we're sad
Everything you touch is a song
You touched my life one day
All my burdens, they just rolled away
They rolled away
You wrote a song that even the bees could hum
Everything you touch is a song
Everything you touch is a song

"Everything You Touch Is A Song"
The Winans

FAMILY

BOOK ONE

To understand who I really am, you must first meet my parents. I have never admired or respected a man as much as I admire and respect my father. I've always had a sense of strength, but I never fully appreciated my source. After hearing his stories repeatedly at family reunions and dinners or in our private conversations over the years, I thought I knew the man inside and out. Then, while writing this book, I researched his life and started to fully grasp all that he's been through. The findings, for me, developed a sense of understanding. Putting everything in context, what he's overcome deserves a standing ovation.

Booker T. Washington said, "Success is not to be measured by the position that one has reached in life but rather the obstacles he's overcome." Success? My father is the Edwin Moses of obstacles. After collecting all of his info, I now understand his breakdown that included tears and a death grasp bear hug that snatched the air out of my lungs at the 1993 NBA draft. He's as strong and loving as they come. This is how he came to be my father.

Mayce Webber Jr. was born November 20, 1946, in Tunica, Mississippi, on the Abbey plantation and raised in a one-bedroom shotgun house. Once we were in Tunica, visiting my father's childhood land, and I asked him what a shotgun house was. He replied with his typical frankness. "Imagine a shoebox. Look at it where length is facing you. That's the shape. Now, imagine if you could shoot a shotgun through the front door and hit the back door. You got a shotgun house."

With the floors suspended on sixteen bricks, four stacked in each corner, the local midwife and expectant mother could be assured the incessant rain that day would not flood my pop's arrival. I can imagine the smile on my grandfather Mayce's face—impatiently waiting on his first-born son, proud the Webber name would go on. I can also envision my grandmother sitting in a chair, rocking my dad back and forth, nursing, and humming a hymn, thankful and grateful for her new baby boy. And I know she was experiencing the torment of a host of different emotions as well: pain, sorrow, and guilt of abandonment—regretting who and what she was forced to leave behind.

At twenty-three, my grandmother Willie Lee (better known as Bill) had lived the lives of a thousand shattered souls. Granddaughter of slaves, a hairdresser and plantation worker by trade, she married at age fifteen, bearing four children in six years. She also endured six years of UFC-type ass-whoopings as the drunken coward relentlessly beat her beautiful, caramel-colored face in.  He would kick her small 5'4" frame or drag her by the hair. And to have irony spit in the face of sympathy, this creep kicked her out of the house and kept all four of her children. As she ran out of the house pleading and crying, he swore to her that he never loved her and she would never see her kids again.

Scared and lost, with no place to go, she got word to her brother Oliver about the situation. He assured her everything would be okay and told her to travel four hours up the road to Tunica. Oliver later introduced her to Mayce Sr., a World War II veteran from Columbus, Mississippi, and the rest is a wrap.

Tunica now seemed to be worlds away from the hell she once knew, and the children she once held. Now in a home she always longed for, this shoebox behind the big oak tree is where she hoped her redemption was being born in my father, Mayce. Shortly after my father arrived, his brothers, Leroy and Paul, and sisters, Mattie and Rochelle, followed. Bill now had four more blessings to the angels she'd lost. And more blessings followed: after my father's sixth birthday, she received a letter saying that her other babies—  the ones she thought she would never see again—would be coming to spend the summer with her! From now on she could see them as much as she wanted. Her beautiful smile (I was told she had one) cracked like lightning in the Tunica night as she had all of her children together for spots at a time.

She regained her soul and continued to give in spite of having nothing. In her community, Bill was known for helping anyone in need by giving food to those who stopped by. My father said he would be jealous of neighbors who came over to eat. "It wasn't like we were better off than anyone," he told me. "She was just kind enough to share. She was also known for her chatter—giving you a talkathon. She would talk your shoes off, talk 'til you fell asleep, and she'd wake you up to talk some more." That's a trait my father gained, honestly.

My father was the eldest on his side and took his responsibilities seriously. Like his parents, he has known hard work his whole life. When he was just two years old, his mother would strap him to her back, walk up and down rows of cotton bushes in the unforgiving southern heat, and pick cotton until the sun went down. At age four, he would have to separate the cotton from the thorns and place them into bowls. By five, he joined the majority of blacks in the south sharecroppers. The conditions of sharecropping were horrific and inhumane. As my father explained it, sharecropping was an evil, rigged system that promised financial freedom but delivered unrelenting work. It became a popular practice in America after slavery. Black farmers were "given" land as a trade to plow the fields of those who owned the plantation. There were several catches:

1. You didn't own the land.
2. You never got to see the books.
3. You didn't know fair market value for the bales of cotton that you collected.
4. You weren't allowed to start a business of your own.
5. Again, you never owned the land. That was a lie.

My father only received about $110 (equal to about thirty-seven bales of cotton) for a year of backbreaking labor. And owning the land was a lie. But you best believe the plantation boss always kept poor sharecroppers hopeful by promising a bigger crop the next year. Doubling as the town's store, the plantation boss would charge you double for medicine. And along with other popular crooked-ass practices, they'd fine you double for work lost on sick days. It's a cold world and dirty game. My father learned that lesson early when the reality of responsibility shook him out of his childhood in one of the cruelest ways possible.

MEMPHIS, TENN
1961

My father was eleven years old and working in the field when his uncle, Ezelle, called out and approached him from a distance. He placed his hand on my dad's shoulder, gently removed the tools out of his hands, walked him behind the old oak tree away from the boys, and said quietly, "Your mother died." She had gone in for an appendectomy, caught pneumonia, and passed away. In that moment, my father's childhood died too. He had no idea how to get in touch with his father, who spent up to four months away, farming oranges in Florida. Young and shaken, my father was unsure how to address the enormity of the moment. Mayce summoned all the strength he could, gathered his four younger siblings, sat them down on the floor, and explained that their mother was gone.

"They really couldn't understand," he told me. "They were only ages five to nine. We cried ourselves to sleep that night."

I spoke to my uncle Leroy about that tragic day. He spoke of his brother with high praise. "All I can say is that your father is an honorable man. Growing up, we children had chores and the adults had their work, but the thing that amazed me was that we had no adult that came and took care of us after my mother died," he said. "For years, it was just us kids. The next morning after the funeral, before the sun came up, I heard your father chopping wood. He came in and started the stove and made breakfast as if he was our parents. And he did that until we were grown."

At age eleven, my father was responsible for doing the girls' hair, washing clothes, making sure everybody went to school, and getting animals fed, fields worked, dinner cooked, homework done, and prayers said, and finally killing all monsters under the bed. He took odd jobs at the dock too, like loading motorboats into the water. This became the routine of young Mayce: older brother and father. He did such a great job that no one in the community realized what was happening...until one Sunday.

"I took my sisters to church, and I did their hair that morning," my father told me. "Well, I guess I scared the church members because the two girls came in the church with horns sticking up on their head looking like little devils, and I guess people knew that our family needed a lot of help and that I was in over my head. So the community organized to help. Sometimes we would be split up and distributed to families that could help."

That was, until Big Mama came to the rescue.

One day, fate would strike and give my father the opportunity to get out of the Jim Crow South. My father's uncle Oliver, who was living with him at the time, told him that he was headed to Detroit to have cataract surgery. Five months after his successful surgery, Uncle Oliver called my father and said, "I like it here in Detroit. I'm not going back to Tunica, but maybe you kids could come here with me."

In came my father's angel, Thelma Watkins, better known as Big Mama. A hairdresser who migrated to the beat of women packing up their families and following their husbands to look for work, she "followed the hair." She moved from Mississippi to Memphis, where there was a lot of working women, and then to Detroit nine years before she invited Uncle Oliver to stay with her. She visited family in Tunica after and was horrified when she saw my father taking care of his young siblings.

In the black community, the Big Mama is the sum of all that is good. Usually a grandmother, great aunt, cousin, or older woman in the family, the respect she commands rivals worship. Good food, good singing, stern with good vibes, and words of encouragement is all that is good in a Big Mama. This one in particular, Thelma Watkins, was no different. Moments after understanding what was happening in Tunica, Big Mama asked my father (now seventeen years old), Leroy, Rochelle, and Mattie if they wanted to come to Detroit. If so, they could stay with her for free. She knew where they could apply for work in her new, bustling city. She understood that the success rate of children raising themselves with partial parental supervision in the Jim Crow South was extremely low.

My grandfather immediately gave his consent. He wanted to get them out of the Jim Crow South. He wanted them out of the environment where he grew up and the overworked monotony where you can't dream. So, at the age of seventeen and with younger Webberites in tow, my father followed Big Mama Moses across the Mason-Dixon line to Detroit, Michigan. Motown. The land of opportunity. All of the children were excited; they didn't have to be told this was a godsend. They had experienced hell.

Many blacks migrated to the north in the early 1960s looking for work. Jobs were plentiful for hardworking men who used their hands for the security of a decent day's wage. When my father arrived in Detroit, he worked at a hotel restaurant right outside of the city as a busboy. He then landed a job at General Motors and never looked back, working there for more than thirty years.

At that time, my father could best be described as a ladies' man. He was tall, handsome, funny, and well-manicured. But after four years of dating in the big city, he finally ran into one woman who wouldn't fall for his game. Her name was Doris.

Big Mama's house was also the local hair salon. Ladies came by to get their "hair did" or their "wigs snatched." Her house was the place to be. It was poppin' with the smell of burnt hair, the latest music, gossip, and the finest women. My father lived with other family members at the time but stopped by Big Mama's house often to get a bite to eat and see if any ladies caught his eye. One day, he set his eyes on a young woman he thought was "outta sight"—my mother. He tried to speak to her, but she would never talk. "She was quiet," he says. "Her head was always buried in a book." He could never make her laugh. If he was lucky, she'd crack a smile, but that was about it. He'd ask her out, but she wasn't having it. He'd ask to walk her home, but she would shyly say no thank you.

My father is no fool…and he's a persistent man. And his persistence paid off. One day, Doris said she wouldn't go on a date with him, but he could come to church with her. "I knew I was in then!" my father says. "I knew she was serious, the marriage type, but I also knew she was the type of woman that could change your world as a man. She was God-fearing, beautiful, and smart. She wasn't like the other women I'd dated. She was special."

My mother, Doris, is definitely special, unique, and set apart. She does not suffer fools and is smart, self-motivated, hardworking, resourceful, sweet, and loving. Though they were both raised in poverty, her upbringing was very different from my father's. Her family believed in self-preservation and developing potential. Her mother, Jannie, who worked as a maid, was window shopping one day, and my mother asked her to buy her a piano so she could learn to play. A piano was an extravagance the family couldn't afford, but my grandmother poured every penny she made into monthly payments for that piano, which sat in their living room on Collingwood Street while my mother practiced on it night and day.

Although Jannie was quiet and polite, she was an unapologetic woman, known to "tell it like it is" and carry a pocketknife everywhere she went. One day she met a veteran and steel worker named Charles. He was sharp and meticulous. Charles was strict and believed in order when it came to himself and his family. He believed in hard work, hated the victim mentality, and couldn't care less about pats on the back. Why would he? He knew survivors didn't have time for the superficial. His background was one of extreme poverty. He had left home at thirteen to make room for more family, and just like that, he was sleeping in the streets and taking odd jobs wherever he could, ultimately finding work digging ditches. At the age of thirty-three, he joined the army and later became a steel worker.

My mom, unlike my pops, was a city dweller, and she grew up in Detroit in the midst of change and turmoil. She was one of the first to be bused from her neighborhood to white schools. Forced to embrace the dissolution of segregation, she had a lonely high school experience. Only a few blacks attended the school, and none were in her class. No matter how close she was with her classmates in school, they never acknowledged her outside the building. Still, she was an excellent student who would forever be in love with education and learning. However, she also continued to work on her music. A wonderful singer and pianist, she shared her talents with many in Detroit and around the world.

Not surprisingly, my pops fell in love with Doris. He asked her parents for her hand, and her father, Charles, said yes with no hesitation. Charles became my father's best friend, and Jannie, who sympathized over the loss of his mother at such a young age, became a second mother to him. She trusted that my father would love and care for her daughter. In fact, when my mother left for France with a traveling choir just weeks after her engagement, Jannie planned her daughter's wedding.

Two years before I would be born, my father (then a waiter) and my mother (a teacher) purchased a small house on the west side of Detroit for $17,000 and set about raising a family.

Chapter 3

I touched down at Detroit's Grace Hospital on March 1, 1973. The birth was a relief for me and my mother. Her doctor said that I was "scrunched up" in her belly, attributing her extreme stomach pains to her baby stretching out in her confined womb. Adding to the doctor's deep medical vocabulary, I was also cramped, hunched, compressed, squashed, and squeezed. He told my mother that I was the biggest baby he'd ever seen and expressed worry that I would not be able to walk because my ankle was wedged diagonally and backward due to my length. Thank God his assessment was off. I was able to walk (and run) pretty well, though I would be plagued by right foot and ankle injuries.

I entered the world surrounded by love. Outside the delivery room, in the lobby, my mother's sister, Charlene, and my father paced. When my pops and Charles arrived in my mother's room, they tried to take over, but my moms (a Chaka Khan's "I'm Every Woman" original) wasn't having any of that. So my father and grandfather took on the audacious task of naming me, going back and forth with terrible suggestions. Finally, my mother took charge and declared, "Because I went through labor, the baby will

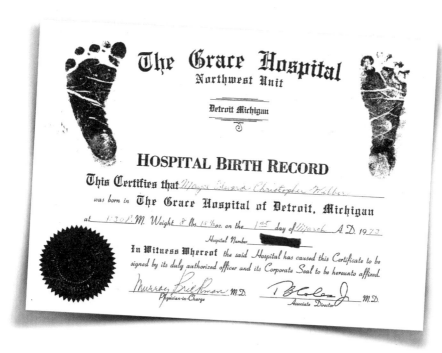

be named Mayce III after his father." I would also carry Edward, her father's middle name, and the name Christopher. Christopher means "follower of Christ," and that was what she wanted her children to be. So there you have it. Though you know me as Chris, my given name is Mayce Edward Christopher Webber III.

I am my father's son, but I am also a proud mama's boy. It came naturally. I adore my mother. She exudes love in every action but was an unrelenting disciplinarian. She's the definition of sacrifice. Through her example, I learned to balance sensitivity and strength. I've never seen her take a drink, and the next time I hear her curse will be the first. I went everywhere with her as a child. She taught at my school. I went to church with her. Grocery shopping, she'd explain to me what to look for in vegetables or when it was time to

catch a sale or buy in bulk. She made all my clothes when I was growing up stitch by stitch, including the red checkered pattern getup on the next page. No matter the occasion—church, school events, play, gym—she was a versatile seamstress.

One of my first memories of realizing I was a mama's boy was experiencing hurt and betrayal. It was the first time a woman cheated on me. It was in the fall, a couple of weeks before Halloween. My preschool had an exhibit, "How Mommies Feed Babies." I was excited when I learned that animals would be used as a teaching tool. First, we had a goat come in with her babies. We oohed and aahed as she fed the cute kids. Then, my mom came in with my newborn baby brother, Jason. She sat in a chair in the middle of the room as we sat around her in a circle, pulled out her left breast, and stuck it in Jason's mouth. As for Jason, well, he went H.A.M. It was like he hadn't eaten for weeks. He must have been starving.

I lost it. I cried and ran out of the room as the children walked around my mom and watched the baby feed under a cloth diaper. After she finished, my mother so gently came over to me and asked what was wrong. She told me that babies are beautiful and that she loved showing how God made mommies so that they could always feed their babies. I bought it, sorta. But I'm sure I thought—with all my four-year-old attitude—"Yeah, but you my mama. Nobody should see them titties but me, the babies, and Daddy."

When she returned to school to obtain her master's degree in education, she'd sit me in the back of the class, explain the importance of being quiet, and hand me a book of simple mazes and a juice box, and I'd sit contentedly and quietly. If she taught piano lessons at our house, she used me as her human metronome, patting students on their backs to the rhythm. I loved this, particularly when the student was cute and female. I don't know how my mom did it: maintaining her schedule, juggling five children, with no time and attention to give to herself. It makes me grateful to call her my mom. She's my example of how strong women really are.

Chapter 4

Superman Is My Brother

I don't ever remember being an only child. I've always been the big brother. My first memory of my brother Jeff, who is a year and a half younger, is taking his bottle from him out of his crib. My mother would put juice and water in his bottle, so the variety was great! I'd have a big brother break by taking a quick swig from the bottle. Whether at church, home, or in the backseat of the car, it was his rite of passage to give me a hit off the bottle.

I didn't know it at the time, but Jeff was not only my brother but my first, best friend. He was the comic relief in our family. He was always on time with an uncomfortable joke in what seemed to be a serious moment. He would upset our father with jokes during Pop's speeches. My father's reactions were so priceless that my mother would join our side and laugh, causing my dad to be that much more upset. But that was Jeff: always entertaining, always looking at things on the bright side and empowering others with his honesty and positive outlook. I can think of no better example than the time he became the neighborhood superhero.

One day, after leaving evening Sunday service, we arrived to find our home had been popped, burglarized. All of our neighbors were outside on the front lawn gathered around our living room furniture. Couches, tables, and dishes. They were all still there because the thieves had been captured. The neighbor who lived behind us knew that we went to church on Sunday evenings. So when he noticed two men at our back door, he came out with a shotgun and told them, "Don't move! I'm too old to run tonight." He laid the guys down and made them wait for the police. I rode with my father to the police station. Of course, he used this moment to reinforce his discipline of *there are actions and consequences.* After we returned home from making a report, Jeff had an announcement to make:

"Mom, there's too much crime. I'm going to make a difference!" he said. Cue siblings' sarcastic laughter. "I'm going to be a superhero!" Cue more laughter, including from Pops.

Our mother always looked for ways to encourage, inspire, and validate her children's interests and imagination, and now Jeff was her project. That night she and Jeff made a checklist of what superheroes needed:

1. They had to be unassuming.
2. They had to possess powers.
3. They had to be careful not to reveal their identity.

Realizing that he didn't have any powers, Jeff agreed to limit his crimefighting to reporting to his special assistant (our mother) and relaying any crime in the neighborhood to the proper authorities. Unless, of course, some unscrupulous criminals backed him into a corner, in which

case he could not be held responsible if he had to kick some ass. During this conversation, I helped my father plug in the TV and watched while they continued their town hall meeting. Jeff's preparation: push-ups and karate kicks, all while watching WWF wrestling. He began drinking Hulk Hogan's raw egg diet. But I was dreading Jeff's superhero debut. To me, it felt like a countdown to embarrassment.

One hot summer day, I was playing in the street when I noticed Jeff patrolling the neighborhood. Keep in mind, our block was always bustling with people. Kids played in the street while parents were on porches snapping peas, listening to music, and talking. School was out, so the block was very active. One of our favorite pastimes was playing football in the street, and during the summer, we had enough kids to have two teams. I played with the older kids, and during our football games, Jeff would play with the other kids. But on this Saturday, he had a different commitment. Jeff was Superman.

Our mother had sewn together a suit that revealed his Superman costume underneath. It was made of a T-shirt and Underoos—underwear. The cool thing was that she also sewed breakaway pants and a Velcro shirt, coat, and tie combination. All superheroes need to be able to make a quick change. The suit made for the unassuming "Clark Jeff" only had two parts: left and right side. The coat's left lapel was sewn into the left lapel of the shirt, connecting the sides so you could break away as a superhero without damaging any buttons. He wore the protective goggles that our father used while working on the line at GM and carried an old suitcase (more like my mom's extra-large makeup case), and in this mild-mannered  reporter attire, he walked around our neighborhood looking for crime. I am happy to say that only a few minor incidents were reported. Jeff—or should I say Superman—was forced to issue a few verbal citations, but he avoided any unscrupulous criminals who would have backed him into a corner (thank God). He would not have been responsible for the terror that he would've unleashed on their asses.

Jeff had the best heart. When our youngest sister, Rachel, took her spankings, it was hard for him to watch. And at times, he'd cry. Jeff would protest and beg to take her punishment, which was no more than a fake pat on the bottom. But Rachel's reactions caused our brother to go bananas. This inspired my mother, who encouraged a family-first attitude, so she allowed Jeff to take Rachel's spankings. Of course, as is true in most societies, corrupt people can turn good ideas into bad situations when they exploit the grey areas. It wasn't long before the rest of us brothers also wanted Jeff's butt to be our immunity. So we paid him to act on our behalf with the same passion he defended Ra-Ra with. After he agreed (and had his conditions met), he made his plea to the man (Mom and

Pops). They agreed—until they found out about our "pay for protection" scandal. Everyone got the black beat off them for inciting family unrest.

Jeff would one day name his first-born after his favorite superhero—Jordan.

Jeff's sensitivity made him a natural protector. Even though I was older, he tried to fight my battles. There were only five other kids at our church: Al and Bukeeka Danforth, and Tony, Mikey, and Lena. Al and Lena were the oldest and laid back, but Jeff would beat up the youngins, Mikey and Tony, every week after benediction, mainly for talking shit about our family. Jeff handed out beat downs like clockwork Sundays at 1:30 p.m. on Tyrone and Livernois streets. Why Mikey and Tony kept talking about my mother's clothes, our bummy van, or what we were wearing every week only to get knocked out I'll never understand. My mother and father tried to address this with Jeff, but he was adamant: "I will never let anyone mess with my family." He eventually stopped handing out ass-whoopins—once they stopped talking.

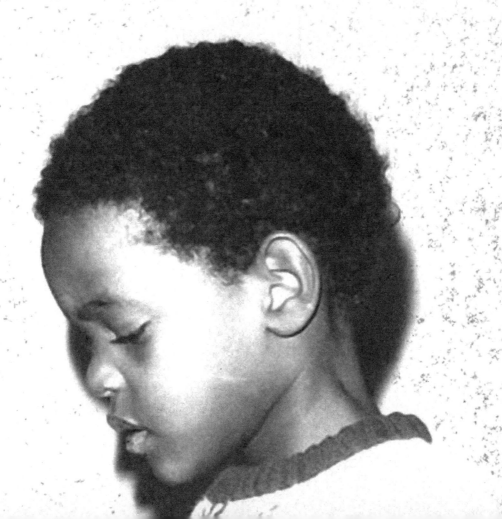

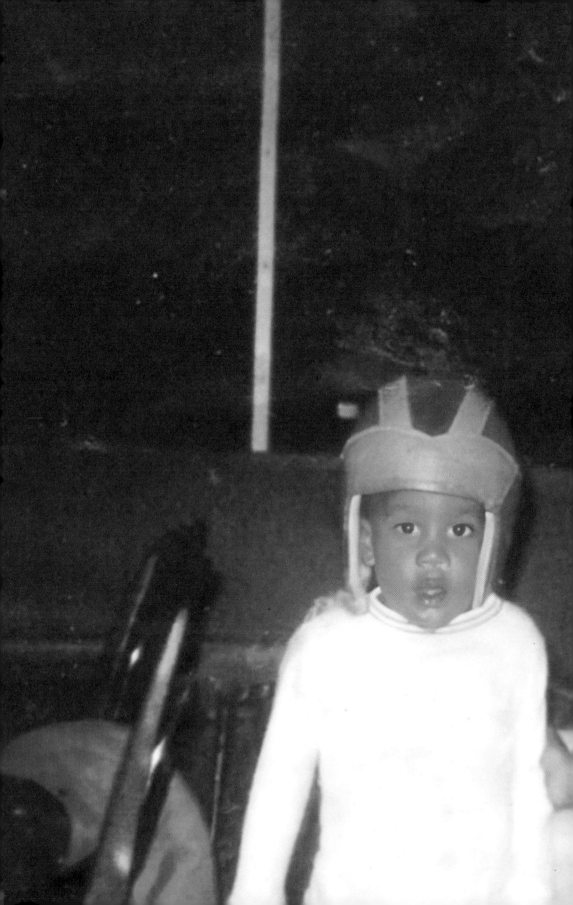

Chapter 5

The Money Box Club

I never received an allowance. My parents would sometimes give us money whenever they had a little extra. But our mother created a way to combat arguments and stretch a dollar among us five children: the Money Box Club. This was the household account for the kids, the stash of money our parents created for us to share. Jeff was the treasurer. As the oldest, I was the president. Everyone voted on what we would do with the earnings. If the Money Box Club had twenty dollars, we could purchase one or two gifts or agree to wait to purchase one more expensive gift together.

This was a great teaching tool by my mother, because we had to learn to negotiate, get along, politic, and develop patience. We always knew the money would be there because of our treasurer, the one responsible for accounting, Jason, a.k.a. Birdie. Once my father borrowed five or ten bucks from the Money Box Club, and Jason charged him interest. In true middle child fashion, Jason was a low-maintenance kid, a finely oiled machine. He didn't seem to require much attention. He was smart, confident, sensitive, stubborn, quiet, funny, and always mistaken for Jeff's twin. They did everything together. Jason is the first sibling that I really have a host of memories of, because I was old enough to be involved with his upbringing.

For example, Jason's first day of kindergarten was a true train wreck. Doris Webber was the only teacher he knew. She taught daycare in the room directly across the hall from the kindergarten classroom, and Jason had been a member of my mother's class for the first four and a half years of his life. But now, all hell was about to break loose.

The first day of school was a big production in our house. We'd lay out clothes, backpacks, notebooks, and supplies. This year, however, Jason set off a first day of school for the ages! Our white 1977 Buick Skylark was packed with four kids as usual and my mom navigating the same route: take Biltmore five blocks to Puritan, make a right across Grand River, go to Rutland, drive five blocks, cross Schoolcraft, pass the big church, and next to the skating rink we would arrive at James Allen Caldwell World of

Learning. JAC was a small Christian school of about 120 students, grades K-12. The teachers were like family, the students even closer, so truthfully it was no surprise when small, quiet, unassuming Jason turned the party out on the first day of school.

Our mother had been coaching and preparing him all summer for his "big boy" day. But Jason wasn't buying it. All summer he told my mother, "I'm not going to school. I'm staying with you." The morning of the first day, he noticed that his green pants and white shirt were laid neatly on the bed next to his older brothers, signaling that he was now one of the big boys. The days of his preschool uniform were behind him. I watched it go down like an Eddie Murphy comedy. We slept in the same bed, so I had a pretty good sense of my young brother's mood. When we woke up, I could feel it in the air. First, he looked at the outfits like, "What, is this real?" He then slowly put on his pants. I helped him button his shirt, put on his socks, and tie his shoes. Mom yelled upstairs, "Ready, big boy?" We were off!

We got to the front door of JAC, and my mother kissed us as usual. Jeff and I slowly headed down the hallway to class, smiling and looking back in anticipation. My mother headed to the right and escorted Birdie to his new class. He was very familiar with his new teacher, Mrs. Gardner; she came over to our house all the time. She was one of my mom's closest friends, but Jason couldn't care less about familiarity. As soon as my mom exited to go to her own classroom and Jason's old stomping grounds and the door closed, Jason went apeshit. Mrs. Gardner tried to prevent him from exiting in search of our mother. She stood at the door attempting to calmly convince Jason that this was his new class and that he would "have a lot of fun."

Jason was having none of it. He shouted, "No, I want my mommy! MOMMY!" He ran around the room, knocking over the cots stacked by the window. The commotion was so loud he disturbed the five classes that shared the hall. Teachers exited their rooms to see what was going on, then students followed. Jeff and I stood there in amazement like "This boy is really going through it." Jeff said, "Let him keep this up. He doesn't want Mama to call Daddy at home." Our father worked the night shift, 10:00 p.m. to 5:00 a.m., so at that moment he was asleep. But after an hour of unrelenting, high intensity protesting, my father was called. Once Pops arrived, he tried to calm Jason down, but to no avail. First, he tried to reason with Birdie for about ten minutes, then he opted for the only reasoning that Jason could relate to: the belt.

Looking for privacy, my father took Jason outside to pick a switch from a bush conveniently located near the front entrance. What Pops didn't realize was that he was giving Jason his licks while the entire class, teachers, Mom, Jeff, and I watched. Fading on intensity of licks, like the end of a well-produced song, our father picked up Jason, hugged him, and brought him back to class. After returning there was no more disruption, just finger paints, puzzles, and naps.

When my third brother, David, arrived, I felt I knew what being a big brother was all about. My brothers and I spoiled David, a.k.a. BumBum. BumBum didn't even have to walk until he was four years old. He had three big brothers to carry him everywhere. But David had an old soul. I never once saw him play with toys; he was mature beyond his age. Things that kids his age were doing he was never interested in. He always wanted to play with the older kids. I'd take him outside so he could sit on the porch with the big boys. In the backyard, he kept score for our baseball games because he was too small to play, but the whole time he was soaking up the energy and attitude of the older kids. When we played basketball, he'd stand on the sideline dribbling, looking all around like he was thinking, "One day I'll get to play, and ain't nothin' gonna save you then!"

Afamous cleaning, whooping, childbirthing combination took place the day Rachel was born, April 23, 1983. I know it was a Saturday because my favorite TV shows were on the night before. I was responsible for running the house while my mother was at the hospital delivering our little sis. We boys were lucky that she was born the youngest because if my father would've had her first it may have been snip snip. He only wanted a daughter.

Earlier in the day, my father had given me a speech before heading to work, saying, "I need you to be the man of the house. You know your mother is nine months pregnant, and anything can happen. Here is a list of phone numbers to call in case of an emergency, and here's what I want you to do…"

I responded, "Okay, Dad. Got it!"

He punched me in the chest and said, "I ain't worried! You know what to do!"

After receiving instructions from my father, I took some personal time to play outside before coming back inside to relax with some good TV. But, of course, my plans were interrupted—not by labor pains or an emergency rush to the hospital, but by my mother demanding that we clean the house from top to bottom so that "when I come home from the hospital, I will not come back to a dirty house with a newborn."

We weren't going to argue with our pregnant mom, so we got to work, but apparently we took too long. Eventually, my mother unplugged the TV and moved it to the corner—a move that would gain our attention. Jeffrey joked around with Jason, not getting any work done, so they both got a pregnant ass-whoopin'. But all the chasing, shaking, crying, and thrashing either upset or excited our sister enough that she tried exiting her temporary home to see what all the commotion was about.

Around 8:30 p.m., in between jokes, whippings, and sweeping, my mother's water broke. I followed my father's instructions. I ran down the street to alert my friend Margo's parents that it was time for my mother to go to the hospital. I grabbed the bag my mom had packed and helped her downstairs to Margo's

father, Mr. Calvin. Once she was settled in the car, I rushed back upstairs to get my brothers together. From there, I plugged the TV in, turned it on, and my brothers and I finished the last ten minutes of watching Boss Hogg, Cooter, Daisy, and all the people of Hazzard County before we went to Margo's house to spend the night.

The next morning my father picked us up, and I finished cleaning. Later he returned with my mom, and I can still picture him pulling up the driveway. I ran outside and saw my friend Wes sitting on his porch and called over, "Look, we got another baby!"

As Wes started to walk over, my mother yelled "Uh, uh! Don't come over here with those dirty little hands. You can visit the baby tomorrow."

My three brothers were waiting in the door as my parents and I approached with the baby, and they started firing off questions: "What is it, Mommy?" "What are we going to name him, Mommy?" "Does he look like me, Mommy?"

My mother smiled patiently and said, "Let us get in the house first, boys."

The anticipation nearly killed us.

We begged and pleaded until my mother said softly, "You guys have a sister. Her name is Rachel."

Jeff screamed "Nooooooo!" as he held his hands over his face. We expressed our displeasure in unison, crying, "Noooo, why?" and harmonizing in a way that would make the Boys Choir of Harlem proud. We cried and cried and cried. We wanted a brother because we needed a fifth member for our basketball team.

But our father had prayed for a daughter his entire life. He had actually wanted me to be a girl. Now, wish granted, he sat us down on the couch and explained to us that we had to protect Rachel. We had to beat up any monsters or bullies who messed with her! Full of excitement, we enjoyed

the newfound responsibility of protecting our sister. We stared and sang to her all night. Meanwhile, my mother looked to rest peacefully knowing the house was clean.

Unfortunately, when you have three older, rough, imaginative, rambunctious brothers, things can tend to go off track. One day, we were playing a game with our two-year-old sister where we would lay in a line on our backs, put her up on our feet and hands where she's in a flying motion, and then pass her to a brother waiting in the same position. Anyway, one day in between a hand-off she was dropped in transition. My mother was out, and my father was home watching us. When my mother returned home, she sensed something was wrong. Before she knew anything, she asked where her baby was. Well, her baby came in the living room limping, and my mother shut the crib down with the look she gave us dumb males who told the toddler to "shake it off."

She then swooped her baby up and headed out the door. When my mother came back from the hospital, she carried in Rachel who was sporting a new cast. Broken leg. Rachel was smiling, and we were ballin'. We had hurt our baby sister, and there was nothing we could do about it. Moms made us feel better, but I try to spoil her to this day because of that botched play.

The Webber household was a home of discipline. Roles were important in our family dynamic and chores were as well. Our home was filled with love and fun, but everyone was expected to contribute. The chore chart was used as a family schedule, and we logged assignments to keep the house clean and in order. To paraphrase 2 Thessalonians 3:10: "If you don't work, you don't eat." It may not seem like a lot of work to keep a three-bed, one bath house clean, but with two adults and five children under the age of nine occupying all of that space, it took the structure and organization of a corporation like Apple to keep that place pristine. And it was pristine.

WEBBER HOUSE CHORES

	SUN	MON	TUES	WED	THURS	FRI	SAT
WASH DISHES		JEFF		CHRIS	JEFF	JASON	
CLEAN BATHROOM				CHRIS		CHRIS	CHRIS
VACUUM			JASON				
TAKE OUT TRASH					JEFF		JEFF
MOP							

I had always wanted an older sibling, someone to teach me all the things I didn't know. I wanted to be able to ask questions that I couldn't ask my parents and have someone to confide in. Still, living in a big family and being the oldest was wonderful, but it did have its difficulties, especially when it came to privacy.

I slept with at least one brother until I was thirteen. In one room, all four of us boys slept in two detached bunk beds. From ages six through ten, I slept with Jason, who peed on me constantly. He peed so much that I kept a towel on the floor on my side of the bed, and when I felt pee that had soaked in the sheets, without opening my eyes, I would reach down, pick up the towel, lift up at the waist, place the towel under me, repeat the routine on Jason's side, and continue my dream in stride. I perfected the move out of necessity. Then, from age ten until I was thirteen, I slept with Dave, who didn't pee as much as his older sibling, but you still couldn't trust it.

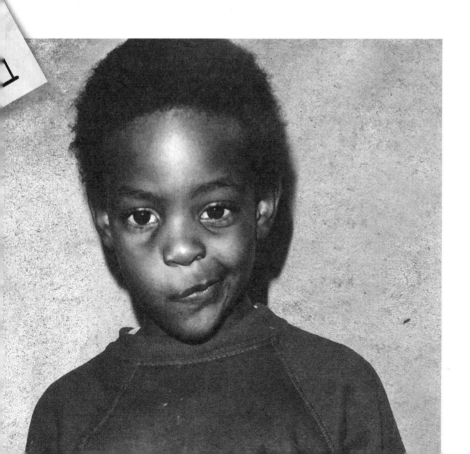

41

My mother has always been passionate about music, and, without a doubt, she unequivocally passed her Jones down to me and my siblings. She played music for me when I was in her belly. In fact, my earliest memory is music: my mother humming softly and singing in my ear. She cultivated the same love in us that she had always harbored by building a home full of tambourines, bongos, flutes, and a piano. We were all encouraged to explore every instrument and sound. Our home was loud at times, but it had an element of peaceful chaos.

I was introduced to many artists and genres, but gospel music is what I remember most. DeLeon Richards was singing "Rainbow In My Window" and "I'm A King's Kid." I loved the Clark Sisters, too, for a couple of reasons. Their vocal harmony in songs like "You Brought the Sunshine" and "Is My Living In Vain" was amazing. They were also Detroit natives who worked at the plant, and my father mentioned he'd seen them. That's all I needed to hear.

Other favorites were the Hawkins family, who sang "What Is This?" and "Be Grateful." Commissioned, Take Six, and "Running Back to You" by Fred Hammond were also on the list of my all-time favorites. Secretly, I think my mother wanted to Joe Jackson us into being like The Winans, the quartet of Detroit natives with the voices of angels. We emulated the Winans brothers: Marvin, Ron, Carvin, and Michael, though we followed BeBe and CeCe later. I used to listen to "Wherever I Go" and "The Question Is" so frequently I could sing every part, in every key, with every inflection, with each member's voice. I loved The Winans.

In preparation for singing, my mother would gather the kids in our small kitchen to rehearse. First, positions and stance. She explained that we had to breathe from the bottom of our stomach. She called it our diaphragm. She would sing a part and ask us to copy or repeat. She'd assign parts—alto, soprano, etc.—based upon the rehearsal. After a little more coaching and housekeeping, we'd learn the words and the song.

We were always at church—for me, choir was the best part about church. I know the message was more important, but the choir was beautiful and entertaining, and the words and melodies

changing the volume of each choir section with movements in sync with the rhythm of the song. The impromptu give-and-take of choir and director as the song being sung was remixed, organically, live, for the first time. Black choirs will stop a song, and then someone in the audience will start it right back up as soon as the choir sits down. I've witnessed the back-and-forth of a song go on for more than an hour—each person singing, praising, and giving their testimony as if they're the only person in the building. This experience gave me chills and goose bumps. This was the first concert I ever attended, and I was a *part* of it.

The workshop lasted for a week, Monday through Friday, 5:00 p.m. to 8:00 p.m. Andraé Crouch worked with a group of choir members from all around the Detroit area. Church would break out in each rehearsal because they weren't just singing, they were praising God. People cried, and someone in the choir would inevitably end up speaking, not preaching, but it was more than a concert. It was a "praise-cert."

Finally, Saturday came, and I put on my mom-made suit crafted for this special occasion. Prior to leaving home, I checked my list and grabbed my tape recorder and Mom's robe, Certs, Halls, peppermint tea, and honey, and we were off. I remember the smile on my mother's face as we drove home from the concert, because the actual concert was just as wonderful as we had thought it would be. Singing, singing, singing, and more singing. My mother sang her heart out and beat the skin off the tambourine. After, I met Andraé Crouch and packed up the tape recorder, Mom's robe, Certs, Halls, peppermints, tea, and honey. We got in the car, grabbed some "Arthur Treacher's," and sang our own little concert all the way home.

When I was nine or ten years old, I had to stand in for my mother's sick vocal partner. I sang "Endless Love" with my mother at a wedding. When we finished, beautiful women would stand, clap, and smile, and men would give me a pound like I was a big fella. It gave me pride performing with my mother. I could see why my mother loved music, and to this day, it gives me peace. My day is steeped in music. I wake up to it, cook to it, and work out to all types of music.

I remember my mother giving me pencil and paper while I watched the movie *Krush Groove*, a movie about two brothers starting a record company. My favorite part of the movie was when the Fat Boys lost a rap contest but got signed to a record deal anyway, sparking a rap compilation with Kurtis Blow, the Fat Boys, and Run-DMC unlike any other. My mom told me to write down all the words from the *Krush Groove* song. She told me that if I wrote them down, I would learn how to write a rap, but

I never shoulda' did that. Rap aspirations aside, my favorite song to perform with my mother and one that was constantly requested by our church's first lady, Sister London, at church was "My Soul Has Been Anchored In the Lord" by Douglas Miller.

Who knew that while my mother was teaching me about music, she was also introducing me to an environment where I could learn about God being my anchor? Who knew my anchor would also be remembering the words to those songs during the worst times of my life? These principles would hold me steady during the unseen storms ahead.

Though the storms keep on raging in my life
And sometimes it's hard to tell the night from day
Still that hope that lies within is reassured
As I keep my eyes upon the distant shore
I know he'll lead me safely to that blessed place he has prepared
But if the storms don't cease
And if the winds keep on blowing
My soul has been anchored in the Lord
But if the storms don't cease
And if the winds keep on blowing in my life
My soul has been anchored in, in the Lord
Oh, I realize that sometimes in this life, we gonna be tossed
By the waves and the currents that seem so fierce
But in the word of God, I've got an anchor
And it keeps me steadfast and unmovable
In the Word of God
But if, if the storms don't cease
And just in case the winds, they keep on blowing in my life
My soul, my soul's been anchored in, in the Lord, in the Lord

"My Soul Has Been Anchored In the Lord"
Douglas Miller

THE BLOCK

BOOK TWO

We lived at 16725 Biltmore Street on the west side of Detroit. Our house was full of love, books, instruments, and toys. Looking back, I knew we were broke, but I was one of the lucky ones. I had two loving parents, a grandfather, and an army of aunties, uncles, cousins, and extended family who reinforced their love and support daily.

My back was had!

Friends that had everything I wanted materially would tell me, "Mayce, we'd trade our life for yours. Your family is tight." But at times, from my child's mind's eye, the double-team discipline of my parents made me feel as if I had two wardens. While the other prisoners on my block roamed, I was confined to the yard, left to decipher and interpret the happenings of the block from solitary confinement. Leading an army of children, my father and mother were efficient with their time and resources. They did not negotiate or sugarcoat when it came to their children. They believed in order, serving God, loving and supporting one another, enjoying life, and doing your best. I knew at an early age that I was loved in this family, but I also knew that I was counted on to be my best and contribute.

♦ ♦ ♦

I first fell in love with competitive sports at Vacation Bible School. We would set up folding chairs in the backyard while Mother made Kool-Aid and cookies. Ten or twenty kids would come over. My mom had a felt board that she borrowed from Sunday school, and when she placed characters like Moses or Paul on the board, it was as if a cartoon came alive. After story time, we would sing a song or two like "I'm in the Lord's Army" or "The Hokey Pokey," and once my mom was satisfied with our participation, and while parents conversed among themselves, we excitedly began the backyard Olympics.

This 'hood classic, hosted by yours truly, commenced with the seriousness of the actual Olympics. Wes and I would stand across from each other and pick our teams from the other Bible class's collection of talent. Games included basketball, football, baseball, badminton, Frisbee toss, two-squares, running bases, skateboard jumps, pogo stick, and men's and women's doubles (including double Dutch and relay). Sadly, the pear toss, which we proposed to see who could chuck a pear over the most backyard fences, was shut down due to Mrs. Mallory's protest. All the rotten pears in her yard drew too many bees. It was cool having a mom who would let you have fun while she was still educating. Or better yet, who manipulated situations to seem like fun, but you were learning.

I remember when Halley's Comet whisked by. My mother saved for weeks to buy a telescope. One neighbor couldn't understand why my mother purchased a telescope instead of some new clothes for her children. Well, she wanted to inspire our dreams. No one in our neighborhood was talking about Mars, aliens, or outer space unless they were referencing a movie. My mother wanted outer space to become real to us, even attainable. One night, for a few minutes, it was. My mother told us to call our friends and let them know that when it gets dark tonight, they should come to the house to witness the phenomenon of Halley's Comet. The comet that only passes through the earth's atmosphere every seventy-four years. When it got dark and our friends came over, she then sat us in the kitchen and told us about space. She asked us if we believed in aliens. How many planets could we name? Who would want to live on a different planet? What do aliens look like?

She asked us questions and listened as if she was our peer, and not silly little children. We then went into the backyard and looked up into the sky. The telescope was not expensive (about $129), so we couldn't see much besides craters on the moon. I don't ever remember seeing Halley's Comet, but the experience I'll never forget. I remember learning about space and the whole neighborhood coming out to look into this telescope as if it held the secrets of the future. For that night, as the kids would say, I had the "cool mom."

◆ ◆ ◆

My mother believed in the communities that mainstream America ignored. She and others like her taught us to believe through their actions. She rarely allowed us to stay over at friends' houses but encouraged us to invite them over to stay with us, no matter the inconvenience of providing food or transportation. I recently had some friends explain to me why she did that. It was to help them. One friend (who will remain anonymous) recently informed me that the only time he'd get a hot meal was when he was over and studied with us. He knew that my mom knew that as well. She killed two birds with one stone: feeding him and making sure he was doing well in school.

Your secrets were safe with mama. She protected every child that crossed her path. When I went to the Philadelphia 76ers, on my first day in the locker room, a rookie came over to me and said, "Man, I love your mother. She was a teacher at my school, Mumford."

I said, "Hell naw! I've been a fan! With you being from Detroit and everything."

We just laughed. I called my mom after practice and asked her if she remembered Willie Green, my new teammate. At first she couldn't remember, then my brother showed her a picture and she said, "Oh yeah, he was so sweet. He was a really nice boy. He was a good athlete but a better student."

I replied, "Mama, I don't care how good a student he was. He wasn't better at books than hooks." And we both laughed.

My mother taught me to face every challenge, embrace the moment, and never run. She said that I could expect good results if I put in the work. My mother always believed in and trusted me. It was February, I was in fifth grade, and for months my mother worked to help me memorize Martin Luther King's iconic "I Have a Dream" speech for a school presentation. My father even borrowed a choir robe from one of the older male members so I could look like a pastor. The day was finally here. It seems like yesterday, the first day of school, September 1st, when I agreed to recite Dr. King's speech in front of the whole school for African American history month.

"Five score years ago... "

"Okay, good, baby. Now learn the next line... " She would gently encourage.

"A great American in whose symbolic shadow we stand today signed the Emancipation Proclamation... "

"Okay, again, but now act like you are Pastor London at church. Imagine you were him!"

"Okay. Ahh, okay. Five score years ago a great American in whose symbolic shadow we stand today signed the Emancipation Proclamation!"

"Amen, baby!"

But now here, six months later, in front of 350 of my schoolmates, I'll recite the speech from the pulpit of our chapel…alone. This doesn't feel like such a great idea now. When I was encouraged to do this, I thought about the fact that we were celebrating Dr. King. The fact that in the second paragraph I was excited to say, "But one hundred years later, the Negro is still not free." Now I'm not so excited to say that, but who cares? The fact that my aunt Charlene had me help her register voters to vote for John Connors, a black delegate from our hometown, didn't seem so inspirational. The fact that my parents told me stories of how bad blacks were treated and how this was a chance to share that with my peers. Well, the great story of Dr. Martin Luther King Jr. didn't seem so great if I were the one repeating this speech. Even thinking it's not so cool to be inspirational.

After a little coaxing from my mother, accompanied by a hug and a kiss, I was ready. Not only did I remember each word, but I tried my hardest to speak with the intensity of a leader who was pleading with the world to love more and love now. I started off slowly, nervous, but as I continued, I got stronger. Repeated each line with the conviction and attention to each word that it deserved. I was interrupted many times with "You tell 'em!" "Preach!" or "Amen!" When I got to the part that said I may not get there with you, I actually saw Mrs. Stearnes, the meanest teacher in the school, shed a tear. After my speech I received a standing ovation from teachers, parents, and kids. My mother came back and gave me a hug and told me how proud she was of me. Seeing the pride in her face became addicting. I wanted to see it as often as I could. Making my mother proud wasn't as simple as repeating lines in a school play. She wanted independent thinkers and men with godly characteristics.

Chapter 11

My parents taught me about mental toughness and where to draw the line. No matter what, no matter where, no matter when . . . they stood on principle. When I say my mother was tough, it's because she had to be. She played many roles: the security guard, referee, and psychologist. I've never seen her back down from a kid or gang, and there were times that scared the hell out of me. For example, my mother taught at my school, and when I was in the fifth grade, there was a high school student there named Scott. Every day, during lunch or after school when kids got picked up, my mother was in charge of selling food. One day after school, she was selling snacks to kids—twenty-five-cent juices, twenty-cent Chick-O-Sticks, penny candies, that sort of thing. Scott came to the table to buy a hot dog. He was a senior and had been suspended numerous times, and he had transferred to our school after being expelled from a different school.

Everyone knew his past. He intimidated the students and even some of the teachers. Scott wore a big donkey white-gold rope with an American bald eagle attached to it. Everyone knew how he lived. He bragged about it and even carried a big knot to put it on display, showing all of us kids "how he got money." When he entered the small makeshift cafeteria, he immediately ordered my mother to give him a hotdog.

She said, "Hold on one second."

He said something back.

She said, "Hold on one second, Scott."

He said, "Bitch."

I was twelve years old. All I thought was, *Why, oh why?*

Now it was on. He approached my mother with money in his hand. She ignored him. She turned around, and he moved toward her like he was going to do something. She grabbed him by the collar, pushed him into the back of a room, and the school janitor took it from there. As Scott was carried out, he yelled, "One phone call. Ima blow this place up!" That threat was often carried out in the '80s.

My mother replied, "You don't scare me. Don't let my husband come up here." (He definitely didn't want that.) Silence fell over the room for about twenty seconds. After the janitor took Scott out, it was like the movie *The Wizard of Oz* when the Wicked Witch dies and all the once-hopeless munchkins come out to sing and dance, celebrating their new liberty. The kids yelled and screamed. Some clapped, looking over their shoulders as if to make sure Scott didn't see them celebrating. They didn't want to get blown up!

I remember a teacher saying, "I told you all that Doris don't play. She'll knock you out!" I was thinking, *Please, you don't know the half.*

When I was younger, I was bullied all of the time by the older cats in my neighborhood. I learned to throw hands from live sparring. I was singled out for a few reasons. I was low-hanging fruit. I was the youngest, frail, and skinny. I was also as tall or taller than the bullies who were four or five years older. Being broke, clothing, and my complexion were all things they poked fun at. It never bothered me. I could hold my own.

One day on the way home from the store, Wes (who lived across the street) and his boys started messing with me. One boy pushed me down, another kicked me. I wasn't even upset. I was just FED UP. I didn't fight back, but I jumped up and calmly jogged home. I knew that my father wasn't home, so I went inside to look for something to end this immediately! A stick, brick, pocketknife, or anything to hit or stick them with. My mother noticed me rambling through my dad's things and wondered what I was doing. I was so pissed that I actually told her the truth in a moment of insanity. I told her what had taken place and alerted her of my immediate plans for revenge. Her response was stern, compassionate with resolve. She said I couldn't use weapons. "Men don't fight like that." *Yeah, okay.* "Your daddy taught you how to fight. And I guess you gotta do that today, 'cause ain't nobody gonna jump my baby."

First of all, I know my mother. There were so many subliminal messages in her statement that it's incredible, but they were all used to boost my confidence. Number one: "Your dad taught you how to fight." (A fact, remind me.) Number two: She said, "Nobody was going to jump my baby." Me being a mama's boy, that was all I needed to hear to help me identify the enemy, and then in my mind I turned into my mother's protector. I was ten or eleven years old, so how much damage can be done in a fight? Right? But at the time, it was as serious a situation as I had ever been in.

My mother walked outside unexpectedly, looked at the boys who were in my backyard circling like vultures, and told them to come over to where she was standing. The boys ran over as if to say "Thank you for letting us continue our previous ass whooping." She said, "Line up. You are not going to jump my baby. If you're gonna fight, do it one by one. He ain't running from anyone."

Right there, I became a man! I can't lie or embellish and say it was glorious and I turned into Superman. What I can say is, I've never ran since that day. I was proud. I must've handled my business 'cause from that moment on, the boys and the block respected me differently. I wasn't "Lil Chris" no more. I learned the lesson that the biggest weight one can bear is fear. Fear brings all the possibilities of failures; failures bring all the possibilities of embarrassment, and embarrassment brings all the possibilities of being inadequate. I'm glad I learned that lesson. I also learned it was worse to be a coward and not face your fears. I don't want to be a man without blemishes, because I choose to thrive surviving scared, avoiding bullies.

It also set a great trend in my life, a great comfort. Whenever my mother was around, I knew I would be successful. Whenever my mother was on my mind, I had no fear. Whenever my mother was around, I could put my love above the fear of what I was going through or facing at the time. She's my life charm. She believes in me and has set standards so high that I can only pray to achieve, but I know she believes I can, so therefore I must! Crazy, because to this day the neighbors on my block joke about me whooping ass that day.

I t was the beginning of it all, the summer that would change everything. The climax of my naïve youth. The last time I'd truly believe and the first time I would know pain. I was becoming a man; nothing would ever be the same.

I was growing like a weed. For two months my knees hurt so much from Osgood-Schlatter disease (an irritation of the patellar ligament caused by growth) that I couldn't walk without limping and experiencing extreme pain. It hurts like hell right under your kneecap. I was now twelve years old wearing a size thirteen shoe and measuring at six-foot-three. When I walked to the store to return bottles (something I did damn near every day for ten cents per), I'd get my daily fix of Snickers, Jays, and Better Made hot chips. I sensed a difference, even in the way neighbors stared at me as if to say, "I know that ain't the scrawny kid from Biltmore."

I was known as Little Chris. There was a Big Chris who lived directly across the street. He was about seven years older than me. Black Chad, Brian, Ricky, Lance, Wes, Larenda, Erika, and Margo were all older. 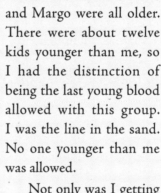 There were about twelve kids younger than me, so I had the distinction of being the last young blood allowed with this group. I was the line in the sand. No one younger than me was allowed.

Not only was I getting bigger, but a little more co-ordinated as well. I started to feel as if I were coming into my own. With coor-dination comes confidence, with confidence comes re-laxation, and with relaxation more confidence. I was get-ting better at neighborhood games. Hide go get it, a game of playing hide-and-seek, except when you find the girl that you were chasing, you get a kiss. Even Larenda, the prettiest girl on my block, could tell I was getting my weight up. Now, I wouldn't just chase her and catch her, but I wanted my kiss. (Never got it.)

Wes noticed my maturity as well. I caught up. When we played pick 'em up, mess 'em up, or football, I held my own with the big guys. I was tall and skinny, but I was just as fast and strong as them. I noticed a change in myself. Wes and I played many games. We competed in everything; he was the litmus test for my athletic ability. The older guy I always wanted to beat, be stronger, and run faster, and I could never do that to him. Although he was two years older, we were best friends. We played games like throwing a Frisbee across the street from my house to his house, sometimes skipping it, hitting the Frisbee in the middle of the street, landing on the front yard. Kicking footballs over the streetlight was another one of my favorite competitions. At night, we had the whole neighborhood sitting as fans, most chillin' on Big Chris's porch. Telling jokes, cheering, or sometimes booing. As long as you didn't hit my father's car with the football, you were okay. If you did, game's over.

Unequivocally, my favorite game was walking the dog. Walk the dog is a game where you measure how far you can dribble a basketball between your legs, doing it at every step, continually. The summer before, I could only walk the ball three or four driveways, from my house to Mrs. Mallory's front driveway. But, that year, I was walking around the block multiple times. Wes could do it as well, so we'd walk the ball in the morning and at night to the point where I couldn't see because the streetlights were off. We'd walk the ball and wave to neighbors and kick at dogs who were barking or biting at our heels. We'd walk the ball while kids in our neighborhood would ride their bikes in front of us, weaving left to right trying to break our concentration. We'd walk the ball in the rain and tried to walk the ball on ice and in the snow. We walked the ball everywhere.

✦ ✦ ✦

We lived in your average, poor, working-class neighborhood. There was some good, some bad, but we were kids and only wanted to have fun. Our block was packed with families, and it's safe to say we had our own culture. Every Saturday morning, from eight years old to twelve, I had the same ritual. I'd wake up around seven o'clock, get a bowl of cereal, go across the street to Wes's or have him come over. We'd watch cartoons from seven thirty or eight until the After School Special was done at about one thirty. We watched *Super Friends*, *Transformers*, WWF, *The Smurfs*, and on a lucky day maybe the Harlem Globetrotters or Evel Knievel would make an appearance on ABC's *Wide World of Sports*.

Afterward we'd go outside and play until the streetlights came on. This was our ritual, something our parents understood. They knew that our weekend routine was part of our God-given right as children. Choir rehearsal wasn't until seven thirty, so I usually enjoyed a full day of fun before leaving heading off to *saaang*. If it was hot, we'd jump through the sprinkler or put water in Ziploc bags to wet each other up. We spent the day playing our favorite games, like two-square. You have a ball, and opponents stand about four squares away, the squares being the imprints of concrete that line the street in front of your house. The object of the game was to hit the ball in your opponent's square in a way in which they could not return the serve, almost a mix between tennis and handball.

Running bases was another game we loved to play. We needed three people for this game. You have two guys standing in two different driveways on the same side of the street, both equipped with baseball gloves and whatever ball was available—baseball, softball, tennis ball, whatever. Another person stands in the middle, and it becomes the baseball drill of the rundown. A runner starts in the middle and attempts to make it to each driveway, or base written in chalk, without being tagged out. This game was particularly good for little fellas with quick feet, like Lance, Hanky, and Mario. We played two-hand touch football in the street and tackle on the side. We played baseball, had water balloon fights, and climbed garages. We would leave the hose on all night to fill the garden up with mud and water; find a piece of thin, flat wood and a couple of cinder blocks to make a ramp; and jump that bitch.

We learned karate in the middle of the streets, literally. A neighbor moved in on the corner who was a sensei. Lance, Big Chris, Wes, Black Chad, Brian, and I got news of this, and we asked his sons to ask their father if he would teach us karate. He obliged. At eight thirty in the morning on a hot June day, you'd have eight kids (including Jeff in his Superman costume) standing in the middle of the street screaming "Yes, sir!" "Huuuh!" and "Haaaa!" Can't blame our sensei for the cries that riddled our neighborhood. Kung Fu movies came on every Friday night. We'd watch them the night before in preparation for getting our Bruce Lee on the next morning.

On this particular Saturday, I don't remember the day's activities. I do remember coming home from White Castle, going upstairs, and turning the TV on. As the day started to cool off, I looked out the window and saw my neighbors arguing in the driveway across the street. Wedged between the garage and side door, I noticed my best friend's parents. As my nosy ass walked downstairs to get a better view, I heard gunshots. I ran to the door . . . his pops had been shot twice by his moms. There was no big crowd or fanfare on our busy block. He was hauled off to the nearest hospital by a neighbor and the block continued on as if nothing had ever happened. We started playing in the street, and rumors swirled around about people "stepping out" or whatever. But who knows? They're still together to this day.

Chapter 14

That summer really got rolling when Timbo, Wes's older brother and my idol, said he wanted to start a singing group. We were supposed to be the second coming of New Edition, and as long as I was Michael Bivens or Bobby Brown, I was cool. Our instructions from our sixteen-year-old leader were to "sing so hard that you can see the veins in your neck pop out." I guess that would indicate that we could really *saaang*.

We learned three or four predictable, fake-ass Temptations steps and were ready for stardom. We went to a manager's house to discuss world domination, but from the look of his house, he needed to manage a mop, a broom, and a paycheck. Anyway, we auditioned for him and returned home. Not surprisingly, after one month of practicing terrible songs led by a sixteen-year-old with eleven- and thirteen-year-old backup singers, our singing careers came to an abrupt end.

Still, summers were the best. Every other Friday I would spend the night at my grandfather's house, or he would just come over to our house on weekends. My grandfather and I were crazy close; he was my man. We'd barbecue, and he would beat us in ping-pong and then eat the eyes out of fried fish to amaze us. Mom would whip up some homemade ice cream, and we'd take chairs outside to eat together on warm, humid Friday nights. I remember him in the backyard with his glasses on, rocking a big tie and his coat dangling on the back of the chair. My grandfather was fresh! Wearing suits and ties only.

He was also lonely. Not because he lacked family and friends, but because his wife had died at the tender age of fifty-four a couple of months after my brother Jeff was born in 1975. The story was already familiar from the death of my father's mother:

a routine hospital visit, an appendectomy, contracting hepatitis C, couldn't even touch her grandbaby, passed away, and nothing the family could do about the negligence. My grandfather stood like a Greek god, six-foot-three and 170 pounds of muscle, the spitting image of my brother Dave. But we would soon come to see that his youth and strength would not last forever.

One day, while bringing my then-three-year-old sister Rachel down the stairs, he dropped her. The entire left side of his body had gone numb. He'd had a stroke. The thing is, the stroke cemented a bond with us grandkids that would never be broken. As soon as my grandfather came home from rehab, I felt like he was my responsibility. I couldn't stand to watch him have a nurse or be that vulnerable, so every weekend until I graduated from high school, unless I was on a basketball trip, I spent the night with him. He had two more strokes, but that just strengthened my commitment. Responsible for bathing him, I would place a milk crate in the middle of the bathtub, sit him on it, and wash his body. I slept in the bed with him, and we listened to baseball games on his radio. I cooked for him. I cut his hair. He was my best friend.

My brothers did the same, and of course, my mother and father were there to care for him as well. But I was his little man. At ten or eleven years old, I would go to the store for him and buy cigarettes and a "jumbo beer," as he called it—a forty-ounce. I would sit in his wheelchair at night and do wheelies as I watched TV. To this day, I'm still very good at popping wheelies in a wheelchair. I watched *The Price Is Right* with him in the morning and *Jeopardy!* with him at night. During the week I'd call him on the phone to check on him. In fact, each of us called him two or three times a day. We would sit and rap about real-life topics. He explained how things were really hard, along with the importance of being a man and having patience.

Back then, my grandfather didn't try to be the most eloquent and didn't use metaphors to get his point across. My grandfather was a cowboy, a talk-about-it-after-you-do-it type of guy. A shake-your-hand, look-you-in-the-eye type of man. A no-nonsense, humble, hard-working, back straight, "word is my bond" type of man. I believe that him having a stroke put me in earshot distance to not only listen to the advice of my wise grandfather but seamlessly learn how to be a cowboy as well. I gained a true respect for age, wisdom, and maturity. I saw his strength, and the neighbors did as well. The 'hood knew not to break into his house, because you never knew what the old man had waiting on the other side of that door. He was respected and returned the sentiment. I was learning a way of life from him.

I remember having one discussion with him in my high school years that involved me not being happy with sports, peer pressures, or whatever the emergency of the day was. I do, however, remember his advice. "Kill yourself!" That's right, kill yourself! "If you're going to keep worrying and not do anything about it, then kill yourself, because you're just going to be dying a slow death anyway. Do something about it or give up. You may have a little time to cry, cry, but after you cry, either do something or kill yourself."

My grandfather could be harsh at times, but that was his version of reality. I never heard my mother curse, and I only heard my father a few times. However, my old-school grandfather, an army vet who had zero fucks to give, had no problem speaking his mind, and you knew it.

"You are special, Mayce." Those are the words one teacher used to grab my attention. She made me feel part of a movement—the movement of those who are called to do something special.

I first heard of the Negro Leagues of Baseball in history class. The first time I would talk about sports would be in this same class. I was in the fifth grade. As class would wind down before recess Mrs. Stearnes, the strictest teacher in the school, would wow us with stories from years past. Like my mother, she was a no excuse, I'll tell your parents, praying, paddling, mad woman, but we knew she cared for us, and we would beg her to tell us more about "the best players to ever play."

Looking back, she took advantage of our eagerness, most of the small talk in break time concerning players, dates, times, and events would end up on weekly tests and some of those heroes we celebrated during Black History Month. We didn't mind. She spoke of traveling all-star teams. She told us that we were blessed and that there was a time when, if we had the obvious talent to compete, there were gentlemen's agreements amongst the owners that effectively banned blacks from the NBA, NFL, or MLB. Many of us heard of the stories of the past tragedies of racism and discrimination, but her vivid accounts made those times come to life like a scary Freddy Krueger movie. She would whisper nightmares of the Klan chasing teams from city to city or recount how it tore and ate at men from the inside not being able to show what they had to the world, to be considered less, or just not having the opportunity to do what they loved. She continued on how most of these players were better than the best players that the media talked about. She said they didn't know. She encouraged us to know our history.

This was an advantage of going to a small black church school in the hood. We were given pride, self-esteem through heroic studies that I would learn would not be taught at the so-called finest institutions in the world. This week in particular, Mrs. Stearnes wanted us to familiarize ourselves with Jackie Robinson. She was proud of this man. She spoke of him with certainty and conviction. One day after class, she asked me to stay after. I was worried because she was close with my mother, and I just knew that I must've done something to get in trouble. Fortunately, that wasn't the case. She spoke kindly and softly and said, "I know you get teased a lot. I see something in you. Everyone does. You have to be like Jackie—strong, and you must pray a lot. They made fun of Jackie all the time, but he didn't care. They never got to him. He showed them all. He was special, and you are special, too." I thought to myself—I didn't play any organized sports at this time—*Why is she telling me all of this?* Then, later...

At the end of our discussion that day, Mrs. Stearnes took out a small box, opened it, showed me a picture, and explained that the man in the photo wearing a baseball hat was Norman "Turkey" Stearnes. Turkey Stearnes was her late husband. He started playing professional baseball in 1920, retiring in 1942. He played for the Detroit Stars and ended his career with the Kansas City Monarchs. He is considered one of the greatest all-around players in history. He batted over 400 three times and led the Negro leagues in home runs seven times. He has the all-time home run record, 176, which is fifty more than second place, Mule Suttles. To supplement income, he worked summers in a factory owned by Walter Briggs—owner of the Detroit Tigers. A team that didn't employ blacks.

This is just a sample of God's grace. I was being filled with the energy of those who had been in the struggle. Not just from family, but from those in my village. Mrs. Stearnes saw something in me before I saw it in myself, before any coach, before any team. Her presence and expectations of my life's potential have stayed with me since our conversation in class that day. Not as a burden, but as validation in times of doubt, holding me to a standard. How could I move forward and not be grateful after hearing first-hand accounts of dreams deferred to the past? How could I not think that I must honor those who paved the way or not pay it forward? I knew the truth. I would never have the excuse of ignorance. Because of conversations with my angels.

Stearnes was inducted into the Major League Baseball Hall of Fame in 2000. Mrs. Stearnes accepted the award on his behalf. I wonder if she thought of those fearful nights fleeing from city to city with the image of a burning cross reflecting in her rearview. I wonder, did she think back to the days when she had to encourage her husband to stay the course while he worked in and was ignored in a factory owned by a man who could fulfill his dreams with one stroke of the pen? I thank God for her. I wonder what she saw in me, the quiet, smiling, loner? I thank her for initiating a conversation that would help frame the way I thought of myself.

That was a rough school year. I learned about death and how cold and calculating it could be. I learned that my friend would never be coming back. "You need to go to the funeral," my mother said. "Matter of fact, I'm going to call your friends so they can go with us and see what real street life is about. Young boys in the streets selling drugs, young boys outside, and parents don't know where they are—who's going to help them? Why are they going through this? They want all black boys dead! Lord help me! What am I going to do? If I catch you selling drugs, I'm gon kill you! And I know your cousins and them lil boys are doing it. Let me catch you! Boy, let me catch you. I promise! God commissioned me to take care of you, and if I can't, he won't mind me taking you out!"

More than a few large school buses filled the parking lot. My mother, Mrs. Butler, Mr. Hill, Mrs. Gardner, and others ushered young students and willing parents on to a caravan of despair to say goodbye to one of our own. "Money" was dead. His funeral, somber. There was a woman who sang "I'll Fly Away," an old church favorite, sending all of us kids into tears. To this day, it is one of the saddest experiences I can remember. There was no light at the end of the tunnel in any of the speeches, just admonishments and warnings. The building was cold. No smiles, no hugs, no explanation. What *is* death? Not goldfish or gerbils dying, but what *really* is death? A person could really be here today and not be back tomorrow? Money, an eleven-year-old who had shared some classes with me in fifth grade, was selling drugs (we called it "rolling" back then), got shot, died, closed casket, and everyone continued with their life.

I remember thinking there should be justice, questioning why no one wanted to do anything about it. Why did everyone just expect him to die? Isn't there something else we could do? This can't be the end, but it was. It was as if everyone forgot about him as soon as they opened their eyes after the funeral's closing prayer. I remember thinking: *This is a cold world!* After saying our final goodbye, we all boarded the bus and cried all the way home.

This was the beginning of it all, the Nancy Reagan "just say no" era. Big Chris and the older kids put me up on game, and I could see for myself that things were changing. Crime went up crazy, and not just on breaking and entering. I mean, cats were getting robbed in front of their houses. Cars were taken out of their driveways. It wasn't safe to go to the store anymore without being crewed up. One night, we went to see *Purple Rain*, and it got shot up during the opening credits. Now, don't get me wrong. It was never sweet where I was from, but something ominous had been released into my community. My family and friends would be devastated by its impact. Around my way, it would never be the same.

Drug cartels used young boys to sell their products, because sentences were less than they were for adults committing the same crime. The thinking was that jurors, police, and court systems tend to be more sympathetic to children. Since juveniles can't be charged as adults, why not use the kids? This was also attractive to the younger boys, because now you could make money and start to have the things that the older kids had or your friends didn't. After a while, everybody wanted to roll in the neighborhood, and my parents were determined to make sure we had other options.

I was coming into my own. I was getting older, and a lot of different things were becoming intriguing. I wanted to be like those older than me in my neighborhood—the ones getting the most attention in my environment. But in this stage of my young life, I thought I knew it all. My parents saw this, and actions were taken. One day, my mother yelled upstairs over the noise of the TV, "Put some clothes on, Chris. Charlene is about to come get you!"

My aunt Charlene was the final member of our close-knit village. She exposed me to so many different things in life. I remember her apartment on Cheyenne, off 8 Mile. It was so fresh, decorated with a seventies flair. Whenever I spent the night over at Charlene's house, we would do little photo shoots. She would make me pose with different expressions. I would sit, and she would click. She pulled all the shyness out of me and installed a quiet confidence instead. She would get in trouble, as any good aunt would, with my mom for letting us watch movies we weren't supposed to. One film on the Do Not Watch list was *Jaws*. Charlene got in so much trouble for allowing us to check it out, because Jeff and Jason got so scared they didn't take baths for days.

Charlene wasn't just about fun. She made sure to take me to art fairs, shows, farmer's markets, and the library. With Charlene it was like I was her little date. It was fun, and she showed me a side of women that my mother didn't have or couldn't show me, because my mother wasn't a single girl in college having fun. My mother was twenty-five, married with two children and three more on the way. As I look back on my relationships with my auntie and mother, I realize they affected the way that I viewed

black women in particular. That's one reason why I hold women in such high esteem: the women in my family are the best.

Charlene would later prove to be one of my closest friends and most trusted confidants. Further down the road, our relationship would be tested intensely by the business of sports, family, and the intersection that breaks hearts and separates alliances.

I always loved it when Charlene came to pick me up. A few weeks earlier, she had invited me out to campaign for a gentleman named John Conyers. The task consisted of passing out flyers to neighbors to help spread the word to get him elected. I had a great time learning about elections and how you can control your own neighborhood by listening and then voting for people who have promised to do things for your community. That was when I fell in love with Better Made hot chips. I love all things hot and spicy, and after campaigning with Charlene on a hot Saturday, I was rewarded with a big ninety-nine-cent bag of barbecue potato chips and a Coke. So when my mother called upstairs, I was excited. If the day was anything like hanging out with my favorite aunt in the past, it was going to be fun.

"Where are we going?" I asked as we settled into her car.

"Jackson, Michigan," she told me. "Here are some brainteasers and puzzles. Sit back and relax. We have about an hour-and-a-half drive."

I had eagerly agreed to go with my aunt, simply to spend time with her, but suddenly I was also an unwitting participant on a "bootleg scared straight" program. I now realize she was attempting to deter any future activity that would land me in the very same facility we were visiting.

When I was growing up, there were two places you didn't want to go in Michigan as a kid. The first place was Northville Psychiatric Hospital, the so-called crazy house. The second was the infamous Michigan State Prison, or Jackson State Prison. More than once, my parents had threatened that they would take me there and drop me off if I ever got out of hand, but I thought it was just that—a threat. Now my aunt and I were actually pulling up to the place!

Michigan State Prison opened in 1839 and was the first prison in the state. By 1926, it was the largest walled prison in the world, with nearly six thousand inmates. As we pulled up, I thought, *What a big building!* There was a big parking lot and a fence that seemed to reach into the sky. The fence had barbed wire, and there were police cars in the parking lot. Little did I know that I was visiting hell on earth.

"This is Jackson Prison," Charlene said.

I thought, *Dang, what happened to the cool aunt?*

We were greeted by metal detectors and guards wearing bulletproof vests. We walked down long, narrow hallways with cells on each side, stacked seven floors high. It felt like we were traveling down the hull of a ship. The inmates were packed in like sardines. As we walked down the hall, I remember the comments hurled at my aunt Charlene.

"Hey, bitch!"

"Look over here, hoe!"

"Hey, little boy, come here!"

I was in Bizarro World. Charlene didn't flinch. She was tough as nails and used to this type of environment. Thinking back, she was probably secretly cheering on the inmates and hoping they would degrade her even more in front of me so she could make her point: this was no place for me. Point made, scared straight, touché, checkmate, and all that shit.

One woman sat next to us. She smelled like she had bathed in a bathtub of hot piss. "Drugs," Charlene said coldly. I didn't look her "client" in the eye, nor did I listen to their conversation. I sat quietly off to the side, stunned and shook. The ride home seemed to take forever. I couldn't wait to get home to tell Wes, Jeff, Big Chris, and everyone else what I saw.

I later found out that Charlene had gotten the idea while attending law school at Wayne State University. Her class went to prison to learn how to interview clients. She said that she had been so disgusted by the experience that the first thing she thought about was making sure that my first impression of that wretched place would not be distorted. I thank Charlene for that experience.

BOOK THREE

NEW GAME, NEW SCHOOLS, NEW RULES

J ust a few weeks after Money's funeral, I tried out for the basketball team. Although this would be my first encounter with organized sports, our school was so small that we had one team that included fifth through eighth graders.

Now, I wasn't good, and I was definitely less physically mature than the others on the squad, but I was still part of the team. We only played a few games, and I didn't get into any of them. But I did get to practice and learn a few things from my coach, Mr. English, like 2–3 zone, 3–2 zone, and help D.

Truthfully, I was lucky to have a uniform. Parish Hickman was our star, a lanky, left-handed scoring machine who was six-foot-seven as an eighth grader and would destroy anybody his age. I can't tell you how important watching Parish was to my development and expectation. I would watch and mimic his moves. He was better than any player I'd seen at that time, anywhere—even Kelly Park, where we played in the summer, in my neighborhood.

Parish was cold. I'd sit on the bus after practice and listen to him hold court on what high school he was going to attend or what shoes he was going to wear next or how many girls he went with. One day after practice, he even came to my rescue after another eighth grader named Dennis tried to stab me with a pocketknife. He was mad becuase I was locking him up. Parrish came over and got in between us then took the knife from Dennis. He told me he liked my heart. He was referring to me being in a fighting stance, but he didn't know that I was scared as hell. I was maturing mentally and physically, but my sports career would have to be put on hold. All because I thought I was Lynn Swann.

Parish was always in my basketball thoughts on my journey because years later he went to Bishop Borgess High School. He was voted third in Michigan's Mr. Basketball and would have a pretty good career playing for Sparty at Michigan State.

Chapter 17

Lynn Swann

It was the first week of school and my mother had a teachers' meeting, so she took us over to the home of a church member, Gracie. We were very close with her kids—Lena, Mikey, and Tony—from Jeff's ass-whoopin' fame, so their house was always a fun place. My mother gave me specific and direct instructions. "Chris, do not go into the street," she said. "Do not play football in the street. Do not throw the football across the street, do not throw the Frisbee across the street, do not race in the street, and do not dribble the basketball in the street!" All of these were my favorite activities. "Are you crazy?"

Of course, I did play in the street! Specifically, I played wide receiver. I was number 88, Lynn Swann. Who would have known that Lynn Swann was supposed to get hit by a car in Detroit that day? I don't remember it being a busy street—in fact, I don't remember much traffic at all. The only thing I remember is opening my eyes in confusion as I lay on the hot asphalt with the whole neighborhood huddled over me. At first, I didn't feel the pain; I was wondering what was happening. Then I noticed my brother Jeff running in circles on Gracie's lawn saying, "He's dead, he's dead!" and Jason following right behind him. That was when I lost it, crying, "Where is my mama? Where's my mama?"

My mother got there as the ambulance arrived, and she said, "Chris, didn't I tell you don't play in the street?"

Relieved to see her but ashamed, I said, "Yes."

She gave me a hug and a kiss, and then we got in the ambulance and rode off into the sunset.

The doctors told me that I had broken my leg in two places and needed surgery. The surgery lasted two hours, and the cast stretched from my foot to my thigh. But then the doctor gave me more bad news: they had set my leg in the wrong place. "We are sorry," he said, "but this happens sometimes, and we can't tell until it's set." I waited a few hours, was reprepped, and then the doctors rebroke and reset my leg. Again, I was given a cast that went from the top of my thigh to the tip of my toes, and my right leg remained straight and constricted for more than three months.

Not only was this a painful lesson in listening to your mother, but its consequences followed me for years. To this day I can't pat my right foot, and I can only raise my right big toe. I have always worn out right shoes much faster than left because I scrape the bottom of my right foot when I walk or run. The break in my leg changed my entire gait for good. I thought about having surgery to cut and stretch a tendon in my big toe to allow more movement, but my doctor said, "If it's broken but doesn't hurt and it works, don't fix it!" But at the time, why would I be upset? I got to wear a cast and chill at home. I was good.

Chapter 18

Basketball Is My Favorite Sport

I've always been a loner. I could be in the midst of close friends and still sit comfortably in the solitude of my thoughts while the world whizzed on around me. Growing up, I was shy, lanky, awkward, and growing like a weed. My height also made me the center of unwanted attention, and I could have done without all the questions regarding my body. Don't get me wrong; I knew that I was cool in my own way. But I came from a big family, and I was used to an even distribution of love and attention. Attention out of proportion, which came whenever I was out with my friends, family members, and classmates, got tiring. I never really learned how to deal with standing out, something I would later be forced to address and accept.

It's funny how misconceptions force you to look at yourself in a totally unflattering way. That's what lack of experience and context does. You become ashamed of your talents and assets. That's why I thank God for having a mother who validated me. My father put me through the rigors of being a man and became my litmus test for what a man really is. One hell of a parenting combination.

There were also wonderful people outside of my family who, through their acts of love, exhibited God's benevolence in my life. Mr. Michael Evans, my soon-to-be principal at Temple Christian, was one of those people. My mother wanted her kids to attend a new school, have better learning tools, experience different opportunities, and escape some of the crime of the neighborhood. There was only one catch: we didn't have the money.

I remember my mother and father huddling us together for prayer so that we could ask God to provide and make a way out of no way. This would be my first true encounter with faith, as I thought there was no way we were going to get into the school. But faith without works is dead. So, I also watched my mom and dad get to work and hustle for their goal.

For extra money, mother did taxes during the tax season, turned hairdresser. My father took on extra jobs—he went to school to get different skills like electrical, plumbing, etc., to provide. I watched it all. Then came the day for my interview, testing, and—if I was lucky enough—orientation. Mr. Evans

asked me a few questions, spoke to my mother, and then, with the heart of an angel, decided my mother could pay the tuition over the full year, not just within the nine-month school window. Mr. Evans knew those extra months were all she needed to pay the full amount. His kindness would set me off on a steep trajectory in education and sports.

God validated Mr. Evans's presence in my life over twenty
years later from the date of his kindness as principal. I was
a member of the Washington Bullets, and we were in Miami to
play the Heat. I was days away from what I thought would be the
worst moment of my life: being traded to the Sacramento Kings.
I was uneasy, and things were just not sitting right with me.
I walked in the chapel to worship and get some peace of mind
before the game, as I always did. And I couldn't believe my
eyes. Who was our chaplain that day? Who was the chaplain for
the Miami Heat for many years? Who talked to me and gave me
godly advice about my unsettled feelings? Mr. Michael Evans.

✦ ✦ ✦

I was excited to go out for the sixth-grade basketball team at Temple
Christian. I would now be one of the guys, not a young, gumpy kid who
got to hang out with the older kids because of being tall and having a
sympathetic coach.

My coach was Mr. Lindsey. He was an ex-jock with a cool personality and
patient demeanor. He needed it with me, because according to my mother, in
games I would stand in the middle of the paint with my arms open, looking
lost. I remember more about the games I played in the streets on Biltmore
on Saturdays than I do about my sixth-grade basketball season, but I do,
however, remember that I used to tape my fingers like Magic Johnson.
Why, I don't know.

Before sixth grade, most of my basketball experience came in my
backyard, where I was Magic and Wes was Bird—or I was Bird and
Wes was Magic, with Big Chris making a cameo as the Boston Strangler,
Andrew Toney. We played games like twenty-one and twenty-one-tip-
out, two-on-two, and one-on-one. We had telephone poles in front of our
houses, and we'd see who could shoot over the electric wire or who could
shoot over the fence from the yard next door. I was just having fun. I didn't
know potential, and potential didn't know me.

"Use the K-Mart super grip."

"No, use the volleyball."

"He can do it with a volleyball. We saw him!"

The day came: March 1, my thirteenth birthday. I'd been telling
everyone in gym class that I was going to dunk soon. Now the moment of
truth was here. "Gimme the K-Mart super grip. I can almost palm it." The
first time, running from the top of the key without a dribble, I got my feet

right, but off the back of the rim—BAM! "Ooooooh!" and "Dang!" came from my classmates. Second time, same ritual. Except this time, BAM— I dunked it!

It was as if we had won a national championship. The class and Mr. Lindsey mobbed me. It was a dream come true and one giant leap for Webkind. I was six-foot-two and lanky. I had on a pair of tan khakis and a fake white polo shirt. I gained so much confidence after that fingertip dunk in that dusty, small gym that it would carry over into the next year. Ultimately, it would be the catalyst for a long professional career. At the time, Dr. J. was the epitome of basketball, and anyone who wanted to dunk wanted to be Dr. J. I was the only kid I knew that could dunk in junior high school. I knew then that something special may be going on.

After that dunk, I was going hard with trying to learn the game. Over the summer I worked out with Wes, Big Chris, Lance, and the fellas and got my game on. Runs on the block or at Kelly Park were tougher physically and mentally than at school. The fellas were all older, and they would foul hard and talk shit about your mama, who they had just hugged on their way into your backyard. It was cold, but they prepared me.

When I got back to school, I was better, and the world (or at least Michigan) started to notice. In one of our first games of the season, the only game my parents ever missed (because my brother was sick), I had my first triple-double: sixty-three points, fifteen rebounds, and ten assists, with fifteen dunks. I was getting better and working on things like passing and ball handling. After all, I wanted to be Magic or Bird. I was taking on my father's personality, at least work-wise. He is more outgoing than I am, but his work ethic was unmatched. He told me that as long as I took care of whatever business I had, I could play as long as I wanted. What was funny was that neither my mother nor father knew how well I was playing until Coach Gilliam called my father two days later to alert him of my Wilt Chamberlain–like game.

"Mr. Webber, I hope you don't mind, but I called a TV news crew to come cover your son and our team tomorrow," he said.

My father asked, "Why?" My father never mentioned the conversation to me, but he was at the next game. I wasn't surprised. He only missed that other game because my brother was sick. That was the first and last game he missed.

That was the beginning of my basketball journey.

Chapter 19

When Channel 7 arrived for the interview, I was rocking a pair of Reeboks Moms had found on sale that were a size too big so that I could "grow into them." The cameraman asked me to dribble in place as he panned from my feet up my stick legs to my nonexistent waist, stopping at my bony shoulders and peanut head. The man who interviewed me asked me, "Do you like playing basketball?" and "Do you think about playing in the NBA?" to which I replied, "I don't know." Then he asked a question that would fuel a long burning debate.

"What college would you like to go to?"

Head down, nervous, I said, "Michigan State."

A day or two later, we sat huddled around our small television to watch my debut. My mother popped popcorn, and we added a combination of potato chips and pretzels, our favorite yellow salt, and hot sauce. My dad came down quiet, slow, and cool. We all knew that he was the most excited of all. When the interview came on, we watched, then cheered, hugged, and clapped, and then huddled up for prayer to give thanks. Then my brothers and I went upstairs and played basketball with a hanger on the door as the hoop and a sock as the rock.

Before I ever thought about what high school I was going to, I received my first college recruitment letter. Jud Heathcote, the head coach of Michigan State, who had led Magic and the Spartans to the 1979 NCAA championship, sent a note to our gingerbread house on Biltmore. He explained how happy he was that I wanted to be a Spartan and that he wanted me there as well. He sent an invitation for me and my family to come up and visit the campus that summer. Of course, I begged to go, and we did. I went with my parents to visit the campus in East Lansing.

We met Coach and his staff at Jenison Fieldhouse, the home of the Spartans. We got to go in the football stadium. I touched the grass, ran end zone to end zone, and looked at all the seats. I was so impressed. Coach then took us back to Jenison Field House. We walked through the locker room, and he showed me pictures and explained the Spartan tradition. The trophies, the players, and the locker room. He even gave me a shirt with my name on the back. I was in heaven.

The best moment of my life, up until that point, happened only a few minutes later. I got a chance to watch my hero, Magic Johnson, along with current and past Spartans, battle live in pickup games. I couldn't believe it. I was actually on the floor, sitting on the same bench the players got to sit on. Drinking out of the Gatorade container that they drank out of. Wiping my face with the same towels. I couldn't believe it; it was one the best moments of my young life. Did I mention it felt like I was in heaven? I was literally hyperventilating on the side, had sweaty hands, and was anxious. I couldn't wait to go home and tell my brothers, Wes, and the entire block about the experience of watching our favorite player up close and personal. The only thing that could've been better was to have the chance to play with the man.

Born only a few miles away, known as the best point guard of all time. The guy in the video with New Edition for the song "Secret." The guy who got out of the limo to meet Larry Bird in the Converse Weapons commercial. The guy with the goatee and signature smile. The tall guy who played the little guy's position. The guy whose father worked in a factory just like my father. It was surreal, something out of a Coca-Cola commercial with Mean Joe Greene and the little kid in the tunnel of Giants Stadium.

Then Magic Johnson looked over with his big grin, smiled, pointed his long, crooked index finger at me, and said, "Hey, kid, you up next." I damn near shit my pants. "Me?" I looked at my father, and he returned the awkward look and smiled as if to say, "I can't help you now, boy." I had on my school uniform—some green corduroy pants that my mama sewed and a fake Izod shirt that my mother bought and then sewed in a bootleg animal emblem the morning of our trip to East Lansing. "Okay!" I shouted.

I remember leaping off the bench, excited and nervous, running as fast as I could, which was slow. Magic was so fast, so in shape, and he talked so much. He had so many different emotions on the court. It was like he had multiple personality disorder. He was happy, mad, and a leader—encouraging his players like a big brother while talking shit to the other team and using his words as intimidation. Hell, he was even like a nun dragging a student by the ear down the hall at Catholic school after someone made a bad play. He was a parent, admonishing his kids for coming in late after curfew for someone not being in the right place on defense. All with a smile. All while competing. I noticed these attributes.

I had two chances to make a play for Magic. The first, I let myself down. Coming down on a three-on-one fast break, Magic tried to hit me with a no-look pass. The ball whizzed through my hands and past my head. I'd had a wide-open layup, but I missed the ball, dropping the pass. I promised myself on the car ride home, while reminiscing over the wonderful time I'd had, that I would work on my hands and never drop a pass again. I saw up close the best passer in the world. So, what's a pass from anyone else? Others should stick to my hands like a fly trap. That was the commitment I made right then and there. I believe that day was the catalyst for me having some suction cups. I regretted not catching a pass from Magic, one of the best—if not *the* best—guards of all time at the age of thirteen. Wasn't that a great regret? Also, a great inspiration.

The second play, Magic beat his defender at the top of the key, went down the lane, faked the ball to his left, and hit me while still looking left. In the back of my mind, I was hoping that he wouldn't pass it while at the same time hoping that he would. I caught the ball, jumped as high and hard as I could, and smacked the glass with both hands. I nervously and excitedly watched the ball go through the hoop. I didn't take a breath until there was a score on the other end. We won the game, of course. Coach Heathcote called me over as I was leaving, and I thanked Magic for allowing me to play; he said it was nice to meet me. I returned the comment with, "Boy I'm tired," and I'll never forget Magic's reply: "You can't get tired until you make $25 million." I knew what he meant. (I'd done nothing yet.)

Amused by Magic's brashness, my father let out one of his big, hoarse "I'm going to embarrass my son now" laughs. We went to Coach's office to talk for a while and returned to the gym. It was about two and a half hours before we left, and we walked through the arena once again. I took it all in. I looked up at the banners that honored Big Ten titles of the past, the championship banners of 1979, and Magic Johnson's retired jersey. I knew that I wanted to be part of that lifestyle. Coach took my parents to the side to talk to them, and I went on the floor with a newfound confidence. Shooting while imagining I was Magic. Dunking and pointing, that day sealed the deal for me. I fell in love with basketball. I wanted to wear green and white. I wanted to be a Spartan. More important, I wanted to be a hooper!

MY GRANDFATHER AND ME

Thank God I had my grandfather growing up. The world was about to get crazier. Fast. When I was thirteen, my grandfather had another stroke, losing mobility on his left side. I felt that this would require even more of my attention. He was vulnerable, and I felt it was my responsibility to get involved. I asked to move in with him, but Temple Christian was on the other side of town, and I didn't have any transportation. So we worked together. My mother and I sewed Velcro straps on his gym shoes. He protested when my father tried to build a ramp next to his porch. "I don't need no damn ramp," he griped. "I can walk." I loved his ornery spirit. I made sure I went to rehab with him.

Our entire family encouraged him to walk, and he did! I made a makeshift seat in the bathtub out of some old milk crates so he could sit up and not slip in the shower. Now every time I see a commercial for the tub that you can sit in, close the door, and then fill up with water, I think what a great invention that my grandfather would've loved.

Getting in and out of the shower would be scary for the both of us. Of course, you don't want anyone to see you naked or help you wash places that only children require assistance with. It was humbling. I admired his will to live. He never once complained or played the victim. I inherited that spirit, proven through the toughest moments in life. I spent the night every weekend, game or not. He continued to cook and clean. Besides driving, I don't really know how much the stroke slowed him down.

He was my second father, and we talked about everything and nothing. At times we would sit for long periods of time without speaking. I miss that. He understood me. He was comfortable with silence. Come to think about it, I know that's where my mom got it from, and I got it from her. I remember one of our conversations when he explained that all of his friends had passed on. He went on to say, "Well, in my life, I've only had a few great friends, and a few great friends are all you need!" I wish I would've asked him to elaborate. I wonder what stories were hidden behind his poker face and mantra.

What a difference the big game had made in my development and confidence. However, my true development started with the "Black Bobby Knight of the 'Hood," Curtis Hervey. Harv and his trusty assistant coach, Mr. Mont, and their team, the Super Friends, changed my life.

My father was at work on the assembly line, when some of his fellow grinders were talking about their kids, schools, and sports. The UAW (United Auto Workers of Detroit), a union that my father was a member of, supported the PAL (Police Athletic League), an organization of police, service men, and regular citizens who coached young people in sports. The police of Detroit's PAL were, in my opinion, some of the best people ever. They were there to raise men. Not pussyfoot. They were very fine men. My father was interested in getting me involved, so he inquired to his fellow GMers. A friend suggested he go to Bishop Borges, a local high school, to watch a PAL game. My father watched a few games, then inquired with the high school's head coach, Mike Fusco. Mike, never seeing me, told my father I was too young but that he knew a coach who was good and coached kids my age. My father came home cautiously excited... what could you expect from a thirteen-year-old?

"I've found a team for you."

"You have? What's the name?"

"Not sure, but it's supposed to be a pretty good team."

My father said that before I could play, he wanted to talk to my mama. I don't know what my parents discussed, but it didn't last long. My father called me downstairs and said, "I talked to your mother, and she said you could play. Practice is next week."

Eagerly, I immediately responded, "Thanks, Daddy!"

He gave me a kind look and a stern warning concerning commitments. My father would often speak of commitments and how most people would break theirs. He explained that the difference between real men and boys is that real men keep their word. He warned me, "It cost $120 up front to play on this team. This isn't about basketball! I have to work hard to make this money. I have other kids to feed, and if you do this, all I ask is that you work hard, just like I do every day. Don't waste our time or my money."

"No problem, Dad. I love to play. I'll do it."

Up until this point, all I knew was dunking, laying it up, having fun, and blocking shorter players' shots—basketball from a lighthearted, cakewalk perspective. I had never had real competition. It was not hard for me to dominate my seventh-grade year at Temple Christian. I was six-foot-three, almost a foot taller than the average seventh grader. I weighed 130 pounds. Even though I was crack-head skinny, I should have dominated. The kids didn't have a chance when playing against me. I was towering over them. My reach was so long that they couldn't even get their shot off.

I never really played organized ball, so I didn't know what to expect. I already knew the players on the teams I tried out for because we went to the same school. I had a comfort level with them. This tryout with this new team, however, would be something I had never experienced.

We pulled up in our Oldsmobile 98 to Lutheran East Church, which had a small gym attached in the back. I walked in with my father and noticed the atmosphere immediately. It was more like my street Biltmore than my new school Temple Christian. Screams of "Defense, checkup, off! That's nothin'!" rang through the gym. I had asked my mom to make me some basketball shorts for team tryouts and had on a burgundy Hawaiian short set outfit that she had just finished sewing the night before (Hawaiian short sets were the thang back then!). I also had a fake Max Julian black coat with a detachable fake fur hoodie. It was raining outside. I thought I was fresh. But looking fresh and having game are two different things, believe me.

I learned that when it comes to basketball, there's no question I'd rather have game. Curtis Hervey, a.k.a. Harv, the head coach of the Super Friends, called me over to participate in a drill. "Okay, big fella, you're on shirts," he said. "Three-on-three rebounding." That's a drill that starts when a coach or player shoots and intentionally misses. The team that rebounds can automatically go right back up for the easy score. It's a great drill to show the importance of offensive and defensive boarding—something I'd later become known for. I took off my six-button Hawaiian shirt, revealing my tank top, ran onto the court, and proceeded to get my ass busted that day.

A kid named Antonio Ragland would box out and foul me relentlessly. He was tenacious on the glass. Jalen was laughing, talking shit, putting a battery in Tones's back. Harv ignored every foul, but he didn't ignore me. "What the hell is wrong with you?" he'd shout. "Dunk the ball—every time! Go up strong! Quit being soft! Box out, jump!"

He kept screaming at me. I had never in my life heard curse words this creative and specifically in these combinations before. I had never heard a curse word directed at me by an adult this derogatory. You didn't curse in the Webber home. Harv was the Shakespeare of cusses. I was in shock. I had never experienced anything like this before. I never expected to be able to do the things that Harv expected me to do either, like dunk everything in the paint. Layups did not count in this practice. Considering I'd only learned to dunk off of a vertical jump four months after my thirteenth birthday, this seemed like a lofty goal to me.

There were about ten guys there: Iyapo Montgomery (pronounced Yop-oh), Kevin Colson, Jalen Rose, Quincy Bowens, Michael Hamilton, Antonio Ragland, Shake, Josh Koby, and the coach's son, Darrell Harvey. We were all only twelve and thirteen years old, but Harv was crazy. He expected us to be crazy too. It was just his style. He was like a mix between Bobby Knight and the legendary coach Will Robinson. Discipline and testing limits of mental strength were his forte. He coached heart and toughness more than strategy.

Harv, an ex-track jock from Jackson State, worked with his cousin, the great jazz artist Earl Klugh who, at times, would also help support the team financially. Harv was a unique individual. He was known for cursing you out in front of your mother, dogging you, and playing mind games with you, but he was also known for doing something most coaches aren't: follow-through. After he broke you down, he'd build you back up. You knew he cared and wanted the best for you. But I wasn't trying to hear that at the time. Not at all. I couldn't care less about him building me up or helping me become a better man. I didn't want none of it. The players were also aware of the Channel 7 interview and were trying and succeeding at proving that they weren't the competition I was used to playing against. They talked cash shit the whole practice. I could feel it was personal but didn't recognize why at the time.

After the last sprints, which were more than I'd ever done in my life, I left as fast as I could. When we got in the car, my father asked, "Did you like practice? How'd it go?"

Rapid fire, I said, "I hate it, I hate that team, I hate the coach, I don't want to go back. They don't do nothing but talk trash and foul and push and try to dog you. They're not even that good. They don't even run any plays. I don't want to go back. Please don't make me go back."

My father laughed—not in an "I told you so" way but in a "We already talked about it, and you better handle it" way. There was no turning back. "Just one season. That's all you're committed to, one season," he said. "Plus, I think you will like it. I think you'll really like it." My father told me to think about what I could do to be better and that "Webbers aren't quitters. We don't jump off of bridges. You gave them your word. You gave me your word."

I'm glad he didn't relinquish. I'm thankful that he didn't change the decision because of guilt or my emotions. I'm grateful that my parents only cared about the right thing, my protection, and what was best for me in the long run. But this was one of those times that I did hold contempt for my father. My mother couldn't have cared less if we played sports growing up. Even though I knew I made the decision myself and my father had explained commitments, I went to my room upset that I had to go back to practice and that my father wouldn't listen to me, that he didn't understand my feelings. How could he betray me? About a half hour later, my father came to my room. Maybe it was because the subject was sports, but that is the first time I remember my father speaking to me like a man.

Most of us are accustomed to hearing the same stories from our parents. Most of the time we look at them as nothing more than manufactured clichés intended to control us. Well, after this late-night talk with my father, his clichés started to make sense. My father, who never gave up much information about his upbringing, began to share. He talked about opportunity and how his were cut short because he had to quit school to work for his family. He continued, "At the end of the day, you're going to have to be committed to something. You might as well be committed to something you love. How will you know if you love something if you don't give it a good try at least once?"

I quickly flashed back to thinking of my father every day when he walked in the house, tired and frustrated from work. He would say, "Boys, find something you love to do. The factory ain't no joke." But that night he was on one. "You can't quit. If you don't go back, that means that you quit. Because of what someone says, you're going to quit? Because it's difficult? Because someone doesn't like you? That's not a man. You make them love you because you are the best or hate you because you are the best. If you don't go back, you will always remember why you didn't, and it was because you were scared. And you don't want that regret. Who cares if you do good or bad? You don't want to regret quitting because of the unknown, and only you will know, and that can be lonely, son."

The seriousness of what he spoke made me wonder if there was something deeper to his words, some kind of pain. I didn't even ask my grandfather. I knew what he thought: "Do something or kill yourself." After the talk with my father, I started to feel better about my commitment. After all, I did ask to play on this team. Practice wasn't that bad, just some loud screaming. It was actually fun. And those guys were cool. I had gone from a frenzied confusion about whether or not I should return to practice to a frenzied excitement about returning. I didn't know that this commitment to playing basketball and going back the next week would be a foundation, or, rather, one of the pillars, in my life. Those pillars—of not caring what people say and working hard at something you love rather than something you're forced to do—have accompanied me throughout my life.

This is why I think sports are so important for kids growing up. At least, the best of sports and the best characteristics of sports. Not only do they teach teamwork and how to win gracefully and lose with the same grace, but they teach you to get back up if you get knocked down. Sports simulate life's curve balls. Getting back on that horse and going back to that practice the next week would be the first lesson for me as a man. My first lesson in sports. With the same passion and commitment? We as kids fight what our parents say, but what better way to reinforce a parent's knowledge and their rules than through sports. With sports you have to be on time for your teammates. That's your responsibility. You have to sustain good grades to be eligible to play; you can't let your teammates down. You have to communicate with members of a team you may not get along with, and for the betterment of the team. I think it's great for kids to be involved in something that's bigger than them.

I thank my father for saying that I had to go back to practice. To this day, it's one of the best life lessons I've learned. When I make a tough decision, I go back to that day because I've seen the process and the proof of the principle that sometimes you have to keep walking forward, even if it's in a sandstorm and you can't see your hand in front of your face.

I returned to the next practice to make the best of a bad situation. All I had to rely on was instinct, but I found myself that day. I walked in wearing the same burgundy Hawaiian shorts set. I just nodded at my new teammates and didn't say anything; I was ready to go. I was focused and understood the weapons they were going to attack me with: not just agility and strength, but a mental game. I was ready for it. The shit talking on the block had prepared me.

Coach Harv called me onto the court just as he did the week before, for the same drill, shouting, "Big fella!" This time I was ready to rock. I didn't dunk the ball every time, but I did leave a few oohs, aahhs, posters, and highlights in that gym. Now I was the one snatching the boards smiling, collecting and-ones. It took me about two hours to establish myself as the best player. I was no longer the awkward, soft kid from the last practice.

Afterward, I sat around and talked with my new teammates. We laughed and talked about schools and our favorite athletes and teams. I became best friends with Iyapo, Jalen, and Kevin.

My father showed up for that practice. All he saw was me smiling, laughing, and looking mean and as focused as he does when he's fixing an engine. It was also the first time he heard me curse. When I said "Checkup, bitch" as I got an and-one on Antonio, I glanced at my pops out of the corner of my eye, hoping that he hadn't heard. I interpreted his poker face as approval. I became more confident, knowing he expected me to give my all, as he does every day at work.

Quickly, the Super Friends became my second family. Mr. Montgomery, Iyapo's father and our assistant coach, would become my second dad and one of my father's closest friends. The team culture was like my family culture: put God first, work hard, make no excuses, enjoy each other, have fun. I cared more about the Super Friends than I did my seventh-grade team at Temple Christian. Who could blame me? The Super Friends took basketball seriously. There was nothing else, no other options. Guys at Temple Christian liked it, but they had choices in their lives that we didn't, so they couldn't muster the same passion and dedication that we did. Our *surroundings* gave us incentive. Becoming great at basketball was a matter of survival for us. The Super Friends wanted to get out of our environment. Our team was special, not just because of the talent that we had but because of our mental toughness.

I SEE DEATH AROUND THE CORNER

We were about to travel out of town for our first tournament with the Super Friends, but we had to make a detour before we could leave from our usual meeting place, St. Cecilia's. Tijuan, a thirteen-year-old friend and teammate from AAU circles, had been shot and killed. No one knew why. Rumors of drug dealing and being in the wrong place at the wrong time ran prevalent. My parents, Harv, and others suggested that we all attend the funeral before heading to Connecticut for the AAU tournament.

It was déjà vu all over again. It was sad. The cries and tears from children and parents alike echoed in the large stone Catholic church. "God is not pleased today," the preacher yelled. The cries turned to wailing. "Tijuan is in a better place, but we are losing too many of our young kids here in

Detroit. We pray God keeps his arm of protection around these young kids and keeps them out of harm's way." With his prayer and a sea of tears, we were off to our first tournament as Super Friends. It's crazy that this was the second of many young friends slain violently, and I was only thirteen.

After a long somber drive, we arrived at our destination in Bridgeport. Entering the gym, the first thing I noticed was a huge picture of seven-foot-seven-inch Manute Bol standing next to five foot-three Muggsy Bogues. Incredible. As the team began to stretch for warm-ups, we watched the eleven-and-under team play, and then the twelve-and-under team. Those young squads had players like Robert "Tractor" Traylor and Maurice Taylor. That was the first of many tournaments from which I'd return home with an AAU All-American medal. We won, and I brought home an MVP trophy, but I don't remember who we played or how many points I scored. What I do remember is the validation. Not from crowd or players shaking my hand but from knowing that I had played well and was going to get even better. Sure enough, in a few weeks I noticed a real improvement in my game.

Let me introduce you to the original Super Friends:

Kevin Colson. Kev was an athletic point guard, a two-way player, and the smoothest one of the team. The ladies loved cool Kev! He thought he was up on everything before anyone. He lived with his mom, Kim, who we were all in love with. One of my favorite Super Friends stories involves Kev. It was 1986, we were in Connecticut, and he wanted the brand-new Michael Jordan white-and-red, patent leather, low-top eel-skin gym shoes. His mother had given him eighty dollars for food, which was supposed to last him a week. Well, Kev bought those shoes for eighty-three dollars the first day of the trip. I can't say that he didn't own his decision. If he didn't eat all week, he just didn't eat all week. He won twenty dollars in a dice game, and that held him over until Mr. Mont heard, told his mom, and held him down until we got home. Kevin was always fresh. He became my closest friend throughout life.

Iyapo Montgomery. An athletic lefty, son of Mr. Mont. He had a dope hi-top fade and was a dead ringer for Special Ed, the rapper, so girls were in love with him and thought he was the cutest guy ever to walk the earth. He was humble, loved Michael Jordan, and did everything like him. His pops was strict, though. The only man tougher than my pops. He didn't allow Yop to do nothin'.

Jalen Rose. Jalen was the lanky left-handed guard equipped with a weird-looking jumper that always fell. He was fast and could pass, was funny, and kept the group light. Jalen was the clown of the group, but don't underestimate his jokes.

Mike Ham. Solid forward, good defender, funny but did everything correct. He was a technician in everything he did, like running and shooting. It made him look robotic.

Antonio Ragland. Antonio was synonymous with fouling and rebounding. He was a tall, funny, big cat who loved hoop, but football was his favorite sport, and that was what he dominated. His mom was often on trips with us, and she was a sweet lady.

Darryl Hervey. Son of Coach Harv and a true warrior. A linebacker by trade, a great defender, and a tough son of a bitch on the court who was not to be tested.

Josh Koby. He was our Larry Bird. A great shooter and the only player from the suburbs who wasn't soft.

AAU trips were the best. Not just because of great competition or a chance to run around the country, but because it was a chance to hang out with your boys. Running out of restaurants instead of paying the bill. Wrestling in your hotel room and eating everything out of the mini bar, then acting like you didn't know what happened. The adventures of the young and stupid. Growing up with friends having these adventures was comforting. It was the environment I had always wanted. Brothers my age, guys to bounce ideas off of and to hear what they were thinking. I was right where I needed to be for the growth I desired. After coming back from Connecticut, the competition and camaraderie gave me a newfound confidence and identity.

Chapter 20

Ed

By eighth grade I was six-foot-five and excited about the newfound possibilities of this sport I was falling in love with. The best thing about AAU was that you could play against the best kids in your state and maybe even in the country. You could see how you measured up against the best of the best. But before you can become the man, you have to become the man at home. I was on my way to doing that. My seventh-grade summer did wonders for my confidence. I had gained weight from working out and lifting, and my game improved. I noticed a change in my posture when I sang solos at church.

Something had clicked. Suddenly I wanted to succeed in all facets of life. I became a competitor. I was committed to discipline, believing that with discipline comes results. I had people around who believed in me and set high expectations. I thrived on them. I couldn't wait to start my eighth-grade season. However, in Detroit basketball circles you can make your name in the summer as easily as you can in the state tourneys, and when it came to those, Coach Harv was old school.

When he took our team to play exhibitions or scrimmages, he had one rule: we had to play against older teams. Let your guys get beat up during the season and then unleash them during the tournament. Our team had a reputation for being tough and playing hard. We'd feel destroyed after we lost, even though we were losing to teams that we shouldn't have even played in the first place. As one coach said, "I don't even know why he lets them get their hopes up playing high school teams." But there we were, in the seventh grade, scrimmaging against high school kids.

It would be then, at a scrimmage for the Super Friends and several middle school teams at Southwestern High School, that I would meet the great high school basketball coach Perry Watson and his main man, Ed Martin. After play, Ed came down and introduced himself to my father. Ed said he was Perry's guy, a coach, and a "man of the community." He told my father he worked at Chrysler, and they hit it off. They were both part of the fraternity of auto workers. I met Ed after the game, and he seemed cool. He had juices, chips, and other snacks in a cooler in

his trunk. He passed them out in the parking lot to kids on all teams as he gave out words of encouragement like, "Keep your head up. Good work. I see you out there; that's the way you play." He was a familiar face at all the area amateur basketball events. He and Head Coach Watson looked like father and son, or older and younger brothers, and their relationship was just as close.

When it came to basketball, Southwestern High School was the most powerful program in Detroit. Coach Watson played for Eastern Michigan's team from 1970 to '72 and then became the head coach of the Southwestern Prospectors in 1979. P. Dub, as we called him, was known for coaching hard-nosed teams and great players, including Antoine "the Judge" Joubert, 1983's Mr. Basketball for Michigan.

Perry was known for always coming close to a title but not ever winning one. He advanced to the Michigan High School Athletic Association state championship title game seven times, only to lose seven times, from 1982 to '89. He was a sentimental favorite, the hood's favorite, and we all wanted him to win. We knew he had fewer resources. However, his workouts were legendary. All his players had to run track and cross-country. On defense he pressed relentlessly, subbed in patterns of five, and his teams would swarm.

That's why it felt so good to play so well at the exhibition at his high school. As I came by his car to grab my juice, he greeted me, "Hey, son." And then he complemented my game. He said he had watched me play a few times and that he'd seen a lot of players, but none could move as fast as I could at my height. He said if I worked hard, maybe I could be good one day. That was the end of it.

Ed Martin was on the pudgy side and always wore a fresh velour jogging suit. He wore dress socks with Jordans, and many times I saw him reach down and pull twenty, forty, or even a hundred dollars out of his sock (he carried a fat knot) and give it to a parent or kid in need with no hesitation. He'd also give money to kids after games for snacks, food, gym shoes, gear, or for them to take home, because he knew most of these kids were hungry. I would later learn that his go-to moves were cakes, pies, and ice cream from the Jewish deli off 8 Mile. Ed would hand out food to neighbors, friends, and strangers alike.

Mr. Martin was the Godfather, the candy man. He drove a gold, late-model seventies Mercedes-Benz. Nowhere near new, but nothing that we would see in our own 'hood on the regular. He was also a diehard basketball fan who knew the players. He would talk about Antoine Joubert and Roy Tarpley and other guys from Michigan who went to different colleges all across the country. He lived in a big, beautiful house on a golf course. He worked in the factory, so everyone was familiar with him, but few people knew about his lifestyle. He said that he'd lost an eye in a factory accident and won a big settlement.

The hood needed a Santa Claus, and Mr. Martin was it. If you needed shoes, he would have a hookup. If people were unemployed, or if it was around the holidays and things were hard, he was there for you. Not just for the best players on the team, but for coaches or parents and people in the amateur ball system that was the word. He seemed to be more than sixty years old when I met him. This made the jogging suits and gym shoes stand out even more, but it seemed to fit him because he loved basketball so much. That was who he was. I would become accustomed to seeing Mr. Martin at all the local hoops events. He knew all the teams and coaches, including the Super Friends and our parents and families. He was part of the Detroit basketball system.

Although I was gaining a reputation in Detroit, it would be a trip to St. Louis, where I got to see the stars of the future, that would inspire me to work even harder. It also showed me that I had a long way to go. The Super Friends won the Michigan fifteen-and-under AAU tournament in Monroe, and we were only fourteen! It was a wonderful feeling winning the champion, but our goal was to win the national tournament.

We worked hard to get there. When I say we worked hard, I mean we *worked hard*. Since we didn't have a track, Harv designated a route through the streets of Detroit for us to run. We would lift weights in the backyard of Antonio's house. Often we would run down the street, and people would yell out of their cars, "Don't kill those boys!" or "Keep it going!" We sold candy, begged, worked, and did chores to raise money for new uniforms. The game in Monroe paid off. I made the All-Tournament Team, and after the champion was crowned, I was named the tournament MVP.

St. Louis, however, was a totally different party. As we sat in the opening ceremonies, I saw a sixteen-year-old, seven-foot-two kid named Shawn Bradley. Jamal Mashburn of the New York Gauchos was on a team of men among boys. Monster Mash, as he was named, put on a clinic in that tournament, posting up, hitting jumpers, and dribbling. He could do more than most players. His size was not used as an excuse or disadvantage. The game was changing, and he had guard-like skills despite his size. I met and became close with a kid from Virginia named Grant Hill. "G Hill" was skilled, athletic, and could shoot the lights out.

I made the All-Tournament Team, a feat I was proud of since I was a year or two younger than the other guys on that coveted list. Everyone on the Super Friends had to reevaluate their game after that trip, not just because guys were older and more mature, but because we saw how good we could be with hard work. I think we came in fourth.

That tournament changed things. No longer would we be concerned about dominating Michigan ball. We wanted national championships. We came away with a better appreciation for basketball and discipline. That trip was one of the best I've ever had in my life, and I'll always remember it for several reasons. First, I saved someone's life. We were outside swimming in the pool, or rather playing around in the pool because none of us could swim, when I saw Mike Ham going under, starting to drown. He was known for cracking jokes, so it took me a while to realize that he wasn't joking.

He slipped from the side and was now in the middle of the eight-foot deep pool. He was reaching with both hands in the air, gasping, and swallowing water. I held onto the side, trying to reach him, but I couldn't grab him. So I blew the breath out of my body, went to the bottom, grabbed him, and jumped up, moving us both toward the side of the pool. Then I went back down again, holding onto him, and repeated it twice until we go to the side, basically jumping underwater. After we made it to the other side, we laughed about it, and I told him he owed me his life. I saw his eyes after we pulled him out. He was scared—terrified. This had been no laughing matter. But we were young, so it was hilarious.

I made it back to the room and earned a scar that I have to this day. I was wrestling in my room with Kevin, and I actually broke the Super Friends record for piledrivers. The WWF and guys like Hulk Hogan, Andre the Giant, and my favorite, the British Bulldogs, were still big around this time. My go-to move was the piledriver, a move in which, while standing, you plant your opponent between your legs with their head between your knees, as they face you, and you proceed to fall, or drop on your butt, ramming their head into the ground. I did this to Kevin eighteen times in a row on the bed of our hotel room. Earlier that day, I bought a cap gun and put the extra caps in the right front pocket of the jeans that I was wearing. Jalen kept shooting the cap gun off. Around piledriver number fourteen, I noticed that my quad was burning—not from muscle fatigue but fire. The gun had seemingly sparked the extra caps in my pocket, and my pants were on fire! Before I knew it, there was a hole in my pants.

I rushed to take off my father's belt that I was wearing. But it was too large, so I cut a hole in the belt with a knife so that it would fit better around my waist. Man I was in trouble because it wasn't that easy to get off. It was stuck! I screamed and yelled. I could not get my pants off until it was too late. White flesh. Somehow, we just laughed and joked about it.

We had a great time in that hotel. It was really nice, and the elevator was staffed with a conductor. We would spend most of the day ringing him from different floors, then running down the stairs so he wouldn't know who was ringing the elevator. I guess by the end of the weekend he was fed up because after we came in from our loss in the consolation game, he refused to let the team on. That was a very bad decision. The elevator man held his arm across the elevator to block our entrance. Harv said, "Let us in!" The conductor said no. So Harv said, "Big fella, let us in." The conductor said no again, so Harv proceeded to karate chop and pull the guy out of the elevator. He then took us up to the floor himself.

In order to appreciate the times then, you must first understand the culture of Detroit basketball in the early eighties and nineties. No matter how good you were, what high school you attended, or your AAU team of choice, if you wanted to make it, you had to go to one place to display your skills: St. Cecilia's. I've traveled across the world. I've seen firsthand how intensely different communities embrace their local homegrown sports. The passion for basketball at St. Cecilia's is comparable to Texas's "Friday Night Lights" with football. Floridians with oranges. Serbians with water polo and basketball. Idaho with potatoes.

This was the local farmers' market for hoops. You could watch the stars of yesterday play alongside the present-day NBA beast and beat up on and inspire the skinny, snot-nosed players of tomorrow. **The Saint is a basketball sanctuary,** a hole in the wall. It's the small gym inside St. Cecilia's Catholic Church, located on the east side of Detroit. It was about ten minutes from my church, which made commutes on Sundays convenient.

There are two small, makeshift locker rooms located in the Saint's basement, though most of us would change in the car in the parking lot. Capacity is around two hundred, including standing room. The "out of bounds" line—which should serve as the "baseline"—is substituted with a home gym knowledge of the court. You don't run your ass into the out of bounds line because it's a brick wall with no warning sign. The restrooms and drinking fountain are located directly next to the bench on the far end. Why is this important? If you're a spectator, you better come down out of the stands, stretch, and prepare to make a break for it.

The far wall, which runs full court opposite the stands, also borders a brick wall. If the ball hits the wall, it's out of bounds, but your back can touch the wall while you let up a three. It's cozy. So cozy that you can't shoot a full-court shot because the low ceiling is like an ode to Mutombo, slapping every full-court heave down at its apex. Lastly, there were no open windows and no air conditioning. One way in, one way out. Hot, humid, and

'He's still so young'

High school coaches pursue 6-foot-5 eighth-grader

BY CLIFTON BROWN
Free Press Sports Writer

If you don't know who Chris Webber is, you've haven't seen him play basketball this season. You'd remember him.

In one game, Webber had 15 dunks. In another game, he scored 51 points. Webber averages more than 30 points a game. His team hasn't lost in almost two seasons.

But here are some other interesting facts.

Chris Webber is 13 years old. He's in the eighth grade. And already, he's being pursued by high schools because of his basketball talents.

"Sometimes, I think all of us forget how young Chris is," said Dave Gilliam, Webber's coach at Inkster Temple Christian. "We look at the kid, and he's 6-5. We think he's a man. But he's still so young."

Yes, Webber is young, but he's good. Good enough to dominate youngsters his age. Big enough to wear size-16 sneakers. Talented enough to make a difference in any high school's basketball team.

Not only that, Webber is an excellent student, personable, and well-mannered – the kind of youngster you'd want your son to make friends with. Webber, who lives in Detroit, will begin high school in the fall, and he hasn't decided where he will go. When Webber decides, one coach will be elated. Many others will be disappointed.

"This is an unusual situation, something I've never been through before," said Mayce Webber, Chris' father. "I mean, there's a lot of pressure on kids today. People have been talking to me about Chris for a while now. My wife (Doris) and I try to protect him as much as we can.

"The main thing we want for Chris it to get a good education. Things in life like basketball can be lost at any time. Wherever he goes, we want Chris to get the education."

WEBBER IS JUST ONE of many eighth-grade players in Michigan being watched by high school coaches. Head coaches, their assistants, and others connected with a school attend CYO games, summer camps and junior high games to find out which youngsters have the most potential. It doesn't matter how young you are anymore. If you can play, the coaches will find out about you.

"You think it's a coincidence that the same high schools have good teams, year after year?" said Sam Washington, director of the nationally renowned St. Cecilia basketball camp in Detroit. "You think it's all just good coaching? No way. I don't care how good a coach you are, you need talent. And the coaches who keep up with these grade-school kids are the ones that win consistently. I'm talking about the private schools, and the PSL."

Most high school coaches don't like to use the word "recruiting." Coaches say that word gives people the impression they're doing something that violates Michigan High School Athletic Association rules, such as offering an athlete free meals or an athletic scholarship. Yet, it's a fact many of the best high school programs in Michigan keep tabs on eighth-grade athletes.

"Usually when you see a high school coach at an eighth-grade game, he's not there just because he loves basketball," said Kurt Keener, head basketball coach at Detroit Country Day.

"As the coach at Birmingham Brother Rice, I'm perfectly within my rights to see an eighth-grade kid play basketball," said Brother Rice coach Nick Conti. "By the same token, a public school coach has the same right to watch a kid who's playing within his district. But I'm not naïve enough to think that no coaches out there have ever cheated."

MHSAA assistant director Fred Sible says he hears very few complaints regarding illegal high school recruiting.

"Every once in a while, a parent will call and accuse a school of recruiting, but the complaints we get can rarely be substantiated," Sible said. "Our rules clearly state that a school may not be involved with any undue influence with regard to recruiting prospective athletes. And any tuition or financial remuneration must be based strictly on financial need or academic merit, not on athletic ability. If we can prove recruiting is going on, we have the authority to make it very difficult on a school."

WEBBER'S PARENTS ARE keeping close tabs on their son's situation, and so far, Mayce Webber insists he hasn't been pressured, or offered anything illegal. And he is determined to do things the right way.

"When you start taking offers from people, it leads to bigger things," Webber said. "People think they can run your life after that. Besides, Chris has the qualifications. We don't need that."

Chris Webber lives in the Redford High school district, but he is leaning toward attending a private school. He is considering Country Day, Birmingham Brother Rice, Detroit St. Martin dePorres and Redford Bishop Borgess. And of course, the people at Inkster Temple Christian want Webber to stay there. Temple Christian is a Class D school with fewer than 500 students in the first through 12th grades. Webber has been there for two years, and he enjoys it.

"People treat me like a regular person here," Webber said. "There isn't a lot of special treatment just because I play basketball, and I've made a lot friends. I might just stay here. I put God first, then my family, then basketball. I figure if I'm good enough, I'll be seen here just like I'd be if I went to a big high school."

The people at Temple Christian know they'll have to fight to keep Webber. And they're ready to do it.

"Believe it or not, I'm not putting a lot of pressure on Chris, because he knows how I feel about him already," Gilliam said. "But we're not going to just give him up. We care about him too much as a person to just let him go. He's a beautiful person, and he has such an impact on other kids at our school.

"All I can offer him is a lot of love. I can't offer him everything that these bigger schools can. We're going to upgrade our schedule, and we'll need to if Chris stays. And the thing is, if Chris Webber plays here, other good players will want to come here, too. It would do a lot for our varsity program."

Webber appears unaffected by the attention he is receiving. All he wants is a school where he's comfortable, where he can get a good education, and where he can play basketball.

"I'll probably make up my mind in May," Webber said.

But get this. Webber has three youngster brothers, and all of them are tall.

Said Mayce webber with a laugh, "I guess we might have to go through this again."

JOHN COLLIER/Detroit Free Press

Chris Webber, 6-feet-5, is drawing a lot of attention from high school coaches but he says people at Inkster Temple Christian "treat me like a regular person here. There isn't a lot of special treatment just because I play basketball, and I've made a lot of friends."

Top-notch eighth-graders

The following is a list of some prominent eighth-grader basketball players in the Detroit area.

Player	School
Chris Webber	Inkster Temple Christian

summer temps were often unbearable—triple-digit readings with the only relief coming from the one open door.

As I got older, I appreciated the sweatbox-styled gym even more. It was a great place to lose weight and get in shape during the off-season. It was the perfect village. Everyone felt safe. You would see the same parents every weekend, serving their three-to-four game bid. The Saint was an all-day name-dropping session. The competition was crazy! If you were college or pro aged, you could play against the likes of Hall of Famer Isiah Thomas and NBA vets like Terry Duerod, John Long, Derrick Coleman, Steve Smith, Glen Rice, Joe Dumars, Doug Smith, and Victor Alexander, to name a few.

High school and junior high students benefited the most from the Saint. We had a chance to sit and watch the best in the game. Study their movements, mimic their body language, and dream of their life. The best of the college and high school guys are far too many to name, but the hoopers I grew up with at the Saint would be at the top of that list: Jalen Rose, Kevin Colson, Iyapo Montgomery, Dre Mitchell, Tony Tolbert, Voshon Lenard, Brian Tolbert, Quincy Bowens, Parish Hickman, Mike Jackson, Howard Eisley, Katu Davis, Boo, Emanuel Bibb, and Shawn Respert. Many of us played pro ball, and all of us were given a chance to get a good education while chasing our dreams.

The Saint was more than an environment. It was our incubator. I looked forward to every minute playing in front of what was our version of the Apollo. Alley-oops off the backboards were like James Brown doing splits. The full-court traps were relentless, like a rhythmic jazz section improvising while staying in tune and on beat. Bad shots or players who consistently refused to stay in their lane and play their role would get booed off the court by our sandman: the crowd. Games often had to be stopped because of fan enthusiasm. These fans were the smartest. They cheered for basketball plays, clapped for bounce passes, jumped for and-ones, and lost their damn minds on any play that exhibited heart. Oftentimes, the losing team (often a younger team that had no right to be playing) were lauded off the court as if they had won the championship. If you wanted respect here, you needed to play with heart.

Another gym we played at was 1300 Beaubien—better known as 1300—where many of our PAL tournament games were played during the year. The unique thing about 1300 was that it was in the Detroit police headquarters. Occurrences at the tourney games could have been a TV show, with all the different angles, story lines, and episodes just waiting to be written. Drama, comedy, and sometimes horror, I got to watch the players in the city of Detroit go at it. The gymnasium had one main floor, with courts expanded parallel sideways, bisecting the main court. Sardine-like bleachers encompassed each of the courts. There was one common entrance, and it was not uncommon to see officers bringing people in handcuffs in to be processed. But I never felt that we were in danger. There were so many policemen at the games—coaching, refereeing, outside and inside. We did see a lot though.

My most memorable Saturday was when a kid named Derrick Grose broke a wooden backboard on a body-to-body dunk. Seeing that sealed the deal. I wanted to be a big man that was powerful and could dunk on you like Dominique Wilkins, Charles Barkley, and Derrick Coleman—the great powerful forwards. Doug Smith, Derrick Grose, D. Lyton, and Terry Mills are who I wanted to ball like from our metro area.

I used to love playing at 1300 for reasons beyond competition. Since the games were downtown, that was a plus. I loved going downtown. Driving past Cobo Arena and going in Trappers Alley and watching them make chocolate, with an emphasis on watching because we never got to purchase the chocolate that looked so good. The workers would mix it in a show-like atmosphere before cooling it and boxing it up to sell. After every game that was close to the first or fifteenth, we would go to Greektown to buy gyros. We'd visit my grandfather and drop off his lamb, and on our way home, we'd drive through Indian Village, a neighborhood in Detroit lined with beautiful old houses. We cruised through neighborhoods, seven people packed into an Oldsmobile 98, dreaming and pointing out which house we'd move in to if we could.

We discussed the architecture and different types of yards; everyone had their own style. Jeff loved houses with big yards in the front, while my mother loved old Victorian architecture. I loved houses with old slate roofs and brick or stone facing. "I'm going to buy you that house when I get old, Mama," Jeff or I would say. Jason and David (and the baby maybe even) had something to say. My mother would say "Thank you, baby," or "Oh, I can't wait, David." We argued over who would buy her the house first or who she would live with, and she'd smile while settling us down.

Chapter 23

Soul Is Not for Sale

It had only been one year, but so many things took place. So much maturity. The death of friends. Confidence gained through hard work. I kissed a couple girls but was still in love with Larenda on Biltmore. I grew a couple of inches, put on a little muscle, traveled a little bit around the country, and made a few friends. I thought life would always be great. Why wouldn't it? I was playing well and couldn't have had better expectations for our team. We'd just been together a few months, so why wouldn't everything keep getting better for everyone? We were a family. We preached family. Everyone did. We spent the night over at each other's houses. We would never split up—not the Super Friends.

In the year to come, I would learn that I hadn't seen nothing yet and to never make assumptions. I had a lot to learn about people. I believed words. I grew up thinking that all cliques and friendships would mimic the dynamics and love of my family. I was naïve. I would soon learn that people lie, and some who call themselves friends can be jealous. There's a thing called ulterior motives, and people will play you emotionally to get what they want. I was just happy I got to travel and make new friends. I didn't have time to take it in. I was in it. I was excited just playing video games on ColecoVision, watching television, playing football in the middle of the street and tackling on the sides, challenging Wes to see how many times we could jump consecutively on pogo sticks, sitting out late at night on Big Chris's porch, and taking care of Granddaddy. I was still a kid. I loved basketball, but I was still a kid. At least for a little while longer.

After another late evening and tough practice, Harv had the parents huddle up at half court. He told them he had an opportunity that none of them (including himself) could afford. He went on about a scholarship program at a high school called Detroit Country Day. He said the school was known for its educational prowess, sports programs, and high tuition—about $20,000 per year. Harv knew that all the parents valued education and that some of the parents already had their kids in private or Catholic schools, but that was $2,500 at the most.

He informed them that the scholarship was based on previous academic records but, most importantly, an interview and four-hour entrance exam. Some parents knew right away they were out of the running, while others were going to make sure they weren't going to miss out. To each his own, right?

Personally, I didn't care about the opportunity. As far as I was concerned, J. Rose and I were going to Southwestern. We had become close friends and wanted to be like Derrick Coleman and Steve Smith, the best guard and forward out of Detroit. We were going to rep Detroit together and bring all of the Super Friends with us. At least, that was the plan.

My teammates and I were not enthusiastic about Country Day, because we made presumptions fueled by ignorance and fear. The fear came when we learned that in order to receive the scholarship, we had to pass a test. My mother was super positive, saying, "I know you'll pass, easy! I taught you to read, write, comprehend, and make decisions. Just trust yourself, baby. Don't listen to all the negative talk that you can hear in your head sometimes. That's natural insecurity. Why not take a test to go to one of the best schools in the country?"

I responded with frustration. "I want to be with my friends!" I said. "I don't want to go somewhere where there aren't people like me. They won't like me! They're all rich. We are broke as a joke! I don't want to be around people that don't understand. They are all stuck-up, entitled, spoiled little rich kids."

"Oh, so you know them personally? You know how their parents raised them? You know how all whites, Asians, and Middle Eastern kids act? You don't even know how black kids act! If they know everything like you, they'll judge you the same. Do you want that?"

Until I spoke to my mother while writing this book, I didn't know that she had been a part of the first few busing waves in Detroit high schools an attempt to reduce the impact of segregation on poorest communities. My mother was involved in the process that assigned students based upon their addresses. Unfortunately for her, she would be the only one in her neighborhood to attend Henry Ford High School, a twenty-minute bus ride from her home.

High school was the loneliest time of her life. Instead of going to Central or Northern High School with friends in her district, she was spending most of her high school moments on lonely bus rides and long commutes. When my mother was young, she hated the fact that no one looked or dressed like her. No one lived close. It wasn't easy to have friends over after school because of distance and lack of transportation. One of her closest friends at the time, who was in the same Christian club, told her, "We can be friends at school, but you can't call my house." My mother was heartbroken. She was sick a lot and couldn't ask her friends for the homework assignment because they wouldn't talk to her. It was hard with her friends in her neighborhood as well. They had different schedules and went to different schools and grooved to different rhythms of life. She spent time with her friends at church, and they would fill the lonely void in her social life. At this time though, I didn't think she understood.

I don't remember it, but my father told me that Coach Keener, Country Day's basketball coach, came over for a visit. Coach Keener came over to explain how good Country Day was as a school. My father said that he had a great visit and that he immediately took a liking to Coach Keener. He and I knew Southwestern High School was still my first choice, but Country Day had an open house in October. The test and interview would take place during the open house.

I was both defiant and excited on the morning of the test. For weeks I'd been threatening to drop out of school and fail the test. I would face my consequences and flat-out not go. The Detroit basketball community knew that I hated the idea of going to this college preparatory school twenty minutes away from home. I loved Will Smith in *The Fresh Prince of Bel Air*, but I didn't want to be him. I didn't want to go to school with a bunch of Carltons. My father's reply was simple and direct: "You will go to the high school that your mother chooses. As long as you live in my house, you will obey our rules. When you move out of my house, you can make your own decisions."

As we drove to the campus, The Winans song "Wherever I Go" played on the shabby speakers of our violet Scooby-Doo van.

My mother started to speak about this song, just talking about how God would be with us through all our ups and downs. She said a prayer with me, asking God to help me remember what I had studied, that I wouldn't be nervous, and to help me make good decisions. She reminded God of the fact that she did not have the resources for this opportunity, and she knew this blessing came from Him. As we hit the top of the hill, I could not believe my eyes. The school was one of the most beautiful places I'd ever seen. The grass was crazy green, immaculate, and cut meticulously. The parking lot looked over the football and soccer fields and huge scoreboard. Inside, the halls were lined with carpet. It was quiet.

Students were sitting on the floor, studying while listening to music. The band and orchestra were practicing the day I arrived for my test. The gym was incredible. It was a picture-perfect moment, though I didn't want to admit it at the time. I hated the school even before I took one step into the building.

Wherever I go, let your spirit follow me
Wherever I go, let your spirit follow me
If in the desert I'll find pleasure
If in the valley, I really don't care
I'll walk through the wilderness
Through shadows of darkness
I'll never falter as long as you're there
Wherever I go, let your spirit follow me
Wherever I go, let sour Spirit follow me

"Wherever I Go"
Marvin Winans

Now, as I looked around the campus, I had to admit that it was more welcoming than intimidating, more inspiring than deterring. Kevin and Iyapo loved it. Kev said, "Man, you see those girls? You see the football stadium? Man, this is the nicest school I've seen."

As I walked down the hall, I saw pictures of athletes from the past. Robin Williams was a famous alum. School legend has it that he was a pretty good wrestler. Actor Courtney Vance and too many others to name adorned the halls like ornaments on a Christmas tree. But there was one alum I was very familiar with: Charles Johnson. He grew up on Gilchrist, just one street over, and won a state championship playing quarterback for the football team. He then went on to college, where in 1990 he won a national championship at Colorado as a backup who started in the Orange Bowl, defeating Notre Dame 10–9. I knew he was a good man from the city, so that helped Country Day in my eyes.

Over the next week, the members of the Super Friends would test and interview to apply to Country Day. I prayed that our whole team would pass or that we'd all fail. That would be the best-case scenario: carpool, AAU practice right after high school practice, seeing the same parents, same friends. I knew that going to different high schools would have separated us due to conflicting schedules and situations. Specifically, when you're a Super Friend, your summers are devoted to the team. All relationships are sacrificed, lines are drawn, commitments have been made, and priorities are set in stone. I knew there would be casualties from this test and interview.

I felt very insecure as I entered the classroom and sat down at the too-small desk for my test. As I sat down, I couldn't help but think of what I was wearing. I was in my father's pants that were too big, a shirt that my mother had sewn, and a blazer from only God knows where. It wasn't in my normal rotation, and it wasn't new, so who knows. Goodwill had been good to me and my family. As I look back, I can't complain, but as a teenager, one can only imagine my sarcasm. After a few more jokes from Kev, I calmed down and settled in. The test took a little under four hours, with two intermissions that we used to go to the bathroom and take inventory of our answers and emotions. Kev was hard to judge because he was always optimistic; the same with Iyapo, but because he was quiet. As I look back, I think I was in awe. In less than an hour, I witnessed more freedom to return to childhood dreams than I had since I lost that magic that every adult loses and that kids from poor environments are forced to abandon way too early. Clichés seemed believable again, like "If you work hard, it will pay off." Not like my 'hood where everyone works hard, but there seems to be little reward for their sweat. Though I had planned to boycott and play tic-tac-toe on the multiple-choice answers or flat-out refuse to test, I didn't. I answered every question to the best of my ability. My pride wouldn't let me fail. I also knew that this was my mother's dream.

A few days after the first of the year, I was sitting in the living room when I heard a knock on the door. It was followed by a hello and the flow of letters through the mail slot of our tiny home. We sat waiting by the door for Daddy to come home, excited about his ritual of good food on paydays. Sometimes we could choose. We were in the middle of brainstorming Chinese, fried fish, White Castle, Arthur Treacher's, Ponderosa on Sunday, and Bonanza, when my mother calmly announced that I had been accepted to Country Day.

My father walked in as my mother read the news. He immediately had us join hands to pray and thank God for his blessing. But I didn't feel blessed. I thought my mother and father were making the biggest mistake of our lives—selling their souls, and mine, for the opportunity to be around rich people. I felt they were valuing people or prestige. I was wrong. They valued education and opportunity, but I couldn't see it. I thought it was against everything my mother and father had worked for.

Before our next practice, I found out that not all the Super Friends had passed the test, and some "chose not to take advantage of the opportunity." But we would not be attending high school together, and the line seemed to be drawn directly down the center of our team. Out of nine players, three went to Southwestern, one went to McKenzie for football, four went to Country Day, and Josh Colby went to school in Farmington. I was hurt. I wanted to go to Southwestern, but my parents would not allow me. Jalen and I planned to win championships together.

That moment changed things forever. Dozens of local and national tournaments couldn't keep the sworn teammates for life, the Super Friends, together. We would have one more summer together.

This hurt me. I appealed to my parents to come to their senses, but they weren't trying to hear it. I explained that my friends were very important to me, and they conceded that they loved my friends, too, and did not want that to change. But my parents were like two trees planted by the rivers of water: "They would not be moved." Instead, life kept moving. On Sunday at church, they thanked God for the opportunity that He had afforded our family. Meanwhile, I was questioning God, wondering if he even heard my prayers or wanted what was best for me. I laugh now thinking about how foolish and naïve I was, being mad at God because he had given me His grace to get me in that school.

Early my eighth-grade year, Ed Martin came over to the house one weekend to speak to my father. They chatted on the porch while I played outside with my friends. I was always excited to see that big body gold Benz swerve up the block like a spaceship. After about twenty minutes of talking with my father, Ed called me over.

"Hey, I got these for you," he said. "Those old Etonics you're wearing are beat up. Your father said it's okay."

"Thank you, Mr. Martin."

"No problem. Just keep getting those good grades and listening to your father. Proud of you."

That would be our first and last conversation about grades. My parents ran thangs at our house and didn't need any help with incentivizing or discipline. I ran upstairs to my room, excited that I had a brand-new pair of shoes. I only had two pair before, my church shoes and my school shoes. Some patent-leather Ronald McDonalds that were one size too small and my gym shoes, some beat-up Etonics. My mother was still sewing my clothes, so even though I was excited about the shoes, I was hoping that he had some brand-name jogging pants to match. I called my brothers Jeff and Jason into the room. "Look at these," I said. "Mr. Martin bought me these. They're fresh."

My brothers and I talked ball as we laced the unlaced gift several times before going to bed. But before I closed my eyes, I thought, *It's really messed up Mr. Martin got me these, and my brothers still look bummy wearing my second, third, and fourth hand-me-downs.* I was so happy about my new gift though. The irony, however, is that earlier that week Jeff and Jason were getting killed in school because they had patent leather NBAs, a cheap sneaker that was a knockoff of the Adidas brand. It was the only thing my mom could afford from the Sibley's shoe store on Grand River next to

Perry Drugs and our *Cheers*—the K-Mart, where everybody knew our name. They were being teased as the kids in the lunchroom announced that NBA stood for "Never Bought Adidas!" I promised myself right then and there that I'd one day make sure the whole family was straight.

My mother was not at all impressed by Mr. Martin's gesture but seemed to let my father handle it. Privately, she said, "I don't like him. Why would an old man be interested in a young boy? Something ain't right."

My dad tried to make sense of things. "You don't know basketball, baby," he said. "That's how it is. He helps these boys get out of the ghetto; he doesn't want anything in return. He's just a good man who loves basketball. He just wants to make a difference." That was Ed's thing, his mission statement or mantra. He didn't need or want anything from anybody. He was paying it forward. He just wanted to help those who were less fortunate. He wanted to help and give back to the community.

Our eighth-grade team went undefeated that season, but I didn't wear my new shoes until the season was over. I wanted to use them for PAL, AAU, and the Saint. Ed started to come over more my eighth-grade year. There were more cakes, pies, two or three jogging suits, and a pair of shoes for Jeff and Jason. Even though he would aggressively push me to team up with Jalen at Southwestern, I still felt that he cared about me and my well-being. Plus, he knew that Jalen and I had promised each other in seventh grade that we would go to the same high school, so recruiting wasn't really necessary. I didn't think that he was recruiting me; we weren't for sale. He knew us. I thought he was just helping my brothers, who were wearing terrible shoes, and helping me look good since he had extra. I knew he wanted me to go to Southwestern, and that was why he gave me things. But I also must say, I felt he would've given me those things anyway, because he did it for players who didn't go to Southwestern.

However, before the end of my eighth-grade year, Ed actually put on the full-court press for recruiting. He would say things like "You know you have to come here and play. Who else is going to get you ready for college like Perry? Save Detroit basketball! You have to help us win a championship! We lost seven times in eight years. You know Jalen is coming; Mike Ham is coming. Don't you want to play with them?"

I was convinced. I wanted to go to Southwestern. I loved the school, the history, the players who came before me, the reputation, the basketball, and I loved Ed. Not because of a pair of shoes, or juices, or the food, but because he seemed to be a nice man. I thought Ed was an extension of Harv and Mr. Mont, who didn't have the money to help. They were giving kids the shirts off their backs—men who cared about the boys coming after them. In one conversation I had with Perry, he said that he could make me one of the best high school players in Michigan. I believed him. My father believed him. But the one problem was my mother, who was in charge of making the decision. This was a promise my father made, or rather asked her to make, when discussing parental responsibilities while dating his girlfriend who was a teacher. She didn't give a damn about hoops, coaches, presses, promises, or potential. She was not changing her mind.

I was only fourteen and felt like I had the weight of the world on my shoulders. The toughest part was that I didn't have any experience or context to help me accept my parents' decision. I felt like I had the responsibility of grown men three times my age. I was told that Perry was going to lose his job if he lost the biggest recruit in Detroit history to the suburbs. They would have me believe that I would be letting the whole neighborhood and community down. Damn, that was a big responsibility for a fourteen-year-old kid.

AIN'T TOO PROUD TO BEG

There was so much I wasn't privy to. I was in junior high. I didn't know my potential. I just wanted to play with friends. I interviewed my father for this book, and his insight gave me so much more context about what was going on behind the scenes in the adult world of how to pimp a young hooper. He told me about a conversation he had with Ed that would establish clear boundaries and set the tone for an unpretending relationship.

His account of a drive with Ed on a cold winter day makes perfect sense, because after that drive, my relationship with Ed and the Southwestern brass would be fractured. It would always be them against me. Southwestern against Country Day. City versus suburb.

Ed asked my father to jump in the car with him and go for a ride to the Jewish bakery on 8 Mile near the fairgrounds. This was something that they used to do: drive around the neighborhood, talk, come back with cakes, and say their goodbyes. But that day, while the route and destination would be the same, the conversation was different.

"Twenty thousand dollars," Ed said suddenly.

"What?" said my pops.

Ed stopped at the light on 7 Mile and Woodward and, to my father's shock, handed him a huge knot. "Count this!"

My father counted the stacks of cold, hard green wrapped in bands that read "Thousand dollars" and stopped before he reached twenty. He told me, "That was the most money I had ever seen in my life. I only made a little more than that for the year!

The thoughts that went through my mind in seconds—wow. I calculated the bills I'd pay, what to put up, what to buy your mama, what to give the church."

Then my father looked at Ed and said, "Man, you crazy. I can't take this! You'd give me this for Chris to go to Southwestern?"

"Hell yeah! Isn't that what Country Day's scholarship is? About 20K?"

Ed persisted, not realizing that he had scared my father with his proposal. "All I know now is that I was being set up," my father said. "I really couldn't believe he asked me at a stop light. I was scared and uncomfortable. It was like a movie." What began as a conversation between two men about basketball had become a transaction, and my father was offended. His upbringing had given him a great deal of pride in his surname, and it was not for sale.

Ed also didn't take into account that my mother openly didn't like him. She knew that his generosity was about more than "helping kids get out of the ghetto." She felt that although he helped some kids, he exploited most. His offer validated her suspicions, bruising my father's ego. Meanwhile, my father felt as if someone was trying to buy his son. He felt that if he took the money for his son, then effectively he would be selling his title and authority over his family and son.

After more badgering from Ed all the way to the bakery, my father gathered his composure, ordered some bear claws and old-fashioneds, came home, and never mentioned Ed's offer. They remained cordial, even close. My father said later that he realized who Ed was and that Ed knew where he stood and respected him. That was good enough for him.

A couple of weeks after that offer, we were at a tournament. Ed, my father, Mr. Mont, and Harv were driving in a caravan back to the city from Monroe, about forty-five minutes away. They noticed a group of kids in basketball uniforms standing outside a broken-down bus on the side of the road. Several cars stopped. Ed offered to buy the kids dinner up the street while they waited on the bus to be repaired. The bill was over $500. That's who Ed was too.

Chapter 24

One of the first lessons I learned about loyalty was that the ones who talk about it the most usually practice it the least. Immediately after I passed the Country Day test, the tides and winds of my environment changed. I noticed a shift in my relationship with Ed. I had always thought Ed helped everyone and was for the kids. I thought our relationship had been sincere—Detroit versus everybody. And now, to think he would be so upset to start acting funny, I was confused and angry. It felt as if Ed had turned against me.

Ed and Perry knew me attending Country Day was my parents' decision and that education came first for them. They knew my parents didn't really care about basketball. But in their eyes, I went from being a fourteen-year-old kid from Detroit, a kid from a sacrificing, God-fearing family to a suburban kid who wanted to play against weaker competition in one bitter lie. Now that I'm older, I get it. It wasn't about me. The cold shoulder, the arrogance, the snickering behind my back, the less-than-flattering words about my parents—those would be things that I would always remember. No matter how far up the mountain we'd climb together later in life, I remembered what they thought about me. I would always remember what I felt: hurt and betrayed.

Still, at the time I only had a young teenager's understanding of the situation. How could I have known that Southwestern had to save face? They couldn't have the best high school player in the country, a Detroit native, refuse to go to the best basketball program in the city of Detroit. That would not have been a good look for them—no matter how many championships were to come. It was business, not personal, and while that was a wake-up call, it was a sad one.

I started to see all through the rhetoric of the past with its promises of future, family, and love. That's how recruiters get you. They talk about us versus them, loyalty, understanding, using terms like *foxhole*. The word *brother* gets thrown around as loosely as darts at your favorite dive bar. What's sad is we kids actually believe these adults; I mean, they're supposed to be the ones who have seen it all.

During eighth grade, in the midst of my loneliness, my relationship with God grew. I clung to the stories in the Bible—stories of David, the great king who had a lowly beginning tending to sheep. He was the youngest and scrawniest of his brothers, and God used him to defeat Goliath. Moses in Egypt, whose mother had to place him in a basket and let him float down the Nile, not knowing where he would end up. The queen found him, and he became her son and lived in the same palace where the leader, her father, issued decrees of death on his people. I often thought of how conflicted he must have felt knowing that he was not one of the rich who had adopted him.

I thought of Country Day the same way. Going there seemed as drastic as Moses being born poor and being raised in a palace. Country Day represented "the man," hoarding education, information, and resources. I thought it was a setup, and I knew I would feel conflicted. I thought I was going to end up being around a bunch of rich kids who would never accept me as one of their own. Meanwhile, my friends would think I believed I was one of the elite. I would be perceived as the "one good black kid" and the rest of my friends looked upon as less than. I worried that my interest and actions would represent a whole culture. Basketball would be the easy part.

I was raised to speak out and to care about those from my environment and those with less resources. I knew Country Day would afford me that opportunity in "injustice's backyard." Maybe I just didn't want the call. I knew what most high school gymnasiums in the D looked like; hell, I played in every one of them in AAU tournaments. Slippery floors and outdated gyms. In some cases, you couldn't shoot out of the corner because there was an old-school track that encircled the gym. It was suspended right above your head, and fans used it as standing room only for the biggest games. We'd actually apply a full-court press in those games because we knew that opposing players couldn't pass the ball over a double team. If you tried from the corners, you would hit the track.

I knew that there was no comparison between the sports facilities in Detroit versus the suburbs. I knew all about Detroit schools' lack of resources, and I also knew that if I went to Country Day, I would become part of that system, an accomplice. I didn't want their help. I had watched my mother every year go through the same routine. She looked at offers from other schools in the suburbs and then pray, as if she were really considering, before deciding to stay in the city because if she didn't, and others like her didn't, who would?

"I could get paid more if I go teach in the suburbs," she would say. Jeff would reply, "Then why won't you do it? We need the money." She'd say, "Because I'm from the city, and I want to help the city and others in the same situation that we are in." With my fourteen years of wisdom, I thought, *Why the hell would everybody think it's so easy for me to move and go play in a community that wouldn't want me if I couldn't dunk a damn ball?* I didn't think about the opportunity; I was too focused on all the battles I knew would be placed at my doorstep. What else is a fourteen-year-old supposed to do but drown in the pool of self-pity?

Ed actually made a *last* last-ditch effort to convince my parents to reconsider. I remember the door in the back of my small church building opening and seeing Ed in a suit, which I had never seen before. I would've been surprised to see him in anybody's church. But what really threw me off was that he'd brought Jalen. I nodded and as they were taking their seats. Just then, I was called by Mrs. London, the first lady of the church, to come up and sing a song: "Jesus, You're the Center of My Joy," written by Richard Smallwood. It was crazy. I was in the middle of a guy recruiting me and a family protecting me, and I was singing my heart out to God.

After church, Ed wanted to talk, and I think they did for a few minutes as me and Jay chopped it up outside. But after this stunt—popping up at my mother's place of peace—I knew with all my heart that there was no chance I would play at Southwestern. I hope my mom prayed for forgiveness that night because I could read her thoughts of wanting to kill the man who came into the house of God on some bull. She saw right through him, and he knew it.

Jesus you're the center of my joy
all that's good and perfect comes from you
you're the heart of my contentment hope for all I do
Jesus you're the center of my joy
When I've lost my direction you're the compass for my way
you're a guiding light when nights are dark and cold
In sadness you are the laughter that shatters all my fears
when I'm all alone your hand is there to hold -
Jesus you're the center of my joy
all that's good and perfect comes from you
you're the heart of my contentment hope for all I do
Jesus you're the center of my joy
you're the reason I find pleasure in the simple things in life
you're the reason for the meadows and the streams
the voices of the children my family and my home
you are the start and finish of my highest dreams
Jesus you're the center of my joy
all that's good and perfect comes from you
you're the heart of my contentment hope for all I do
Jesus you're the center of my joy

"Jesus, You're the Center of My Joy"
Richard Smallwood

Damn, I grew up in a great era. Whistle Pops, swim mobiles, ice cream trucks, Adidas Top Tens, BB guns, Pop Rocks, water balloon fights, pogo sticks, Pole Position, Zaxxon, *Star Wars*, *Gremlins*, $100,000 Bars, Chick-O-Sticks, penny fish, belt buckle name plates, WWF, IntelliVision, Atari 5200, and the new cable with antennas on the roof. Sheepskins, three lines in my eyebrow, water wave, tick, cardboard boxes, nunchaku, karate shoes, high-top fades, *School Daze*, *In Living Color*, *Soul Train*, *The Cosby Show*, *A Different World*, The Box, Karl Kani, Kangaroos, Starter jackets, colored Lee Jeans, Michael Jackson jackets, Gandoffs, Max Julian's, windbreakers, Suzuki Samurais, Honda Elites, Nitro Tour, Donkey Kong, ColecoVision, Tahitian Treats, Sergio Tacchini, the Fat Boys, the Rappin' Duke, roller skating, *Beat Street*, breaking, fresh fest, firecrackers, jumping through the sprinkler, Edge Water Park, *Fraggle Rock*, Gary Gnu, fat laces, gold on a roll, *The Wiz*, and Saturdays.

Chapter 25

Mens Sana In Corpore Sano
("A healthy mind in a healthy body")

—Country Day School Motto

Some events can change your life forever, and I was very aware of that during our twenty-minute drive to my new high school. Take a left on 6 Mile, then a right onto the Southfield Freeway. Take Southfield Freeway to the lodge, exit at Lasher Road, and make a right. Drive approximately three to five minutes and make a left. You're at Country Day High School in Beverly Hills, Michigan.

The directions seemed simple enough, but it represented a galaxy far, far away. Proximity and how long it actually took to get to school didn't matter; I was going to be spending my days in an entirely different world. We made the short drive to Country Day in our Scooby-Doo mystery van: my mother, three brothers, sister, and my boy, Kev, made the journey on the first day. Our Scooby-Doo van was no mystery machine. It was more like the vehicle of chaos. With gospel music playing in the background, it served as a wrestling ring, lost and found, team van, homework station, choir deployer, and Meals on Wheels truck. We hauled bake sale goods and juices that my mother sold at school. The color of the part-time mobile sewing unit was somewhere between dark purple and burgundy, with two captain's chairs and a bench that converted to a bed. It was a necessity in our large family, and the van was well appreciated.

That is, until we pulled up to the car show in the parking lot of the high school. Damn! Honestly, I don't remember much about the actual drive to school. I know Jeff cracked a few jokes, my mother threatened to slap the black off of us, and Kev was brushing his hair. He was obsessed with waves. I was nervous, but easily hid behind my anger and resentment at going to the school. I didn't say one word, but when I saw the Jags, Porsches, Honda Accords, and Jeeps that filled the lot, I was thinking, Man,

even the "regular cars" are new. The student parking lot looked better than
that of the teachers. I knew I was in trouble. My mother proudly pulled
around all those beautiful cars, right to the front door, and told me she
loved me. Kev opened the door, and half of our house fell out of the van.
After picking random items up off the ground and after a couple of parting
shots from Jeff, we started our voyage into the unknown.

Kevin set the tone for my four years of high school. He welcomed the opportunity to go to school at Country Day. He was excited, but Kev was excited about life, period. It didn't take much. He was geeked about the new pretty girls he planned to slay as school king. He was committed to expanding his horizons. He felt he had been set free. Me? Well, I felt like I was beginning a prison sentence or being exiled for four years from those I loved most. But Kevin's constant confidence and exuberance couldn't help but be anything other than contagious, though it would take more than a year for me to be convinced.

Kevin seemed to know that this was our time. He Diddy-bopped through the front door, just as comfortable as the lifers, basically announcing, "I'm here, so get used to it!" I, on the other hand, did not want to make friends. I did not want to fit in. I did not want to become one of "them." I knew I could never be one of them or on their economic level. I wasn't desperate to be accepted among the elite. Kevin wasn't either, but I had a different weight on my skinny-ass shoulders.

Coach Kurt Keener walked in and introduced himself to the class of about sixteen as our homeroom teacher. He explained that every morning at 8:00 a.m., we would meet in this classroom for fifteen minutes before starting our daily sessions. At that point, I stopped listening. I remember sitting there on the first day thinking, Coach, you won. You got me here. You got my parents and my boys brainwashed. Just let me be. I wanted to forge my own identity, no matter what school I attended. I was at that age in which I was becoming a man. I felt that I had to stay focused and self-aware in this new, intimidating environment. No matter the school, I wanted to be one of the guys and make mistakes. I did not want to be constantly tailed or observed, and I thought the school put Coach in that class to do that. The next day I had Kev switch homeroom classes with me. It was great, because the teacher was cool, but also now Iyapo and I were in the same class. I didn't want to let anyone get close enough to me to change my view on Country Day. I did not want to like it there!

Though I would've sworn otherwise at the time, the kids in my school were just like all the other kids I'd gone to school with. The social dynamics were the same as well. You had jocks, rich kids, nerds, rebels, outsiders, artists, poets, protesters, punk rockers, Jews, whites, Muslims, Christians, Arabs, Asians, mama's boys, spoiled daddy's girls, elites, snobs, poor kids, grunge, class clowns, politicians, pretty girls, popular guys, and rich lifers. You could tell who they were because they all clumped together in little pockets like a bad pot of grits. There was also a wonderful mixture of those combinations, mainly because everyone had to play sports, and everyone had to study their ass off if you wanted to pass. Of course, I was comfortable hanging in my group with the athletes and my AAU teammates Kevin, Iyapo, and Darrell. Luckily, I also made two friends, Vince and Adrian, on my visit during orientation the previous year. They became lifelong friends.

My first year of high school was a one-man wrestling match. I was mad at God, my parents, everyone. I found out Coach Keener would also be my history teacher; it was as if he was following me. I would try to skip his class. I wanted to show him "You're cool with my parents, but not with me." The only problem was my plan couldn't work because Doris Webber wasn't having it. My mother made it clear and plain that if I didn't get the grades she expected, I would not be eligible to play. She had shown me many times that grades came before play. I was both mad and defiant, but I ain't no fool. I swore to never speak to my dad again out of protest, for allowing this bull to happen. This lasted for eight or nine months. I didn't initiate conversation and would avoid him. He really didn't care, and he made it clear. The last thing on his mind was kissing my butt. He and my mom were a team. I appreciate that now.

Country Day boasted a 98 percent graduation rate. Classes were small but competitive. For many students, it was Ivy League or bust. Now I didn't just have discipline at home. I had to deal with the school rules as well. No facial hair allowed. (It was hard to abide by that one when having facial hair is your ultimate goal in life.) Your shirt had to be tucked in. You had to wear a tie and blazer. No gym shoes were allowed. We had three hours of mandatory homework a night. We had to attend off-campus events such as plays and the opera. We had to engage in internships, and volunteering was encouraged. Grades were grouped: summa cum laude (a 4.0 GPA and above), magna cum laude (3.8 to 3.9), and cum laude (3.5 to 3.7).

School was different as a whole. I was used to teachers babysitting and constantly reminding you of projects and deadlines, but the teachers at DCDS were tough. No excuses, no reminders, and definitely no babysitting. You received your syllabus at the beginning of the week and were expected to turn in your homework on time. There was no special treatment because you were an athlete—everyone was. Every student was required to play at least two sports at the time, and if you were on scholarship, you had to play three. We all had to deal with schedule issues because of games, meets, and competitions. You had to learn to manage your time.

The first semester was incredibly difficult. I had to get used to new teachers, students, different cultures, shorter days because of the ride to school, and practicing in different seasons because of the different sports I was playing. Three hours of homework meant I couldn't spend that much time with Big Chris, Wes, and the boys on Biltmore. I felt as if I was in the middle. At school they didn't want to accept me, and my friends at home felt like I had deserted them. After all the talk about recruiting in basketball, I didn't understand why Country Day would want someone like me and not my friends. I knew I wasn't a better person; I could just play basketball. I would often think about the opportunities I received as opposed to others around me, how the system was unfair, and how if I couldn't play basketball, I wouldn't have had those opportunities. That was usually when my mother would smack me on the back of the head and say, "That's why you've got to get good grades. Nothing is promised just because you have this opportunity, so you better work."

My family didn't have the means that the other kids did. It was incredibly embarrassing. The distinct divide in resources was illuminated and put on display daily as a reminder that I didn't belong. Truthfully, I truly didn't know how much we did or didn't have until I walked into that building. That started my resolve. My classmates had houses with indoor pools, private jets, and trust funds. We had love, hand-me-down clothes, and a Scooby-Doo van.

✦ ✦ ✦

I was ready for basketball season. Our expectations were high. Harv set the bar high for us, saying, "This ain't AAU, but you guys are on the team, so you better win the state!" Short and sweet. Led by Jimmy Bolden, our six-foot-one senior point guard, we were ready to take off. I found Coach Keener to be a damn good coach and an informative teacher. He knew what we were made of from watching Super Friends games, so the respect was mutual. He graded tough, but his history classes were an easy listen. He wanted input from the students and seemed to respect everyone's opinion. As a coach, I found him to be sincere. His knowledge of the game dove deep, and he wanted the best for his players, giving us as much information as we could handle. I'm sure on a personal side, he was just trying to keep his balance on a tight rope. He was a white man who was married to a woman who happened to be black.

Looking back, I see why he was understanding. I wonder how tough it was for him. I'm sure he caught hell from both ends of the color spectrum. To make things worse, his wife, Nedra, was a former hooper herself. She was lovely, sweet, and loyal, "the team mom," with a personality that combined Mother Teresa, Joan Rivers, and Steve Harvey. She could be a one-woman show at games. If a ref made a bad call, she'd let him know it. She would have the crowd cracking up, but there was no one more caring about those boys at that crazy school. She also made some of the best food you ever tasted in your life.

Coach Keener worked the hell out of us while teaching us the game. While playing professionally, I never learned a major basketball concept or principal that he hadn't introduced to us first in high school. We worked tirelessly with a purpose. One of my favorite drills was the low-block drill: six offensive players would stand on the right side by half-court, and six defensive players would start on the left side at half-court. Players on one side would start dribbling from half-court with the purpose of laying the ball up.

On the other side, the players would try to cut a player off while blocking the shot low. We used the same concept and tried to get in front of the dribbler to take a charge. I remember these drills getting the team hype because it was playing defense on the ground. Coach emphasized this concept because he believed that defense had nothing to do with athletic ability, but, rather, your thought process. You had to know where to be ahead of time, know your man, and play each offensive player according to his skill set.

We did shell drills, three-on-two, two-on-one, and every player practiced in every position. I loved this because he allowed me to play the

middle, which meant drills pushing the ball on fast breaks. Back then, it was unheard of for a big man to do this. This helped me become comfortable with my ball handling in game situations. Coach loved catering plays and systems for different players. An ex-basketball player himself from Division III Whitney College, he had always loved the game. He was very organized. After going to college and then the pros, I saw that he ran his practices just like those systems. Not one minute was wasted, and every minute was scheduled. We began the season with two-a-days, where he expressed equal emphasis on defense and offense. He specialized in "team first" basketball—assists, playing fast, taking charges, creating turnovers, and making plays for others.

He wanted to make players better with purposeful thought and action. To know where players were, to know my personnel, and to know who to trust in which position. If Harv set the tone for my heart and courage, Coach Keener set the tone for my basketball IQ. He watched film with us and called everybody out. He pushed the right buttons. You gave Coach Keener everything you had, because you enjoyed playing for him.

✦ ✦ ✦

Coach was amazed at the maturity that Kev, Yop, and I brought to the team. We challenged the seniors. We were our own gang. We

traveled together and had played (and been beaten by) some of the best high schoolers when we were in junior high. We damn sure weren't going to be intimidated now. We were the first in the gym and the last to leave. Kev was always first in sprints, and I was always the first big man in running drills. We wanted to study tape and learn more. Coach knew we were leaders-in-waiting.

THE ART OF THE INTERVIEW

One of the things Coach did that helped me the most, and impacts my life to this day, was understanding my personality. He knew that I really wasn't interested in small talk or fake responses, so he insisted that we go in his office after practice to work on mock interviews. He sat me down and said, "You'll be doing a lot of interviews in the years to come."

Coach, a history major, understood my potential more than I ever did. He had a video recorder set up in front of me as he played the role of a reporter. We went through many different scenarios. We had just won. We had just lost. I played great. I played terrible. He asked questions like, "Kevin couldn't hit a shot tonight. Iyapo Montgomery fouled out, and you missed the game-winning shot. How does that feel?" He asked questions that were meant to set me up for a bad or questionable response.

He also explained that the moment should never speak for me, I should speak for the moment. "The best have to be able to handle the pressure. Pure and simple," he said. He knew I would face tough questions. Together, we watched the tape back, evaluated, and went through the process again. This two-hour session with Coach was better than any communication class that I've had to this day.

Then, finally, it was time. After everything I went through—the speculation, rumors, being recruited and made to feel guilty by the grown men who were recruiting me, the declaration that I would never be a Michigan great in hoops, suits and ties at school, three hours of homework each night, and the rest of the madness—it was time to get down to business. Our first game was here. When you hear players talking about how the game is their safe haven or sanctuary, it's because of the sense of peace and enjoyment you get as soon as you step on the floor. There is no time for distraction because you're in the middle of a great distraction already, enjoying the rules of engagement. I can't recall ever being on the court in the middle of a game and thinking about something that happened in real life. Maybe a flashing thought, but never an in-depth, in-head discussion. When I stepped on the court that night, I was focused and ready to go, eager to show what I was working with on this new level.

We ran out of the locker room to an overcrowded gym. Standing room only! Our pregame routine was organized, and we thought we looked good as well. We'd run in a single-file line (guards to bigs) out of the locker room to half-court. Then the team captain stood in the circle as the rest of the team circled him giving him dap. From there we headed straight into a tip-drill, and after the last man tipped the ball in, we split up seamlessly into two-line layups. As I ran out on the court, I saw Bill Frieder, the head coach of the University of Michigan, out of the corner of my eye. I couldn't believe it. The first coach to come watch me play. He was standing in the corner by the door on our side of the court. It was standing room only, but he had picked his spot carefully. He was damn near under our basket. He wanted to be seen. He was the star and had on a maize-and-blue jogging suit with some dope Nikes.

As I get to the other side of the layup line, Iyapo smoothly gestures with his head to look in the direction again of Coach Frieder. He wanted me to see the man standing next to the man: White Boy Rick. White Boy Rick was an urban legend in the flesh. He was standing next to Frieder by the door. He had on a fresh red, white, and blue jogging suit with low-top gymmies to match. He had two beepers, a brick cell phone, and one of the biggest dookie gold ropes I'd ever seen.

Frieder was signing autographs, taking pictures, and laughing extra hard. The adults were going gaga; it was brilliant. His message was, "See, kid, I'm the coach of Michigan. We're bigger and better. You want to have some fun? You want to win? Don't forget about me. Don't forget about us."

That got me hyped. I was going to show him something. Kev and Yop were geeked too. We were thinking, *This is what we've been dreaming about. Let's go!* I made sure I gave Coach Frieder what he came to see and more. I was pumped. I tried to tear the rim off the socket a couple of times. Led the break, hit jumpers, and rebounded like a madman. The fans saw some stuff they'd never seen before, and we got the win.

Personally, I went on to have a successful season, but we lost the regionals to Tony Tolbert and DePorres. Tony Tolbert was one of the best scorers in Michigan's recent history. Around six-foot-four, he could jump out of the gym and shoot threes better than anyone I'd seen. They pressed us, and we turned the ball over. As the Super Friends, we played against their players all of the time in the summer. We lost that game on heart alone, and I tried to warn the fellas that it was a different animal we were going up against. Our dreams of being state champs ended quick. Still, I ended the season averaging 21.3 points, shooting 65 percent from the field, snagging 10.5 rebounds, and collecting 2.8 blocks per game. I was named to both the All-County and All-State teams.

Chapter 26

Agreements & Commitments

A fter my freshman year, my ice-cold feelings toward my parents and Country Day began to thaw. Interacting in sports, school, clubs, or class, I saw the true personalities of my classmates. Some of them were all right. I got used to the school's culture and rules. I got in a rhythm with the school… and vice versa. I also found time to hang out with Big Chris, Wes, Lance, and everyone else on Biltmore, just like old times. More importantly, I made some serious agreements.

After my freshman year, I made an agreement to trust God. To let go. I didn't have control anyway. I was taught to believe the words of the Bible and to memorize verses in scripture. But it wasn't until this moment that I had to have a personal relationship with God. I had felt abandoned when I came to Country Day. I was hesitant to make friends, and I didn't want to be in this environment. But the experience was turning out to be different from what I thought. I promised from that point that I would rely on God, not me or man.

I also trusted my mom. The one who would encourage me to stick to my guns. The one who embarrassed us every Sunday at church by crying and lifting her hands to the sky, oblivious of those around her. The woman who wanted her children to be educated so we would have many options to be our unique selves. I trusted my father, the man who didn't have the luxury of having a dream, having dropped out of sixth grade to take care of his family. I would ride with that man, who sacrificed for his family at a young age and committed to being a provider. The man with the strongest work ethic that I've ever seen. A man who always kept his word. I would honor him.

I had to trust; I'd been raised that way. I believed that I was part of something bigger. It's not just about me. I knew the stories of faith, humility, pride, arrogance, and downfall. I knew that I couldn't explain my feelings to anyone. I knew I had to be a man and accept things. Embrace them. Embrace now. No excuses.

I was tested, put in the fire, and forged into a man because of the actions of some I didn't know and some who I loved. Basketball was now my friend, my safe haven, and the hardwood became my sanctuary. I was quiet and chill off the court, skeptical of anyone I didn't know. On the court, I was charismatic, focused, and expressed my emotions effortlessly. Just three years earlier, I had started playing this game. In such a short time and at such a young age, I'd already lost friends to the streets, been ostracized, learned to stand alone, learned how to ignore ridicule, and was misrepresented and lied to because I didn't do what others wanted. I was fifteen, about to be a sophomore, with only one toe in the water. I wasn't even ten toes deep in the game. Besides my family, Harv, Mr. Mont, and a few others, most of the people I experienced were fake fortune tellers who offered unfounded advice and deconstructed clichés. There were conditions for loyalty, and adults set mental traps for manipulation.

I have always valued family and friendship, but now I started to develop *discernment*. I was constantly in different situations with all kinds of people, and I started to take note of differences in sincerity, conversation, values, and personal attention. I had started to be able to see through people. I could sense sincerity, and I prayed aggressively for wisdom. I did not want to ever depend on anyone, because I saw that they wanted you to depend on them so they could own you.

My mother and father only asked that I be respectful of people no matter how I felt about them—to "stick to innocence." They never wanted me to sink to the level of the people who tried to manipulate me.

About this time, I started reading a chapter of Proverbs at night before I went to sleep. It would comfort me, settle my nerves, and calm my anger. I treated that book of the Bible like a playbook. Proverbs was more like rules for navigating through life. Reading Proverbs helped me realize that I had to accept my current situation with humility. I wasn't wise enough to understand why I was at Country Day, so to pout would be foolish. I didn't know enough to have an expectation, good or bad. I had to be humble and accept that there was something larger than me going on—something God had planned for my life. I had to trust and understand that I had no control and needed to surrender.

I could no longer complain or use my silence and disappointment to detach and become aloof and uninterested. I had to be all in. I had to be a man. I had to emulate my father, the man I didn't speak to for most of my freshman year. I had to invoke his focus, thick skin, and work ethic to move forward. I had to grow a pair. Continuing to sit around, being a victim, clinging to teenage depression or anger, or doing nothing was no longer an option. I really started to understand some tough lessons that I would use for the rest of my life.

I swore to put all negativity behind me that fall as I headed into my sophomore year. I made a commitment to embrace Country Day and any challenges on the road ahead. That summer helped confirm that I was not the only one in a similar situation with similar expectations.

I was invited to many camps over the summer: Five-Star, B/C Reebok, Slam and Jam. Back then, those were the biggest. I didn't go to any of them. My coach redirected my thinking, and instead I chose that path. I attended an invitation-only basketball camp at Princeton University. The only freshman from Detroit and youngest participant, I was proud to be a part of something that boasted the top 150 players in the country from grades nine through twelve. It was the Nike ABCD camp. The camp emphasized academics and had classes designed to prep us for college. The classes were actually cool. We had great speakers like Spike Lee, Dick Vitale, and others.

The camp was convenient for coaches and recruiters. It coincided with the first week that college coaches were permitted to evaluate high school prospects, July 10–31. Those were the NCAA rules at the time. I heard many parents talk about it like it was a meat market, almost like a high school combine. I didn't care. I was excited to play against the best. I wanted to see how I measured up. It was also the first time I'd slept in a dorm. Unlike the ones at Michigan State, these seemed to be two hundred years old. They were beautiful on the outside, and dusty as hell on the inside. And no air conditioning, so our room was a sweatbox. But I loved every minute inside that sweatbox. I ran into friends like Grant Hill, Jamal Mashburn, and Conrad McRae.

I also made new friends. This big-eared cat from Chicago who had the words "Big Nook" shaved in his head. The words were in cursive and, I thought, *dope!* We were standing in the lunch line, and I thought he was a senior because he had a thick-ass goatee. I could barely sprout a shadow. We hit it off automatically. We became quick, lifelong friends. "Big Nook," otherwise known as Juwan Howard, was from the South Side of Chicago. He lived with his grandmother in the projects. He was given nothing in life. Juwan was six-foot-nine, funny, full of heart, crazy, and compassionate. We'd stay in touch over the summers ahead. I found out we were in the same grade, both from the Midwest, and cut from the same cloth.

My first game at that camp would be remembered as an epic battle. It was one for the ages. Not because of anything I did, but because of who was headlining. Two of the top seniors in the country were facing off against each other, both point guards and both from the New York–New Jersey area: Bobby Hurley versus Kenny Anderson. Later in college they'd meet in the ACC as Bobby's Duke Blue Devils faced off against Kenny's Georgia Tech Yellow Jackets.

Talk about a new level. I was glad to be part of it. I'd never seen nothing like this before in my life. I was on Bobby's team. His quickness, precise ball handling, shooting, and passing were incredible. I had to have my hands ready at all times. I had a couple of great plays in the game. One I remember specifically—a half-court alley-oop from Bobby that I caught with one hand and flushed with force. A scout later told me that after he witnessed that play, he dubbed me "the man child." Meanwhile, I'd never seen anything like Kenny Anderson. He was a freak of nature with his quickness and handles. I'd say he got the best of Bobby that day, but I think we won. Kenny was a one-man show, though. He could get anywhere on the court with or without a screen. Later on in my career, I'd see New York guards who reminded me of Kenny and the moves introduced to my generation, like Stephon Marbury, who's had great success in the NBA and is now a legend in China; God Shammgod; and Kyrie Irving, a.k.a. Uncle Drew himself.

I left camp with a new respect and reverence for the game. I saw what the future of hoops looked like. Quick, athletic, hybrid wannabes of the best players in the NBA. I wasn't the only big man emulating the small guard ways and passing ability of Magic, or the only kid counting down in their backyard and dreaming of posting up and hitting a deep three à la Larry Bird. Why not? If they can, I can. So I came back with an even better work ethic. I knew what I was up against, and it wasn't just the kids in Detroit. It was a great experience because it gave me a healthy context—one that extended beyond my environment. I was blessed. I became addicted to weight lifting, not necessarily just for the results on the court, but because of the girls. I was tired of being skinny and scrawny. I wanted the pecs, the horseshoe on the side of my arm. I would lift in between classes, before and after lunch, and after practice. I'd do one hundred push-ups a night, then lift every day. I went from a skinny 210 to a solid 225 in a matter of nine months.

My mother cooked very healthy, but because she had so many kids, she knew how to make the most of a meal. We had a lot of sides with our main dish so we would be filled. Cornbread, potatoes, beans, cabbage, greens, sweet potatoes, soups, and broths (from leftovers). I gained so much muscle there were rumors that I was on steroids. That's when we first started hearing about those crazy supplements and remedies. I laughed it off and was actually kind of proud. I was constantly sore and tired. It took a lot of energy and discipline to sustain.

YOUNG, DUMB, AND DOING STUFF

Kev and I would sit in the basement and watch a show called *The Box*. It was a video channel that let you order a music video over the telephone: three videos for $1.99 or one video for $0.99. It was on! We ordered videos over and over again. The videos seemed to be programmed according to regions, so if you waited long enough, your video would most likely come on. But we weren't that patient. MC Lyte, cha cha cha, EPMD "You Gots to Chill," Special Ed's "I Got It Made," Too $hort's "Life Is... To Short" and Big Daddy Kane's "Smooth Operator." We watched them all... but my father had to pay for them all. He lost his mind when he saw the extra $200 on the phone bill. An extra $200 we didn't have. But for the first time, my father was actually calm in a situation where I messed up. He calmly and deliberately spoke to me like a man. He let me know that I had taken resources that we didn't have from the family. He reminded me how much he hated his job. He kept the incident between us, which made it hurt even more, because this was serious—so serious he didn't want to bring it to the family to cause worry. I had received $2,000 from an insurance settlement after being struck by that car three years earlier. I had to put half away, and my parents released $40 to me every month. I paid my father back out of that stipend.

S tarting my sophomore year at DCDS, I played football. Neither my father, Coach Keener, nor the football coach wanted me to play. I loved every second. I came out a couple of weeks late but played well enough to have my own play, "19 Waggle." I caught nine touchdowns. I had good speed and great hands. I loved the experience: bus rides, practices, wearing your jersey to school on game day—I enjoyed it all. Well, except the "clip block." I was a big target—my shins couldn't take it.

Things at home were still the same. I'd spend the night at my grandfather's every weekend and take care of him. I'd babysit during the week when Dad's schedule at the plant changed or Mom got extra work or went to school to get more plaques.

On our block, things had started to change rapidly. We had witnessed the start of it all with the introduction of crack just four years earlier. In a short time, it destroyed families and delivered crime and death to our doorstep. Timbo, my childhood hero and ex-bandleader, Wes's older brother, was arrested and sentenced to four to twenty years for multiple armed robbery attempts. Watching him get pulled away from his family was shocking. I knew it would never be the same for them. I felt sorry for my best friend; I knew how much he admired his older brother.

All I could think about was my frightening trip with Charlene, where those high tiers and endless rows of cells housed inmates at Jackson State Prison. I wondered—if he had had the same opportunity to see what I saw at that impressionable age, would he have thought twice about being a stick-up kid? Though I might have had it in my mind to embrace Country Day and the different cultures, situations like this made it tough. I had survivor's remorse. I kept thinking that Timbo was so creative— what if he'd had the opportunity to attend a school like Country Day? What if he had been rewarded for his hard work and exposed to the best teachers, tools, and education? What kind of options could he have had in a different setting?

Socially, I was coming into my own. I had a small group of friends who shared the same interests: sports, hip-hop, girls, and video games. For Homecoming 1988, I performed a song called

"Parties are Ill," with my friends Nate Johnson (a.k.a. Shaheed Shabazz) and his cousin Carlos (a.k.a. Los a.k.a. Razzaq Rahim), who didn't attend the school. We turned the crowd out. I was Big Daddy Kane, just as in the backyard I was Magic, or Lynn Swann in the street. We each spit sixteen bars and the hook repeated the phrase "Parties, parties, parties are ill." We shut it down. Country Day ain't never seen nothing like that before.

Along with hoops, I became a big football fan. During the season, I went on unofficial visits to Michigan and Michigan State to watch games. It was exciting to see so many fans in one place. The fight songs, excitement, and the "We'll die if we lose" mentality around campus was contagious. I enjoyed those times out in the sunshine, in the stands with my parents and the other hundred thousand fans. Since the basketball coaches were on football time, they introduced me to the football staff that I'd come to know over time. I became familiar with Coach Heathcote by way of his assistant coach, Tom Izzo. Izzo was young, brash, and exciting. He believed in the way of the green and white at Michigan State. He never undersold Heathcote, who was becoming more of a scapegoat. He never talked bad about the Wolverines either. Quite honestly, I liked him out of the gate, even more so than the school. Michigan's head basketball coach, Bill Frieder, was leading in communicating his desire to have me play for him more than any other coach though. I knew he wanted me. It wasn't just because he showed up at my first high school game. He sent me handwritten letters, and his familiarity with Detroit and the inner city gave him credibility. His school wore Nike; Michigan State, Converse. Frieder and Michigan had the upper hand in this early race. Then it all changed.

The Tuesday after Selection Sunday (the teams for the NCAA basketball tournament were announced), Bo Schembechler, University of Michigan head football coach and athletic director, banished Coach Frieder from the university's basketball facilities for accepting the head coaching job at Arizona State University. Bo was livid! He said, "Only a Michigan man can coach a Michigan team," and named Steve Fisher, Frieder's longtime assistant, as interim head coach. The timing was terrible. Frieder's team was ranked nationally as high as Number Three early in the season. The team had crazy talent and terrible chemistry. They were said to have multiple personalities.

That team included Glen Rice, a previous Michigan Mr. Basketball; Terry Mills, a future high draft pick; Sean Higgins; Lloyd Vaught; Mark Hughes; and Rumeal Robinson. It was too much talent for one team. There was one ball, and everyone wanted it. Coach Fisher somehow got the attention of the team and narrowed their focus for six games. He begged them to use this as an opportunity to prove everyone wrong. They listened and responded. Against all odds, they dusted off Xavier, then destroyed South Alabama. They got rid of North Carolina in the Sweet Sixteen before getting a chance to play Illinois in the Final Four. The Illini had defeated Michigan at home on senior night, and this would be the Wolverines' chance at revenge.

Ironically, I was a big fan of the Fighting Illini. They had high school phenom Marcus Liberty, who, in my head, had a finger roll as legendary as George Gervin's. They also had Kendall Gill, Nick Anderson, and Stephen Bardo, all around six-seven with the ability to switch on D. I was pumped. I knew the history and what was a stake: a chance to advance to the national championship game. I watched at home with my brothers, and at halftime, while I was shooting socks into a hanger on the door, the phone rang. It was Coach Fisher.

"Chris, just letting you know we are thinking about you."

Stunned, I responded, "Uh, thanks, Coach. Good luck."

"Thanks, and if you work hard, you can take us to the Final Four one day."

My jaw dropped. I ran around the house screaming. Dunked on my brothers and tore the hanger down. Got in another hundred push-ups and watched the rest of the game. My favorite play, and a move I permanently borrowed from Sean Higgins, was the behind-the-back layup. It happened in that game. Glen Rice went bonkers on an incredible scoring run, pushing Michigan past Illinois.

In the national championship game, the Wolverines knocked off a good Seton Hall team on a pair of famous free throws by Rumeal Robinson. I was happy Michigan won it, but I would've been just as happy if Michigan State had pulled it off. But something about that halftime shout-out from the locker room stayed with me. To be thought of at that moment! I didn't take that lightly.

✦ ✦ ✦

I stopped counting the letters I received from coaches and recruiters when Jeff and Jason told me that I had received fifty in one week. I would sit in awe on the floor, reading letters from the likes of Duke's Mike Krzyzewski, UNLV's Jerry Tarkanian, Georgetown's John Thompson, and Syracuse's Jim Boeheim. We'd eventually pile the letters in a closet at the top of the stairs, hoping to fill that big space to capacity.

Meanwhile, Harv kept in contact with everyone on the Super Friends. He had us study over at his house for midterms and finals. We studied early, listening to Al B. Sure!, Guy, or some other R&B. Then Mrs. Hervey, Harv's mom, would serve us food, and then, like clockwork, an NBA regular-season or playoff game would come on. I appreciated Harv for giving me one of the few chances to escape my personal labor camp back on Biltmore.

They laugh at me because I'm different;
I laugh at them because they're all the same…

—Kurt Cobain

Ed started coming to my games again in my sophomore year. I noticed him in the stands talking to my pops at the first game of the tournament. Ed, still upset I didn't attend Southwestern, threw a hissy fit and did not show up to any games my freshman year. I saw him flip. I was cool on him. I didn't want him around after I saw the drop off or insincerity. I was pissed because, in an effort to undermine any validation of me attending Country Day, he projected me to be "one of them."

I heard all of the "not from Detroit," "won't be as good," "thinks they're better than us," whispers. I went to Southwestern games and watched Voshon, Howard Eisley, and Jalen play, and ball they did. Perry subbed five players at a time, and their press would make Rick Pitino say "Hot damn!" They had shooters, finishers, and heart. Unfortunately, they were upset in the tournament again, missing out on the 'chip for the second year in a row, and that killed me. The media and public went off. I took no pleasure in watching people's satisfaction in watching them lose. It hurt because Southwestern was representing the D, and I felt no one cared about Detroiters. Kids, schools, job growth, whatever—we were the underdogs. I was from the D, and they might as well have been talking about me.

Back to Ed. I thought it was his way of apologizing, but it was much more. "I bought you a car," he said proudly. It was a used '86 Honda Accord. I smiled ear to ear. I couldn't believe it. A car? Man, every kid old enough to drive had a car at my school. I couldn't believe it! What color was it? Blue? Wow! All I could think of was me driving my new blue Bronco with the driver's side window down, left hand on the wheel, leaning to my right bumping EPMD's "You Gots to Chill."

Then reality shivered my spine when I thought, *Wait, how is this going to work? You must not have asked my parents because I know my moms wouldn't have let this go down, period.* I asked him, and he said no. I didn't have the balls to even suggest the possibility of this extravagant present. He looked at me in shock, as if to say, "Oh yeah. I forgot about that woman." That was the end of that conversation. When I got home, I begged my father for a car on my sixteenth birthday, foolishly asking for a 1986 Honda Accord I had seen for sale.

He responded, "Do you have some Honda Accord Money?"

That was the end of that.

The basketball season was redemptive and rewarding. After losing in the regionals my freshman year to Tony Tolbert and DePorres, we licked our wounds, returned with hunger, and won the state championship. I was proud to have won a championship—that's all I heard Magic talk about. Winning—that was all I heard Isiah Thomas and others on the Pistons say they wanted every time they lost to Boston. I did it! The school was proud, and my family as well. It was also a relief because after hearing all the outside chatter about not being able to maximize my potential at Country Day, I felt like I was proving that theory wrong. However, since we won the title in Class C, there were those who felt we still hadn't accomplished anything.

Our school had fewer than five hundred students, so we weren't in the pool of Class A schools, whose student bodies can exceed three thousand. Some tried to discount our winning. I took note of that. That was the main excuse of public schools, some that we actually beat during the season or that I'd given the business in summer league competition. Proving others wrong would become a habit for me, and I wanted to address this. I asked Coach if we could move up to Class A. He explained that we couldn't move up two classes in one year but that we could indeed move to class B. I was excited with that solution. I averaged 25.3 points, 12.5 rebounds, 5.1 blocks, and 2.1 steals. With room to improve, it was on to the next level!

Chapter 29

The Worm & Coach

Sophomores with transportation were allowed to leave campus for lunch. I was pumped to be old enough to inherit this responsibility. My father let me drive his beat-up burgundy Corsica, and I loaded it up with Kev, Yop, and whoever else would fit. I drove it back and forth from school and AAU practice too. When I was grippin' that car, you couldn't tell me nothing. We made it our personal pimpmobile. I kept it washed, waxed, and clean at all times. The cloth seats were always vacuumed. I even had a special mix tape for the ride. Gas was ninety-nine cents a gallon, so I wasn't tripping on taking a spin.

At lunch on school days, we'd ride over to the Tel-Twelve mall down the street from school to hit up the food court and play video games. There were rumors that it was also Dennis Rodman's hangout, and every time we went for lunch, we were on lookout hoping to spot the Worm. After about two months of quarters and burgers, we finally spotted him. Or, shall I say, he spotted us. He came over while I was playing Millipede and said, "What's up?" to me and the crowd that surrounded the game. We said, "What up?" and tried to keep our cool. We didn't bother him and let him play his games, even though I'm sure we kept looking over our shoulders to see what he was doing. Just as we were finishing up, we noticed him headed our way. He asked me, "Kid, how tall are you?"

"About six-eight."

"You play basketball?"

"Yeah…"

"Wanna work at my camp?"

"Yeah…"

"Okay, give this guy your number, and he'll call your parents."

Just like that, I met a hoop hero of mine, a guy who played on my favorite team with my favorite player, Isiah. It was surreal. I made $300 for one week of work. My father joked that I made more than him and didn't do any real work. I really didn't. I just soaked up the gym. The camp was for kids ages five to fifteen. No real serious hoopers. We just rebounded and wrangled kids for lunch and bathroom breaks.

Rodman came in for about an hour, spoke, and left. I was bummed, because I wanted to talk, pick his brain, and get advice, and that wasn't happening. But on the last day of the camp, he came in early and said to me, "We are gonna have some fun today. We are gonna have a dunk contest. Can you dunk?"

"Yeah," I said. But I really thought, *Hell yeah, I can dunk! I'll dunk on you!* Well, after seeing the display of dunks Rodman had, I was embarrassed about my private thoughts from earlier. I watched him stretch, and his muscles were bulging out of his skin. He walked and ran on his toes. He was cut up with seemingly no body fat. I was in awe. He dunked with ease. Dunk contest dunks—I couldn't believe it. I didn't know what real athletic ability was until I saw him that day. He was kind to us kids. He thanked us and left. I appreciated that Dennis. That Dennis was a kind spirit. This meeting would also give context and confidence as time would go on too.

I KNOW WHERE I'M NOT GOING...INDIANA

At the beginning of my junior year of high school, Andy Slovis, my old point guard, asked me to come up and see him at Indiana University. It was his freshman year, and we had grown close over basketball workouts during our time at Country Day together. He was excited about school, and I was excited for him. One weekend I drove up to Bloomington just to hang out with my former teammate. It was their homecoming, so the campus was poppin'. I dropped my stuff off in his dorm, went to a class or two with him, and then he asked, "You wanna see a practice?" Now that I look back, I should have put two and two together and realized this was a setup—an "unofficial visit." I was young and glad to be alive. Plus, I really didn't think that I was on Bobby Knight's radar. I wanted to go to the practice, so we did.

The trainer let us into Assembly Hall, home of the Hoosiers. Practice was in full swing, and the ringleader of this disciplined circus was standing at half-court in his famous red sweater with his arms folded and a scowl on his face. Lawrence Funderburke, my teammate from Nike Camp a year prior, noticed me and gave me a nod and a look like "Watch this bull." I noticed that there were five to seven trainers taking stats in practice of every drill. Turnovers, misses and makes, deflections. Knight yelled most of the practice. I took note

of the discipline. I also took note of how his team did not
seem to be enjoying practice. No smiles, no trash talking, no
encouragement, nothing. Just one guy holding court, cussing
players out. I was not impressed.

We were asked to come into the locker room after practice,
and we had a front-row seat at a film session. As I entered
the film room, I said what's up to Calbert, Lawrence, and the
rest of the team. I had on a Pistons hat with a red bandana
under it. Fundy warned me to take off my hat before Coach
came in there: "Hey, Webb, you better take off that hat and
bandanna before Coach walks in. He's crazy!" The room agreed
in laughter. Coach Knight walked in; I didn't realize he was so
tall. Six-seven, six-eight. He asked how I liked campus so far.
I said, "Cool!" He said good, and that was about it. He went
back to cursing his team out. Simple.

Chapter 30

Whitley Gilbert

The summer of '89 was mine. I was coming into my own. I was sixteen, and my high-top stayed fresh, courtesy of Shaheed Shabazz or my man at Dixon's barbershop on 7 Mile and Livernois. I was filling out nicely, the result of lifting weights every day. Mentally I embraced becoming a man. I also enjoyed being a teenager. I was walking a fine line. I was given more responsibilities and more freedom. I learned that the more trust, the more responsibility. If I had to be home by eleven, I was home by eleven. Being allowed to have a curfew and go out was better than losing the argument and the war.

I went to Nike Camp again, and that was a blast, as usual. This time, I wanted to dominate and show that I had improved as a player. I wanted to be different from the average tall stiff and separate myself from the herd. Between the factory and the city, I had started to understand what my parents had always said about effort and passion. Though I should've seen the connection between my effort and my improved grades, it made more of a difference to me on the court.

I was more confident after winning the championship at Country Day. Now I reacted to concepts and situations on the court without thinking. I also realized that I loved being booed. I think I got that from the Pistons and their "Don't care what you think" style of play. Being booed was a badge of honor. I was the best player on a team that was kicking ass, so I got booed all the time. I knew I could finish with and over the best in the paint. I played against local legends like Derrick Coleman, Doug Smith, and Daniel Lyton. I loved to rebound because that was the only way I could emulate Magic on the break. If I snagged a rebound, I was pushing it.

During the summer after junior year, I caught back up with Granddaddy, spending weeks over at his house. Same routine—talk, laugh, cook, bathe, change, talk, laugh. I also started sneaking girls over to his house at night. It was the easiest crime ever, since his movement was limited and he went to sleep like clockwork around 7:00 or 7:30 p.m., after the news and *Jeopardy!*. Around

8:00 or 8:30 p.m., girls would come over, and we'd watch TV, kiss, or whatever. Sometimes my grandfather might have thought he heard talking, but I'd always tell him it was just the TV.

They weren't having it anyway, not with Granddaddy just a few steps away, and I wasn't taking that risk. He probably would've shot me had he walked in on me and a girl. He was truly old school. Don't disrespect the man's house. But he never once got out of bed at night. He'd just lay there with his gun on his dresser, the radio on low. He'd wake up every morning at 5:45 a.m. on the dot. With that, I didn't have time for much else besides basketball and girls.

That summer, Harv took the Super Friends on a college tour. It was one of the best summers I can remember. Two coaches and a dozen players driving across country visiting five colleges. It introduced many of us to college life and opened our eyes to the world—not as athletes, but just as kids. The trip took the intimidation out of big and small campuses, and for many of us, that comfort level opened a new door. Some of the guys on our team had never thought that leaving our 'hood, let alone attending college, was really possible. We thought the trip would be more about ball, and it was definitely about ball. Everything was with Harv. But it was about more too.

✦ ✦ ✦

Our first stop was the University of North Carolina. I was geeked as hell. We went into the Dean Dome; it was quiet and regal. Carolina Blue all over the place; banners lining the rafters. Two of my favorite players had played here: James Worthy and MJ himself. I sat at half-court and gazed into the stands. I took quick note of the differences between this shrine to hoops and the dilapidated field house in Lansing. There were rumors that college and NBA floors had springs under them, so without a basketball I jumped a few times as Kevin and Iyapo let me know how far my head was from touching the rim. We concluded that the floor in fact did have a little more spring. As Harv started to leave, Kev and I did a quick suicide drill on the court, confirming that this was the same size gym that we practiced in. Young, dumb, and full of energy.

We followed Harv into the locker room, where we met legendary coach Dean Smith. He showed us around the arena, pointing out his favorite trophies and sharing his fondest memories. One particular moment memorialized in his office was forty-yard dash and mile times.

I'll never forget when he said, "This is the reason I respect Michael so much." He had us at *Michael*. "He worked his ass off." I looked at Harv. He pounded his chest and smiled as if to say, "I told you, boy. Let's do this." I'm sure Coach Smith talked to me, but I really don't remember. He had been writing me personal letters since ninth grade, so I believe he did. All I really remember is where Michael's locker used to be.

We headed down the road to Durham, home of the Duke Blue Devils. At this time, I knew nothing about Duke except that they played in the ACC and had a pretty good program. They didn't have the championship résumé they boast today, but the Blue Devil mascot looked dope on the sidearm of the Starter jackets everyone wore at that time. We walked the campus, and since I'd always loved architecture, I fell in love with the campus's stone structures. I liked that the campus seemed small, cozy, and intimate. The gym, where Duke players and students would anger and embarrass some of the greatest ballers of all time, was tiny, like a little bowl, more appropriate for boxing. I couldn't believe it. We walked through the locker room in awe of their trophies and mementos before heading back on the road.

I called my mother to tell her how I loved the architecture at Duke, and she noted that the architect of Duke's campus was Julian Abele, the first black student to graduate from the University of Pennsylvania with a degree in architecture. History—and, more important, black history—was plentiful in my home. We felt the expectations and inspirations of our ancestors, from the Nubians, who created the oldest recorded language in Africa, to our Northern Egyptian ancestors, who pioneered everything from brain surgery to folding chairs, gold sandals, paintings, and even the calendar we use today. My parents believed we were resilient, magnificent people who should know our history and emulate greatness. So did I.

Hampton University, an HBCU and our third stop, was filled with that greatness. No disrespect to my man Michael, but even he had nothing on the Hampton Pirates and the familiarity of the campus. We visited classes and joked about the faculty because you could easily find a professor who looked like someone's mama—plenty of fuel for jokes. We even went to a party at the student union.

Kev announced at that moment, "I'm going to a black college!" He wasn't lying, either. Three years later, he was a freshman at Florida A&M, an HBCU in Tallahassee, Florida. But the athletic facilities at Hampton were both small and outdated. If they'd had half a gym or a decent basketball program, I would've signed before I went home; I liked it that much. I left the campus of Hampton University in love with every girl who passed my way.

Off to Georgia Tech. I will always have love for my man Dennis Scott, the six-seven Orlando Magic forward who hit a then-record eleven threes in a single game. Anybody who knows D knows that he's funny, kindhearted, and a plain fool. I met him at Georgia Tech. Bobby Cremins, head coach of the Yellow Jackets men's basketball team, greeted us in the lobby of the arena. I was hoping to see my ex-Nike campmate Kenny Anderson, who had just committed to Tech, but Coach told us most players were home for the summer.

We walked around, and I was shocked that the campus was right off I-85, in the heart of the city. The arena was nice, though it looked almost

as if it were buried in the ground. Coach Cremins gave us the usual tour of the football field and other athletic facilities, but we were anxious to get into the gym. Coach didn't disappoint. As we filed into the gym, we noticed a tall dude at the other end of the court. We couldn't tell who he was because he had his shirt off. Kevin then said, "Y'all see where he's shooting from?" We looked and were amazed. It was Dennis Scott. He took the time to rap with us, and he had a fan in me from that day. But what I couldn't believe was how tall he was and playing the three, the small forward. I was maybe an inch taller, and I was a center. I had an epiphany: I should master my skills in all areas of the game and not worry about a particular role. It's not just about being athletic.

Dennis said, "Let me talk to the kids for a minute." Then he sat us down and dropped a few jewels. "Man, look. Y'all are gonna love college," he said. "You get to ball all the time, hang with your friends, and girls are way prettier than in high school. Just make sure you work on your game. It's not just about dunking. You want to be complete players. Work on the part of your game that's lacking, not just what Coach tells you. Stay hungry and stay focused. I know y'all got boys back at home getting in trouble, but stay focused." We thanked him, and as we left, Kevin stayed behind talking and watching Dennis drain deep three after deep three. We had never seen anything like that in person. We were inspired—and a little afraid of how good you really had to be to ball at this level, and in the pros.

Our last stop was Georgetown University, home of the Hoyas. I was pumped to visit the place where John Thompson and his towel reigned. We drove by some monuments to give us a bearing on how close the campus was to the center of Washington, DC. Georgetown's campus was beautiful; the architecture reminded me of Duke's historic look. We walked the campus and then headed to McDonough Arena, and I noticed a three-on-three game going on, with two of the largest humans I've ever seen going at it. It was Patrick Ewing and Dikembe Mutombo. Out of all the visits, this was the only place we saw pro players go at it, and boy did they. They were fouling the hell out of each other. No jumpers, just taking it to the hole. It was as if a personal challenge had been issued to every player, daring them to take the ball to the cup. The big guys on our team huddled together to take notice of how real it was at the next level, especially in the paint. Their practice reminded me of a Super Friends practice.

Coach Thompson reminded me of my father. Tall and kind, commanding respect upon entering the room with a no-nonsense approach. He took us to his office, sat us down, and talked to us about college life and the responsibility of being a man. He hit on the pressure of being a young black man and how even though the world is unfair, we couldn't use that as an excuse. He wanted us to always be disciplined, focused, and prepared. While he spoke I thought, this sounds like the speech I get every day at home. I thought, *If I come here, this would be like playing for my father. Ain't no way I'm coming to play here.* One thing I did take away was that I had to become more physical. I couldn't be satisfied with my development.

After the college tour, Grant Hill called and asked me if I wanted to play on his AAU team in Arkansas at a national tournament. I asked my parents. Surprisingly, they consented. I felt guilty because I was going to miss my first Super Friends tournament, but I was crazy excited that I was going to get to play ball somewhere new. I'd become close to Grant at Nike camp. He was a basketball nerd, a film watcher, quick to quote a "historic moment," and a "remember that game?" type of guy. I was the same way.

So, after our second annual Nike Camp trip, it was off to Jonesboro, Arkansas. We played in the tourney and killed it. I brought the house down with a few dunks, and we filled the break and ended with *SportsCenter*-style highlights. It made me think of what we could be and how good we could be together. The time before the game, however, was more memorable than the game itself. I was introduced to the governor of Arkansas, Bill Clinton and his wife, Hillary. Mrs. Clinton was roommates with Mrs. Hill at college. Grant and I watched them laugh and interacted with them for a few minutes. I still remember their kindness.

We went back to Grant's house to spend the night. We watched a bunch of NBA and college basketball games on tape (I couldn't believe he had Beta): Big Monday, Big Ten, old dunk contest, bloopers. I loved Mr. and Mrs. Hill. They'd been kind.

Anyway, after some time, Grant asked his mother if we could go to a party so he could show me around his neck of the woods. His parents gave him the exact same speech that my parents gave me: "Who's going to be there? What's their number?" Grant gave the same lame responses as I did and made the same pleas for extra time. I was in shock. It was just like my family!

I didn't realize exactly how much like my family they were. I thought, since his father was a professional football player and his mother was an all-around brilliant woman, that somehow he didn't have to adhere to the same discipline as I did. I thought he had it easy and could do whatever he wanted. That could not have been further from the truth.

We drove to a party to look for girls, as teenage boys do. After some time there, Grant looked at his watch and said, "Time to go." As if to say, *You know the drill. I don't want my parents mad at me.* But I said, "Man, I'm having a good time. What's your address? I'll get a ride home."

I don't know who I thought I was. Maybe it was that I hadn't been away from home for any extended amount of time. Maybe it was the pretty young thangs at the party. Something made me lose my rabbit-ass mind. Grant left like it was nothing. He knew the drill. He was not gonna get in trouble, so he just jetted back to the house. He got home, and his mother asked him, "Where is Chris?" He told her, and she lost it. "What do you mean you left him there? He's going to find a ride back home? You go back and get him."

Grant rushed back and told me what happened. I was scared shitless. What if his mother told my mother? I walked in the door and proceeded to get an earful from Mrs. Hill, who was on the phone with my mother. Grant and Mr. Hill looked on, each with a smirk that said, *You brought this on yourself, lover boy.*

I thank God for the village he put around me. Most were extensions of my parents. They shared their belief system, and that, to me, ensured trust. I thought my parents were crazy and too strict. I thought their theories like "work harder than anyone," "prioritize," "focus," "know your history," and "respect all and fear none" were typical clichés. We were broke. Where was the proof that those theories would work? I thought we were just poor and proud. I had no idea they were instilling in me the pillars of being a decent human being.

✦ ✦ ✦

Legendary basketball icon Will Robinson would often talk about the importance of being a good man and standing for what you believe in. At that time, I just thought of him as a nice man, which he was. I thought he just worked for the Pistons as a community ambassador because everyone in the community loved him. Later, when I found out he was basketball royalty, his character was tangible.

Will Robinson became the first black coach in Division I history when he accepted the head coaching job at Illinois State University. He was also the first African American high school basketball coach in Michigan, winner of two state championships. He was basically given the job at Detroit's Miller High School because he was able to calm down racial tensions in the neighborhoods after the race riots in the city. And for sixteen years, he was the only black coach in Detroit. Can you imagine the pressure?

Coach Robinson represented the change that was to come, which was more diversity among coaches. Talk about a rock and a hard place. He coached Spencer Haywood at Pershing High, where Steve Smith attended. He was the first black scout in the NFL, discovering Hall of Famers Charlie Sanders and Lem Barney. Now that I'm older, I can imagine how much he had to overcome to be the first at what he did. He was placed in vulnerable situations where no one understood. He was focused only on the task at hand. As a boy, I did not understand the full context of his words of encouragement and wisdom, but I did sense the meaning, and it strengthened me at the time. I appreciate his words more as each day passes.

✦ ✦ ✦

Bo Schembechler, Michigan's head football coach, was always kind and encouraging to me. Long before I finalized a college decision, we had somewhat of a relationship. On September 27, 1989, I witnessed his kindness before and after one of the biggest games of the year. The game was a brawl between number-one-ranked Notre Dame against his second-ranked Wolverines at the Big House in Ann Arbor. Coach first asked my family if we wanted to come to a game, and of course I did. My mother couldn't have cared less, so my father and I made the trip, just us. It was raining that day, so the weather wasn't optimal for sitting in the stands. I still had a blast. I went into the locker room before the game—same as the year prior—and watched the players smack each other on the shoulder pads and slam their helmets into the lockers. Some did stand quietly, as if hypnotized and staring into the future.

Bo came over by the equipment room and greeted my father. Then he came to me. A pat on the back accompanied with a "Hey, kid." He asked me who I thought was going to win. I answered quickly, "Michigan." The game was exciting. I had to hold in my enthusiasm for great football. I witnessed Rocket Ismail run two punt returns back to fuel an Irish victory.

As the fans trickled out of the stadium, their heads hanging in disappointment, one of the assistant coaches asked me if I wanted to go in the back. I thought, *I hope he doesn't mean the locker room. I saw the way the team behaved before the game. I don't want to be around them now. They probably don't want anyone in there.* But the coach assured me it would be okay. In the locker room, we saw Bo again, and he greeted my father with, "Well, Mr. Webber, our boys played hard." Then he said to me, "Well, kid, we are going to have some tough practices this week.

We have some work to do." Then he smiled, suggesting that though they needed to address some things, they were going to be good. He patted me on the back and disappeared off into the steam of the locker room. I remember looking around the room, soaking everything in. The reporters, the players, their lockers, their muscles, the way they interacted.

On the way home, my father, who was a big Bo fan, gave me a sermon with a message of "Why I like Bo." He went on to describe Bo's type of discipline. How he was old school and held his players accountable. My father preached the same sermon at the end of that season, when the Wolverines won the Big Ten football championship. They won ten in a row after that loss to Notre Dame. Guess they did have a great wealth of patience.

A few months before the start of my junior year, I was blessed with a personal angel. Isiah Thomas reached out to me through a couple of high school coaches. I couldn't believe it. I mean, what would Isiah Thomas want to do with me? He called our house and spoke to my mother and father. I was entering my last couple of years of high school, and he wanted to talk to me about "basketball and the world of basketball." If it was okay with my parents, he'd love to come over and talk to me. They were ecstatic that he even wanted to reach out. They were honored and told him to come over.

My parents sat us all down and told us that the captain, number 11 for our Detroit Pistons, was sliding through. We went berserk! Screaming and high-fiving. I broke out in push-ups, and after we calmed down, we were sworn to secrecy. We could not tell the block. My mom reminded us that "Isiah doesn't have to take his time to do this. He is very busy and doesn't need the whole block knowing he's coming over." After our meeting adjourned, I ran across the street and told Wes and Big Chris that Zeke was coming over.

Zeke pulled up in his new black 1989 Toyota Forerunner. I was outside on Big Chris's porch talking to my friends, playing it off, waiting for the man. I wanted to give them a front-row seat. I told them to wait out here until we finished. Then when they spotted him coming out, come over and handle their business. Zeke got out of his truck and waved, and the porch started cheering. Zeke hit them with a fist pump and his signature smile and went into the house.

I couldn't believe how cool he was. He talked with my father about the factory and with my mother about his mother and how hard it was growing up poor in Chicago. I could immediately feel a kinship with him and almost understood why he was concerned about me. Isiah saw himself in me and all the little black boys trying to make it. After he and my parents spoke for about a half hour, he spent a little time with my brother and sis. Then just Zeke and I sat in our small living room, and he asked me to spell out my dreams.

I told him how I wanted to play in college and win a championship like him and Magic. I told him I wanted to play in the NBA. He told me stories of how some guys had talent but lacked work ethic and a high basketball IQ and how because of that, they hadn't made it. I asked him what the difference was between great and average. He told me, "Most greats are leaders." He got up to finish the conversation, wrote his number down, looked me in the eyes, and slowly said, "If you need anything, call me. Be careful who you have around you, who you let help you, or those that come out of nowhere. This is the only family you need."

I couldn't help it. I wanted to get out all the thoughts I'd had over the past five years; if anyone could understand, he could. For the first time, I felt I had someone who could understand what I was going through. I spoke about my uncertainty about where to attend college and that I wanted to make the right decision. He said that I had a bright future. He told me to watch whose advice I listened to and reiterated that if I ever needed anything to call him. He gave me a pound. He was gracious to the whole neighborhood, which showed up at my doorstep. Signing autographs, engaging everyone. My boys told him, "Watch out for Boston and Chicago!" and Isiah replied, "They don't want none," and hopped in his truck and was gone with the wind.

That convo with Isiah Lord Thomas changed my outlook on everything. It's hard to explain, but it took the pressure off. I knew that I had someone who cared about me and didn't need anything from me. That was a liberating feeling. It gave me the confidence to know that I had an NBA great at my fingertips who could give me advice. I knew that was an advantage. I also had someone I would not be afraid to ask for help.

I was young and feeling invincible and pumped up for the new school year. I did not expect to hear the words "You may never play again" roll off the lips of a doctor. But I was at the gym on a Saturday with all the usual suspects (Yop, Kev, Darrel, Vince, Corey) getting in a workout. Our routine was to stretch, lift for a couple of hours, and jump with the heavy rope, and then we had free throws and shooting drills, ending with five-on-five. I went up for a rebound and came down on someone's foot. I was used to twisting an ankle or stretching a ligament, especially on that uneven concrete grass combo in the backyard. I'd even done so several times in games and practices, but something was different about this one.

I didn't feel anything snap, but in minutes my ankle had swelled to the size of a grapefruit inside my Michigan-maize-and-blue Nikes. I'd never seen the color it was now turning. I went to the doctor, who was the father of a friend, and after looking at MRIs and X-rays, he said, "It seems as if this ankle has been habitually damaged. You have torn and partially torn ligaments in your ankle. I honestly can't say that the ligaments will heal properly."

I immediately asked, "What does that mean? Will it get better?"

This sucker actually said, "You may never play again."

I burst into tears. He was single-handedly taking away my dreams with his half-wit diagnosis. My mother consoled me, both with love and a mistrust of the doctor. Thank God, we found out later that he didn't know what he was talking about. I was on crutches for a month and my limited mobility helped put everything back into perspective, but after rehabbing I was balling just like before. I was ready for my junior year.

Junior year was more than basketball, girls, or books. I was coming into my own as a man and student. At times I spoke on issues, despite feeling powerless or embarrassed to be the only one with an opinion. For example, at the end of the school year, sports and school club banquets were an everyday occurrence. Country Day's policy was that if you were a student on scholarship, you had to be a server at these dinners. But after I put on a white jacket, my mother became livid. She said that serving was not a requirement of a scholarship; grades and behavior were. She was furious at the "outing" of those on scholarship. I took action when she and other parents, and even faculty, called the school headmaster.

I spoke on behalf of those on scholarship, both academic and athletic, explaining how we felt. Being forced to be servers was demeaning to us and gave validation to the narrative that we didn't really belong at the school. I said that I would not take part. I explained that the policy created different social groups in school, became a point of contention and separation, and established a platform for bullying. The school agreed and changed the longtime tradition.

I was excited for my junior year. I was growing as a basketball player. I had learned that not only did I need to improve, I had to make my teammates better in order for us to win. That meant knowing their skill sets, because that helps you put them in a position to be successful. Not only does that help define roles, but it encourages guys to get to their sweet spot, play efficiently, and not try to reinvent the wheel during games.

Our team had moved to Class B that year, and the competition was different. The schools had larger student bodies and a larger talent pool for sports. We started the season off with a loss to Saginaw Buena Vista. I could not hit a free throw to save my life. Still, we were ranked number one the entire season, and in the playoffs we beat Grand Rapids Northville by twenty points at Crisler Arena, earning a rematch against Saginaw Buena Vista in the championship.

This title game took place at the Palace of Auburn Hills. Home of the Pistons. The gym where the Jordan rules were created. The place where Isiah mesmerized defenses with his dribbling and the rim that Rodman rebounded on. I stood on the spot where Kareem hit his patented baseline hook shot. I hoisted threes from behind the official NBA line that Bird owned. I walked over to the corner where Bill Laimbeer swung on Charles Barkley. I was in heaven.

Before the Palace opened, I entered a contest for a chance to win lifetime season tickets. Fans were asked to suggest names for the new arena. I suggested "The Gym" because I thought it was short, sweet, and to the point and that it represented the city's hard-hat mentality. The closest I had ever gotten to the Palace was sending that letter to the arena suggesting the name. Now, I had finally arrived.

In the locker room, I immediately sat down at Isiah's locker. I closed my eyes and imagined what he would be thinking before the game. I went with "Be a leader and have confidence." I knew we were in for a battle. I knew I had to keep everyone involved to maintain confidence. I also knew that I would have to hit my free throws, something I hadn't done in our first loss to Saginaw Buena Vista. I went through Isiah's locker looking for anything I could get my hands on. I found some tape, tore a piece of it off, and put it in my sock. To channel his energy, I guess. Now I could hear the crowd in the locker room.

After Coach gave us his usual calm, methodical "how to kick their ass" speech, we got hype. The arena was packed with 19,186 fans, reminiscent of a Pistons-Bulls matchup. The whole city had been clamoring for me to play against better talent. Since 1931, no team had won back-to-back championships in different classes.

It was a close game throughout. I gave the crowd what they had come to see with a few dunks that even the best college players didn't attempt in games. I scored thirty points and pulled down fourteen boards in a 59–53 victory. Redemption from our previous loss. Saginaw Buena Vista hacked the hell out of me, as they should have, because my free-throw percentage was in the fifties. But I set an MHSSA record with fourteen straight free throws made. I missed my first two but stuck with a focused mind-set

and stuck eight in the fourth quarter alone. I received tournament MVP honors, All-State, All-Metro, and All-American. We ran back to the locker room, danced, and sprayed each other with water bottles. Some of the best times as a teammate aren't in games or on the floor, but during those times in the locker room when you're sharing a victory.

PROM NIGHT

I was excited that my junior year was coming to a close. However, there were a couple of events that needed to take place before becoming a senior. First was junior prom. I was looking forward to dressing up and going out and all that good stuff. So Kev and I secured dates and put the wheels in motion for the evening.

We went to Northland Mall to rent tuxedos. Swung by the barbershop to get some fresh cuts. Ed let me borrow his Benz. We went to pick up our dates and were on our way. I remember thinking, *Damn, I'm going to get one of these.* It drove so smooth, like butter. We listened to Rakim, looking through the sunroof at the stars.

We headed to Greektown for food and, when we left there, headed off to the festivities. But prom was much worse than advertised. I got up and sat down like a seesaw depending on which song was playing. There were three or four different cultures, so you had to get in where you fit in. Our dates also seemed less than interested, not just in the whack music, but in us. Bored or indifferent—it was something.

Kev followed me to the bathroom and said, "Maaan, this is boring. And the girls are bored too. Let's get up out of here."

I thought, *Okay.*

So we headed back out to the party and asked if they wanted to leave. We dropped them off at home, hit a liquor store, bought two forties of Old E, and went to the drive-in to see *House Party.*

Around this time, I was starting to receive recognition as the best player in the state, and that got me talked about in the same sentence with some other great players. Across the country there was talk about Glenn Robinson (Gary, Indiana), Alan Henderson (Indianapolis), and my boy Juwan Howard (Chicago). I got to know these guys from the class before and after ours through summer camps and AAU. Juwan called me up to let me know his team was coming to Michigan to play us in an AAU tournament early in the summer heading into our senior year.

Nook and I were as close as two kids in different states, with no money to pay a phone bill, could be. It was in our nature to be competitive, but we never competed with one another. Nook's team came to Orchard Lake St. Mary's, a popular spot for AAU tourneys, and I remember how pumped up everyone was for the game.

Don't get me wrong; you always play hard. But anytime there's city pride on the line, you played *extra* hard. It was like his team wanted him to win it more for him than he did, and my team wanted to win it more for me than I did. They all wanted to prove that the number-one player played on their team. Well, after a close first half, the trash talking hit such astronomical levels that a fight started, and both teams had to be calmed down and warned more than once. Nook and I made sure to be there for our teams, but we avoided each other during the melee. My team got the win—and of course, I talked trash to Nook about that— but we knew the AAU game. You may lose, but you have to keep it moving.

Nook was a great defender. I admired his anticipation and discipline. I was more athletic and used my jumping ability, anticipating help from the weak side. So, after the game when he and I discussed summer plans and players, I was shocked at the praise this defensive demon heaped upon Glenn Robinson. "Whew, that boy Glenn—he can go. Score from anywhere, dog!"

There was no internet; back then, it was all word of mouth, and word of mouth isn't as reliable as your personal eye test.

"Dog, he can dribble outside, post up, shoot, and dunk," Nook told me.

"Damn, dog, he's that good?"

Nook nodded. "Ole boy can go!"

I felt like I had been put on notice. Harv had a plan for the Super Friends. Let us lose every game—so what? Make us play against older and better talent, and even in that scenario there were no excuses allowed. This put us in position to have small victories, which is why I fell in love with "the process." The process is not sexy. You get no pats on the back during those lonely moments of discipline. Working out, push-ups, calf raises, lifting, shooting, scheduling. Playing against Derrick Coleman at age sixteen and seventeen, when he was six years older than me and had just won Rookie of the Year for the New Jersey Nets. They were all small victories. Boxing him out and winning a single rebound against him was monumental—a little something positive to store in my memory bank on days when guys who couldn't carry his jock strap tried to step up.

I watched Steve Smith change the game with his height at the point. Once, my father took me to watch Steve at Callahan Hall. He got a steal right before halftime and threw it off the backboard to himself for a dunk as time expired, and then kept running into the locker room.

SUPER PREP

Country Day's Chris Webber wrapped up Mr. Basketball Award a long, long time ago

By Mick McCabe
Free Press Sports Writer

Early next month, the members of the Basketball Coaches Association of Michigan will receive their ballots for the state's most coveted award — the Hal Schram Mr. Basketball Award.

It will be a waste of postage.

Can we be honest? Does anyone really believe someone other than Chris Webber of Birmingham Detroit Country Day will win?

Even our dear departed Swami wouldn't need his crystal ball to know who will get the award named for him.

Even the coaches with outstanding players know the winner is a lock.

Face it, it's a bad year to be a senior.

"There's no question — no doubt in anybody's mind who's the best," Albion coach Milton Barnes said. "Anybody with any damn sense knows Webber is the best. I don't care who anybody else has, he's the best."

And the best, now a 6-foot-9 senior center, keeps getting better.

"When I first saw him as a sophomore he seemed a little timid," Saginaw coach Marshall Thomas said. "He was being a little bit of a nice guy, but he's gone beyond that. When I saw him in the first game of his junior year I didn't know how he'd ever make a free throw; he was atrocious. Now, all of a sudden, he's made a 200 percent turnaround."

Sometimes a player who is bigger and more physically mature early in his career gets labeled as the best in his class and wins Mr. Basketball simply because of outstanding sophomore and junior seasons. That might have happened in 1986 when Romulus' Terry Mills won the award instead of Detroit Northern's Derrick Coleman.

Or in 1985, when Detroit Southwestern's Antoine Joubert won over Traverse City's Dan Majerle and Flint Central's Darryl Johnson. Or in 1987, when Saginaw Buena Vista's Mark Macon won even though Detroit Pershing's Steve Smith had the incredible senior season.

But not in 1991. Webber is finishing his career as he began it — as a terror.

"I think he's dominated high school basketball for four years," Country Day coach Kurt Keener said. "The mark of a true player is, do they also lead the team to championships? Chris led Country Day to our first two state titles ever.

"Chris was a dominant player as a freshman. I thought that isn't the case. He's maintained it and even widened it. He's a man playing with boys."

And so, in a little less than two months he will be selected the state's Mr. Basketball. A few weeks later, he will announce his college. As of Sunday, Webber said he was still considering Michigan, Michigan State, Duke, Minnesota, Kentucky, Detroit Mercy and Liberty. But he is expected to eventually choose between U-M and MSU.

Webber's shoo-in Mr. Basketball status does present a problem: BCAM officials ask members to vote for three players. Who do you vote for after Webber? Here is an alphabetical list of the next nine candidates — all exceptional players who just started school the wrong year.

JAKE BAKER, 6-5 forward, Plymouth Salem: The western suburbs have a versatile candidate in Baker, who signed early with Central Michigan. He can score inside, but he also has a good mid-range jumper and has extended that to three-point range (14-of-22) this season. "If you're going to be one of the top 10 players in the state you've got to be a complete player; you can't be one-dimensional," coach Bob Brodie said. "We ask Jake to bring the ball down the court, we ask him to shoot and we ask him to rebound. Over the last 2½ years, with Jake as a starter, we've only lost six games."

EMMANUEL BIBB, 6-1, guard, Detroit Denby: He is on track to win the Detroit Public School League scoring title for the second straight year. He has recovered from an early-season ankle injury and continued to dominate. He signed with Detroit Mercy. "He's an explosive player; he really can't be stopped," coach Rueben Washington said. "He goes to the hole very well. If he gets to the hole he can't be stopped. He has great upper-body strength; he's got a Rumeal Robinson-type body."

JESSE DRAIN, 6-7, center, Saginaw: Last season he helped the Trojans reach the Class A finals. Always an intimidating big man, he has developed his perimeter skills. "Jesse is playing with a little more intensity," Thomas said. "He's not so willing to be stopped. He can put the ball on the floor and take it up to the basket or pull up."

VOSHON LENARD, 6-4, guard, Detroit Southwestern: Many coaches think he is the most valuable player for Class A's top-ranked team. He is certainly the most versatile. Not only does he posses a good jump shot, but he can take the ball to the basket. "He can do it all inside or outside," coach Perry Watson said. "His defensive skills are as good as his offensive skills."

TODD LINDEMAN, 7-0, center, Iron Mountain North Dickinson: He is the best Mr. Basketball candidate ever from the Upper Peninsula. More than a shot blocker, Lindeman has refined offensive skills and moves well on the court. He signed with Indiana. "Todd's got real soft hands and catches the ball real well," coach Don Beattie said. "He runs the court real well; he really

hustles. He's well-coordinated; he could be 6-2 or something. I think he's a diamond in the rough."

ANDY POPPINK, 6-7½, guard/forward, Tecumseh: They haven't invented a position he hasn't played. A year ago he was the driving force behind Tecumseh's run to the Class B quarterfinals before losing to Country Day. He signed with Stanford. "He can do everything," coach Ed Oxley said. "He handles the ball like a point guard, he passes like a point guard and he posts up like a big man. He's defended guys 6-8 and guys 5-10. It depends who the other team's best athlete is, and that is who Andy guards."

JALEN ROSE, 6-8, forward, Detroit Southwestern: He is probably the state's best pure shooter. The son of former Piston Jimmy Walker, Rose could end up at guard in college. A first-team all-stater as a junior, he has excellent jumping ability and led Southwestern to last year's Class A title. "He is gifted with talent," Watson said. "He is equally capable of scoring on the perimeter as he is on the inside. He is very tough in the clutch and has the ability to create his own shot."

DAVID WASHINGTON, 6-6, center, Albion: Albion is 53-10 with him starting. A Central Michigan signee, he is one of the state's top shot blockers. His offensive game progressed remarkably over the summer. "His offense has developed so that he's a definite threat every time he touches the ball," Barnes said. "Teams are double- and triple-covering him and he still delivers. He can jump and has good timing."

THERON WILSON, 6-8, center, Royal Oak Dondero: One of the success stories of the season, he moved from Detroit to Royal Oak and committed himself to academics and basketball. He signed with Eastern Michigan and could be an impact player in the Mid-American Conference. He is a dominating defender and an offensive force inside. "I think Theron is a potential big-time player," coach Jerry Barich said. "He's probably the most intense player I've had, whether it's in practice or a game. I keep telling him it's just a game, but he says: 'This is more than just a game. This is what we do.'" Special writer Rich Hava contributed.

MR. BASKETBALL CANDIDATES

PLAYER	SCHOOL	FG%	FT%	REB	AST	AVG
Jake Baker	Salem	55	75	10.0	5.0	18.0
Emmanuel Bibb	Denby	44	68	6.4	4.3	26.7
Jesse Drain	Saginaw	57	76	13.1	2.0*	19.9
Voshon Lenard	Southwestern	57	85	7.0	7.0	22.5
Todd Lindeman	North Dickinson	67	69	18.4	4.6*	28.0
Andy Poppink	Tecumseh	48	74	10.0	4.7	21.5
Jalen Rose	Southwestern	54	83	9.0	4.0	22.9
Chris Webber	Country Day	64	64	15.7	4.8*	29.2
David Washington	Albion	47	75	11.8	4.3*	16.4
Theron Wilson	Dondero	56	60	10.3	6.3*	22.9

* Blocked shots

I played in the Sandy Sanders camp against local college guys from Eastern, Central, and Western Michigan University, which gave me experience, toughness, and resilience, but most important, I was gaining confidence.

We went to Chicago to play Glenn "Big Dog" Robinson and his team. We had a blast on the short four-hour drive to the Windy City. Harv let us control the radio while Kev and I (we always had something on hand) supplied musical entertainment. We had slow-jam mix tapes, hip-hop mix tapes, West Coast mix tapes, East Coast mix tapes. We put crazy time into making the tapes, recording everything off the radio. The patience, the precise timing of pushing the record button simultaneously with the play. It would take weeks to make a good one, not just one regurgitating radio's "Top Eight at Eight" show. We had the whole van rocking. It felt good that we were all together before our senior year of high school. We had gone through so much, both individually and collectively, that the fact that we were all together put everything in perspective. Some had lost family members. Some had experienced the harsh realities of divorce or parents or siblings going to jail. But when we came together, we were on a mission. A beautiful distraction. A new summer, a new chance. We wanted to win a national AAU championship. We had won locally and regionally, but not nationally.

Photo courtesy of the Detroit News

I was the only All-City, All-American, all-anything on the team. We weren't built like most teams, stacked with the city's elite. We were a ragtag bunch of players who had (minus a few guys) played together since we were twelve. We'd begun with a promise from Harv: "If you do things the right way, sacrifice and focus, you guys will win the national championship." We all bought in, though we were let down in four straight years.

Games like these were always fun for me, for a few reasons. I loved going out of town and getting away from my small, crowded house. I also loved playing hoops. I would've stayed at home or gone anywhere to jump it up. I loved the competition. I was addicted to it, and I was familiar with all of the guys I played against locally, so testing how I was against the nation's best was something I loved. I looked at it like my play was adding to the legend. One game. You'll go back and spill the beans. Word of mouth was my ally. And I was pumped up to play Glenn. I heard so much about him and was starting to feel like, "Damn, okay, he ain't Superman." I had never heard this much about any player in my high school years.

"Yo, Kev," I said. "Wait 'til they come out and warm up first. I want to see what's up."

"All right. Bet."

I watched Glenn's team come out in warm-ups and tried to gauge a feeling on how good they were. The building was packed with basketball heads and the 'hood's finest. I was amped, but I'll always remember the atmosphere as much as any game I've ever played—the combination of anticipation to see who this great "Big Dog" was to the fact we were at a gym in Chicago that resembled St. Cecilia's. The energy was hype, and everything was special. The icing on the cake sent my emotions over the top. All of a sudden, someone had a boom box and was playing Public Enemy's "Brothers Gonna Work It Out." Now, anyone who knew me knew that I had been playing Public Enemy's *Fear of a Black Planet* and Ice Cube's *AmeriKKKa's Most Wanted* for months. When "Brothers Gonna Work It Out" dropped, the fellas looked at me like *Oooooh!*

Our team went to the side to huddle up before the tip. Harv punched me in my chest so hard I lost my breath, but I swallowed it. He gave a speech about heart. He was screaming about walking in the lion's den and taking the beating heart out of a lion and eating it in front of his pride. He asked us if we had the balls for this life. Balls for commitment? "It's not an easy road, nothing's promised," he told us. The music got louder, and one guy started hopping up and down. The music got even louder, and then three or four guys were now bobbing in sync. It seemed as if there was a DJ in the stands turning up the speakers and playing with my emotions. I went blank. I was hype.

Next thing I knew, I was in the middle circle with Glenn. The crowd wouldn't sit down or shut up. Glenn reached out to shake my hand, and I gave him a pound. The ref blew his whistle, alerting both teams to the ensuing jump ball. He tossed the ball up perfectly, and I…didn't jump. I just looked at Glenn like "What?" Glenn, whose long arms were outstretched, pulled back in midleap and came down and stared at me like "What?" We stared at each other. The place went bonkers, with the ball bouncing in between us at half-court. The refs didn't know what to do, so they warned us. Of what, I don't know. But warned us, nevertheless. The refs had to clear the floor of passionate fans who ran out on the court with excitement. Glenn and I gave the people what they came to see.

Juwan was right about this man's offensive skill. I was in awe. I'd never seen anything like it. I never had to step out on a big man shooting a jumper. That just wasn't a thing back then. Glenn was stepping back and hitting threes off crossovers. I drove down the lane and wind-milled so hard that the refs had to stop the game because fans ran onto the court again. One guy came out of the stands, ran full court, and smacked the glass with two hands because he was so pumped. That may be one of the best moments of appreciation I've ever received.

Glenn repaid the favor, hitting bucket after bucket in mesmerizing ways. More than once, we all had to go to our respective corners so the crowd could gather themselves. We both scored over thirty. There was nothin' I could do with him or vice versa, but we won the game. We were proud of that, but the experience is something I'll always remember. Glenn and I hugged and exchanged home numbers after the game. I made a lifelong friend that day.

I got back home and told my father that I wanted to get a part-time job to make some money. He laughed and said okay. A friend at school worked for a lawn-care company and said he made $100 for work on the weekend. I wanted in. My career in landscaping lasted one whole day. First off, I had to get there at 5:30 a.m. Living in the city, that meant I had to leave at 5:00.

I didn't understand why my father was so eager to drive me that early, but I realized that he was happy that my miserable, sleepy ass got to see how life was on the real side. Coffee, son? Funny, Dad.

My first and only day was horrible. Carrying bags of hot shit around in the hot sun, my allergies killing me. I should have thought about that. The final straw came when I was cutting grass outside a community next to Detroit Country Day. There was no gate, but it had an entrance and was less than one mile from my school on the same road. As I hopped back on the lawnmower, a car drove by, and two or three people yelled out, "Nigger!" Five minutes later, as I was standing with my friend, a different vehicle came from the opposite direction. Someone yelled out, "We don't like niggers around here. Go home, nigger!"

I couldn't laugh it off. I kept thinking that my school was right down the street. Then, after a third motorist flattered me with curses, I just got off the mower and hollered at the crew I was working with. They understood, and then I proceeded to walk my black ass down the street to the school. I went swimming and waited for Pops to get off work. I just told him that they didn't need any more help for the job. It was a harsh reminder that I was a part of the school but not the community.

During senior year, I went to Northland and bought seventy-five dollars' worth of gold on a roll. That's the fake gold chain or link that you purchase by the inch. I paid three dollars per inch. I didn't have enough to get what I wanted, so I came away with a choke chain and a blue jean jacket with my face spray-painted on the back. That was the fun part about youth: being creative. But I was well aware that I was embarking on a new beginning with college and all, but despite complaining about my little brothers and sister, or the fact they used to follow me around, or the lack of privacy with seven people sharing one bathroom, or that I was always in church, or that my father was too strict, I was depressed because I understood that this was the last time we'd live together as one family.

I knew things were changing. My family, my support system, my team, even my friends. Kev and Iyapo were chasing their dreams of going to college, getting a scholarship, and maybe even playing in the pros. I was just aware of the fact that one stage of my life was coming to an end. Who would watch over my brothers and sister? Who would escort Mama when she came home late from school or choir rehearsal? Who would watch Granddaddy? I'm sure I overexaggerated my importance, but I knew we all played vital roles, and now mine would change forever.

Chapter 35

I cut my picture out of the issue of *Sports Illustrated* I'd just purchased and posted it to my wall of fame in between Barkley and Jordan. It was a sweet picture of me laid out doing a backward dunk and was the only picture of me on my walls. Every other inch of the room was plastered with greats from sports, hip-hop, and film. My mother had let me turn the attic into a bedroom, and I had a lot more peace and quiet. Every night, same routine: push-ups, turn on some Anita Baker, and do homework, dreaming of my future.

Things were getting real. After all the camps and high school games, after all the rankings and all the calls and letters from coaches, this was it. Deciding which college to attend. My mother and father would give me all the advice that I needed, but they made it clear that it was my thing. "You have to make yourself happy," they said. I had a busy year ahead: five official visits, a couple of unofficial and home visits.

I was a big fan of UNLV and Arizona, but I knew they were too far away. I didn't think much at all about the other West Coast schools. I heard Pepperdine's campus was the nicest, along with Hawaii, but I knew that wasn't realistic. I also thought about Howard and Hampton for a good minute, but I decided that I wanted to play for the best team and situation for me and stay as close to home as possible. Any campus within a twelve-hour drive was in play. With the Big Ten and ACC schools, it seemed possible to have it all—school, hoops, and mama's cooking. After crazy deliberation, my final five schools came down to Michigan State, Michigan, Duke, Minnesota, and the University of Detroit.

I had time to make my decision because I was not going to declare early. If I had signed early, I would have gone with my gut—with Michigan State. I was thinking of waiting to the end of the season in March to announce. The timing of declaring is a personal decision. If you declared and the coach who recruited you got fired or took another job, you could not transfer to another school. I had friends who declared early, and the coach still recruited players at their position. I was in no rush, and truthfully,

besides dreaming and kicking it with the boys, I never really thought about declaring with any seriousness. First things first. The countless calls and letters I had gotten from coaches over the years gave me confidence that I would have a spot at somebody's program.

Let's go college shopping. It began with home visits from head coaches…

University of Detroit Titans

The University of Detroit was first on my list. I was a big supporter of Titan basketball. My father had taken me to games, and the gym (Calihan Hall) was one of my favorite places to work out and play. It was two blocks from my man Mike Jack's house, and we'd go there three to four times a week to hoop. I knew the history as well as anyone. Dave DeBusschere, Earl Cureton, and John Long had played there. I didn't seriously consider U of D, but I wanted to be supportive of Detroit, the school, and Head Coach Ricky Byrdsong. I knew that the fact that I came on a visit there would help in recruiting, and it did. We attended the same church. His assistant coach, Scott Perry, had recruited me since the ninth grade, and we had a great relationship. They appreciated the gesture, knowing that the home and official visits would help them recruit others in trying to rebuild a once-great program.

University of Minnesota Golden Gophers

Minnesota coach Clem Haskins was relentless in his recruiting. I don't think he recruited through an assistant coach. He called and wrote constantly. I loved the Big Ten. Minnesota's gym was interesting, in part because the court stood about five feet off of the floor. I hated the cold and I heard that the winters in Minnesota were near impossible, but something about his style garnered my attention.

Sparty

Michigan State. Honestly, I was theirs to lose. After the seventh-grade interview, visiting their campus numerous times, playing with Magic, and, most important, my relationship with assistant coach Tom Izzo, I already felt like I was a part of their program. I was so familiar.

When a player is recruited, he or she, most times, will have a better relationship with the assistant rather than the head coach. This is no slight to the head coach. It's just that most communication before arriving on campus is through an assistant. Assistants study the players, host them on visits, and talk to them on the phone. The assistant can make or break a deal, and I wanted to play for Izzo. I just knew him better than Coach Heathcote, who was aging and I perceived as old school. Izzo was honest, had fire, and was going to let me run point like Magic and Smitty.

JOHN COLLIER/Detroit Free Press

Webber: "I want to have things balanced. In case one thing leaves me — like basketball — I don't want anything else to collapse."

Stalking Chris Webber

Fame brings bids, but precious little time to be a kid

By Mitch Albom

One coach, upon learning that Chris Webber goes to church every Sunday, dashed off a letter saying, he, too, was a regular churchgoer: "The other night we were singing a hymn, and I had the joy of Jesus in my soul — and then I started thinking about you, Chris, and how, if you played basketball for our school, it would bring joy to my soul, too"

Chris threw the letter away.

Another coach got wind that Chris was sensitive to family matters. So he phoned the teenager and began moaning about his divorce, how it was tearing him apart, affecting his work. "Chris," he said, nearly breaking into tears, "if you came to our school, it would make my life so much *better…*"

Chris handed the phone to his father, who told the guy no thanks.

There was the coach from Southern Cal who wrote how he loved watching Chris play basketball, and how he had followed his career since junior high school – except that he spelled the name wrong, over and over, calling him "Weber" instead of Webber.

And then there was the coach from a college in Nebraska who called the house and couldn't get anything right.

"So, Chris, you guys play Class D ball, right?"

"No, Class B."

"Oh, right. So, how do you like living in Birmingham?"

"I live in Detroit."

"Oh, right. Say, uh, how's your Dad? I spoke with him just yesterday."

"My Dad's been out of town all week."

"Well, listen, we sure would like you to come to our school…"

On it goes. Behind Chris Webber, in front of Chris Webber, above Chris Webber, below Chris Webber — this endless parade of college basketball characters. Coaches, recruiters, alumni, boosters, all tripping and stumbling and generally embarrassing themselves, chasing any lead, swallowing any tip — "*Where will he go? Which way is he leaning?*" — all because this tall, graceful, well-mannered son of an automotive worker can play basketball better than any other high schooler in the country.

He can swoop and dunk. He can pass like a point guard. His body, long and thick, can find the ball through any crowd of defenders, two, three, four, they can't stop him. One game, he scored 58 points and sat out the fourth quarter. Another, he had nine dunks by halftime. In a playoff game, an alley-oop pass went too high, over his head, but he just hung in the air until the ball ricocheted off the glass, then he grabbed it and stuffed it. Amazing. His coach at Birmingham Detroit Country Day, Kurt Keener, says Chris Webber plays the game "as if God built him to do it."

But God never had recruiting in mind. You thought *you* had a hard time getting through high school? Here is a teenager who has actually *removed* the phone from his bedroom because it never stops ringing. He has keys to four of his friends' houses — which he goes to even if they are not home — just to escape the madness. When he goes to school, people ask, "Which college have you picked?" and when he goes to the video arcade they ask, "Which college have you picked?" and when he stops at the supermarket they ask, "Which college have you picked?" — as if their lives will change with his decision.

Sometimes, he makes things up, just to throw them off. They swallow it anyhow. He could say he was going to Mars and recruiters would scurry to find what Mars was offering.

"It's embarrassing," Webber say. "All these grown-ups making this big fuss over me."

Embarrassing, yes. Also silly and sad. This is a story of the biggest prize in high school basketball

See MITCH ALBOM, Page 6C

Our house was spotless, but I was still embarrassed that the coaches got to come see where I lived. I wasn't ashamed of my family, but our financial portfolio wasn't anything to brag about. It wasn't anything period. Both Coach Heathcote and Coach Izzo sat in our small living room as my mother offered them something to drink and ordered me to get two chairs from the kitchen. The MSU staff spoke to my siblings, exchanged pleasantries, and got down to the get down. I noticed they approached my family the exact same way the other four would. They addressed my mother on the educational benefits of the school and told my father how they would complete his job of raising me to be a respectable man.

Coach Heathcote got right to it, saying that he understood my family. He said my family was blue collar like his and that of his most famous recruit, Magic—whose father, like mine, lived that cold factory life for the betterment of his family. He assured my parents that they could come to campus anytime they wanted and that he would call them directly about any behavioral issues. My parents loved that. What I loved most about the pitch was that Coach Heathcote told me his plan for me on the court. He said, "I want to make you a point guard." I tried to fight a smile as it wrestled through my lips. *Point guard.* You're a great passer, and I know passers. We'll work on your shooting and dribbling." He reminded me of my grandfather, and that's always a good thing.

The Maize and Blue

Michigan head coach Steve Fisher came to my house with his assistant too. Fish was cool, professional, and to the point. He had an easy sell. It went something like "Michigan is one of the best academic institutions in the world. The campus is only thirty minutes from your home. We play the best competition in the best conference, and we need you to get back the glory we once had. We believe in you. Will you please believe in us?" That was a serious question considering the 1990-91 team didn't seem to have much of a shot for the upcoming season.

Duke University Blue Devils

Coach K didn't know that he was entering hostile territory. As he got out of his car, he was greeted by boos from neighbors gathered across the street at Big Chris's house. My block hated Duke. We all cheered when UNLV beat the dog snot out of them in the 1990 NCAA Finals. I, on the other hand, was seriously considering becoming a Blue Devil. I liked their playing style and head coach. I also played with Grant Hill and Bobby Hurley, so I knew playing with them would be exciting.

Coach K came in with an assistant coach and a video recorder. I'd never seen a portable video recorder before. I was more fascinated with how he used it to show me where I would play in their offense. It was dope. He showed me tape of Christian Laettner and proceeded to tell me how well he saw us working together in a three-guard, two-forward offense. Like Coach Fisher, he had a rather easy job discussing the educational benefits of attending the school.

With my home visits out of the way, my official campus visits were next. I was closer to deciding where I'd sign. The whole process of recruiting was wearing on me. In the papers there was constant speculation and updates on the speculation. The media tried to compare, contrast, and incite competition between me and Jalen. They tried to make it a big deal on who was the best player in the state. I never fell for it; he was my boy, and I wanted to be the best in the country, not just the D. They were always asking what we thought about it. I refused to get caught up. I understood that there were many great players out there, and if I got caught up on myself or anyone else, I was gonna get caught slipping, and I was not about to let that happen.

University of Detroit Titans

Every campus has a different pulse, language, and energy that usually reflects the pulse of the area it inhabits. Official visits serve the purpose of getting a kid acquainted with the campus—dorms, workout facilities, arenas, etc. Although it was unexpected, my first visit turned out to be my most exciting one.

Coach Byrdsong and Coach Perry played it smart. No pressure, just a conversation about possibilities. They focused on everything that I didn't know about the school or Detroit. I went to the museums, met business leaders, went to classes, and saw the underground college community that I didn't know existed in the city. We talked about how I would fit in and what would be expected of me. Finally, before the end of my visit, Coach Byrdsong thanked me for sacrificing a visit to bring awareness to his program. He knew that I was doing it for Detroit and because my boys had signed there. I also knew his resources were limited, and I wanted him to succeed as a coach. He knew the game and was a good man. After we came to the conclusion that I wouldn't be attending U of D, I called a couple friends to come to the Pontchartrain Hotel downtown, where I was staying, to eat some free room service. Lo and behold, next door to my room, it was going down.

I heard loud music bumping through the walls and asked Kev to turn the TV down to see if he heard what I did. It was knocking! Then, girls' voices. I was in a suite, and my room shared a door with the club next door. I could swear I heard a familiar voice…it was Luke Skyywalker of 2 Live Crew. But it was probably just the music. I went out into the hall and saw the man himself! He said, "What up? fellas? What y'all up to?" We said nothing, and he waved us over. He told us he'd just had a concert and that we should come in and grab some food, girls, or whatever we wanted. I walked right in; Coach Byrdsong couldn't have set this up. Plus, Luke was a Miami Hurricanes fan. Kev and I chilled, watched, gawked, and imagined, trying to hide our expressions but mouths wide open on the inside. Any official visit after this would definitely be a letdown.

Later, I told Coach how much I loved my visit. He replied, "Really? Us? But you know Detroit as well as anyone."

I just laughed and said, "Trust me, I'm not lying, Coach."

♦ ♦ ♦

I had grown up watching Steve Smith play basketball for the Pershing Doughboys. So when I was told that Smitty would be my host, I was pumped. He drove me around, and we talked a little about games and players from State. Truthfully, I couldn't have cared less about being shown around. That didn't matter. I was hanging with a childhood hero. I watched him shoot some jumpers in the gym. That was all I wanted: to talk, play, shoot. I went to some classes and truly felt I belonged there.

Michigan State was laid back, unpretentious, come as you are, and I could dig it. After going to a Spartans football game, I sat in the gym for about twenty minutes, moving from seat to seat, looking at the rafters— specifically at the banner from Magic's 1979 NCAA championship team. I closed my eyes and imagined life as a Spartan. I talked to Coach Izzo before I left and told them they were number one with me. I was starting to think about committing early.

The Golden Gophers

It was November 9, just ten days before the early signing period. Minnesota was freezing as usual. As I exited the airport, the cold air hit my face, and I said, "No way! No chance." I questioned why I even came on the trip. From that point on, I just tried to enjoy it. What I didn't know was that this visit would be the ultimate deciding factor in my choice of school.

I had a great time with Coach Haskins and his wife. I went to his team's practice, and it was okay. I just remember a ton of fouling. I thought how my neighbor, Voshon Lenard, was seriously considering going there and that made it easier to consider. I was a big Willie Burton fan. He, too, was from Detroit, but he had already moved on to the NBA. Walter Bond took me out, and I had a great time, but during the visit I was just uninterested, respectfully going through the motions. We headed out to the Metrodome to attend the football game, and, ironically, the Golden Gophers were playing Michigan State. After attending games at Michigan and Michigan State, I wondered why the school would put its average football team on display to help recruit. I thought they should have gone in a totally different direction. With the tradition of the Spartans and the Big House that sat over a hundred thousand Wolverine fans, they should have kept their hidden gems to themselves. The game seemed uneventful. Michigan State put a whooping on the Gophers, 28–16. It was a really boring game.

Webber in NCAA probe of Gophers

Free Press Staff and Wire Reports

St. PAUL, Minn. — Birmingham Detroit Country Day basketball star Chris Webber Thursday was linked to what might have been a minor recruiting violation by the University of Minnesota.

Webber was Gophers basketball coach Clem Haskins' guest in a Metrodome luxury suite for part of the Nov. 10 Minnesota-Michigan State football game, the university said in response to an NCAA inquiry.

MSU officials occupied the adjacent suite, and Nancy Weaver, wife of former Spartans athletic director Doug Weaver, said she recognized Webber.

"We were only there five, six or seven minutes," said Webber's father, Mayce. "I don't know what's wrong. We've been doing the same thing at Michigan and Michigan State — going to the press box. It's no secret; I'm not trying to tell on them. Maybe there's some jealousy between schools."

The most serious charges against Minnesota deal with former administrator Luther Darville, who allegedly gave athletes cash, loans, meals and merchandise. University officials say Darville acted alone, although he denies that. He has been convinced of stealing $186,000 from the school.

The university report also said former football coach Lou Holtz, now at Notre Dame, has admitted giving former running back Roselle Richardson $10 or $20 while talking to the recruit in a car outside his Warren, Ohio, high school in 1985. Holtz said it was to replace a wallet that was lost or stolen when Richardson visited the university several days earlier.

We decided to leave to get a bite and just get away from the game. As we were walking up the long row of stairs headed to the concourse, we passed a section of suites. Specifically, a suite filled with people. I was with Coach and the host—I don't remember who, I don't know who they were. A coach asked me to say hello, so I stepped in with the Minnesota contingent, shook a couple of hands, and left. I continued up the stairs and gave the thumbs-up sign to a suite containing Spartan fans.

I'd say it took me less than two minutes. No harm, no foul, so I thought. That was until I went home a couple of weeks later and word that I might be under NCAA investigation was circulating.

On January 4, I read an article in the *Detroit Free Press*, and I couldn't believe it. They said I was associated with a scandal. Why would my name be associated with a scandal? I did what they had asked me to do: say hi. If I saw those people again, I wouldn't have remembered their faces. A violation? On me? Not the ones who asked me to say hello? For a handshake? Nothing was discussed. What, they made me an offer in those two minutes? What the hell? The source was the bigger issue and changed the dynamics of everything. Michigan State had called the NCAA. The article said that the wife of the former athletic director at Michigan State had noticed me at the Metrodome and informed the school. Michigan State, the front runner at the time, the school I was most familiar with and had the most history with. Michigan State, whose coach I loved. At that time, I had been ready to declare with them early. They lost me right then and there.

I was told that MSU had summoned a reporter and had her take pictures from across the arena with a long-distance lens through a Coke bottle. The NCAA called and asked for a meeting with me, my father, and Coach Keener. They had the pictures and for a couple of hours asked questions. Stupid ones. I got up several times in the meeting and yelled, "You're treating me like I did something wrong! Why not punish the school? What was I supposed to do?" What would you tell your child to do in a situation like this? I didn't know. I was being lied to and decided, *I'm not going to either one of those schools.*

I went from announcing early that I would be attending State to leaving it wide open. I truthfully distanced myself from them. That was the best thing that could have happened for the University of Michigan. Coach Heathcote and Izzo were livid. They understood my feelings of betrayal; they called me and verbalized my confusion better than I could. They also took responsibility, though I knew they had no control over the actions of others. It was just messed up, and we knew it. It was as if they had tried to eliminate the competition by any means, no matter who became a casualty of friendly fire. That one event changed the course of my chances of ever becoming a Spartan.

University of Michigan Wolverines

At the start of my campus visit, I didn't have much of a connection or vibe with the University of Michigan. Coach Frieder had gone to Arizona State. Mike Boyd, the assistant coach, had been hired by Cleveland State. But I was familiar with the school. I loved going to the campus, and the students showed me love. At any game I attended, I felt like I was already part of the student population. The problem: there wasn't a player on the team with game who I wanted to host me. The team was straight whack! On other visits, teams had players with an NBA future or players who I wanted to emulate. Michigan State had Steve Smith. Duke had multiple

All-Americans. But Michigan was in total rebuild mode, and the players there weren't interested in having me take any of their time.

Instead, I spent a lot of time with the coaches, which was good because I got to know assistant coach Brian Dutcher. Coach Dutcher's father was a longtime successful coach, so he really knew the game. He was funny, had a cool wife, and guaranteed that with hard work, the sky was the limit for me. In the locker room, he presented me with a Michigan jersey with my name on it and a spotlight on my locker. He then walked me across the corridor to the football game.

Well, one hundred thousand fans in one place is a sight to see. A sea of maize and blue. People of all ages. Different generations engaged in fellowship. The best fight song known to man. I was in heaven. I was excited to watch the game. The love I received from the fans that Saturday was incredible. They shouted "Webber...Webber" as I walked up the aisle to my seat. But I felt that the staff was uncomfortable trying to make a connection with me. I'm sure they were desperate to get me to commit. Then, a few minutes into the game, we made a small but lasting connection.

A fan was booing Coach Fisher as we walked up the stairs. As coach and his wife stayed off to the side, this man went on a rant, attacking Fisher while pleading for Frieder and the good old days. I saw the disappointment and embarrassment in Angie Fisher's eyes as the belligerent ass held court with other drunk bastards, who were laughing and egging him on. I also saw her look at her husband and whisper "It's gonna be okay" while she patted him on the knee. I fell in love with her and Coach right there. I saw their love for each other. I felt their resolve, and I loved her dignity in that situation. I was used to people lying and making things up, so I didn't care about someone's random opinion. I was interested in seeing how others handled adversity. I took that as encouragement. I also took it as encouragement that Coach Dutcher's wife had to be rushed to the hospital where she delivered a healthy girl.

Duke University Blue Devils

My next destination was Durham, North Carolina—home of the Blue Devils. Duke was in my top three and at the time was ranked fifth in the nation. Earlier in the year, I watched on TV as they beat Michigan 75–68. I spoke to Grant before the trip, and we were both pumped about the visit. The first place I got to see was the gym. I was familiar with it from

a visit just months before, but this was the second real college practice I got to observe. It was only a shootaround. No hard play, considering they were playing Shaquille O'Neal and LSU. I went to some classes with Grant and Christian Laettner, who served as my host. That was cool. The whole campus was cool. The coach was cool. The vibe was cool. There was no feeling of pretentiousness. Just feelings of respect, focus, and determination. Nothing arrogant or personal. I liked that. I got to talk to Coach Tommy Amaker, who was their great assistant coach at the time. I bonded with him, almost like with Coach Izzo. I felt that he understood the delicate balance of my situation at school and my home and environment. He knew it could be tricky. Another plus was that Cherokee Parks had also committed to Duke, and I had bonded with him at Nike Camp. I knew it would be fun to play with him, and I loved his skill set.

On game day, I got a taste of college basketball pandemonium. It was as good as any ever sampled. The coordination of the fans is unexplainable, and the small size of the gym serves as intimidating, instead of embarrassing. I noticed crooked rims on the visitor's side, not that it mattered. You had to shoot on both ends, but for some reason, I took a mental note. Now at this time, I had never really heard of Shaquille O'Neal—the dominant big man from LSU, otherwise known as Shaq. Most college ball on TV was regional, so I was more aware of Acie Earl from Iowa. I could not believe my eyes when Shaq came out on the floor to warm up. He was seven-foot-two, weighing in at 295. I seriously contemplated if I was in the right place and playing the right sport. Physically, I had never witnessed anything like him. Why weren't more people talking about this phenom? He was leading the nation in rebounding at fifteen a slice and averaging twenty-seven points. Not to mention he was only eighteen. Mental note: *Get your game right.* It ain't a game outchere.

The game was exciting, but Duke beat the breaks off the Tigers 88–70. Laettner scored twenty-five and ripped eleven boards. Duke held Shaq to a season-low fifteen points and ten boards. I knew that Duke had done their due diligence on me and my family. As I was hanging with Grant and Christian at a Duke party, Laettner said, "This is whack. Webb, you want to go to another place?" I'm like, "Cool." We jumped in his car and went a few minutes up the street to North Carolina Central University—an HBCU. That visit showed me that I could have it all. North Carolina Central felt like home. I was familiar with both scenes and could escape comfortably into either environment. I was feeling Duke, its players, and campus. I wished it wasn't so far away.

With the official visits to each campus behind me, I was able to settle down and concentrate on being a senior in high school. I went into my senior season relaxed and confident. I loved my teammates and my school. The talk with Isiah had really calmed my spirit. It gave me mental freedom because no one had more than Zeke. It helped me relax and focus because he told me how he had decided to attend Indiana. He told me to write out the pros and cons and go with my gut. I believed he'd be there if I needed him, and though I'd be too scared to call him my senior year, I was satisfied with the fact that he understood me. For once, someone outside of family didn't want anything from me.

I went home and immediately got back to working out with Kev and Mike Jack, running through the 'hood like Rocky with no kids following us. My school load was down for the first time in three years, so there wasn't a lot of academic pressure. I'd made close friends in an environment where I was the outsider and never looked back. This was my school as much as anybody's. I put in just as much as they did. That experience would forever make me proud of who I am, unashamed and humbled. I never wanted to be "one of them" who prejudged, knew every answer, or thought their success was something that they had earned all on their own. I didn't necessarily know who I was yet, but I knew who I was not going to be, regardless of my level of success.

◆ ◆ ◆

My mother passed me the phone; it was Juwan. He had called to tell me how excited he was for the season, and we talked about camp and expectations and laughed after he brought up how we supposedly cheated him and his AAU team this past summer. He also mentioned how it was crazy because he'd always wanted to play for the Illini and now he couldn't. In 1990, the NCAA announced that the Illinois team would be penalized for recruiting violations:

- The team could not play in the 1991 NCAA Tournament.
- The university could not offer more than two basketball scholarships in the 1991–1992 and 1992–1993 academic years.
- In 1991, basketball coaches were prohibited from recruiting off campus.
- The university was barred from paying for official visits by potential student athletes during 1991.

And those were just some of the sanctions! It was easy to see why Big Nook had crossed them off his list. He was leaning toward Michigan, but he knew that he'd be alone and couldn't recruit others to play with him. So he started recruiting me. "Dawg, you know Michigan ain't that good this year, but man, if you, me and Jay…man, me and you could switch everything defensively, and we could own the paint." The possibility of Michigan started to come alive.

Meanwhile, I was excited about the start of the season. I felt like this was going to be my best year ever. Since entering high school, I had gained twenty-five pounds. I had worked out with and against NBA players. I was familiar enough with the game to know I was good, but I also understood that I had miles to go. But I'd proven myself against the best and knew that I belonged. In the first game of the season, a rematch with last year's runner-up, I had thirty-eight points, hit a couple of threes, and knocked down my free throws. Steve Fisher, Jud Heathcote, and Clem Haskins were all sitting front row.

As I continued my senior season, my relationship with the media made me cautious of them and their motives. They became bored with the story of the good kid. I became a commodity. I heard their slick remarks, and I ignored their provocative questions, like "How does it feel to be the best player in the country?" or, "Who's better, you or Jalen?" I got it. I went to the rich school with the haves;

Webber gets 38; Country Day wins

Chris Webber, one of the top prep basketball players in the country, scored 38 points as host Birmingham Detroit Country Day, state Class B champion, opened its season Wednesday with a 77-51 victory over Saginaw Buena Vista, the Class B runner-up.

Webber, a 6-10 all-state center, hit 14 of 20 shots from the field, including two three-pointers, and eight of 11 free throws, in three quarters of play. In attendance were coaches Steve Fisher of Michigan, Jud Heathcote of Michigan State and

METRO/STATE

Clem Haskins of Minnesota.

The Yellowjackets led, 16-14, after one quarter, and put the game away with a 28-12 margin in the second quarter. Webber had 27 points in the first half, including 16 points in the second period.

Senior guard Shawn Jackson had 19 points for Buena Vista.

he went to Southwestern. So the "me versus him" narrative worked. This was suburbs versus Detroit. But I wouldn't play. Even though I played with the haves, I was from the land of the have-nots. I wasn't afforded the luxury of forgetting that while attending Country Day.

What made things worse from a press perspective was that Jalen and I were scheduled to play each other on December 22 in the Big Michigan Shootout at Cobo Arena. The city was hyped. We were too. We were competitors, and both of us wanted to lead our squad to victory. Whoever won this game had a great chance of winning the national high school title. Jalen and I both had a great game, but we lost that night to Southwestern. Still, I loved playing in Cobo, in front of what seemed like the entire city. All I had ever wanted was to do my thing in Detroit, to show the city I loved what—or rather, who—they produced. I tried to tear the hinges off the rim on every dunk and no-look every pass. I tried to Russell every shot and Isiah every handle. But I was disappointed after our loss. It was my chance to prove that I had made the correct decision on school, education, and hoops.

Though he would still hit me off with a pair of shoes or I would get a jogging suit and sweatshirt on his tab, my relationship with Ed Martin was strained. After my talk with Isiah, I was more confident. There were no awkward feelings when he cheered in the stands for his team and then came over and spoke to me after the game, congratulating me on my effort. I was more hurt that we had lost, but now I was looking forward to the future. The next level, a fresh start.

Webber and Rose:

"We should be able to just play, and then talk about who's the best after the season. Don't make two young people clash or pit them against each other. It's just not right."

— Chris Webber, prep phenom

But state's top players weary of comparisons

BY SCOTT WALTON
Free Press Sports Writer

Before they were teenagers, or the stars of their state championship teams or unanimous mentions on recruiters' Top 10 wish lists, they were friends.

The national acclaim will last a while for Birmingham Detroit Country Day center Chris Webber and Detroit Southwestern forward Jalen Rose, but not forever. The friendship forged as 12-year-olds, in AAU summer basketball, however, will last a lifetime.

Although the public insists, Webber balks at making comparisons and citing what distinguishes him from Rose. Maligning Rose won't

legitimize Webber's status as possibly the No. 1 prep senior in the country.

"People have already tried to play me and other players against each other," said Webber, who at 6-feet-9 shoots, rebounds and dribbles equally well. "It's always, 'Who's the best, Chris?' or 'Can you check him?' Whether they mean to be divisive or not, it's unnecessary. We're just 17-, 18-year-old kids."

Rose, considering first what's in the best of interest of their friendship, usually withholds comment when such questions are raised. Rose, the state's No. 2 prospect, didn't raise his team to the top of USA Today's national poll alone *or* with his mouth.

"Of course, I'll try to play the best I can,"

We continued to improve and stay focused the rest of the season. We wanted to win back-to-back titles in Class B. The MHSSA was upset with us because after winning the Class B championship a year earlier, we petitioned to move up to Class A. I guess they read that as an insult, but we just wanted to compete against the best and make history. For me, it was personal. I wanted to prove that I was not only good enough, but smart enough and able to make the players around me better—so much so that a school with fewer than four hundred students could take down Goliath.

During the season, the press coverage was suffocating. I was called everything from "God-sent golden child" to "Just an okay player." The media said I spoke well and couldn't believe I was from the ghetto. I hated who they presumed me to be. My emotions callused. Rumors were rampant that I was going to Kentucky, that I was definitely not going to Michigan. During all this, I was very aware of what was happening in the college scene. Shawn Respert was doing well at Michigan State. Michigan played hard, but their record was terrible. Duke seemed to be headed toward

Friendly rivals

Rose said with a what-a-stupid-question-to-ask look on his face. "But I won't be trying to just outdo Chris. I'll try to do to the best I can to help my team win."

The boys high school basketball season officially opens Tuesday across Michigan, and Webber and Rose are the season's most compelling figures. Neither has decided which college to attend. Both are already weary of the time-worn question: Who should win the Mr. Basketball Award?

Rose won't concede the prize to Webber, but he doesn't covet it, either. Webber wants the award, but not at all costs.

"I'd love to win Mr. Basketball," Webber said. "But I'd much rather be successful later on in life. Derrick Coleman didn't win Mr. Basketball, and look at him today."

Said Rose: "I really don't think about it too much. Since I play every day, of course, I'd like to win, but I won't be heartbroken if I don't."

Class A Southwestern and Class B Country Day will play Dec. 22 at Cobo Arena in the second Michigan Shootout. The event features four other games — including a fine matchup between Saginaw and Detroit Pershing — but they will hardly receive mention because of the Webber-Rose confrontation.

Webber resented the pregame hype when he played another good friend, former Pershing center Lorenzo Orr, in last year's Shootout. He is determined it won't happen again.

"At the end of the game I was mad at myself for letting the media play with me," he said, "and mad at myself for probably not playing up to my potential."

He vented his anger that evening with a rim-wrecking dunk as time expired.

But that was last season. Let the new one begin.

a championship run. Iyapo signed early with U of D. Mike Jack was holding out for Michigan, and I wanted them to recruit him. Kev signed with FAMU. Things were moving quickly.

I was getting closer to making my decision. I just felt a certain peace about a certain school, but a call from Juwan would seal the deal for me. In March 1991, Coach Keener called and told me that I had won the Mr. Basketball award for the state of Michigan. It was sweet to get the news from him because only he and Kevin knew how bad I had wanted to win it. I wanted the validation. I wanted the statue to show that I had fulfilled my potential, regardless of where I attended high school. I wanted the trophy to concede that the rhetoric that my parents were fools was straight bull. I wanted it. But when Coach told me that I had won it by the largest margin in Michigan history, I was shocked. On March 18, we headed to the press conference to accept my award. When I got home, I got a call from the best recruiter of all.

"Congratulations big dawg!" Juwan said. "I know you were killing them out there. Look, Michigan sucks. We can go there and start and play together. You don't want to go to State. They tried to make you look bad. That shows how they will treat you. You know I'm better than Peplowski, and Respert is all they have. Duke's a good team, but you know you don't want to go there. Come to Michigan. Me, you, and Jay—you know what we can do? We will all have a chance to start and play together. It's only thirty minutes away. Your mom can bring us food all the time."

The moment I hung up, I was a Wolverine. I didn't tell Juwan, but I already had a sense of peace about it. Juwan had filled in the recruiting holes, the excitement gap. I was seeing the university through his eyes, and I knew that he was going to make the best of it. I thought that the chance to play with Jalen had passed, but maybe not. I could play for my city and my state. I was pumped. My siblings were important to me; I wanted them to be able to come to games. I wanted to keep as much normalcy as possible. Plus, we were a close family, and my grandfather's deteriorating condition was my tether. I was at peace with attending Michigan.

My mother and father called a family meeting. I alerted everyone that I wanted to talk about colleges. I asked everyone what school they thought I should attend and why. My mother said that she had prayed on it, and this was something I needed to decide, so that I'd always be clear and would never have regrets. My father ignored her revelation from God and said, "I like Coach K, but Michigan or Michigan State. I want to see you play." My siblings were split two-two, Michigan versus Michigan State. Finally, I told them how I prayed every night that God would help me make a good decision and that I felt at peace. For the first time, I said I was a Wolverine.

My mom smiled. Pops jumped up and said "Yeah!" Two kids cheered while two booed. I told my parents that I planned to make my announcement after the championship game. It wasn't hard to keep a secret. Only family knew, and I had less than a week to announce.

Michigan's head assistant, Mike Boyd, who had recruited me and who I had formed a bond with, had been hired by Cleveland State, and there were rumors that Perry Watson was going to be given the Michigan assistant coaching job. Michigan knew that I had wanted to play for P. Dub. I knew that if that were to happen, Jalen would go there. I knew what the deal was. I knew we would all be together. Two games to go until I'd announce to the world I was attending the University of Michigan. I went into my final two games as happy as I'd been in a while. I was a kid with a secret. What could be better?

The first of my last two games was against Bridgeport in my new home at the Crisler Center. I was hyped in the layup line, imagining myself in the same spot with the Wolverines. I spotted my locker in the corner—the one I had when I won a championship and two regional finals. The one I decided I'd ask Coach if I could have next year. We put a monumental beatdown on Bridgeport, 78–44. I had twenty-five points, seven blocks, and nine rebounds. I was three for three from deep.

Undefeated Albion (26–0) was the final test en route to ending high school with three consecutive state championships. Game day, I was just as excited about the game as I was about announcing my decision. Isiah and some Piston teammates were there along with boxer Tommy Hearns and some other Detroit sports dignitaries. I was young and invincible. Nothing was going to stop me.

Twenty-seven seconds into the first quarter, I went up for a block and came down on a teammate's foot. I hit the ground in pain. It was the same ankle I had hurt months earlier. I couldn't believe it. This was not how I wanted my high school career to end!

I was carted off the court and went back to the locker room to get retaped. As I walked out, I saw my mother, Mrs. Keener, and about three other women gathered outside the locker room in a prayer huddle. I was encouraged by their presence. I knew I was going to be okay, and okay I was. I finished my career with a win and poured in twenty-seven points and grabbed twenty-two rebounds with a partially torn ankle ligament. All in a day's work.

I'd done it. We'd won three state championships—one in Class C and two straight in Class B. We'd accomplished what others couldn't even

1. All-State 1988–1991

2. First team All-State for a record third time

3. All-Metro 1988–1991

4. All-Suburban 1988–1991

5. Dream Team 1988–1991

6. Parade Player of the Year

7. Gatorade Player of the Year

8. USA Today Player of the Year

9. McDonald's All-American and MVP of Game

10. Michigan Mr. Basketball (by a record number of votes)

11. Third all-time in scoring (2,628 points)

12. 1,300 rebounds

13. Most rebounds in a season: 344 and 425

14. 252 career steals

15. Most blocks in a season: 143 and 142

16. 479 career blocks (second all-time)

17. 102 games played (second all-time)

18. Finals record fourteen consecutive free throws

19. Finals record twenty-two boards

conceive. I was happy for our coaches, our school, and our team. As for me, I set a lot of records along the way.

On the way to my press conference, I called Coach Izzo and explained that I wouldn't be attending Michigan State. I wanted to tell him first. I didn't know what to say. I didn't want to call, but I knew it was something my father would say a man has to do. Besides, I really respected him. We talked, and he was gracious. He knew they had lost me on the Minnesota visit. He sounded as if he was crying, or maybe I was just hearing myself. I realized after our conversation that my decision was real. I called Izzo before I called Fish. I didn't want him hearing from anyone but me.

We pulled up to the 1940 Chop House in our Scooby-Doo van, and when we got out, the whole house fell out with us: paper towels, notebooks, juice boxes, basketballs, footballs, and hymnals. I felt great, despite the crutches. Everyone was seated. I walked in, and it was a love fest. It was all of my family, church members, neighbors, and friends from Country Day. This was the moment I'd been waiting for. Reporters had followed me to the movies, tapping me on my shoulder whispering, "So where are you going?" I had to spend the night at friends' houses to avoid the phone calls. Finally, it was time to embrace a historic moment for my family. I limped up to the podium.

"Hello, everyone. Thank you." Then, for some reason, I quoted a song I sang regularly at church. "Lord, I'm available to you, my will I give to you, I'll do what you say do. My soul has been emptied, and I am available to you." The words, sung by Reverend Milton Brunson, were my inspiration. I was exhausted, relieved, and thankful. I wanted to tell God, in front of everyone, that I thanked him for keeping me sane through this process. I saw my mother tearing up, and it took everything in me not to let go.

I then thanked everyone for coming and announced, "Next year I will be a Wolverine! A Michigan man." Which was a shout-out to Bo, who had played a big part in recruiting me. My sister, who was sitting on my brother's shoulders, lifted up both hands, made two thumbs-up signs, and turned them upside down in protest. She definitely wanted me to go to Michigan State. All I could do was laugh. The crowd cheered in approval.

I can't say that I knew the impact we'd have on the college landscape or that we'd earn a nickname, but I was the last of the "Fab Five" to sign with Michigan. My father, however, was cussing someone out on the phone. A member of the media was standing next to my father, who was on the phone near the bathroom. The reporter told me that he heard my father say "My child is not for sale." That was something I heard him say often. I knew that I was not for sale. None of my parents' children were. My father had turned down many financial deals since the days when recruiters tried to convince us to move to a different state for middle school. This was nothing new.

MR. BASKETBALL

Senior Chris Webber has averaged 24.5 points and 12.8 rebounds in his career at Birmingham Detroit Country Day.

Webber wins award in a landslide

BY MICK MCCABE
Free Press Sports Writer

Every high school basketball fan in the state *knew* who this year's Mr. Basketball would be except Chris Webber

"I know nothing is ever a lock," Webber said.

This was. Webber on Monday become the 11th recipient of the Hal Schram Mr. Basketball Award, given annually by the Basketball Coaches Association of Michigan in conjunctionwith the Free Press.

Webber, who led Birmingham Detroit Country Day to two state championships in his first three seasons, received 695 points, almost 500 more than runner-up Jalen Rose of Detroit Southwestern. He won by the biggest margin in the awars's history.

"It's an honor, " Webber said. "I remember when Michael Talley won and he was so happy. Guys like Sam Vincent, Demetreus Gore and Mark Macon were great players. The only thing that will mean more is winning a state championship."

But he already has two state titles.

"I don't want to lose my last game," he said.

Fat chance. In his four years — all as a starter — Country Day has gone 92-12. Webber has scored more than 2,500 points — 24.5 a game — and grabbed more than 1,300 rebounds — 12.8 a game.

Webber, a 6-foot-10 center, said he probably would hold a press conference to announce his college. He said his finalists were Michigan, Michigan State, Detroit Mercy and Duke.

Webber's parents, Doris and Mayce, proudly attended the presentation press conference at the Free Press.

"I think it means for us and our other children that hard work pays off," Doris Webber said. "Chris has worked hard. When other people were at the movies, Chris was at practice or at a camp."

Doris said she was as equally impressed with her son off the court. "He's a delight," she said. "He's very demanding with his brothers but very encouraging, too.

He helps them a lot. He's definitely a Mr. Basketball son."

But does he clean his room?

"On occasion," she said with a laugh. "But when he does, he demands that everybody else in the house does, too. His job around the house is to wash the pots and pans. He does them several times a week. He does them or he'll pay one of his brothers to do them."

Mayce Webber called Chris an ideal son. He does the pots and pans and takes out the garbage.

"Him being 18 doesn't mean anything," Mayce said with a laugh. "As long as he's living in this house he has to live by our rules. He's obedient and gets good grades. There's nothing else I could ask for in a son."

Monday's affair was a pleasant diversion for the Webbers, who have been feeling the effects of the Chris' recruitment. Because of the recruiting process, Mayce asked not to be photo graphed.

"My picture was in the paper a couple of weeks ago," he said. "People started recognising me anywhere I went. They were alumni. They offer things. I'd like to leave it at that. When this first started it was fun, but it's not anymore."

Recruiting also has taken its toll on Chris. He gets most upset with constant media speculation on which college he will attend. He said because of it he decided not to major in journalism or communications.

"I couldn't be a part of that," he said. "Anytime someone can take this quote about me loving some coach over something that happened two summers ago and somehow connect that with today's happenings is irresponsible journalism.

"Once you make a person look like a jerk you can't change that. The rebuttal is not as big as the original quote."

If journalism is out, what will Webber do?

"Maybe I'll go on the progold tour," he said with a smile.

Not until he does the pots and pans.

After the announcement, I had a couple of months of school left and a senior project working at my mother's school. Country Day seniors must intern off campus for two weeks and write a paper about the experience. My experience at Mumford High School in Detroit added levity and made me even more grateful.

Mumford, home of the Mustangs, is located in Detroit on Wyoming. It was approximately a five- to ten-minute drive from my house. I finally got to see the world that my mom and her comrades navigated on a daily basis. We entered through metal detectors and were welcomed by security. The first thing I noticed was the large number of students. It had to be two to three times the number that attended Country Day. My mother was a special needs teacher. Mrs. Linda Adams and Mrs. Claudia Burton, members of our church, allowed me to work in their classes. I had a blast. I knew many of the kids who passed through the halls since we lived around the same block, hung around the same movie theaters, Coney restaurants, and arcades. I had never attended a school where a uniform wasn't mandatory, so I was happy to wear jeans and gymmies.

But the lack of resources was appalling. Old books in classes and libraries. No air conditioning despite being in one of the most humid cities in the country. Old, dilapidated desks. It was like the two schools represented the same picture of education in Detroit, but Country Day was in color and Mumford was in black and white. Where were the resources going? Not into the schools, that's for sure.

The teachers I volunteered with were hard workers who always took their work home. Like Isiah, they were sources of safety and inspiration. I teased the ones I worked with that they had definitely incurred recruiting violations due to their resolve to help kids. They laughed, but during those two weeks I saw many reduced to tears out of pain and frustration.

One student had three children of her own, and I was amazed at the teamwork between her and the teachers. There was no judgment, just solutions. The teachers would drive to her house if she missed school and take her homework to complete, but also bring formula, diapers, and food and still hold her accountable to the graduation standards. There were students on dialysis and another whose sickle cell anemia had become nearly debilitating. One student passed away during my time there, and the school family was heartbroken. But they knew the drill. Loss happened every year, whether due to violence, sickness, or just a student quitting school without explanation.

This is the story and sacrifice of many teachers throughout America. Seeing the daily impact those teachers had on students who statistically weren't supposed to make it made me want to do something. They were serving a higher purpose. I remember my mom sewing a dope prom dress that the teachers had purchased for a girl who had a terrible home situation. The moment of seeing her smile and then screw up her makeup crying was priceless. These teachers helped parents learn to read so they could help with their children's homework. They did it all. The experience made me proud that my mom was a teacher.

My senior paper was called "America's Bias: How America Purposely Disperses Education Based on Income and Zip Code." I wrote about the educational disparities in America for black and brown people and correlated it with the unemployment, welfare, and incarceration rates. I got an A.

I was excited about graduation. I was happy for my parents. I was happy for Mr. Mont and Harv, who had sons walking that night. For Mrs. Colson and Kevin, who was leaving the D for Florida. I was happy for my other teammates and friends: Myron, Adrian, Backus, and Vince. This was our time. We walked down the aisle with our backs

straight and heads held high. Walked up the stairs, shook hands, and grabbed our diplomas. I was nostalgic; I knew things would never be the same. I understood that things change and life happens. I closed my eyes throughout the night, trying to take mental pictures of my last day as a kid.

I was also excited to play in the **McDonald's All-American Game.** I had watched many of the games on TV and wanted to do my thing.

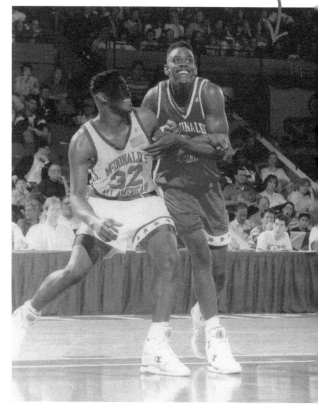

It would be the first time any of us had played on national TV, and that was a big thing; all our family and friends would see us. I was also looking forward to meeting new players and reconnecting with some old friends: James Forrest, Travis Best, Glenn Robinson, Alan Henderson, and, of course, Juwan and Jalen. Juwan introduced me to Jimmy King as soon as I got to the hotel. I roomed with Glenn, and we all had a blast.

One of our first commitments was to visit the Ronald McDonald house, a wonderful, peaceful place. It was the opening year for the Springfield, Massachusetts, house, and after meeting children with terminal illnesses or in cruel pain and seeing their smiles, resolve, and hope, I was inspired. I honor the staff at places like this. Their daily love, compassion, and professionalism, despite constant heartbreak, is commendable.

The next day came the big game. I played for the West and scored twenty-eight points, the second most ever in a game behind Michael. I added a game-high twelve boards and made the game-winning shot on a dunk, my tenth of the night. I was named MVP. My ankle was still hurting, but I tried to rip the brackets off the rim on every flush. It was a moment I'll never forget. Glenn Robinson dunked on Donyell

Marshall off a crossover so hard that it was embarrassing. Juwan gave 'em a smooth sixteen points and eight rebounds. J. Rose hit 'em with thirteen and eight, and Jimmy dropped off a cool eight. After that weekend, I finally began to understand what Juwan was talking about. Out of our recruiting class, we had four McDonald's All-Americans and should have had five. I was happy for the opportunity to play in the McDonald's and Dapper Dan games and show my skills nationally, but I still had one more box to check off my life: winning an AAU national title with the Super Friends.

I received the inspiration of a lifetime. A confirmation that it was okay to head to college, the next level. Rick Mahorn, a supporter of the Super Friends and Bad Boy champion, brought his close friend by my high school to say what's up. I was in the gym lifting, and I couldn't believe my eyes when Rick said, "Yo, Chris. Come over here. I want to introduce you to somebody." It was the Chuckster himself.

Chuck introduced himself to me, and I shook his hand in disbelief. My favorite player—the one whose posters were on my wall; who won the NBA rebounding title; the one I stole my game from, from rebounding to dunking on suckers. He was standing in front of me.

He looked at the weights that I was lifting and said with a laugh, "Yo, slow down." He gave me some great words of advice and told me to keep working hard. I don't remember saying anything. I just remember staring at him. I thought he was so much taller, so much bigger, and I was thinking to myself, how can he dominate in the NBA when he's shorter than me? He was taking pictures and telling jokes. He left me with two impressions:

1. He's cool as hell.
2. Shiiiiiid, I got work to do.

The Super Friends were so close, and unlike many teams, we weren't stacked with all-stars. We were a team once made up of twelve-year-old friends who were now eighteen with one box left to check off. But before I could win a title with the Super Friends, I tried to recruit Juwan to win an AAU title for team Michigan. I had always wanted to play for team Michigan, which comprised the best players from the Detroit area, but I didn't out of loyalty to my team after our eighth-grade split. But now I was happy to represent Michigan.

I called Nook up and asked him, and he came through. Our team loaded up the bus and hopped on a plane to Jacksonville, Florida. We went 6–0. Juwan, Voshon Leonard, Jalen, and I beat our longtime nemesis, Indiana, 116–112. I was tournament MVP and had thirty-one points and fifteen rebounds. Jalen had twenty-eight and eleven rebounds, and Juwan scored twenty-two. After the tournament I called my dad and told him how Juwan might have been the best passer that I'd ever played with and that he had thrown me so many oops it was unbelievably easy to score. I came home happy about the win, but I felt like I had cheated. I had skipped to the front of the line and played with an all-star team.

Next, we were headed to Florida for the AAU national championship tournament, but we didn't have enough money to go. Then the Pistons' Rick Mahorn donated $1,000. We were a ragtag, car-washes-to-raise money-for-travel, cookie-sales-for-uniforms type of team. A buy-your-own-shoes team. We'd had our heart broken many times: qualifying, not having money to go to tournaments, getting beat at the last second on a crazy shot. No one knew about us except for the teams that we played our hearts out against.

I wanted this championship more than I wanted the one in high school. I wanted to play the assembled All-Star teams and see if they could put their hearts on the line. I knew the win meant more to us. We hopped in our van, removed the back two rows, put blankets down, and drove nineteen hours for the tournament.

We played the first-ever game in Florida's St. Petersburg Arena. I wanted to win the first tip and score the first bucket, and when I did, I tried to tear the rim out the brackets. I also threw myself an oop off the backboard just to give the people their money's worth. Super Friends win, 95–75. I had thirty-eight points, Yop had twenty-one, Kev had twelve, and after six long years, we finally won! Crying on the podium with Kev, Harv, Iyapo, and my teammates is all that I can remember. Harv and Mr. Mont deserved it! I wanted to win it for them. They didn't get the credit of the other coaches, but they were the ones who really developed our talent.

I wanted my loyalty to mean something more than just watching their kids move on to college. I wanted to leave them with something. I wanted them to see that their words mattered. Their love mattered. Their presence in my life meant something. Winning it all was the only way I knew how to say thank you. That was my moment of true release. I felt like I had taken care of all my unfinished business. Best of all, I was staying home

in Michigan for college and could drive to Detroit on weekends to grab some of my mama's cooking.

Jalen and I were having a combined graduation party, and we knew Juwan was coming to town to play, so we postponed it until the weekend he'd be in town. Jalen and I invited all the kids we knew and threw it together. I walked to J's crib, which wasn't surprising to my parents because I went to his house often to switch shoes, polish shoes, or talk about shoes. However, this day was different. It was hot, and we started drinking at his house around 4:00 p.m. Ice Cube had been representing a new malt liquor called St. Ides, and we thought we'd partake of his new beverage. I drank a forty and a half and was straight gone. Jay was a little cooler with his. I fell asleep on the porch in the sun. I did wake up refreshed, and my boy

Jay was in full throttle on his third forty. We were ready to get dressed and get picked up for the party.

The room had no decorations, just tables and a DJ. We waited for the festivities to begin, but then Jalen started to throw up viciously and violently at the table where we were sitting. After laughing, I immediately jumped up to avoid any shrapnel, made sure he was good, and then went to check on our guests, who had started to arrive. I came back to check on Jay, and some girl was sitting there kissing him, tongue on nasty tongue. After I threw up a little in my mouth, I got back to partying.

About two hours into the party, I heard what sounded like my father. I was sure that my mind, or the St. Ides, had been playing tricks on me. But then I heard his voice again. After a few more seconds, the music stopped, and I definitely heard my father on the mic saying, "Where the hell is Chris? Jalen? What the hell are you doing?" Everyone stopped dancing and stood in shock. I ducked under the table and ran out the back. I saw Juwan as I was running out the door and told him my pops was about to kill me. He just looked confused. Kev made eyes with me and, not wanting my father to body slam him, ran to the back door as well. I jumped in the car with Kev and spent the night at his house. I called my brothers to let my parents know where I was, but I was definitely glad to be moving out of the house, or I might have gotten whacked by my pops in my sleep.

Ed had given us some money for the party, and later he told my father about the festivities. I guess he thought we'd told my father what we were planning. Must have slipped my mind.

Growing up can be a pain
You're not a man until you come of age
We've given up our teenage years
In the effort to pursue our career
Who assumes responsibility
Of having to support our families
Who's protecting us from harm
Is there anyone around
That we can trust
So, we search for answers to our questions
Looking for the answers
No answers but are taught a lesson every time
Through mistakes we've learned to gather wisdom
Life's responsibility falls in our hands
Keep on learning
Keep on growing
'Cause wisdom helps us understand
We're maturing
Without knowing
These are the things that change boys to men
Oh, the goals we set may exceed reality
'Cause failure always is a possibility
Who can tell us that we're wrong?
It's up to us to figure out
What life is all about
So, we search for answers to our questions
Looking for the answers
No answers but are taught a lesson every time
Through mistakes we've learned to gather wisdom
'Cause wisdom helps us see our responsibility

"Boys to Men"
New Edition

THE FAB FIVE

BOOK FOUR

I was the first in our class to get to campus. I don't know what was up with the rest of the crew, but I wanted to get away from home and head to freedom as soon as possible. My family pulled up in our Scooby-Doo van to the South Quad dorms, everything fell out on the ground, and all the kids got out to see my new spot. Dorm life. There was no cable in the building, but at least it was coed, so I could deal. My room was on the seventh floor, right over the basketball court—the perfect omen. After some jokes and hugs with my family, we held hands in a circle and said a prayer, and there it was. I was a college freshman.

I had a couple of days on campus to myself before the fellas got in. I just slept and saw a couple of friends from high school. College life was everything I'd hoped it would be. The black sororities and fraternities were just like what Denise Huxtable, Whitley Gilbert, Dwayne Wayne, and Ron showed us on *A Different World*. Friends came up from Michigan State to visit. I had friends from Country Day, like Vince and Darryl Walker, on campus to hang out with me. Eastern Michigan was about fifteen minutes away, and a bunch of friends from Detroit went there, so I couldn't complain. I was also close enough to home that I could get to my mama's fridge in thirty minutes.

Finally, the five of us were on campus. Jalen was my roommate, Juwan and Jimmy roomed together, and Ray roomed with another Texan, Rich McIver, a sophomore on our team. I was excited to finally meet Ray. He arguably made the biggest first impression out of the crew. We dapped and hugged, Ray said "What's up?" in his southern drawl, and all five of us headed directly for the outdoor court.

Chapter 39

Dorm Life

A couple of kids there from Country Day, along with some other students, filled the court outside the South Quad, and the Fab Five was born. Besides the fact that we could hear our radio clear as day, blasting out of our window, I don't remember much except saying to Juwan, "I've never seen anybody jump as high as Ray." He smiled and said, "Told you, dawg!" Ray was catching oops and was built more like a linebacker than hooper. We hit it off right away.

The yard had filled up with people watching us, so we all had to put on a show. The students got a hell of an exhibition that day. This was the first true time all of us would start, and kids were going crazy. They sensed and we sensed that something was different. I remember Ray going up and catching an oop and thinking, "This can't be real. He jumps as high as Jimmy." We were dunking, shooting, trapping, throwing oops, laughing, and talking light smack. We had chemistry from the first hour, minute, and second of Day One.

At times, my college classes seemed easier than those at Country Day, mainly because of our schedule. I was shocked to learn that we didn't have a class every day of the week. Plus, the three hours of nightly homework from high school helped prepare me for the college grind. In the classes I had with Jalen, one of us would take notes and the other would write a rhyme and then pass it to the other to read. "Study table" also gave me confidence that I could finish all my assignments. This was a scheduled time of day when players studied in a controlled environment. I loved it because it helped me stay focused. Usually starting after practice around 6:30 p.m., players had to meet with teachers and tutors to finish our homework and start projects. After an annual evaluation, you could be released from the study table if deemed fit.

We got a lot of work done and cracked a lot of jokes in these sessions. Juwan seemed to be the most serious about school. We'd joke that it was because he came from the school in *Lean on Me*.

I loved dorm life, but we had a problem with our residential assistant. The only time Coach had a problem with me was when Jalen and I butted heads with our RA. She would always warn us for playing loud music, and after many warnings, she finally wrote us up. After our third write-up, she called to inform our coach. He brought us into his office and told us that we had to turn the music down and that he was getting complaints. *Oooh.* We apologized and then headed straight to the store to get firecrackers.

The bathroom was down the hall from our room. Really far down the hall. Jalen and my lazy butt would drink and then keep or collect forty-ounce beer bottles so that when we had to piss, we had a pot. We rarely if ever emptied the bottles; we just stacked them against the wall. We had bottles and bottles stacked in our room. Now that I think about it, that was nasty, but hey, we were kids. We decided to pay back our RA for snitching on us with a prank that neither she nor the seventh floor in South Quad would ever forget.

Late that night (or early that morning), Jalen and I tiptoed down the hall and taped firecrackers to the RA's door. Then we stacked bottles and cans of piss and placed them gently against her door, which opened inward. We lit the firecrackers and jetted back to our room. All I could hear was screaming and thunderous popping as I ran as fast as I could. Our friends at that end of the hall complained to us the next day of the stench of piss in their room and in the halls. Needless to say, we had another meeting with Fish, except this time there was no understanding. Just a whole bunch of laps.

I'd never known the type of conditioning that we did at Michigan. It was the hardest conditioning program I'd ever been a part of. The previous season, the squad had gone 14–15, so Coach Fisher's practices were demanding. He expected us to be precise and detail oriented, and he encouraged us to ask questions to better understand new concepts. One

of his goals was for us to be in excellent shape, so we were by far the best-conditioned team in college hoops. Our conditioning program was crazy.

The worst drill was on the track: we had to run ten 400s, each one time around the track. The forward and centers had to run in under 1:20, and when you finished one, you walked around the track to the starting point and started again. If you did not complete your ten under the designated time, you had to come in at 6:00 a.m. and then in the evening to complete another ten. I dreaded going back to the dorm on some of those days because sometimes the students played around and got the elevators stuck. Sore and hurting, we'd have to walk up to our floor.

I remember thinking, *I can't wait until hoop season, because this working out is killing me.* The weight lifting, the running, and the workouts made us eager to start the season. We figured the games had to be easier than running just to run. But looking back, it was fun. Between the pranks, complaining, and swearing to take out our pain on another team, we were building chemistry. There was a change in the air. Everyone around us could feel it. They might not have known where it was coming from, but we did. It was coming from us.

Chapter 40

The Birth of the Fab

We weren't recalcitrant, though that was how most wanted to paint us. We were all about paying homage to the game. Not the media or the so-called traditions. We knew that if you loved the game as much as we did, you had the right to "Expect the Impossible." Our war cry was "LET YOUR NUTS HANG!" We set the tone in that first pickup game. We also became such close friends that you would never see one of us without at least one of the others. Most of the time, all five of us hung together.

It really started on a Saturday in the fall. A football Saturday. *Nothing* beats a football Saturday in Ann Arbor. Some of the upperclassmen wanted to go to the football game, but the freshmen came to Michigan to hoop, and we couldn't wait for pigskin season to be over; we wanted to get it in. Our home base, Crisler Center, was the site. All the players were shooting and stretching, anticipating a run. No coaches, just us. Usually a couple of guys picked teams and the games began, but this was far from usual. We were in the middle of a friendly let-a-guy-shoot, jog-to-the-other-end, jaw-at-each-other pickup game... until Chris Setter, a senior, set in motion and started something he could never take back.

Chris considered himself the quasi-leader of the team. He kind of had an asshole personality, but he wanted to win, so I understood what was in his bag. However, what he did not anticipate was that even though we were freshmen, we were a bunch of hyenas. You might hear laughing and chatter, but we would come take your food! He ignited the fuse. I don't exactly remember what happened, but he fouled Jimmy hard and said something to the effect of "I don't care who you are, freshman!"

I was standing under the rim on Jimmy's team. When I heard him say that, I immediately thought, *I know if you're saying that to Jimmy, you must be saying that to me, and I'll make you care about who I am.* Everyone paused for a moment, almost in shock. This must have been the moment that the seniors and others had been waiting for—a challenge. Jalen looked at me, and looks went around among us newbies, and almost immediately, in sync, we said, "Freshmen versus everybody."

Jalen was familiar with Mike Talley, who he played against in high school. Jalen and I had played together forever, Juwan and I had already formed a bond on the court, and Ray and Jimmy were about to show everyone what Texas was all about. I jumped ball and won the tip, and it was over. Jalen played point and pushed the rock so fast we were on a constant fast break. The times that the ball went out of bounds or action was stopped and we had to play in a half-court set, Juwan would throw oops to me in the post or go to work himself with jump hooks and up-and-under moves, killing the taller forward and centers. No guard could seem to get past Jimmy on D, and Ray did everything—rebound, start, and finish the break. After dunking on them, throwing shots in the stands and telling them to get that shit out of here, we won a few in a row before they quit. We talked *so* much; I know I did. "Why you leaving? We ain't done. Let's go! Tony…Mike, you know we're from the Jungle. You better warn them about us!"

That day we sent a message. *We're not your typical freshmen.* We lived life, real life. What's school when you've seen the type of shit we've seen? We may have had all the talent in the world, but we lived like we had nothing to lose, because we didn't. We had that attitude around campus. Our music was different. We were from a different place and weren't ashamed. We actually wanted to share ourselves and our interests with everyone. By the time the season started, the players had developed a mutual respect for one another, although from time to time egos would be bruised.

We had seriously competitive practices. I mean guys going hard, diving on the floor. Guys didn't want to lose, and Coach Fisher found out early on how to keep us motivated: *keep score.* Whenever we had a drill and Coach kept score, the energy went up a notch. Pride led to bets. "Bet your pizza card we win!" "Bet five dollars y'all lose this drill!" Whenever the drill was over, the losers begged to complete the drill again to win. Competitiveness was our glue.

A perfect example of that theory was our favorite teammate and "glue" guy, walk-on Freddie Hunter, who we voted to be our captain. Freddie wasn't on scholarship; he actually had a job. Coach found Freddie in the intramural league; his team was Freddie and the Seven Dwarves. Freddie didn't give a damn about anything except making and then helping the team. He inspired us with his play. His leadership shined through his effort. The team's identity was established in the locker room and on the practice floor. No matter the name on the back of your jersey; if you were on this team, you were expected to be a dog on the court. No suckas allowed. Fred always played hard. He was a tenacious defender and was quick to dive. Through his work ethic alone, he gained our respect.

Fall of 1991. Our game uniforms were being handed out in the locker room. It's hard to describe the excitement of seeing your name on the back of a college jersey. But after trying on the uniforms, we freshmen began negotiations for a shorts exchange with our older, larger teammates. We all wanted to move up a size, so we'd do damn near whatever it took. I never negotiated as hard as I did with Chip Armor and Eric Riley. But after I tried their shorts on, it was like air being let out of a balloon. They wouldn't work. I had always loved the longer shorts worn by Illinois and UNLV. So we begged Coach for longer shorts.

All five freshmen had the same cry: "Coach, can we get longer shorts? These are nut huggers. I don't want to wear any John Stocktons. We'll get a yeast infection. We can't go out like that!" After weeks of tough practices, a million laps, and a few games, our wishes were granted. A cool extra four inches in the inseam did the trick.

Our first game was one of the most memorable for me. I was home and starting off my college career in front of my family and friends at Cobo Arena against the University of Detroit. I'd played more than a few games at Cobo. That was the arena of the people. What was also dope was the fact that I was playing against Iyapo, Mike Ham, Mike Jack, the Super Friends, and Detroit. It was all Detroit. I couldn't wait to play in front of my people, ten thousand Detroiters. My family was there, cheering me on in the layup line. That was why I'd chosen Michigan—to be close to my family.

Our starting lineup consisted of me at the four, Juwan at center, Jalen at two-guard, Mike Talley at point, and Freddie Hunter at small forward. Though Ray and Jimmy could have started out of the gate, I really felt bad for Eric Riley. Eric had led the Big Ten in blocked shots the previous year, and he was skilled at center. In my mind, he was the only one who had a true gripe, because Juwan and I were taking his playing time. But Eezzo, as we'd call him, was a cool soul. He gave us rides on campus when teammates couldn't be found, came to parties with us, and introduced us around campus. He was like the sixth member of the Five. His humility, along with some of the others, made us who we were.

Our first game was exciting. We scored a ton of points and had a host of highlight plays, but Juwan and I had thirteen turnovers combined. Still, our talent peeked through the cloud of ugly play. My first college bucket was a three-pointer, and I finished with nineteen points and seventeen rebounds. Juwan had thirteen and nine, and we both fouled out. But we won, 100–74. The icing on the cake was the fact that my mom cooked food for the entire team and staff and packed it in to-go boxes so she could send us home full. She continued to do that for every team that I played for in my career. One of my favorite platters was baked chicken, potatoes, salad, green beans, and buttered rolls.

The team loved their new (my old) private chef. Funny thing is, though we won, the reaction wasn't all positive. We weren't what the media and basketball old guard were used to. They needed a minute to digest it all. It seemed that after watching us play that night in Detroit, they didn't know how to interpret what they saw, because they'd never seen anything like us before. Not just the style, swag, or long shorts, but our style of play, which was a mixture of fundamentals with some extraterrestrial shit.

✦ ✦ ✦

We took every game seriously. The common denominator was putting our honor on the line—our character. However, some games seemed more important than others because of timing, ranking, or hatred. Undefeated, but only four games in and still building team chemistry, we had to play against the defending champs, Duke. Even though I had been close to choosing Duke, I became defensive about Michigan being compared to Duke. Everyone acted as if it was crazy harder to get in Duke as opposed to Michigan—as if the Duke players were smarter or inherently better. More experienced? Yes. Smarter? No.

Duke was ranked number one in the country, so of course there was extra motivation to upset them on our home court. This was also our first game on national TV. To say I was pumped would be an understatement. Coach prepared us both physically and mentally for the game. We were focused, knew every play call, and knew the importance of attention to detail and preparation. Bobby Hurley had played all forty minutes in the Final Four just a year before. Christian Laettner was last year's Final Four MVP and in the midst of a legendary college career. A young Grant Hill was a beast, earning his stripes in the season prior.

We were excited about unleashing new gold uniform. We knew we were fresh. We got in the huddle before the game as everyone chimed in, and all I could say was, "Yo, this is on TV. Our families and the 'hood are watching." I was excited to see Jim Nance and Billy Packer, who I had watched for years, calling the game. When my name was called, I came down the line in introductions and stopped at the end next to my man, Sam Mitchell. We cursed each other out: "You ain't ready for this, you're soft, they gon' destroy you, young and dumb!" We loved the haters. It felt good to hear that before the game. I can't explain it, but I've always embraced the boos in sports. After the introductions, Jim Nance went to break saying, "We'll be right back with the Fab Five against America's finest!"

The game started off shaky for both teams. I started off with a turnover, and neither team could score. Travels, bad passes, charges. Juwan was the best defender I had ever played against, and he started off on Laettner and did a crazy good job on him. But Bobby Hurley started off killing. He had ten of the team's first nineteen points, hitting threes all over, pushing the pace and getting others involved. I started to heat up—first defensively with a couple of blocks, then of course I had to dunk on a few cats. Jimmy came in and did work in the first half, driving and hitting threes, but Duke got up to a seventeen-point lead. A couple of calls were so suspect in the fans' eyes that they started throwing stuff on the court, until Coach Fish had to grab the mic like a true MC and "move" the crowd.

It was the first season that the student section was moved closer in the lower bowl, and I never heard a crowd that loud in a college arena! I believe they believed, but they only had a four-game sample and they really didn't know what to expect. You could feel the bleachers rattling. I knew this was my coming-out party. I loved our team, and I wanted to make sure all the universities that I said no to understood that I was number one in the country. I mesmerized the crowd with a couple of grown-man dunks over Laettner, and as the camera zoomed in on my lips, you could see that I was having fun talking some grade-A shit. "Oh, this is what you wanted? Freshman? Checkup." But we needed to do more than talk; we went into halftime trailing 43–33.

Laettner was talking smack as well. He felt he was the OG. But neither one of us took it personally; it was business. We were cool. I respected it. I also wanted to make my name against him. The second half, we came out more poised. I had three quick dunks. While staring at Laettner, I ran down the court and made a "lock my lips" gesture after promising myself not to speak in the second half. J. Rose, who was in foul trouble in the first half, found his rhythm offensively. We came all the way back, and I made a three to give us the lead. The game was a back-and-forth affair in the final minutes. My last-second half-court attempt hit the rim, and the game went into OT. Momentum was on our side, or so we thought.

I fouled out with twenty-seven points, twelve rebounds, and three blocks, and Laettner fouled out right after I did. Hurley had a career-high twenty-six points and seven dimes. We fought hard and fell short of a win, but I knew that I had proven that I belonged that day. No one on the floor had a better game, and that was a great feeling, but it wasn't enough. Our first loss in college may have been to Duke, but it hurt. We were too young to understand that we shouldn't have won, but we were wise enough to understand that something special was brewing. We were young and hungry.

You cannot fit in and stand out at the same time.

—T. D. Jakes

All five of us freshmen were chomping at the bit to start. We were a team within a team. We played for and better with each other. We would earn Coach's trust and then lose it just as quick with turnovers or the typical freshman mentality. But we were slowly winning him over. On February 9 at Notre Dame, I was focused on getting a win but also going up against LaPhonso Ellis, a top-five player in the country. Funny how things go in sports. First, you're a fan and admire the skill of a player, like I did the last two years with Laettner and Ellis. Then you get on the court, and you want to take their food.

Coach Fisher's father loved Ray Jackson's toughness and heart and wanted Ray to start. He called Coach and told him he should start all five freshmen. Fish knew the ridicule, hate, and racism that would come with that decision, but we had hit a bump in the season and needed a spark. Coach did not mention his conversation with his father on the flight to South Bend, but in the visiting locker room, just minutes before the game, he revealed the lineup. He didn't say, "You freshman are starting." He just went down the Fighting Irish's scouting report and assigned a defender to each opponent. Juwan, you have Ellis, so on and so on, just like that.

I was sitting in a chair in between Juwan and Ray when Coach said it, so casually. "Ray, you'll start at the three." I kept my head down, but my heart was beating through my chest. My leg was bouncing. Juwan grabbed it and gave a hard-ass squeeze as if to say, "This is our moment." All five of us on the floor. This was the moment he spoke of in the first few practices. Finally, that day was here. We came out like gangbusters. I caught a one-handed alley-oop for the ages on a pass from Ray and ran down the court laughing with pure joy, happy because my boy was happy. We had the Fighting Irish crowd screaming and cheering for us. Anyone in the building could feel that this was something special, something different, something awesome. We were playing hard for each other, communicating on D, switching, and making extra passes. I dunked one so hard the rim got stuck. I was disappointed I didn't shatter the glass. I was trying to, especially on TV. We won 74–65, but what was just ridiculous was the fact that the freshmen scored *Every. Single. Point.* I had seventeen, Jalen twenty, Juwan fourteen, Jimmy nineteen, and Ray four.

Sometimes the media loved us, but most times they hated on us. Billy Packer, Al McGuire, and others said we were trash-talking front-runners. After we shaved our heads, Bill Walton said we looked like thugs. But we knew what time it was. This was a time when players couldn't speak their minds. We spoke our minds and were unapologetically black. We were not only representing ourselves; we were part of a greater movement.

There was another shift happening too. Our generation, Generation X, was taking over. From sports and entertainment to business, we were out to get it, and we were a part of that independent train of thought. We had been the first to feel the effects of crack in the neighborhoods—how it affected families, neighbors, and friends. I was a product of the "Hope to make it to eighteen" generation. We grew up on *Do the Right Thing*, Public Enemy, and KRS-One. Culturally, things were going to change, and every individual in our generation was doing it in his or her own unique way. We embraced our role—to be us and not to assimilate. We knew that we were special and relished it, even though so many of the questions and insinuations were disrespectful. We knew what time it was. We made the most of it and enjoyed every second.

I was named Freshman of the Year in college basketball after averaging seventeen points and ten rebounds. I became the first freshman in Big Ten history to lead the conference in rebounding. I also led the Big 10 in steals, becoming the first player in conference history to lead the league in steals and rebounds. We went into the NCAA Tournament with a record of 20–8. We'd had huge wins against Bobby Knight and the fourth-ranked Hoosiers, Michigan State, and Iowa and were expected to be a three seed in the upcoming tourney. We weren't. We ended up the sixth seed in the Southeast region. We couldn't believe it! But the low seeding ultimately proved to be a blessing. Our attitude was: "Okay, they won't give it to us? Let's take it."

After landing in Atlanta for our first game, we were hit with a sign from heaven. I was walking through the hotel lobby with Chip, a senior big man. I heard him say, "No way!" I asked him what, and he said, "I just saw Muhammad Ali!"

I ran over to Ali. He spoke and then asked the team to come up to his room. He was kind and engaging. He did some magic tricks and then discussed the Bible and Islam. After Ali threw a few jabs and smiling combos, the team left, but his assistant asked me to stay behind. When we were alone, Ali looked at me, poked me in the chest, and said, "Good man! Good black man!" Then he smiled and acted as if he was going to knock me out so the compliment wouldn't go to my head. I smiled. His assistant told me that Ali watched a lot of sports and loved our team. He listened to my interviews and loved that I was a strong black man.

I wondered, *What interview? What did I say to get the champ's attention?* I was so pumped I went back to the room and cut my head bald. No one was doing it then. I remember people thinking I was crazy. But I didn't care how I looked. I was hype and ready to play. Now that we have that straight, let's go to work!

Our first game initiated us right away into the world of the NCAA tourney: rough, rugged, and no joke. John Chaney, coach of the Temple Owls, had it out for us. Their matchup zone would confuse and contain us at times, but we won 73–66. Again, the freshmen scored most of the points. Another sign that we were ready to lead! We ran through East Tennessee State in our second game of the tourney, which was a surprise. I assumed we would be playing against Arizona, ranked number one earlier in the season, but East Tennessee State brought them to their knees. The Buccaneers had two guards under five-eleven, played hard, and loved to let threes fly, but we beat them 102–90. I gave 'em a thirty-piece, feeling as good as ever on the court.

One of the reasons I believe we gained so much popularity was because all season long, the press had been hating on us. Bill Walton said we weren't disciplined and went on and on with his exaggerated statements. Dick Vitale and others fired shots at us. Some hated that we didn't fit into the old whack ways and were scared that we'd influence other players. All we knew was that all the big names and surefire NBA lottery picks were getting shipped home. Shaq and LSU were knocked out, and 'Zo and Georgetown got the gas face. After our first two wins, we went back to Ann Arbor to prep for the Sweet Sixteen.

I wanted to beat the hell out of legendary coach Eddie Sutton and Oklahoma State. OK State had an All-American named Byron Houston; another chance to prove myself against the best. They had been ranked number two after winning their first twenty games of the season. I was in foul trouble the whole game and only managed to score four points, but we squeaked by the Cowboys 75–72 thanks to a big game from Jalen and E Riley, who was hitting his patented turnaround jumper and blocking shots. On to the Elite Eight!

The winner of our next game would earn an invite to the Final Four. We had Jim Jackson and the Ohio State Buckeyes standing in our way. The Buckeyes were the Big Ten champs and had had preseason aspirations of ending the year number one. They'd beaten us twice during the Big Ten season, but we were sure that the third time, for us, would be a charm. I loved playing against this team, even though we didn't have much luck playing against them. The Buckeyes knew my disdain for them; in a nationally televised game in Columbus, I'd put a 360 dunk down, shaking the souls that filled the arena. That was the first 360 I'd ever seen in college. In the papers, I promised that we were going to beat Ohio State—and senior All-American guard Jimmy Jackson and his grown-man game to go with it.

The game went back and forth, and neither team showed signs of surrendering early. It was late in the game when a player gifted us with momentum. We were down two, and Coach called a play. Lawrence Funderburke, who I was familiar with from Nike Camp, had transferred to Ohio State and was talking so much smack that I couldn't hear the play call. "We gonna beat y'all sorry-ass freshmen again!" We loved it. The talk kept us going. I screamed, "Yes!" Okay, that's what they want?

I caught a pass, split a couple of defenders, and tried to tear the screws from the glass. I could hear the supports shake like a squeaky mattress. "Tie game, what now?" We went into overtime, and a few guys seemed to be tense. Usually the serious one, I wanted to break the tension, so in homage to Magic and Isiah, our two favorite players, right before the tip, I walked over and kissed J on the cheek. Jimmy said "Ewwww," we all laughed, and that might have been the distraction we needed. We played tough D and finished plays with rebounds. We passed and found the open man, executing with purpose, and pulled out a 75–71 overtime win.

We had made it to the Final Four. I immediately ran over to the bench players to say thank you. *Thank you for shutting out the voices of people saying you should play more. Thank you for your sacrifice. When we win everyone gets credit.* I then ran over to J and Juwan, who was doing the sweat dance and the cabbage patch. I had long dreamed of cutting down the nets and heading out to a Final Four. No one had expected us to win. The feeling was incredible.

Funny thing is, Coach Fish had predicted this moment. Remember, during the 1989 Final Four, he called me from the locker room at halftime while in the midst of coaching his team to his first NCAA championship. He told me that if I worked hard, one day we would be right here. Well, here I was at the top of the ladder, with scissors in hand, blowing kisses to my mom. I didn't know it was exactly one year to the day since I had been surrounded by friends and family at the 1940 Chop House restaurant, formally committing to Michigan. So much had happened in a year. I had matured a great deal, yet we still had a long way to go.

With a fresh bald head and goatee that barely connected, I packed up my Nintendo with *Tecmo Bowl* and headed off to the Final Four. There was a lot of hoopla and attention, but no more than we were used to. Game recognizes game, and we respected Cincinnati and Coach Bob Huggins. His team was a family of castaways and "left for deads." They were rough on D, and, like us, weren't easily intimidated. They had outrebounded each of their opponents in the games leading to this matchup.

In the papers, guard Nick Van Exel and company said they believed they would win. Their big fellas were talking in the paper about how I wouldn't be dunking on them and how they were the better team. Their confidence, honesty, and brashness mirrored our own. I remember sharing

a laugh about that with Jim Nance at our Final Four practice, where we put on a dunk show for the ages. Our pride and manhood had been called into question. We had to be smart, but this was now personal.

The game started off with Coach Bob Huggins instructing his team to press. They wanted to keep the ball out of Jalen's hands so that he couldn't control the pace and use our height advantage. Nick started off the game killing us, scoring seven of their first nine points. This was his team. Since he'd taken over the starting job, the Bearcats were 18–1. We started the game five for five from the field, but it was a back-and-forth contest that transformed into a game of runs: 9–0 for us, 11–2 for them. We also had a scoreless stretch that lasted four and a half minutes. We committed twelve turnovers, and neither team held the momentum.

Then Jimmy came in balling. Hitting threes from everywhere and ending the first half with a crazy dunk! I made sure to make a liar out of Erik Martin and Corey Blount, who had said I wouldn't dunk on them. Playtime was over! The refs had to warn both teams over and over to quit the chatter and trash talk. But all the talking in the world couldn't help us hold a lead. We trailed at halftime, 41–38.

Van Exel was a monster in the second half, hitting threes and driving to the cup. But Jimmy Voskuil came through for us. Voskuil, who had started the season off as a starter and was our best shooter, single-handedly won the game for us. He was hitting jumpers, driving at will, and knocking down free throws. That's one thing about the Fab Five: we would never front and not acknowledge the rest of the fellas on the squad. We won as a team, and everyone contributed. Mike Talley, another former starter, came in and played big minutes breaking the press. After the Voskuil run, we never relinquished the lead. In the end we were too much for the crew from Cincy. I remember Juwan yelling as we headed to the locker room, "We're going to shock the world!" The feeling was inspired by our surprise meeting with the Greatest, but Juwan really believed it. Before we had had one practice, he saw us going to the championship.

Minneapolis, Minnesota. More than fifty thousand fans at the Metrodome. I had never played in front of so many people. It was an amazing atmosphere. This was the rematch we'd been waiting for since late December. The veteran-laden Duke roster had already shocked the world by beating the UNLV Runnin' Rebels when they were heavy underdogs. Fresh in our huaraches and blue unis, we got off to a great start. Juwan played incredible D on Laettner, frustrating him throughout the first half. Laettner had the worst half of his college career, and that's saying something for one of the best of all time. He had more turnovers than points in the first twenty minutes of play.

The game didn't have any kind of rhythm. It was ugly. Both teams played great D. I remember watching Jimmy catch the most beautiful oop, thinking, *This looks like slow motion.* I was controlling the boards and putting rebounds back up ferociously. I was jumping out of the gym, playing on the largest stage in the world in a game I loved. I took a rebound full court, hit a defender with a crossover, and hit Pelinka with a behind-the-back pass in full stride. He caught the ball and after a 180 spin, laid it in. We were hyped. We held a 31–30 halftime lead.

The second half proved to be drastically different. I was called for my third foul early in the half. Jalen had four fouls with ten minutes remaining. Laettner woke up and started playing like one of the best college players of all time (which he is). He hit jumpers and a big three at the top of the key. We kept the game close, down three with 6:51 on the clock. Duke started to stall and took thirty seconds off the clock on each possession. So we started to press. Literally and figuratively. There was nothing we could do, and just like that, the game got out of hand.

Hurley and Grant attacked, and the next thing I knew, I was on the bench crying as garbage time was well underway. Just like that, we were down twenty. Duke was the better team. They proved they were worthy of being the first team since 1973 to repeat. They defeated UNLV and us. Their win was well deserved.

Losing hurts. I hate losing more than I love winning. We wanted to win for the students, the alumni, and our coach, because he believed in us. We wanted to win for our families, friends, each other. The crazy thing is, just two years after sitting on his couch watching reruns of past finals, Grant Hill (who flat-out destroyed us) and I were the players of the game.

I lost myself on the way back to the locker room. The weight had taken its toll. I was in tears, walking and screaming down a hallway full of cameras and reporters. "So, y'all got what you wanted?" I shouted. "We lost. Come on, cameraman, get a close up. I'm a man! You want to see a man cry?"

Ray grabbed me, and we continued into the locker room. I was proud of my personal play in the finals, glad I made the All-Tournament Team, All-American, and Freshman of the Year, but I wished I had kept that to myself. There was no excuse. I was tired of all the hatred and the constant criticism from the media. I was just an idiot who had embarrassed my family.

I apologized to my parents, and of course they weren't proud of my actions, but they forgave me. It all got to me. I also wasn't used to losing championships. Apparently, through embarrassment, I would learn patience. After the press conference and hoopla, my youngest brother, David, and I were out talking in the hall. Grant's parents saw me and came over to console me. Grant followed. We dapped and hugged, and then he looked down at my brother Dave and gave him his game uniform still drenched in sweat. For a half a second, David stopped crying and smiled. G is a real one through and through.

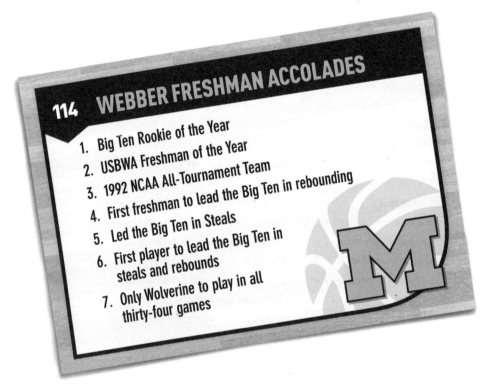

114 WEBBER FRESHMAN ACCOLADES

1. Big Ten Rookie of the Year
2. USBWA Freshman of the Year
3. 1992 NCAA All-Tournament Team
4. First freshman to lead the Big Ten in rebounding
5. Led the Big Ten in Steals
6. First player to lead the Big Ten in steals and rebounds
7. Only Wolverine to play in all thirty-four games

Chapter 44

Money Ball

I never took a dime to attend the University of Michigan. Not in middle school, high school, or college. I never thought of going pro after my freshman year. I could've left straight out of high school like Kevin Garnett, Kobe, LeBron, and Moses Malone, but it wasn't like that then. I couldn't name one freshman who went pro when I was in college. I did, however, know that I was going to work to be the best, and someday they would have to deal with me at the next level. Rumor had it that I could already go in the top three or four in the draft. So I wasn't pressed, but I was frustrated.

I was moving off campus with Myron Potter, my former teammate from Country Day, and I needed transportation. I was also starving. Myron and I were on a diet that would not help me make it to the league: ramen noodles, bacon sandwiches—not exactly healthy food for an athlete's body. I ate that way because I was broke. I received about $625 a month and the rent was $700, so Myron and I split it down the middle. I told my father that I didn't want to scrape at school.

An article tells of how a friend and I walked off campus and went into a restaurant. We ordered before realizing that we didn't have enough money to buy a good meal for both of us. We ordered one plate instead, split it, and left. With our stomachs growling as we passed by the campus store, I looked through the large window and saw three people in line with my jersey. Don't get me wrong—it felt good, but I was hungry at that moment. For the first time, I correlated my performance with branding and the business of sports. The Fab Five was a jackpot for merchandisers! I could see our pictures everywhere, including on basketball trading cards and T-shirts with our likeness being sold at the football games. I saw baggy shorts being sold as well.

Over the summer, I saw my jersey at St. Cecilia's; meanwhile, I didn't have one for my brother. I was immediately pissed. There was even a "scandal" over pizza cards. We were issued pizza cards as part of our food program. Most of the time when you use the card, it's for a large pizza, but sometimes you can't eat a whole damn pizza by yourself. So we would split cards and order an extra-large pizza with everything on it and would never order anything smaller than an extra-large because it felt like a waste. That way, we could stretch the cards and eat more. Suddenly, we were told by both the restaurant and school that we couldn't do that, and the rest of the cards were canceled. Couldn't do what? Things like that will get to you when you come home from practice hungry as a muggg!

There were reports that enrollment was at an all-time high. I knew that was partially because of our popularity in the state. But what about guys unlike me, who wouldn't play professionally? They had to study as hard as any student, practice up to four hours a day on a year-to-year scholarship (no college scholarship is for four years), and if they got hurt, there was no guarantee that the university would continue their scholarship or take care of the medical costs associated with the injury. I had friends with babies and bills and family back home that needed them. What the author of the article couldn't report was the conversation that I had with my father, who understood my frustration. We were clear on my potential but also the reality of the present moment. The only thing we could think to do was call Isiah Thomas.

I called Zeke up and explained my situation, and he listened. He then told me to put my father on the phone. Isiah had experienced what I was going through at that time. He asked my father if he could help me on one condition: that we don't owe him anything and to never discuss this again. My father had a condition: Loan it to me and write up a contract. My father went to Toyota and bought me a truck. Who cosigned? Isiah! He's the type that would always make sure you were straight. What freedom he allowed me to have! I didn't owe anyone. I could continue playing college ball in peace. I didn't have to sell my soul.

THE BANK OF BLOOMFIELD HILLS

505 NORTH WOODWARD · SUITE 1300

BLOOMFIELD HILLS, MICHIGAN 48304

———

TELEPHONE (313) 644-2301

TELECOPIER (313) 644-7107

November 11, 1992

Dear Kevin:

Per our conversation, please find enclosed a financial statement to be completed by Mr. Thomas and Mr. Webber. If Mr. Thomas has a financial statement already prepared, it should be acceptable in lieu of filling out this form.

Please let me know when it would be convenient to get together. I look forward to hearing from you soon.

Sincerely,

President

DTP665

My net worth exceeds   #1,000,000.00

My social security number is ▓▓▓▓▓▓▓▓▓

Isiah Thomas   11-29-92
_____   _____
Isiah Thomas   Date

DREAM TEAM

Our team went to Europe on a tour during the summer. We were exhausted and complained most of the time, but I know I appreciate the trip more and more as years go on. Much more than I did then. We went to Italy and played against professional teams. We were recognized by the natives there, who would scream out "Fab Five!" in their native tongue. We walked around the towns freestyling to whoever would listen as we faked like we were taking in the sights. It was a cool trip overall.

When I got back, I was informed that I was under investigation because Donny Kirksey, a friend of Juwan, had supposedly paid me to go to Michigan. They said they had a record of him calling my house. I said, "It could've been him or Juwan calling me-I don't care. They're my family." I didn't hear anything after my convo with them. I then was accused of going to Michigan because of Perry Watson, even though he was hired months after I signed. I was very suspicious of that.

During all the hoopla, I was called and asked to work out against the USA Olympic team. I was told that this would be the first year that professional players would participate in the Olympics, and since we would have been asked to be on the team originally, we were invited to camp. We were pumped. My teammates were old friends: Bobby Hurley, from Nike camp and college; my man G. Hill; Eric Montross, whom I'd known forever; Rodney Rogers; and Jamal Mashburn. We were excited to be part of this experiment. We were in hoops heaven. We got a chance to play against the best players of all time, the Dream Team. We knew what an opportunity it was.

I arrived at the airport, and a limo driver was holding a sign that said Bird/Webber. I damn near fell out. I grabbed my bag and went to the man holding the sign, and lo and behold, sitting next to him reading a paper was the man himself, Larry Legend. I shook his hand, and he said, "Hey, Chris." I couldn't believe he knew who I was. He didn't say much in the back of the limo, but when we got out at the hotel, I got a glimpse of the legend unfiltered. "Make sure you get some sleep tonight. We are gonna bust y'all asses tomorrow."

I nervously replied, "Yeah, right." I was confused, happy, and insulted. Happy to be insulted. Happy he knew who I was, and nervous he was gonna try to prove a point on who he was. I said something quick back like "Larry, you know your back is already messed up. I'll take it easy on you."

He laughed. I exhaled and called my pops and told him Larry Bird was talking trash to me.

Our first practice was monumental. First, as college players, we wished we could play in the Olympics, like collegians had before us. Second, we knew we were privy to something special, the greatest team in the world, so we were going to make the most of this moment. This was bigger than the Duke game for Bobby, Grant, and me. At least at that time. We all huddled up and proceeded to have the best practice of our lives. We were talking on D and getting out on the break.

Bobby's speed was paralyzing. He was actually attacking Magic, getting into the lanes, and hitting me for dunks. Grant was getting to the cup on Jordan. We couldn't help but smile as we huddled up, and Coach Daly told us to keep it up.

We did not speak one word of trash on the court; we weren't no fools. After a few more buckets, the scoreboard read 62–54, and we won the practice. Seriously won. It was the first practice for the Dream Team, and they didn't have any chemistry, but I was nineteen, and we were kids playing against our heroes in an official capacity. We went back to the hotel and binged on pizza and B-ball stories. Friends, then enemies, and now friends again, Grant, Bobby, myself, and everyone else reminisced on our scrimmage. We dreamed aloud of going to the NBA. We laughed about one play when Rodney Rodgers rotated to the corner and went for a Larry Bird pump fake. While he was in midair contesting Bird's shot, Larry looked up and said, "Welcome to the parachute club," and hit a three in his mouth. Those were the war wounds we'd go home and brag about.

The next day we were back to reality when we didn't score one bucket in a twenty-minute scrimmage. That week of practice was the first time I allowed myself to think about the "what if" of the next level. I had played with my heroes. I knew their games better than they did themselves. I studied them. I was able to talk to the pros, ask questions, and get great advice. I also played pretty well at camp. Enough for Chuck Daly, whom I'd known for a while, to tell me he was proud of my improvement. I left La Jolla, California, with a deeper maturity.

Chapter 45

The Road to Redemption

My sophomore year felt like one of redemption. We were a year wiser. We hoped we could talk some trash, be ourselves, and stay away from the haters. I toned down my antics and was all about business. I kept it simple. I already had the individual awards, so there was nothing else to accomplish but winning a championship. But now we had gone from being the hunters to the hunted. That took some getting used to. We loved being the underdogs, the ones nobody believed in. Well, that was then, but not now. Now there was a target on our backs. We took everybody's best shot. Coaches, teams, journalists, leeches, you name 'em. We were changing the game, and *everyone* knew it.

We were in Ray and Jimmy's home state of Texas, getting ready to play Rice University. We were pumped to play in

Houston. Any team with good chemistry loves playing in front of a huge crowd, especially in a teammate's hometown. You want to show out. Go back and dominate with them, add to the legend, and show the people who supported them some appreciation. The fellas did it for me when we played against U of D or Michigan State; they would make an extra pass or get me some easy buckets. We wanted to do that for Ray and Jimmy and all their people in the South. We ended up beating Rice by only four, 75–71, but it was a win. I had twenty and nineteen boards, but the game was a side note to our style.

Ray and his boys hit the mall to get some socks before

the game. Ray had been going through it. Though the season was young, he was thinking of transferring because he felt he deserved more playing time, and he was tired of Coach Fisher and his criticism. Ray decided that he wanted to stage a silent protest against the University of Michigan's men's basketball program. The only question was: what color socks would he use to break protocol? He bought two pair, grey and black. While he was contemplating in his hotel room, Juwan walked in and said, "Damn, those are fresh," referring to the socks that Ray was holding up.

Juwan, Jalen, and Jimmy ran across the street to the Galleria Mall and bought us all a pair. Me? I was in my room asleep. When I woke up, I saw the fellas with the socks, and they had my pair ready for me.

I thought it was the dopest shit I'd ever seen. We all did. We wanted to keep our secret to ourselves, so we kept our warm-ups on—something we didn't usually do. When we pulled off our warm-up bottoms and walked to half-court for jump call, I could see Coach Fisher, his face turning red.

Coach Fisher was a fair man, but he called a timeout the first chance he got and cursed us all out. He was livid. He couldn't believe that we would unilaterally not give a fuck and make a decision like this together. We won the game.

Later, when we were on the bus ride to the plane, he pulled me aside and said something to the effect of, "Chris, we don't have two teams, the Fab Five and others. You're from a big family. You understand how large group dynamics work. You must continue to lead like that. Everyone can wear the socks or no one can."

Ray's plan would backfire. Instead of his actions opening up a way for him to leave, to get out, the sock situation sealed our brotherhood. We weren't listening to him and some protest. He couldn't go anywhere else. Period. We said so!

I responded without hesitation. "My bad, Coach. You're right. I got you!"

The socks were a hit. Nike reportedly sold close to two hundred thousand pairs the following week. Everyone criticized us for our style, but we'd expected that. The youth got it, but that's how it always goes. Young people get it; the adults complain and then act like it's news later. Our style could be best described as "We don't give a fuck about other people's opinions." We weren't trying to be accepted by anyone or gain their unwanted approval. That's why I loved us. We loved us, and that was enough for me.

We started off our sophomore season 4–1. We knew that nothing was guaranteed as far as getting back to the Final Four, but we also knew that we had to come with the same heart. We beat three Top Ten teams in three nights in a tournament in Hawaii. First, Nebraska. Then we beat North Carolina 79–78 on a last-second tip-in. Finally, we beat second-ranked Kansas 86–74. We lost by one to Bobby Knight's Indiana Hoosiers and my friend and old nemesis Alan Henderson, who blocked my frantic putback attempt at the last second. Even though we had some big wins and hurtful losses, the year wasn't as much fun as our freshman year. Even in victory, the media did their best to defeat us. We knocked off our in-state rivals, Michigan State, but Juwan and Ray put up middle fingers, and the media ate that up. (I still can't help but laugh at that one.)

In the tournament, we earned a number-one seed, but our first games were out West. We would be tested early. We started off against Coastal Carolina, torching them with a well-balanced attack and walking away with an 84–53 victory. Up next was UCLA. Prior to this meeting, Michigan had never beaten UCLA. We were 0–6 all-time head-to-head. Early on it seemed like the ghosts of UCLA's past were in Tucson at the McKale Center. The speed of their tough, small point guard, Tyus Edney, proved to be a problem for us all night. Ed O'Bannon, fresh off knee surgery, played one of the best halves of his life. We started off focused, and the game was tight in the early going. I tried to saw the rim in half with a windmill dunk. We were moving the ball but didn't realize we were falling into the Bruins' preferred pace of play. Ed went on to score in every way possible. First, an offensive rebound followed up with an and-one seemed to get him going. Then Ed drove, then stepped out and drained a three. He was all over the place.

The arena started to give the Bruins the West Coast advantage they'd been praying for. Arizona fans hate UCLA, but not on that day. They were letting us have it, all while supporting the Bruins. We were tied at ten, and then, just like that, it was 49–30,

NCAA TOURNAMENT 1993

then 52–33. Mitchell Butler played some great minutes, driving and hitting tough layups. O'Bannon went on to score ten of the team's first sixteen points and seventeen in the first nine and a half minutes. Their big man, Richard Petruska, even hit some timely threes, drawing our big men out of the paint. I noticed, around the four-minute time-out in the first half, that the coaches for UCLA were jumping up and down high-fiving like the game was in hand. Bad move.

I tapped Juwan, pointed toward the bench, and after he nodded in acknowledgment, he gave me this crazy-looking serial-killer smile, and I immediately felt better. We were playing sloppy, committing seven turnovers to start the night. We were lucky that Ray kept us in the game in the first half by grabbing some tough rebounds, converting and-ones, and getting layups. We went into halftime down 52–39.

In the locker room, our maturity came to the forefront. Jalen and Juwan gave the halftime speech. I don't remember what they were yelling about. I was staring at the wall like a zombie across from Ray, who kept repeating, "What you got for me, big dog? We need you! What you got for me, killer? You're Detroit's finest, aren't you? They don't make no hoes in Detroit!"

Coach didn't say a word. I went back on to the court with tears in my eyes. Not feel-sorry-for-me or I'm-scared tears. Mine were tears of defiance and destiny. It was not time to go home. We played inspired ball in the second half, slowly walking them down. The pro-UCLA crowd started cheering for us because we were the underdog and showing heart in a hell of a comeback. It was Rocky versus Ivan Drago in Russia. I scored on dunks inside. We slowed the game down and exploited the zone with Juwan turnarounds. Jimmy came out of the gate and hit a couple of threes, and O'Bannon wouldn't score for most of the second half. We turned the D up and put the kibosh on that. We went on a 23–4 run at one point. J. Rose hit two threes in a row, and Jim Jam saved the day on two big plays: a steal to send the game into overtime, the first of the tournament. In the second, the game was tied at 84 with 9.6 seconds on the clock. I caught the inbound pass and executed a dribble handoff to Jalen, who I knew would be strong to his left. Jay attacked and shot his patented floater but missed, and Jimmy followed up with a tip-in to give us the lead. The only question was, Would the replay show that Jimmy had beaten the clock?

It would. He had. We won.

We were beside ourselves. The UCLA coaches argued with the refs in disbelief. I scored twenty-seven and added fourteen rebounds. Ray had nineteen and five. We moved on and disposed of Yinka Dare and George

Washington. Juwan, Eric Riley, and I took it personal that Yinka, the big man for G.W., was getting a lot of hype, as if he was going to shut us down. We beat them 72–64, and he did not score one point!

Then it was Temple. Temple, Temple, Temple. We must have been a thorn in their side. I remember asking Juwan what was wrong with their coach. Why did they hate us? We'd already shown them last year in the tournament that we didn't play, and all that loud, raspy, screaming wasn't doing nothing. This wasn't personal for us; this was about getting back to the Final Four, and they were in our way. We attacked and defended. I had five blocks, led the team in assists, and pulled down twelve boards. Despite great games by Aaron McKie, Rick Brunson, and Eddie Jones, Temple lost, and Coach John Chaney refused to shake Fish's hand after the game. We couldn't have cared less. We were cutting down the nets, and it was off to the Final Four again. What a feeling. More of a relief than celebration. We still had unfinished business.

Kentucky, the number-one overall seed, was the best team we played in our sophomore season. Coming into the game, we each had thirty wins. They were coached by Rick Pitino and pressed full court throughout the entire game. Offensively, they pushed the ball fearlessly, and each player had the green light from beyond the arc. They were led by my boy from the fifteen-year-old AAU Tourney in St. Louis, Jamal "Monster" Mashburn. We knew that averaging 17.8 points, seven rebounds, and 4.5 assists, he'd be a top-five pick in the upcoming NBA draft. Our goal was to send him to the lottery with a loss, courtesy of the Fab Five.

Kentucky was known for getting out to quick starts. Coming into the game, they had averaged thirty-one-point whoopins versus their opponents. But we had won eleven straight and were confident. No one thought we'd get past the Wildcats, so much so that my father took a bet that if we won, he'd shave his head. This was a *big* deal. My father had rocked the same Cassius Clay, army high-top his whole life. He wanted us to play so hard, he added an incentive.

The game against Cincinnati and their press a year earlier proved helpful in preparing for Kentucky. We knew their game was to get you into a frenzied running match. Practice the week before was tough, but we had to strip ourselves of all pride in order to beat them. The Wildcats wanted us to take a quick shot or try to break the press with a fancy pass or too much dribbling. We had to listen to our coaches, who always drew up the best plays. We were focused and hung on to every word of coach's game plan.

We entered the game as seven-point underdogs. As we walked through the back halls on our way to the court entrance, I kept screaming, "Rumble, young man. Rumble!" I was heated. I was talking to our team while looking reporters in the face, saying, "We are seven-point underdogs? They want us to lose or forget who we are?" Both sentiments are unacceptable.

When the game started, Mash introduced himself to our team with a wicked crossover. He scored thirteen points in five minutes, and the pace was in Kentucky's favor early on. I remember being as tired as I have ever been in any game in my life. Juwan and Jimmy played exceptional D, and Kentucky's bench, which averaged thirty-seven points, was held scoreless. We went into halftime with a 40–35 lead, but we were far from satisfied.

We knew what we were dealing with, and it was a seesaw battle down the stretch. The game was tied at seventy-one with ten seconds remaining. J. Rose received the inbound pass, dribbled up the floor, spun off of a defender, avoided a charge, and called time-out with just three ticks left. Kentucky played suffocating D on the final play, and J. Rose missed a jumper for the win. On to our second overtime game of the tournament.

In OT, Ray played big with some hard-fought rebounds, putbacks, and tough drives. Jamal fouled out on a Juwan shimmy and turnaround J. With thirty-eight seconds left in overtime, I put us ahead on a baseline spin move I stole from James Worthy. Now, up three with four seconds left, I blocked two inbound passes and stole the deflection. We won, 81–78! Back to the championship game! In what felt like a heavyweight fight, Jamal had finished his college career with twenty-five. I had twenty-seven and thirteen and was exhausted. After the game I hugged Jamal, and we reminisced about his days as a Gaucho and mine as a Super Friend. He told me, "Don't be stupid. Come to the league; don't get hurt!" After one huge comeback and two overtime wins, we were finally back! The wait was worth it! We had a shot at redemption.

The day before the big game, I sat in the mall with my youngest brother, David, and a friend, catching up and dreaming. David's twelfth birthday was a couple of days away, and I wanted to buy him a birthday gift. He told me he needed shoes, clothes, etc. I was supposedly "the man," but I couldn't even buy my brother some kicks, shorts—nothing. I couldn't help him, and I knew the feeling he was experiencing, forging his own path through the loud barking. He was becoming a lil beast on the court, and I knew all that came with that. It's hard to explain how helpless I felt. I felt like I was missing out on my younger siblings' lives but couldn't help when I was with them. That moment would stick with me.

God has not promised me sunshine
That's not the way it's going to be
But a little rain (a little rain)
Mixed with God's sunshine
A little pain (a little pain)
Makes me appreciate the good times
(Be grateful) be grateful
God desires to feel your longing
Every pain that you feel
He feels them just like you (just like you)
But he can't afford to let you feel only good (only good)
Then you can't appreciate the good times
(Be grateful) be grateful
Be grateful (be grateful)

"Be Grateful"
Walter Hawkins

Yoda was on his deathbed when Skywalker pleaded, "But I need your help. I've come back to complete the training."

Yoda replied, "No more training do you require. Already know you."

Luke happily replied, "Then I am a Jedi."

Yoda damn near had a heart attack and replied, laughing. "Not yet. One thing remains: failure. You must confront failure. Only then, a Jedi will you be."

The North Carolina Tar Heels were the last team standing in the way of being crowned national champions. In a televised game sure to break sports broadcasting records, everyone who was anyone was seated in the Louisiana Superdome in New Orleans. Earlier in the season, we had met up with the Tar Heels in Hawaii, in a game we won on a last-second tip-in after trailing by one. Just a year ago I had promised myself we would get back here. The only thing that could have made this moment better was if we had played the Blue Devils for revenge. But I was more than comfortable going up against the Tar Heels. I'd scored twenty-seven, grabbed thirteen boards, and added five blocks in our first meeting.

I was familiar with Carolina's seven-foot center, Eric Montross. We were cool from camps and had stayed in touch as early as my tenth-grade year. His grandfather and father had gone to Michigan, so I thought he was going to sign with Michigan. We had also been teammates the past summer on team "Crash Test Dummies" for the Dream Team. I knew Carolina had hoopers. We had all grown up playing at the same camps. Clifford Rozier, Derrick Phelps, Brian Reese, and Pat Sullivan were considered the number-one recruiting class the year before ours. They could go.

Any true basketball fan knows the name Dean Smith. Not only has he coached greats like Worthy, Perkins, and Jordan, but at the time he was the winningest coach in college basketball history. We had no margin for error. As the announcer began player introductions, we walked out on the court in a serious, stoic manner. Just as in high school, we were letting our opponents know, "This ain't no game, and we ain't no gimmick!" We gathered in a huddle, hugged, and screamed, "Let your nuts hang!"

The game started slow for us. I felt good, but it seemed like we had to pick things up. We were exerting more energy than usual. I missed a three to start the game. Teammates missed easy buckets. We attacked the basket but got whistled for a charge and had some sloppy turnovers. It started out as a game of runs, but we were clearly out of sync. It didn't matter. I knew this was our night, and at worst one of us would will the team to victory. After some ugly plays, I dunked on Montross, and it got our game going. It felt good, and everybody knew it. It was a statement for the world: *The one you love to hate is back!* I heard one of the North Carolina players scream, "Got damn!" as if I hurt them by dunking so hard. This was not a night to regret; we had to leave it all on the floor. As I ran up the court, I gave the Tar Heels my stank face. I was yelling, "Get used to this! I'm coming all night!" This was for 6 Mile, Biltmore, Wes, Big Chris, Lance, Lorinda, Margo, and the crew. Those who supported us because they *were* us.

The first half was a game of spurts. I provided a few spectacular plays on the offensive end with vicious dunks and defensively by blocking shots. We went into halftime down 46–36. I started off the second half with a loud dunk. I really wanted to get us going, but you have to credit Carolina for their stifling defense. As a result, they led most of the second half. The Tar Heels would switch back and forth between zone and a full-court press. We were forced to call a time-out after their well-executed press, and that time-out would prove costly.

Then Carolina guard Donald Williams caught fire; he couldn't miss. Both teams responded with runs. Play got physical, and I had to stop Juwan at one point from stomping a mud hole in Montross's ass. We were down one with 2:28 left when George Lynch hit a tough shot to put the Tar Heels up three. At this point, every second was key. With 1:18 on the clock and down by five, we went into desperation mode. Carolina thought it was over, but Ray hit a big shot from the corner to bring us within three. We went into a full-court press. Ray and I double-teamed Lynch, forcing a turnover. We were in the midst of a miraculous comeback. Down three, we inbounded the ball, the shot went up, and I got one of the toughest rebounds and putbacks of my career. Within one. Pelinka fouled Sullivan, an 80 percent free-throw shooter, with twenty seconds left on the clock. My life would change forever in those waning seconds.

Sullivan stepped to the line and made the first of a one-and-one. He missed the second, and I grabbed the board over Lynch. I looked to my right, and I wanted to get the ball to Jalen, but I saw that Lynch had stayed up and stunted at Jalen, causing me to stutter step. After the travel, instead of being patient, I tried to get across half-court as fast as I could to avoid a ten-second backcourt violation. I then ran to the right corner, closest to our bench, and I heard and saw teammates signal me to call a time-out. Trapped in a Lynch–Derrick Phelps double-team, I looked at the referee and called for a time-out. In the midst of it all, I remember realizing my mistake. *We were two points down with no time-outs left.* My time-out call resulted in a technical foul, placing a nail in the coffin of our comeback.

I couldn't believe it. I immediately looked at the bench and yelled, "Why the fuck did you tell me to call a time-out? Why the fuck did you tell me to do that?" I wanted to fight. I was so livid. Coach had to motion some of the bench players, giving them permission to return to the huddle. Coach and players tried to calm me down. But the truth is that I was the leader. I was supposed to know better. I should not have dribbled into the corner. The disaster was no one's fault but mine, period.

The Tar Heels were awarded two free throws, which Williams knocked down. We lost, 77–71. I finished with twenty-three points, eleven rebounds, and two blocks. I was named an All-American and chosen for the All-Tournament Team. I'd had one of the greatest team and individual runs in NCAA Tournament history...but none of that meant anything.

The best of my yesterdays couldn't outweigh this feeling. In the words of one of my homies, "One screw up kills a million attaboys." I was overwhelmed with disappointment. I was stricken with grief. Immediately after calling the time-out, I remember putting my hands on my hips and taking in a deep breath, wishing I could inhale my mental lapse and exhale a new ending. I could hear myself breathe. Silence echoed throughout my soul. My heart was beating so hard it felt like it would fly out of my chest. Then it stopped. Sorrow seeped into my being. I was in such shock and disbelief that I couldn't cry right there on the court. I simply had nothing. It was surreal. It was a moment and space in time in which the truth of the situation was not in sync with my understanding of what had occurred. It felt like that nightmare when you try to scream so someone will hear you and shake you into consciousness, but you can't muster up enough breath to utter a sound. I was just waiting to wake up.

APRIL 5, 1993

Louisiana Superdome, New Orleans, Louisiana
National Final

77

Basic Box Score Stats

Starters	MP	FG	FGA	FG%	2P	2PA	2P%
Derrick Phelps	36	4	6	.667	4	5	.800
Donald Williams	31	8	12	.667	3	5	.600
Eric Montross	31	5	11	.455	5	11	.455
George Lynch	28	6	12	.500	6	12	.500
Brian Reese	27	2	7	.286	2	6	.333
Reserves	**MP**	**FG**	**FGA**	**FG%**	**2P**	**2PA**	**2P%**
Kevin Salvadori	18	0	0		0	0	
Pat Sullivan	14	1	2	.500	1	2	.500
Henrik Rödl	11	1	4	.250	1	2	.500
Matt Wenstrom	2	0	1	.000	0	0	.000
Dante Calabria	1	0	0		0	0	
Scott Cherry	1	0	0		0	0	
School Totals	**200**	**27**	**55**	**.491**	**22**	**44**	**.500**

71

Basic Box Score Stats

Starters	MP	FG	FGA	FG%	2P	2PA	2P%
Jalen Rose	40	5	12	.417	3	6	.500
Jimmy King	34	6	13	.462	5	8	.625
Juwan Howard	34	3	8	.375	3	8	.375
Chris Webber	33	11	18	.611	11	17	.647
Ray Jackson	20	2	3	.667	2	3	.667
Reserves	**MP**	**FG**	**FGA**	**FG%**	**2P**	**2PA**	**2P%**
Rob Pelinka	17	2	4	.500	0	1	.000
Eric Riley	14	1	3	.333	1	3	.333
Michael Talley	4	0	0		0	0	
James Voskuil	4	0	1	.000	0	1	.000
School Totals	**200**	**30**	**62**	**.484**	**25**	**47**	**.532**

LINE SCORE

3P	3PA	3P%	FT	FTA	FT%	ORB	DRB	TRB	AST	STL	BLK	TOV	PF	PTS
0	1	.000	1	2	.500	1	2	3	6	3	0	5	0	9
5	7	.714	4	4	1.000	0	1	1	1	1	0	1	1	25
0	0		6	9	.667	2	3	5	0	0	1	0	2	16
0	0		0	0		1	9	10	1	1	2	1	3	12
0	1	.000	4	4	1.000	4	1	5	3	0	0	2	1	8
3P	**3PA**	**3P%**	**FT**	**FTA**	**FT%**	**ORB**	**DRB**	**TRB**	**AST**	**STL**	**BLK**	**TOV**	**PF**	**PTS**
0	0		2	2	1.000	2	2	4	1	0	1	0	1	2
0	0		1	2	.500	0	1	1	1	0	0	0	2	3
0	2	.000	0	0		0	0	0	0	2	0	1	0	2
0	0		0	0		0	0	0	0	0	0	0	0	0
0	0		0	0		0	0	0	0	0	0	0	0	0
0	0		0	0		0	0	0	0	0	0	0	0	0
5	**11**	**.455**	**18**	**23**	**.783**	**10**	**19**	**29**	**13**	**7**	**4**	**10**	**10**	**77**

3P	3PA	3P%	FT	FTA	FT%	ORB	DRB	TRB	AST	STL	BLK	TOV	PF	PTS
2	6	.333	0	0		0	1	1	4	0	0	6	3	12
1	5	.200	2	2	1.000	1	5	6	4	1	0	1	2	15
0	0		1	1	1.000	4	3	7	3	0	0	2	3	7
0	1	.000	1	2	.500	5	6	11	1	1	3	1	2	23
0	0		2	2	1.000	0	1	1	1	1	0	2	5	6
3P	**3PA**	**3P%**	**FT**	**FTA**	**FT%**	**ORB**	**DRB**	**TRB**	**AST**	**STL**	**BLK**	**TOV**	**PF**	**PTS**
2	3	.667	0	0		1	1	2	1	0	0	0	1	6
0	0		0	0		2	1	3	1	1	1	1	1	2
0	0		0	0		0	0	0	1	0	0	1	1	0
0	0		0	0		0	0	0	1	0	0	0	0	0
5	**15**	**.333**	**6**	**7**	**.857**	**13**	**18**	**31**	**17**	**4**	**4**	**14**	**18**	**71**

He who learns must suffer. And even in our sleep,
pain that cannot forget, falls drop by drop upon the heart,
and in our own despair, against our will, comes
wisdom to us by the awful grace of God.

—Aeschylus

I walked off the court into the tunnel and toward the locker room with my head down. Accompanied only by freshman Leon Derricks, I remember thinking, *I can't believe this. This didn't just happen. God, why are you letting this happen to me? Why? You're supposed to love me. You? Not you? You know how I've worked for this! Why? How can this be right? What did I do to deserve this? I can't believe this! Where are you now?*

The booming sound of the North Carolina band playing their victory song was drowned out by the deafening voices of personal vitriol in my mind's stadium. Only Leon shared the stroll of shame with me, as his arm hung around my shoulder, patting me on the head and exhibiting support. Still, I was lonely. Steps after, with my mind still racing and questioning myself on the last moments in repugnance, I felt an overwhelming sense of love and calm approach me on my right side. It was my little brother, David, running to catch up, hugging me around my waist and patting me on my back. It was April 5, 1993, his twelfth birthday. He sported a big crocodile smile. Besides the day before at the mall, for an hour or so, we hadn't seen each other. It had been weeks. He was happy to see his big brother, regardless of the circumstances. For a few seconds, I forgot all the pain. After reaching the locker room, I stepped into the training room and broke down on the training table. I was inconsolable.

After I'd tried to compose and gather myself, my father came in to console me. I thought about his life, ways, and rules. It felt as if he had prepared me for this moment. He and my mother often spoke of tragedy, and when it visited, they didn't act out of self-pity. They never let us blame others, and no matter how terrible the situation seemed, they prided themselves on control and trust in God, not anger, revenge, or blame.

I thought about my grandfather's advice for dealing with adversity: "Kill yourself, then." I even laughed sarcastically, punching a wall.

I reached the podium both mentally and physically exhausted. I sat down at a table filled with a forest of microphones and looked out on the dozens of reporters. Most had sympathy in their eyes. Some had tears. I noticed their compassion. I told them it was my fault. I don't remember most of the questions, but I was aware then as the best player on that team my words would speak volumes about my character. It was on me, so I did not want to blame anyone. I could handle the blame.

I called it. As I came out of the press conference, my father met me in the hall. He rubbed the back of my freshly shaven, sweaty, bald head and wiped away my tears. "I'm proud of you, son. That's what a man does... I know! I'm proud of you." The more time that has elapsed from that day, the more that statement has meant to me. He was proud of how I handled adversity, and now I'm proud of that too. But right then...if my pops hadn't had one firm hand on my sternum and one over my right shoulder, I would've fallen to the ground. The fetal position seemed natural. One of my father's favorite sayings was "We don't jump off of bridges. We trust God, get up, and trust God some more."

But how could I trust God at this moment? It was as if everything I knew about him was a lie. He had left me for dead in front of millions of people. Only twenty years old, my goatee still unable to connect.

When asked about that night, my mother "remembers the quiet." She had witnessed how loud the team could be—at holiday dinners, during games at Crisler, or just at personal gatherings. The silence that night scared her. My father was fighting through the traffic back to the hotel. This was a job for Mama. Coach let her and David ride back to the hotel with me on the team bus, which was against the rules. But Fish knew I needed her. The three of us burrowed into a seat for two as she whispered prayers while rubbing my head. I don't remember any specific consoling words from either of my parents, but I knew they would take away my heartache if they could. I knew they had trained me to depend on God. I was just young, hurt, and in a bad place.

I got back to the hotel drenched in sweat and tears, and not just mine. Before a few friends from Detroit came back to my room to say what's up and offer support, the Fab Five had what would be our final moment together. We were in my room. I apologized to my brothers, crying, saying, "It's my fault. I promise we will win the championship next year!"

Juwan immediately cut me off. "Shiiiiid, you need to go to the league and send me back some money and some clothes. I'm tired of being broke," he said. Ray said to me, "Shut yo black ass up." A few more hugs and dap, and that was the extent of our philosophical conversation. We had an unbreakable bond. We were different. We knew it was us against the world of insincerity and ass kissing. No explanation was needed. There would be no excuses or blame. Our brotherhood had been forged in high school, in AAU, in the dorms dreaming, at practice, at parties chasing girls. I was proud to have lost with them. I wouldn't have traded that screw up to be the hero on any other team. They knew that. They also knew I'd do anything to take the moment back.

I felt the love and support from the fellas. The pain was still there. It wasn't even a question in my mind of not returning the next year, but Juwan was right. I was tired of being broke, and our families were in need.

THE UNIVERSITY OF MICHIGAN
BASKETBALL
HEAD COACH STEVE FISHER

Thank you very much for your note. It makes me proud to know people such as yourself are behind us. We wouldn't have been able to accomplish so much for Michigan without your support.

Keep cheering for the Wolverines! GO BLUE!

Sincerely,

Chris Webber

Chapter 49

Coach Wooden

I t was uncommon for players to enter the NBA draft prior to completing their senior year. Magic Johnson was the last player selected with the number-one pick as a sophomore, back in 1979, and Shaq was a junior when he declared. He too was the number-one pick. I didn't dare to dream of that. Detroit's own Derrick Coleman left after his senior year. So did UNLV's Larry Johnson and Duke's Christian Laettner. So not returning for my junior year was not even a possibility in my mind. After more hugs and pounds, we all headed out to Bourbon Street. Even though I had just turned twenty, I needed to get drunk to stay sober. Jalen and I collapsed on Bourbon Street, where we slept for thirty minutes or so.

We landed back in Michigan and took the team bus to the Crisler Center. I was a dead man walking, a zombie. As I walked into the gym with the bleachers pulled back, I thought, *This is where our celebration was supposed to be. I can't believe I let Michigan down.* My team, the Fab Five, Coach Fish, Coach Dutch, P Dub, all the students back in South Quad and at the Student Union, the girls at Wellesley Hall, the alumni, the sororities and frats, the kids at Eastern Michigan, only a few minutes away. I let them all down too. I went back to my locker, grabbed a few things, and made my way to my apartment. Myron greeted me at the door, almost as if he didn't want anyone to see me, when he heard keys jingling and me fumbling with my bags. He didn't say anything but "What up?" with a look of support and some dap. That was what I needed. Not sympathy. I made a fried bologna sandwich with a side of Better Made hot chips covered in hot sauce. Then I took a shower and slept for a couple of days.

Coach Fisher called and wanted me to come down to his office. We discussed the decision for me to attend the College Player of the Year awards—the Wooden Awards. He knew that I would not be excited about any award, though my numbers would warrant consideration. Fish said, "This would show your character." He meant by attending the award presentation in the midst of my hardship. I'd also be honoring John Wooden. He ended with "I think your father would want you to go as well."

He knew with this statement that he had me. First, my father was a big fan of Coach Wooden, and I was as well. Also, he knew that I wanted to make my father proud, especially in this difficult situation. I understood that the hardest thing to do would be the right thing. I discussed with Coach how I wanted to be strong and handle this horrific moment correctly, but I didn't want awards, accolades, attention, or sympathy. I wanted a rematch, but I couldn't get one and didn't deserve one. That's sports. It's fair to all because it's unfair to all. I didn't want to run from this, but I needed time. I wanted to heal and lick my wounds. But sometimes you have to do what you have to do.

I attended the event, which was made up mostly of media. Jamal "Monster" Mashburn won the award. I wasn't mad; I knew how good he was. Jamal, the other nominees, and I sat in the back and dreamed together about the next level. Then Coach Wooden came in the room, slowly walked over, and tapped me on my shoulder, summoning me to a private room. We spoke for seven or eight minutes that seemed like forever. I fought back tears as we talked. He told me that he was proud of the way I handled the situation and that I would inspire many. We hugged, and I left.

The support back on the Michigan campus was amazing. It felt like family. I did not feel any negativity, only encouragement from students, friends, and frats trying to throw parties in my honor, showing they didn't care. I tried to go to class a couple of days, but it was just my body in the seats. How could I concentrate? I hadn't even begun mourning this loss. I wasn't interested in hanging out, parties, or the college scene. I felt older. Pain ages you. Now I started to hear that I would definitely be the first or second pick in the NBA draft if I chose to make the jump.

Chapter 50

The People's Champ

The 1993 NBA draft was June 30, which gave me less than three months to make a life-changing decision. I got back to my apartment and reflected on the past twenty months. From my first day at the South Quad dorms to our first win at Michigan State, or beating Ohio State, even dancing on top of the scorer's table to "Hip Hop Hooray." The football games and frat parties, practicing against the Dream Team, college girls, traveling to Europe with the squad, jumping out of a cab with the fellas in Monte Carlo, the frustration of watching my jersey being sold for crazy dollars and I was broke, the study tables, the laughter. Man, the laughter.

I thought about Sam Mitchell, our happy-go-lucky ex-teammate, who passed away after transferring to another school. I thought about missing my brothers and my mother, who passed through metal detectors as a daily routine as a high school teacher in Detroit. My father, who still worked at the factory. My grandfather, who was at home and could barely get around after his house was broken into a couple of times in the last year. I thought about my small church and how everyone at Faith Baptist on Livernois and Tyrone was proud. I thought about my Big Mama, Mr. Mont, and Harv, all the people who really cared. Then I was overcome with a feeling of thankfulness. I felt so good that within these twenty short months, less than two years, I made an impact in college sports. I made lifelong friends who never capitulated. I made my parents proud.

I asked myself a familiar question for the first time, "If I would've known before I embarked on this journey that everything would've happened the way that it did, would I have still signed up for this?" The answer was an easy yes! It was right then, in that small apartment in the shower, that I decided to take a leap to the pros. It felt right.

◆ ◆ ◆

I could hear Mary J. Blige's *What's the 411?* album blasting from the living room. I called my dad to let him know that I was going to the league. He asked, "What league?" stealing the surprise with confusion. I then realized he was joking because he was so happy he couldn't contain it. He said, "Well, son, if you think that's what's best, we support you." My mother, on the other hand, wasn't so sure. In her eyes, graduating from college was bigger than any Final Four appearance. Now, she's a very practical woman and would be the first to say that you go to college, among other reasons, to learn to make a living. I could definitely do that with what that NBA was paying these days, but I promised my mother I'd graduate college one day.

I called my aunt Charlene and told her that it was official. I wanted to go to the NBA and didn't want to talk to anybody. She said, "That isn't possible." She had been in contact with top agents: Leonard Armato, Shaquille O'Neal's agent; Drew Rosenhaus; David Faulk, the superagent who had Michael Jordan; and Aaron Goodwin and Bill Duffy, two young, talented brothers who had come together to start an agency, among others. I needed to interview them. I told her, "I understand that's how it works." But what I thought was, *I need to get myself together. It's just a few days from our last game. I have to get right. I need to be alone. It feels like I'm building a fire in the rain.* She was quiet for a few seconds and then alerted me that a card company had called and offered me a "high six-figure deal." That sped up everything.

I went to Fish's office and told him about my decision. He was supportive. I told the fellas, and they were just as excited as I was, almost as if I was testing the waters for them. They knew they were just steps behind me. I vowed to try to win them a ring next year, and they vowed the same. We'd had a great run. We'd changed the game with our style and brashness. We alerted the world to a new kind of kid, a different athlete. We were hip-hop, loved, and disliked and loved it. For some, we were uncomfortable to watch but unquestioned in our effort. I loved us.

When I left campus that day, I had tallied the following accomplishments:

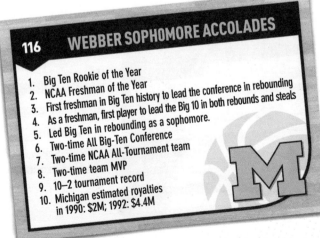

116   WEBBER SOPHOMORE ACCOLADES

1. Big Ten Rookie of the Year
2. NCAA Freshman of the Year
3. First freshman in Big Ten history to lead the conference in rebounding
4. As a freshman, first player to lead the Big 10 in both rebounds and steals
5. Led Big Ten in rebounding as a sophomore.
6. Two-time All Big-Ten Conference
7. Two-time NCAA All-Tournament team
8. Two-time team MVP
9. 10–2 tournament record
10. Michigan estimated royalties in 1990: $2M; 1992: $4.4M

Mayce Webber

"Here, Dad, hold this," I said.

"Hold what?" He looked down at the check and said, "Oh my God."

"Why don't you hold this for a couple of days." My father kept the $700,000 check nervously in his worn-out wallet for a week. I did not get much pleasure out of buying things for myself but got joy out of seeing others receive. Back home in Detroit, I slept in my old room, ate Mama's cooking, hung out on the block, got joked on by my brothers, spoiled my sister, and started to heal. Being home was different. I had left as the big brother and protector and came home in need of love and care. I got a letter of encouragement from President Clinton. Jackie Joyner-Kersee sent shoes and a letter. I was honored; I needed the pep talks.

My mother and I started to talk about the neighborhood, the kids, and the schools, and we decided that we would start the Timeout Foundation, a charitable organization that provides positive educational and recreational opportunities to underprivileged youth. She believed my situation would be inspirational. "How many kids do you think will listen to you because they've seen your embarrassment and want to hear how you got through it?" she said. "What the devil meant for bad, God meant for good."

She then pulled out a "Time Out" license plate she had ordered for her car. She was saying, "I can't be

273

embarrassed by my son. He's mine, he did it, we own it, and we will keep it moving." My mom has so much heart! Seeing strength like that help me start the healing process. It wasn't hard to remember my old routine. Mom's cooking was a highlight. I also watched my father get up at 6:00 a.m. and start his trudge to the factory. His sacrifice made more sense to me than ever. I was no longer sad. I was thankful. I had a great opportunity ahead, and to not embrace it for the sake of my family would be sinful.

My brother Jeff had matured into a young man and pretty good hooper who signed with Aquinas College. Jason was the same happy, independent, make-everything-look-easy self. David was obsessed with hoops, and I could see a familiar look in his eyes. My sweet Rachel was growing up, and I hated it. I hung out with Wes, Big Chris, Lance, and the crew on Big Chris's porch. It was my training camp for my new life. I knew that the NBA would be a different lifestyle, and this was real. I reconnected with home and sincerity. Home would be my lighthouse. If I got off course in the future, I could use it as a point of reference and get back on the right path.

I'd heard all types of crazy stories about guys who left for the league only to come home having lost their souls. That was my biggest fear. I had been around adults who manipulated me with a "them against us" mentality, only to turn out to be part of "them." I was tired of taking the high road with jealous comrades who turned life into a competition—who embarrassed you in public but cried on your shoulder behind closed doors. I was no longer naïve and no longer wanted any part of people or things that were fake. I needed support, love, laughter, honesty, and accountability. I would only allow myself to be around people who loved that way in good or bad times. I was ready to get on with life.

THE WHITE HOUSE
WASHINGTON
April 9, 1993

Dear Chris,

I have been thinking of you a lot since I sat glued to the TV during the championship game.

I know that there may be nothing I or anyone else can say to ease the pain and disappointment of what happened.

Still, for whatever it's worth, you, and your team, were terrific. And part of playing for high stakes under great pressure is the constant risk of mental error. I know. I have lost two political races and made countless mistakes over the last twenty years. What matters is the intensity, integrity, and courage you bring to the effort. That is certainly what you have done. You can always regret what occurred but don't let it get you down or take away the satisfaction of what you have accomplished. You have a great future. Hang in there.

Sincerely, Bill Clinton

I needed to slow everything down as much as possible. Less than two years out of high school, I was about to embark on some real grown-man business. I knew that I needed to address and embrace the new possibilities of this opportunity, but also the pain, anger, bitterness, blame, and victimization that were still with me, trying to keep me in a moment that was already disappearing into the past.

Just because I handled my crushing disappointment well right after the game didn't mean that I was over it. I needed time to sift through my emotions. I needed to pray. I felt like I couldn't move forward until I addressed what had happened. When astronauts return to Earth, they go to a decompression chamber, which allows their bodies to recalibrate to the current environment. I needed to decompress mentally. Alone.

I took the check from my dad, met with a financial adviser, and got an apartment downtown. Less than a week out of college, I had a contract for three-quarters of a million dollars with a trading card company. It was more money than I had ever dreamed of. I dreamed of making the league and being in the Larry Bird–Magic Johnson Converse commercial. I dreamed of screaming "I love you, Mama" like Isiah Thomas did after every game. I dreamed of hoisting the Larry O'Brien Trophy. I never dreamed about the money—or maybe I did and just didn't realize. I wanted to get my mother a big, beautiful house, even nicer than the ones we saw while driving through Indian Village. I wanted to buy my father a real Rolex instead of the fake gold watches he'd rock at church. I wanted to buy my brothers some real sneakers, not the knockoffs that got them bullied constantly. But I had to get me right first.

You may encounter many defeats, but you must
not be defeated. In fact, it may be necessary to
encounter the defeats, so you can know who you
are, what you can rise from, how you can still
come out of it.

—Maya Angelou

I lit the joint, inhaled deeply, closed my eyes, and leaned back, resting the back of my head on the black leather couch. Coltrane played softly in the background. My thoughts would soon drown out the sound of the trumpet and piano. It was the first time I'd been alone with my thoughts with no interruption. Out of school, a man now. I was about to reach my dream of becoming an NBA player. It was the first time I had money and had it in abundance. Enough to purchase my heart's desires or help others, but no matter what I did or could do, I couldn't enjoy the moment. I was hurting. Lesson one of success: money does not make things better, and it cannot erase the past. Note taken.

The exposed brick walls in my large industrial apartment were plusher than any I'd seen. I was steps away from the Detroit River, a place I'd walk and frequent on early mornings and late nights, trying to flag down each thought racing through my mind. I must have been fighting with depression. I felt like I really could've lost my mind. I needed to examine every feeling and thought. I required something deeper than rhetoric. If I made it through, my surviving would be pure testimony. It felt like I was void of being hurt. What else could hurt me? I'd already seen the worst. I was void of feeling. The worst had happened. What do you do when you're there? There being the place you feared so much that you wouldn't even let your mind acknowledge that there was a there. I was there. What do you do when you can't fix something? When you can't do anything for the betterment of the situation that you're responsible for? When you have to wait?

I stumbled on the following epiphany: "Waiting is an action; all I can do is what I can do." Writing this down, I acknowledged that I needed to continue to work out, live in the gym, and stay mentally and physically ready for basketball. Anything else, like trying to go back to the past and fix something, or sit with regret, was a waste of time. I've always been about solutions, and nowhere in that equation was the solution to "Question the past and pity yourself." I didn't want a single moment ossifying into a lifetime of misery, questions, blame, and regret. I needed to maintain the correct perspective. I needed to pray.

Prayer is communicating with God, emptying your soul of all its worries. It is acknowledging that there is something far greater than yourself that you can depend on to help you. It's humbling. It is being grateful. I came to God broken, a stubborn, angry, confused, and disappointed child. My self-hatred was growing. I was punishing myself by living in pain. It's easy to live in pain. You have no expectations, no hope, no wanting anything good, no enjoyment. During those months after the tournament, I distanced myself from family and friends. Instead, I performed surgery on my soul. I had to remove the self-hatred. I had to discard all emotions so that I could deal with the bare truth. I didn't want to be attached to an illusion. I didn't have the capacity to be consoled, so I had to sit in it.

What did I do to deserve this?
Why me?
What am I being punished for?
How could I have done that?
I should've known better.
I should go back and try to win one.
Can I go back after declaring?
One more year of school wouldn't kill me.
We would definitely win this year.
I just turned twenty.
What am I in a rush for?

The truth is, God's grace is sufficient. Time, not just one moment, would define me. I did it, it's over. What now? I was stronger than I was acting. Or would I rather have my father's misery, losing my mother and my future at twelve years old. Would I rather be my best friend who was in jail for life at age twenty-one? Would I rather be dead, like Tyquan or Money Dixon? I thought about my father saying, "We don't jump off of bridges!" Or my grandfather's favorite quote, "Kill yourself." Both encompass the will, strength, faith, and perseverance of men. Forge ahead or give up. No in-between.

They raised me for a time like this. They taught me about God. They showed me what hard work, dedication, and sacrifice were. They lived them every day with no expectations, fanfare, or entitlement. As I decompressed, I clearly saw my situation. It was not as ugly as my emotions would have had me believe. I couldn't change what had happened, and I couldn't choose my memories. Scars are proof of pain, but they are also proof of healing. I should be excited about the future. I should be happy about the present because this was what it was all about. God was about to answer my prayers. I would not carry the burden of resentment. I would redefine this moment. The challenge was to get back up. So I did.

Philippians 4:6–7 says, "Do not be anxious for nothing but in everything by prayer and Thanksgiving let your request be made known to God; and the peace of God which surpasses all understanding will guard your hearts and minds in Christ Jesus." I always wondered what that verse meant. Now I know. I prayed that God would take away the anxiety, anger, and fear and give me strength to move on, and he did. It was a transfer of energy from depression to power.

God gave me peace. I would not think about the time-out constantly, until eventually I didn't think about it at all. The pain remained, but I began to think about it in terms of what a blessing, opportunity, and challenge it was. I thought about how many people would kill for the opportunity to ball like I did. To be part of a legendary group like I was. I had accomplished things in college that no player had done before. One mistake did not change that.

I've never been uncomfortable addressing the time-out, and I immediately started speaking to encourage others through my story. I would speak about how everyone has a time-out in his or her life—the "before and after" of a tragic situation. The key is how we define it, not how it defines us.

Things would get better because the one thing I was good at was basketball. If I worked hard enough and stayed dedicated, I'd have an opportunity to further distance myself from my past mistake through great play. This message translated in my neighborhood and others like it across America. People watched me in the midst of my tragedy and wanted to see how I handled it. They wanted to know how it would turn out. They were used to disappointments as well. My pain was accepted as social currency. I can never really explain it, but the pain did take something away from me. Maybe an inherent unconscious joy? I have that joy, but I'm always aware of how good things are because of how potentially bad they could be. I was also aware that I could overcome anything once I made it through this. I was at my low point, and through the Grace of God, I was going to be okay.

Now that I had taken care of myself and cleared my mind, I wanted to enjoy myself. I also wanted to show everyone I loved my appreciation before I left for the league. I was the infrastructure for my family now, and I wanted to show my parents that their love and sacrifice were an investment that was paying off. For many friends, I was their dream achieved; their hope; their bragging rights, war story, and fishing tales. I understood this and relished the role of giving them a water-cooler-hall-of-fame, unbelievable, "you had to be there" story.

Vestiges of depression resurfaced from time to time. Self-pity, thoughts of trying to correct the past, and wondering what if; however, I did notice that it never reappeared when I helped someone. I got a lot of joy out of giving, putting a smile on someone's face, watching tears roll down their eyes, knowing they were on their last leg with bills, thanking God that he used me to answer one of their prayers. Those moments were priceless.

"I make the money; money doesn't make me," is a saying I love to quote. I didn't want thank-yous and pats on the back. I just wanted to help. If anything, I was savoring the smiles of the recipients. I inherited that giving spirit from my parents. I'd seen them give, having much less than I was newly blessed with. Giving was an honor. I was thankful for God's grace and the people he put in my life.

Even on the business end, my good fortune would be a positive influence. Some agents made promises; others wanted to use their clients as leverage to ensure a high draft position or trade. Some talked endorsements, legacy, and their relationships with the league. My mother, father, Charlene, and I decided that the right choice was Aaron Goodwin and Bill Duffy. It was cool because they were young black agents, and at the time you could count the number of black agents in the NBA on one hand. I received a lot of criticism, but my skin was already thick. I couldn't care less about racial comments or what people thought when I had just navigated the worst tsunami imaginable. I also knew that I had been raised to make positive change. If I, the number-one pick, could show others that it was okay to choose who would represent you, I was honored to manage that responsibility.

I was at home, seeking peace. I turned down an opportunity to be in an upcoming movie, *Blue Chips*, starring Shaq and Nick Nolte. I was offered a leading role, if I could leave Detroit for a few weeks. I said, "No, thank you. I'd rather spend time in my little apartment." I figured if I played well in the NBA, then opportunities like that would present themselves often. I felt that I needed to stay home. I'd find out later that not agreeing to this off-court opportunity would come back to bite me in the ass on the court, though.

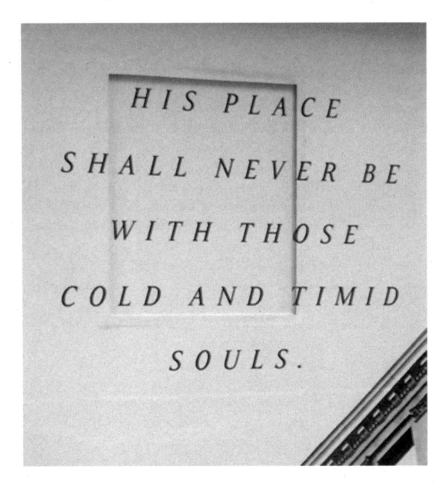

HIS PLACE SHALL NEVER BE WITH THOSE COLD AND TIMID SOULS.

Pick yourself up. Dust yourself off. Start all over again.

—Nat King Cole and George Shearing

I went to a local dealer and purchased a white Chevy Suburban. I immediately took it to the nearest audio sounds store and asked the cat behind the counter if he could give me the loudest truck in the world. He laughed, so I left. I went to another audio store where the cat behind the counter smiled and said, "I've been waiting for a project like this."

He removed four of the eight seats. The rest of the truck was pure sounds. I had to get special windows because they were cracking from the vibrations. I said, "Forget it. I live in Detroit; just make 'em bulletproof." You could hear me coming from a mile away, and the bass on my exits seemed to resonate even farther. I would set off car alarms on purpose because of the bass. I was like a kid in a candy store.

I believe the total speaker inventory included two subs, eight twelves, and four sixteens. I also added a gun compartment, a secret space in the vehicle that could only be opened by completing a combination of adjustments to controls of dashboard instruments. I had a compartment that would release nails if a button was pushed, and another button that released an oil slick, but that caused a problem because the oil was so heavy that it would flatten my back tires. Before I got to the second audio store, I also made a quick detour to buy a pair of pink "gators" and a burgundy suit. Anyone who was anyone in Detroit at the time had a pair of gators, fine men's alligator dress shoes made by Mauri, an Italian shoe designer. They were a symbol of success. Usually colorful and single- or two-tone with trim, they were worn by preachers, principles, pimps, lawyers, and distinguished men of all types, including those who were faking it, or faith-ing it.

I went to the Renaissance Center in downtown Detroit, where I had
a bank account. I called one of my boys, who was strapped like Rosco P.
Coltrane everywhere he went, to accompany me on this Santa Claus/Robin
Hood mission. I was going to withdraw the biggest amount of money I'd
ever seen in cash, $30,000. Riding through the 'hood unprotected would
not be advised. My mission was simple: hit everyone I could think of with
a nice piece of change and dart out before they saw me. I thanked the teller
and took the large bag with the bank's name and logo and placed it in my
recently purchased backpack. I couldn't help but smile as I thanked the
valet, imagining how much fun the next few hours would be. These were
the moments I had dreamed about—coming home blessing the block like
the Pope.

I went back to Biltmore, my street, my home, and my 'hood, going
house to house hitting everybody off. 1G here, 3Gs there, this bill, that
bill, exchanged for this hug and that hug. Somebody blasted the radio,
now it's a full-out block party. I ordered food, and people started dancing;
it was all love. One of my favorite memories was taking my brothers and
the cats from Biltmore to go eat lobster. Now, since I maybe had had
lobster once or twice in my life, I was the expert. We went to Red Lobster

and ate like kings. You couldn't tell us nothing. We were in a seven-star restaurant and not afraid to eat. Cheddar biscuits, the Admiral's Feast, and two orders of lobster apiece (for the virgins). I'll be on my deathbed laughing at that scene.

Another memory that will last was going to a restaurant we could never afford when we were younger, Fishbone's in downtown. While sitting at the table talking trash, I made a hot sauce cocktail out of seven different sauces in a sixteen-ounce cup. I filled it to the top and told Wes, "If you drink it, I'll give you ten thousand dollars." The table was lined with six witnesses, and before I could say "psych," he began to drink it to a cheering crowd. I gave him a check the next day…but I had to slide it under the bathroom door.

◆ ◆ ◆

I drove by Ed's house, grabbed a few stacks, put the money in a paper bag, and placed it near the bushes on the side of his porch garage area. I called him a few minutes later and said, "I got a package for you outside on the side of the garage." He later called back, sobbing. "Thank you. I'm sorry for everything. I'm so proud of you. Thank you." I felt good that I could show him how much I appreciated him in my life. Though I hadn't really messed with him since high school, I loved him. He knew I was doing the same for others who I felt had been there for me.

This was the beginning of the "unfaithful friends and loyal enemies" portion of my life. I was making tough decisions. Sifting through sincerity, peace, love, and pain and preparing for the next level. Ed was relieved that I called him. I hadn't communicated with him for some time. He knew he'd left me hanging when I was in eighth grade and didn't attend Southwestern High School or play on his AAU team. He was just happy that I hadn't told anyone my feelings. He knew me, and that scared him, because he knew that once I see who you are, I will compartmentalize you as such. My thank-you was more of a goodbye, "Don't say I owe you anything" gesture.

I thanked him for his time in my life, for the gym shoes he bought me that I damn sure couldn't afford, for the jogging suits, for the cash, for letting me use his car to go to prom, for the doughnuts, cakes, and pies—all of it. It really meant a lot to me. But he knew that I was very clear about our relationship.

Gifts couldn't work with me, because what would I do with the gift? It wasn't like he could give me a new TV, fridge, car, watch, or household appliance. I couldn't use them without alerting my parents. I was lucky to get the clothes and shoes. Because he couldn't fill a void and build a pseudobond, Ed didn't have control over me. He knew the gym shoes and jogging suits weren't enough to claim space in my life. He realized that the best way to stay in my life was to be a kindhearted soul, like when we first met. He knew I was figuring it out and finding myself.

DIAMOND IN THE BACK, SUNROOF TOP

My mother called me at 7:00 a.m. and asked, "What's up with your father? He was outside at six o'clock this morning fiddling around, now he's cutting the grass."

I said, "I told your man that Magic was coming by the house today to talk to you guys about the ups and downs of the league and what to expect as parents."

"Well, is he coming?"

"Who? Magic?"

"Yes, Magic."

"Uh, no. I just told Dad that because I have a surprise for him later today. I figured he'd believe that stuff about Magic because Magic is close with Isiah, so it could make sense. Plus, Magic's father worked in a factory, so I don't think he'll mind if I use his name for today."

"Boy, you gonna give that man a heart attack," she said, laughing. "I know our neighbors will be upset because he was whistling before the birds this morning." My father was known as the president of the house, and he would regularly say that we were his cabinet. His wife was the first lady. He felt he knew everything and everyone's business as it pertained to the United States of Webber. I made the real boss of the family, Mama, promise not to tell her man the plot. She obliged.

I walked into the car dealership, and everyone left their desk to come say hi, even the customers. The warm greeting made me feel welcome. They came over because they knew who I was, but more importantly they knew my father worked for GM. They also knew why I was there. They understood that a factory worker with five kids would never see the light of day in a Cadillac. There was no negotiation or hassle.

They helped me pick out the best ride for a man whose sweat and tears, like many of those in Detroit, had helped sustain an iconic American jewel. This ranks as the second-favorite moment of my life (number one came for my mother about three years later). They sold me a fully loaded, black-on-black, four-door Fleetwood STS Cadillac. It was a thing of beauty. I drove it off the lot and thought about how my father would come home from work over thirty years and say to me, "Chris, no matter what you do, work hard and find a job that you love." I thought about how those were testimonials, engulfed in pain and monotony.

My dad once told me the story of a lineman who'd had a breakdown on the assembly line. My father said this guy's job was to screw in eight screws every time a certain piece of equipment passed by him. My father said, "Imagine every day drilling in eight screws. That's it—every forty seconds." He said that one day, the guy lost it. "He just snapped, ran out screaming, 'I can't do this! I can't take this!' and ran right out of the building. Never came back. No one ever heard from him again." I thought about my pops and the many others like him who drank poisonous fumes from the exhaust every day or inhaled metal that was ground so fine you couldn't see it with the naked eye. Who knew when the effects of those long hours would kick in? I thought about him at all those UAW meetings, or how they were feeling effects of the strike as well. GM was my father's extended family.

I knew he would be excited.

I drove the Cadillac off the lot, tilted the seat all the way back and leaned over to the right with my right forearm on the middle armrest. I thought, *I'm gon' open this up one good time.* I knew my father's meticulous, precise slow driving would never challenge the horses under the hood. I slowed down around 6 Mile and silenced the radio as I approached my street, and I was overwhelmed with emotion. I said a prayer of thanks and drove down the street, up the driveway, and right up onto my father's freshly cut lawn—a move that could've gotten me killed.

My dad ran out of the house and screamed, "Get off my lawn!" My brothers had sworn some of our neighbors to secrecy, but now everyone came outside. For many of them, my dad was their dad, their personal mechanic or electrician or handyman, and they wanted in on the lovefest. Before my father could say anything else, I stepped out of the car, threw him the keys, and said, "It's yours, Pops."

Without saying a word, he stopped in his tracks and locked eyes with me as to say "Thank you. I can't believe it." Was there a long, tearful hug of gratitude? No... he moved me out of the way, jumped in the car, fired up the engine, and took off through the other side of his lawn, down our neighbor's driveway, and into the sunset. As everybody shuffled back to their houses, I sat on the porch with my mom. We just laughed and smiled. My father drove back around the block, rolled down the window, and asked, "What time does Magic get here?"

I laughed so hard I almost gagged. I shouted, "It was a JOKE, MAN!"

He said, "Oh," and then he skirted off again, smiling.

Chapter 54

Gators for Everybody

I heard the sounds blasting from my truck. I loved to run downtown on Jefferson late night or early morning just to think. The draft was just a week away, and I had run through the full gamut of emotions over the last three months, or, as Lauryn Hill said in her song "Rebel," "He's moving me and purging me around." I was going through a thang; I couldn't believe that the draft would be held in Detroit, at the Palace of Auburn Hills. I was undefeated at this arena, winning two state championships in that very building. I knew everything from the locker rooms to the parking lot. I was proud to be reppin' the city of Detroit and the University of Michigan one more time on one of the largest stages in sports and entertainment: the NBA draft.

Of course, I had thoughts of who I'd like to play for, or *Wouldn't it be fun to play with this person or that person?* Or *Wouldn't it be great to live here or there?* But none of that mattered, really. I was just happy to be living the dream. A few weeks prior, I watched the draft lottery with my family in the living room of my apartment. Orlando, who had picked Shaq number one in last year's draft, held a 41–41 record, the best of all the teams in the lottery, but they defied the odds and netted the number-one overall pick for the second year in a row.

I was ecstatic about the chance to play with Shaq. I thought, *I will average a triple-double.* Juwan and I formed the best-passing big-man duo in college, and I wanted to take that skill to Orlando to throw oops to the big fella. Shaq called right after the drawing and said, "I'm looking forward to playing with you. We should do some damage." Of course, I agreed!

I bought a tan striped suit with some rust gators to match. This was going to be a night of all nights, and I was going to be fly as fly could get. Cleaner than the board of health. Gators for everybody! I bought my brothers and father suits as well. I took Jalen to a spot and got him fitted for the special night. I knew his time was coming soon, and I wanted him to enjoy it. I did this for many friends and family members. On this special day, I wanted them to feel like a million bucks.

The night started with a welcome from David Stern: "Good evening, and welcome to the Palace of Auburn Hills!" The crowd went wild. "Home of the two-time NBA champion Detroit Pistons!" The crowd went crazy. David Stern was a better hype man than Flavor Flav. I got the chills. He continued, "So let's get started!" A video tribute to past greats and future hopefuls played on the scoreboard. The thirteen thousand fans erupted when an excerpt in the video showed me finishing a vicious dunk on an opponent. I could feel the goose bumps on the back of my neck.

There had been rumors swirling that a trade was going to happen between a couple of the top teams in the draft, but which ones I didn't know—and truthfully, I didn't care. I was just geeked to be in the building. The moment was more than surreal. I was twenty years old in the middle of a dream. I wasn't the only one. Sitting in the green room in the back of the arena, I nervously joked with future draftees like Jamal Mashburn, Shawn Bradley, Penny Hardaway, Bobby Hurley, and Rodney Rodgers. We were finally here. No one looked as cool, smooth, or confident in that green room as they were accustomed to feeling or as they were on a basketball court.

I got back to my table seated with my family, friends, and pastor and tried to calm my nerves. I just sat there and thought about all the good. I thought about all of my coaches. I thought about running in the street to the sympathy of neighbors who were telling Harv, "To take it easy on those boys." I thought about the twenty-four-hour practices with the Super Friends. I thought about my mother and her prayer warriors, praying huddled in a corner of the same arena when I tore my ankle ligaments during my high school championship game. I thought about my grandfather at home on Collingwood, hoping that he was watching. I thought about working out with Iyapo, Mike Jack, and Kev. I was just so grateful.

David Stern said, "With the first pick in the 1993 NBA draft, the Orlando Magic selects Chris Webber from the University of Michigan!"

The crowd erupted. It was the loudest crowd I'd ever heard in what was the most serene moment in my life. The deafening cheers turned to still and silence. Then, my father hugged me with all his might. I felt his tears through my shirt. He leaned his head on my right shoulder, an exact opposite of that fateful night in New Orleans. I felt him exhale. I felt pain, anxiousness, and relief exit through this long embrace. Pastor London, his friend and witness to life on the terrible plantation, consoled my pops. Probably for the first time since his mother's death all those years ago, he let go. I told him I loved him while trying to escape his bear hug; crying is contagious, and at that time I did not want to catch his disease. I couldn't look at her for fear of crying, but I hugged my mother. She whispered, "I love you. God is good."

I hugged the rest of the table and then headed the wrong way behind a curtain and up some stairs. I was so excited, thankfully an NBA usher redirected me toward the stage. I didn't care. I wasn't even there. I was on cloud nine. I walked with my newly appointed guard through the green room shaking hands with some of the players. On the way out of the green room, I slapped Acie Earl, the shot-blocking center from Iowa, on the back of the neck and said, "What up, doe!" He laughed. Before making it through the tunnel, I doubled back to Bobby Hurley, reminding him of our time out with the Dream Team. That gave both of us a chance to let off nervous energy with a laugh.

I folded the brim of my new black-and-turquoise hat with the word "Magic" on it like a pitcher. I came out of the tunnel and nodded to the crowd. I was so hype, and they showed me so much love. The last time I'd been in front of a crowd like this, it was silent. I'd been embarrassed, humiliated. I lost. I made a mistake. Now, just weeks later at home, I couldn't have written an ending—or beginning—this gratifying.

I knew it was love. I was receiving the admiration from my home and that was unlike any feeling I'd ever experienced. I continued to walk up the stairs toward the commish, tightly grasping the side rails. I couldn't help it. I was humbled. As I reached the top of the stairs, the moment climaxed. After being acknowledged by the fans with a crazy roar, all I could do was throw up the peace sign to the crowd to say "I love you." The crowd went bonkers. Completely apeshit. This was the crowd's moment as well. They had watched me grow from a twelve-year-old on the local news. They had prayed for me. The factory workers in the stands saw themselves in my dad's shoes and related to his grind. The teachers and community leaders cheered for my mother. They understood her sacrifice. The churches were busing kids to the arena to show them an example of perseverance. My mother's current and former students wanted to show her support. They had experienced her discipline, so they could relate to me and empathize or sympathize with me. This was truly a moment to celebrate.

My memory of the rest of that evening is like trying to catch a bullet with your hand. Impossible. Everything was moving too fast.

I headed over to do an interview with the less flashily dressed Craig Sager of TNT. He started off: "Well, two years ago you're winning high school championships, and now you're the number-one pick in the NBA draft. What can we expect?"

I replied, "Well, first, I'd like to thank God. I'd like to thank God for blessing me, giving me the ability, and when people doubted me, he stayed by my side."

At the end of the interview, Craig said, "Well, congratulations. The clock worked in your favor this time."

I replied, "Yeah, it definitely did."

There's five minutes between each selection in the first round of the draft. I went to the back to do some interviews and then head to my party—or at least, that was my plan. After the interviews, I sat with my agents to discuss rumors. Orlando was $4 million over the salary cap, and that caused speculation that they couldn't pay me.

The commissioner returned before the five-minute time slot for Minnesota's fifth pick ended. There was an excited rustle among the crowd. "Ladies and gentlemen, I'd like to report a trade," he said. "Orlando"—the crowd started to boo—"has traded the draft rights to Chris Webber to Golden State in exchange for the draft rights to Penny Hardaway and three future first round draft picks"—the boos got louder—"which will be exercised at the earliest in the years 1996, 1998, and 2000."

I sat at the table with my father and tried to digest the information, but as I tried to explain to him what I thought had just happened, an NBA official came and got me so I could exchange hats with Penny onstage in a photo op. I had no time to be shocked. I quickly went through my mental inventory of who played for Golden State. Chris Mullin, a knockdown three-point shooter. Billy Owens, Mr. Do It All. Victor Alexander from Detroit, who could shoot from outside. Tim Hardaway, one of my favorite point guards, "Mr. Crossover," a three-point shooting, ankle-breaking Chicago kid making a name for himself. Sunny weather, West Coast… I could deal with that. Penny and I hugged it out in the back halls of the Palace, both excited about our futures.

I was not offended by the trade. If I were Orlando, I would have done the same thing. The combo of Penny and Shaq had Magic-and-Kareem potential. Shaq would eventually tell me that he got close with Penny in Hollywood on the set of *Blue Chips*. The cast members of ballers would hoop after each day's taping, he said, and Penny was killing everyone in those games: dropping dimes, throwing oops, hitting jumpers, setting him up, so Shaq told the organization to draft Penny. Meanwhile, Ernie

Johnson was interviewing Don Nelson at a draft celebration dinner. I was even more humbled when I found out that the reception in Detroit might have been trumped by the excitement in the Bay Area and my new home of Oakland, California.

I left the draft and went straight to the party at the State Theater... it was sick! A line of hundreds outside who couldn't get in. Inside, what was more amazing than the support was the fact that the party people had on Golden State Warriors hats. How the hell did they do that? What store was open? Which hustle man hit a lick? Anyway, with thousands of friends, family, and strangers, I partied the night away. What a difference a few weeks made.

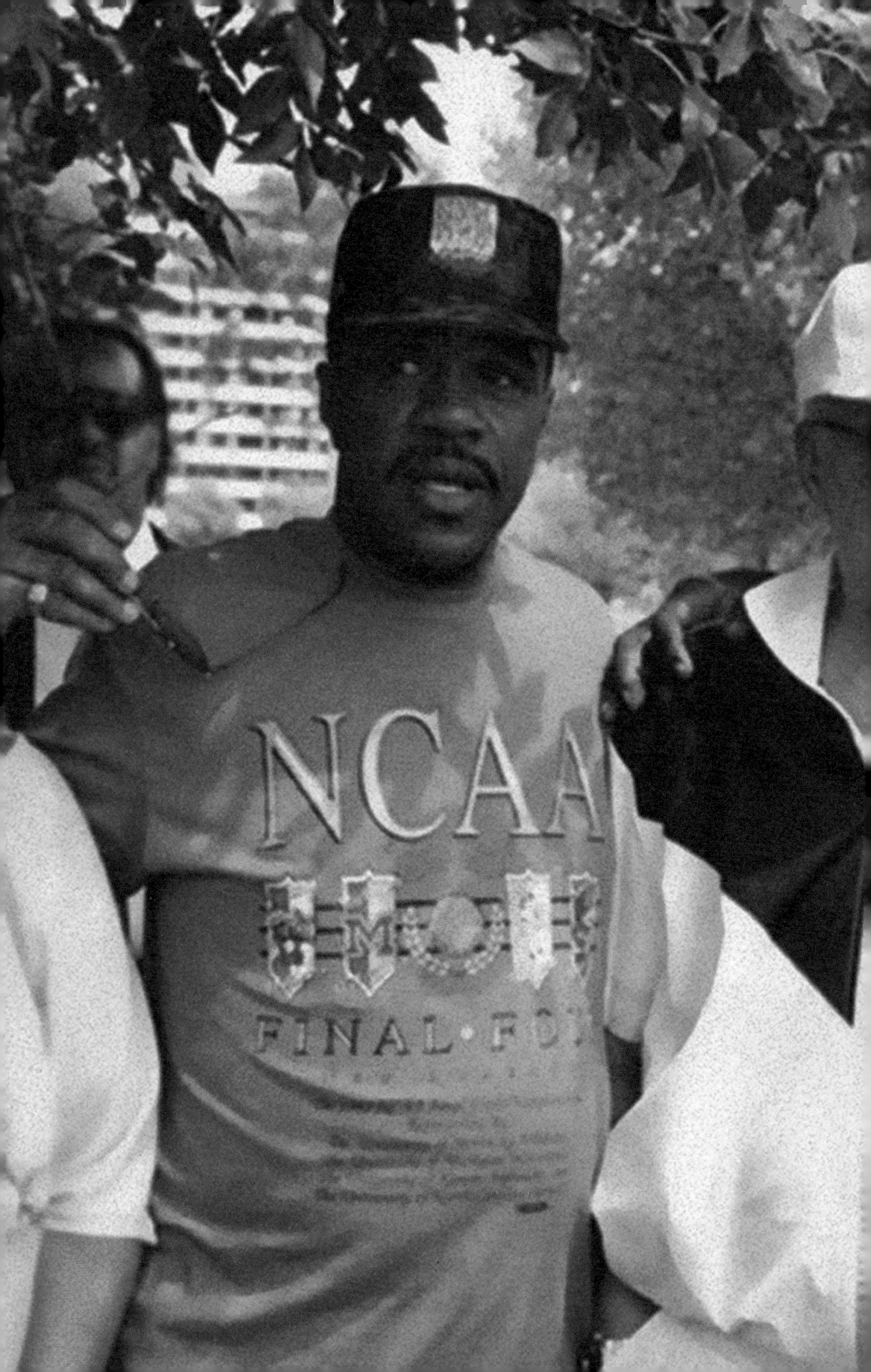
NCAA
FINAL

THE LEAGUE

BOOK FIVE

Every day I was finding out about how my embarrassment encouraged some people to keep going no matter their miscues. It was rewarding. It was a great moment in my life, a wonderful time. The personal letters from President Clinton and Jackie Joyner-Kersee had such an impact of positivity and strength, they encouraged me to give others that same feeling that their gifts of kindness gave me.

I was ready to move on. However, there would be a few speed bumps before I'd get to California. There were rumors that my agents were going to break up, so I chose a local accountant/lawyer, Fallasha Erwin, and paired him with veteran agent Bill Strickland to work as a team. It wasn't so much an obstacle as it was accepting change.

I also had to get an emergency appendectomy just a week before training camp. The appendectomy was a real setback because I'd had great workouts and played basketball all summer and was in really good shape. Having to sit out after the surgery, I feared I'd lose my wind. I saw my father cry three times: upon the death of his father, on draft night, and on the night of this surgery. It's funny when I look back, but it was not funny that night.

I called my father from my downtown apartment in extreme pain. I was having excruciating cramps on the right side of my lower abdomen. I felt like I had to throw up, felt like I had diarrhea, and I couldn't do either. I was drenched in sweat and couldn't stand. My father took me to the hospital, and the diagnosis was that I needed to have an emergency appendectomy. OK, anyone can go through that. But the biggest pain of the night came just after I had the procedure. I came out of surgery feeling pretty groggy and sat in the hospital room as the doctors waited for the anesthesia to wear off. They wanted me to use the bathroom, but minutes went by, then thirty minutes, then an hour, then two hours. No pee.

Here's where the fun starts. They informed me that I had to release the poisons inside of me and they could help me do it—with a catheter. Not knowing what a catheter was, I said, "Sure."

Worst mistake of my life. As they inserted a plastic tube into my penis, I let out the biggest scream of my life. I only stopped to laugh when I saw my father making the funniest face with tears running down his cheeks.

A few days after the surgery, I had to report to training camp. I had already missed a few days. I was anxious and excited to get to California, even though I had another week before I could get on the court. Instead, I needed to use this time to take care of a couple pieces of business while I was out there—purchase a house and sign my contract. Everything was in order when I left Detroit. I said my thank yous, even some goodbyes begrudgingly, but the one person I was upset with was my mother. I wanted her to move. I wanted to buy her a house. Charitably, and selfishly. I wanted to fulfill the dream we all had while packed into that van, driving through Indian Village, gawking at houses that we wished to one day own. I wanted to get her off our block immediately, STAT.

She told me with her frustratingly calm demeanor, "I have to pray on it. I want to ask God which house would be best for me and my family. I'm not going to rush out and choose the first thing I see. I love our neighbors; there's no hurry." The only funny part about it was that everybody in my family was frustrated with her, even my father, who had to live with this decision and put on a good face while doing so. My friends on the block and those same neighbors she loved were frustrated with her. *If only we had the opportunity to get out of here*, they'd say. Well, it would be three years before they moved away from the neighbors she loved. I had the house under surveillance most nights. I knew it was real on the streets and had to have some feeling of control or comfort then, and that helped me sleep.

◆ ◆ ◆

I loved California, especially the Bay Area. The people were laid back, the food was good and healthy, there was more sunshine than in the Midwest, there were mild winters, and the sports fans were crazy. The plane landed at Oakland International Airport, and we drove up to the arena for the press conference and the signing of my new contract. My father was very excited. During the limo ride, he seemed to be recounting the numbers in his head that my agents told me I'd be signing for. We had come straight from Nike headquarters in Portland, where I was designing my signature shoe. Bill Strickland told my father, "That's right, Mr. Webber. The contract is for fifteen years."

"That's a long time," my father replied.

Fallasha Erwin, Bill's partner, chimed in. "Don't worry, Mayce. He has an opt-out after the first year. You know what that means?" My father didn't. "It means that Chris can opt out for even more money after his first year. No rookies have an out after their first year. It's a risk, but there's a reward as well."

On October 18, I signed a contract for $75 million for fifteen years—the largest rookie contract at that time. It was great that I had $75 million guaranteed, considering two months ago I didn't have anything but a loan from Isiah without the scratch to pay it back. It was a brilliant idea from Fallasha. But the best part about the contract was the out clause. After one year, the clause allowed me to opt out and demand top pay as a second-year player, a tool that usually only veterans had.

Of course, there was a risk in being locked into a contract for all those years. Who knew how many times the market would change in that amount of time? There were also rumors that Coach Nelson wasn't too happy that I had thought outside the box with my contract. He thought it could set a precedent and inspire other players to do the same. He also wasn't happy about kids getting younger and going pro. I heard many whispers like "These kids are getting so much money now. Shaq messed it up." I laughed every time I heard that.

I was happy to be shaking things up a little bit. This was the nineties, and things were changing. Young players wanted more independence, empowerment, inclusion, and expression. Everything we sought at the University of Michigan, I wanted to seek professionally. I'm happy Fallasha Erwin and Bill Strickland helped me think that way in the beginning.

Now that I had the business of basketball out of the way, I was excited about getting down to business and playing some ball. However, I learned the first day on the job that even the legacy of greats can be cut off in a blink of eye. I walked into Oracle Arena, where the team was holding practice. Coach Nelson blew his whistle and gathered everybody at center court. He called me over to meet my new teammates. I gave some dap and said wassup, and then went back to the sideline to watch the rest of practice. But before I even got the chance to sit on the bench, I heard a scream. I saw the trainers running from the sideline to attend to an injured player. It was Tim Hardaway. Mr. Crossover had torn his ACL in a drill. This injury changed the trajectory of his career, and he was forced to sit out my entire rookie season.

I was devastated, even though I didn't know how serious the injury was at the time. Coach called off practice and guys went their own way. I really didn't get to speak to anyone, because everyone went to check on Tim. I left practice, went house shopping, and flew back to Detroit to get my things.

The main reason I went back home was to try to convince my mom, again, to let me buy her a house. The only stress I had that year was worrying about my parents back home. I felt that she didn't realize (Pops did) how they could be sitting ducks for any evil mind that wanted to rob them, set them up, take advantage of them, or do something crazy. We'd seen more done to people with less. She didn't bite. So I made some calls, set some rules in place, said my goodbyes, and jetted off to adulthood.

Becoming a man entails many different things. Perseverance, adaptability, self-discipline, pride, humility, staying focused through pain, accepting responsibility, and providing were just a few traits I had to learn, in an eighteen-month span, through trial by fire. One trait I had to learn was going it alone. One reason I went to the University of Michigan was that it was a thirty-minute drive from my house. I always had my support system around. I wondered what it would be like to be two thousand miles from home, with more temptations than any man could handle. But I was blessed because I would have teammates who would fill the role of big brothers for me, the youngest player in the NBA.

My first practice was incredible. Everything I dreamed of. High-fiving, trash-talking, pushing, and jostling with some crazy characters. It felt like I never left Michigan. But NBA basketball was so much different than college, even though the basics were the same. The most notable difference was the speed of the game. The pace, it never stopped. There was no slowing down to set or get a call from the sideline, and no walking it up in this high-powered offense. The athletes were so much better. They jumped higher, ran faster, and were much stronger. I was playing against guys ten years my senior. I wasn't even fully developed.

The league encouraged physical play back then. It looked good on TV with the Bad Boys and their physical defense, or in the highlights with guys on fast breaks. Then I had to play against it. It was no joke. I would catch elbows, wrestle with big fellas in the paint, and there were guards stronger than forwards and centers I played against in college. The one constant was the energy, camaraderie, and chemistry that I've shared on every level that I played. This time it was so much better—the playing was much more fun.

If you broke someone down while penetrating and made a pass, most open shooters would knock the shot down. If you threw an alley-oop, no matter how high, the players were much more sure-handed that you could trust that they would finish. For me, it became follow the leader with Chris Mullin. He really embraced his role as a vet. He taught me how to practice and how to take care of my body. In his distinctive Brooklyn, New York, accent, he would say, "Young fella, follow me." Then he'd perform a ritual of going back and forth between a hot tub and a cold tub three times apiece for a three-minute dip. "You might not appreciate it now, but one day you're going to need this," he told me. "I call this prevention."

I'd sit in the second-to-last seat in the back of the bus and let him hold court, telling me stories from his days in college and the pros. He'd take me to dinner, and even with my first triple-double, someone whispered, "Webb, you need one assist." I told Mully, "I'm going to hit you with the handoff. Knock it down and give me my first triple-double." He obliged. Mully was *smoove*. A left-handed, jump-shooting, back-cutting, low-top-shoe-wearing, run-like he-tiptoeing, buzz-haircut prototype of what a hooper should look like.

I watched him in shooting drills, counting the numbers of consecutive and total makes. I'd never seen anyone shoot like him. I was in awe. Most of the time in college, a shooter would make eleven or fourteen out of twenty, and that was considered great. Mully was hitting seventeen, eighteen, *nineteen* out of twenty from three-point range. Anything under fifteen, he'd repeat the drill.

Billy Owens and Latrell Sprewell served as my brothers. Not only would they help me become a better player and take on the role of guys in the Fab Five, but they would serve as road maps on how to get acclimated with the league. Billy took me to buy my car and furniture and showed me where all the restaurants and clubs were. Where to go and not to go, though that really didn't matter because I never went out unless it was with Spree, Billy, or Mully anyway. Billy O. lived in one of the most beautiful houses I'd ever seen in Oakland Hills, overlooking the city. His lifestyle influenced my goals.

I was just as close with Spree, a basketball and car junky from Milwaukee. Spree didn't even start playing basketball until his senior year in high school. A great cat who looked at the world differently. One time after a game, I came out of the locker room ready to go to dinner with Billy O. and Spree. Billy was looking for Spree, but we couldn't find him. After about thirty minutes, the parking attendant told us to check the lot. We got out there and noticed that Spree was under the hood of my car fixing something, I still don't know what it was, but I know that he had oil on his hands and a few of the engine parts resting on the asphalt. I couldn't believe it! He said, "Where have y'all been? I've been waiting on you." Billy and I just looked at each other and didn't say a word.

I had made lifelong friends in a day. It was a vibe, energy, and spirit. I was familiar with it. I could feel it then. It was something special. We all had similar family situations and backgrounds. I knew their story; they knew mine. There was a comfort and an inherent trust with that.

We played for each other. No one really cared who was going to score. We just wanted to push the rock. Our practices were intense, and Nellie often had to cut runs short because he knew we were competitive and had personal bets on whose team would win a drill or scrimmage. Coach wanted us to save some for the game. I mean, we took these bets seriously. Funny, there we were, millionaires betting on who would pay for dinner after practice or who would pay for food on football Sunday, and dudes were going at it. It was like playing in the backyard. No hatred, no bad will, just "checkup." All of the starters were extra competitive, and true to Don Nelson teams, everyone had a complete skill set. So you had to play defense or get embarrassed. Latrell Sprewell, Chris Mullin, Billy Owens, Avery Johnson, and I served as the starting lineup for most of the season. I started at center. The times I didn't, Victor Alexander would, and I'd start at power forward. We were a fast team…

I remember my first game. We were playing against Hakeem Olajuwon and the Houston Rockets. I was feeling pretty good, considering I only had a couple of practices under my belt. Hell, I was so excited it really didn't matter. I wanted to be out there on the floor. I was about 75 percent healthy, but the adrenaline would get me through. That night I was playing against "Hakeem the Dream," and I couldn't believe it.

A ball boy casually mentioned to me that chapel was down the hall and asked me if I wanted to go. I didn't know the NBA had chapel. Chapel was a safe place. Usually a chaplain or pastor conducted a fifteen-minute worship service or discussion in a small auxiliary area of the locker room. Players from both the home and visiting teams could attend. I attended the first of many that night of my first game. Reverend Earl Smith was our chaplain, and he also ministered to the San Francisco 49ers. But his real job, for over two decades, was as chaplain of San Quentin, one of America's most menacing prisons. He tried to preach God's message of love, repentance, and forgiveness to some of America's most notorious criminals, including Charles Manson and Stanley "Tookie" Williams.

He introduced himself and passed out a syllabus with a summary of our discussion and scriptures to follow up with at home. It was great. A compact service message, but it allowed me to center myself before every game. I waited for everyone to leave, then approached Rev. Smith once chapel ended. I asked him to pray for me. We held hands in the middle of the small locker room and prayed. We prayed that God would protect me physically and mentally. We asked him to allow me to have a long and prosperous career. We thanked him for the moment and his blessings. After we said amen, I ran to the locker room to get ready.

I repeated my pregame stretching routine while Coach gave instructions. We'd gotten a scouting report at practice the day before, that morning, and during shootaround, but this pregame talk was different. Coach walked up to the chalkboard and reiterated a couple of key points. Then he said, "If we score this," as he wrote the number 125 down and circled it, "we will win." Then he walked off, as cool as a fan. I looked at Spree, Mully, then Billy, smiling from ear to ear. They smiled back at me with an "I told you so! We do it different here," expression on their faces.

I was a half a year away from turning twenty-one, but I was playing a man's game now. I didn't have time to worship a future Hall of Famer; he was now the enemy. **Olajuwon** and I got in the center circle and gave each other dap. This was everything I'd been waiting for. Practices, training camp, commercials, notoriety—all that was fine and good. But you're not in the NBA until you play your first game, and my first one was here.

I jumped center and tried to tap the ball back behind me, but it went right to Otis Thorpe. Houston set up in their offense, and the first play went to Hakeem on the right block looking in. He took one dribble baseline with his left hand, faked, and lost Victor Alexander coming back shooting middle over his right shoulder. The net didn't move, two points. The second play on offense, I was guarding Otis, who went across the paint to screen for Dream. I was supposed to switch with Victor, but I didn't. By the time I caught up with Olajuwon, I was fouling him on a jump shot. He had five points. On the third play, Dream beat me down the court, dunking an oop from Robert Horry. I couldn't believe the pace; it was even faster than practice.

My first points as an NBA player came on a fast-break dunk, assisted from my man Spree, who led the break after a steal. Later, in a one-on-

one play where I drove straight to the basket from the top of the key for a tear-drop finger roll, Hakeem blocked my shot. In the second half, however, I dunked on him. In the end, I survived a lesson from one of the greats, but we lost. Dream had thirty-two points, eleven rebounds, and four blocks. He hit jumpers off the crossover, baseline right shoulder jumpers, baseline left corner jumpers, fake left middle jumpers, and fake right middle jumpers. I'd never seen anything like it in my life. He drove to his right, to his left, and played like the reigning Defensive Player of the Year in the paint.

I had seventeen points, nine rebounds, and six assists, but I'm glad that I got schooled in my first game. It set the tone for my year. I became relentless. After watching tape the next day, I realized that I had to learn how to slow down in the post on offense. Defenders were so good at anticipating your next move that you had to throw them off with a different cadence. It wasn't like college, where you could crab dribble twice, jump over someone, and shoot. You had to have a rhythm and a second and third option.

I loved to watch film. It was something I learned from Coach Keener at Country Day. Film could tell me all the things that I didn't know about how I was playing, including how I were feeling at a certain time. Posture, body language, fading on free throws—film let me see what I was doing wrong so I could change it while providing encouragement for what I was doing right.

◆ ◆ ◆

The league was a completely different world. We played eighty-two games as opposed to the thirty-something I had played in college. There was no babysitting, no one waking you up, no one feeling sorry for your sore aches and pains. No one cared that I was the youngest player in the league. I was a pro, and they expected me to act as such. But it really wasn't that tough because I had good teammates. Spree and Billy would throw my twenty-first birthday party, a night I'll always remember. One time, during a party that was absolutely poppin', Spree's father tried to jump from the balcony of my house into the swimming pool, missed the pool by three feet, and shattered his left ankle. The funniest part about it was that everyone saw it happen, paused, collectively made a sound like "Auugghh…" and then just got back to dancing. Spree felt no sympathy for his father and told him to get a ride to the hospital, because he had warned him earlier to quit trying to show off.

When we played against the Detroit Pistons in my hometown, my mother cooked for the entire team. She got a room at the hotel and made baked chicken, potato salad, corn bread, rolls—you name it. The fellas loved the food. It was a long road trip, and everybody craved some home cooking. Game night was different. Almost the exact same thing that happened during the high school championship a few years earlier happened again. First quarter, I grabbed a rebound, jumping as high as I could to show my athletic ability. The next time I came down the court, I tried to do the same thing, and Bill Laimbeer stuck his foot out so that I would land on it and twist my ankle. Which I did. A dirty play.

We played the Pistons again in January, and this time we beat them by sixteen. Isiah had fourteen points and five assists. Joe D. had thirty-two. I had twenty points, eleven rebounds, and five steals. At one point in that game, I did Isiah's signature "fake behind the back and bring it back" layup, and Zeke fouled me. He laughed.

I got a lot of respect from the other players in the league. It was great to find out that basketball players were fans of each other. They had followed my college career just like I followed their NBA careers. I was part of the fraternity and didn't even know it! The year was filled with highlights. Anything positive was a highlight. Any day I was smiling was a highlight, and I smiled a lot of days.

It was a new experience living alone. I got a chef and put myself on a schedule. I was used to schedules. At the University of Michigan, Coach Fisher had us scheduled to the hour. I liked knowing the rules. Structure allowed me to do what I needed and plan my time for relaxation, which I would turn out to need just as much. I even got a Rottweiler puppy, Zeke.

Chapter 57

The NBA season is like a triathlon, a grueling race in multiple stages with brief respites throughout. Training camp is one stage, the start of season to the All-Star break is another, the final stretch to the playoffs is another, and then the playoffs are toughest part of the race. With all that, I couldn't wait until Christmas. My parents and siblings were coming out to see me. This would be the first time we actually shared in some of the benefits of my new income. When they stayed at my house, everyone had their own room for the first time. It was the first time we had more than one bathroom. We finally had a big enough table to seat all seven of us.

I'd been excited to purchase the new house in San Ramon, in Blackhawk subdivision about thirty minutes east of Oakland. My neighbors included Chris Mullin, John Madden, a beauty from an R&B group, and some friends who were ginormous in the tech industry. This place had the most beautiful homes I'd ever seen, with the nicest manicured lawns you could ever ask for. I settled on the last house at the top of the subdivision, a beautiful, modern design situated on a grassy hill. I made sure I got everything I'd ever dreamed of, though I didn't really need most of it. I wanted to play for Golden State my entire career. The seven-bedroom house had a beautiful pool, an indoor spa, a gym, a large family room, and a humongous kitchen. I didn't buy that house for myself; I bought it with my family in mind. Even though they wouldn't be there more than a couple of weeks a year to share it with me, it was really their house.

The limo bus picked my family up from the airport while I stayed at home to get everything ready. For most of them, this would be their first trip out West. I realized that they had made it because the doorbell was being struck frantically. I let them in, and my brothers and sister rushed me. But just as they were about to give themselves a guided tour, my parents asked everyone to pray and thank God for his blessings, right there in the foyer. It's hard to get off track with that philosophy.

After the prayer, the race began. We literally had a relay race throughout the house, passing a rolled piece of paper as our baton. It was my house now, and my parents couldn't say there was no running. I was so proud of that house, and my mother loved it: the wood and stone floors, the slate roof, the fixtures, and architecture that she knew came from her influence and her comments while driving through Indian Village in Detroit.

Considering the amount of time and sweat he spent on our small lawn, I thought my father was going to pass out after seeing those lawns and trimmed bushes. Cows grazed down on the side of the hill every day, and my father would make his cup of coffee, jump over the fence, and walk with them. You can take the man out of the country, but you can't take the country out of the man. The funniest and best part about their visit was that every day during their week's stay, the siblings all slept on the living room floor like we used to do when it stormed at home. The big house didn't matter to our happiness. We missed each other. We were together.

I had a hot tub and sauna in the master bathroom. I remember my sister with her dolls, and my whole family sitting in the hot tub. As we were talking and laughing, I pushed a button that made the roof retract. They were speechless. I wish I could have videotaped that moment. The silence was broken when my father said to my mother, "See, B. We need to move. We could be doing this at home." Everyone broke out laughing except my father, who didn't see the humor in it. He was dead serious.

My mother spent most of her time cooking—more for some of my teammates than for my family; they loved her food—singing, walking through each room in the house praying. I wish I had purchased a grand piano for her to replace the finely tuned but shabby red one we had in our basement at home. Those are some of my favorite memories. I felt truly blessed. This was true success. There was no talk of money, no bickering, nothing except being excited, geeked, and thankful to be surrounded by love.

Don Nelson was known as a very good coach. A player's coach. By the time he retired, he had amassed the most wins in NBA history. Prior to his coaching career, Nellie played the game. He had a hell of a career at the University of Iowa before winning five championships with the Celtics. He was a big man with the stature and cadence of a sad grizzly bear. But the rumor in basketball circles was that the game had evolved, and Nellie didn't want to adjust. I didn't know what that meant, because when it came to Xs and Os, he was an innovator. The game had to catch up with him, or so I thought. I think it had to do more with the front office, TV, and the notoriety of players and their brand. Nellie was pissed with the business of basketball.

I had had only had a few coaches in my lifetime, but after a while I realized that Coach didn't like me. Worse, he hated it that the team loved me. Nellie was very moody. I didn't mind that; I was used to coaches yelling and screaming. But he loved playing mind games. Games that would hurt the team, not bring us closer together. The day before Christmas, during a practice in Alameda, coach separated the big men and the smalls at different ends of the court. On our end we discussed things that we needed to do as a unit better. Box out, talk on defense, get the ball out of bounds faster to the guard, things like that. On the other end, I would find out after practice, they were having a much different conversation, and I was the subject.

Jeff Grayer, a stocky two-guard from Flint, Michigan, whose high school career I followed growing up, called me to his car after practice. He sat me down in his Benz along with Mullin, Spree, and Billy O. Jeff and the fellas explained that Nellie told them I wasn't a good fit. He wondered if I would continue to listen with all the money I could potentially make. He noted that I was uncomfortable playing center. Hell yeah I was! I was the youngest player in the league, and every center seemed to be at least seven one and outweigh me by thirty pounds. I was just six nine, so I was at a disadvantage every night. I was

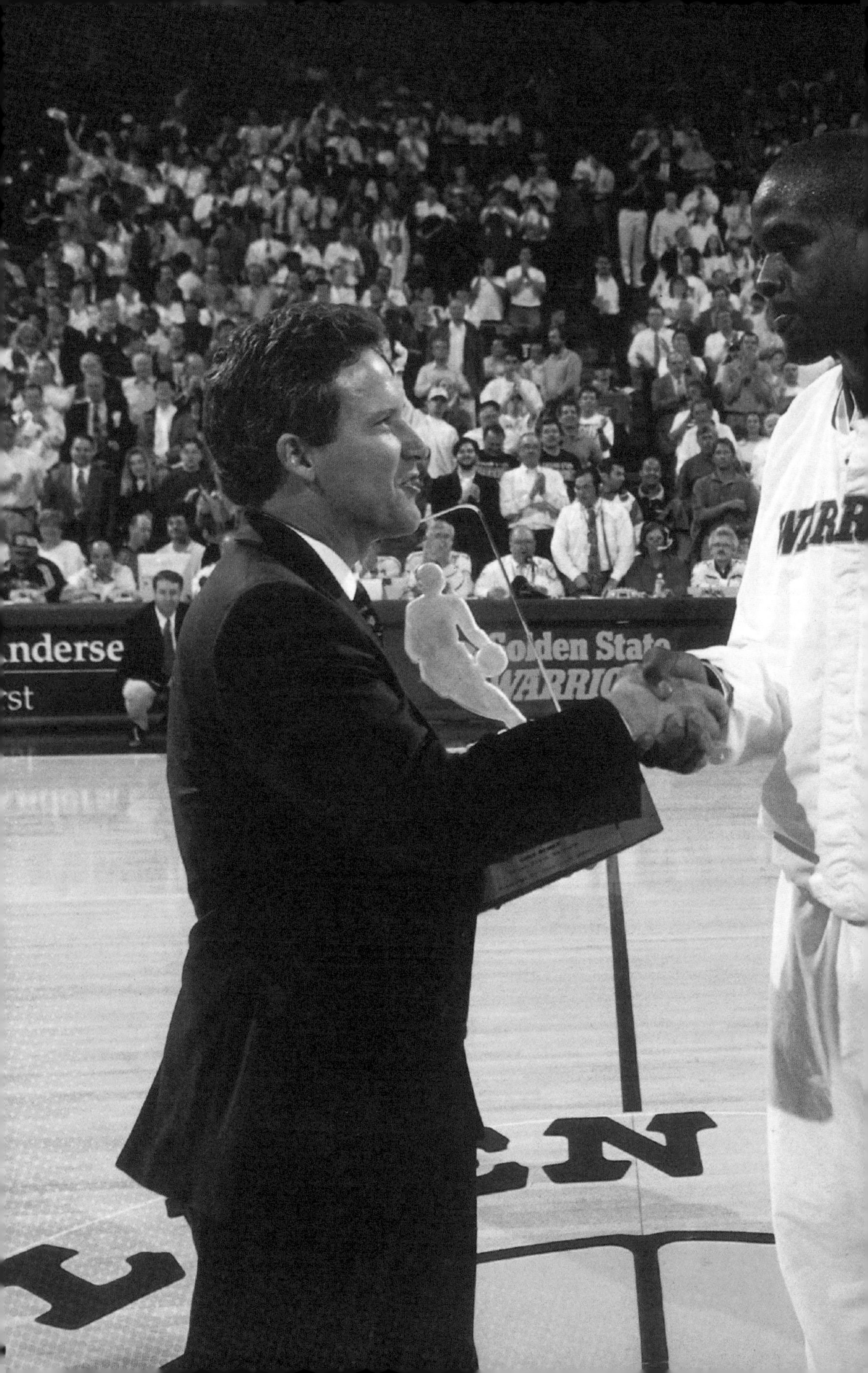
anderse
st
Golden State
WARRIO
WARR

fighting for my life, but it wasn't like I made a big deal of it, and eventually I figured out that my quickness gave me an advantage on offense.

One night we played Dikembe Mutombo and the Denver Nuggets. As I said, Coach was innovative and creative. He started me at point guard. Before the game, he just looked at me and said, "You can dribble, and he can't keep up with you. Make plays, and when someone else has the ball on our team, stay behind the three-point line and space. We'll get an illegal defense called on Mutombo because he's not used to defending that way."

At that time, zone defenses were not allowed. You had to be within six feet of your man. If I stayed behind the three-point line, there was no way Mutombo could help on penetration. We could negate his shot-blocking ability in the paint. That night playing point was one of the best of my life. It felt like all my practice, all the time playing with the guards, working on my dribbling back on Biltmore with Wes, was paying off. However, Coach also had his dark days. Avery Johnson played point for us all year, but come playoff time, Coach barely got him in a game. We were confused by the move and played like it. We didn't have a floor leader because Coach refused to play Avery.

It was hard to understand Nellie sometimes. We'd joke and say he needed a hug, but I needed a hug after that conversation in Jeff's Benz. I didn't know what to think. I had just been told by teammates that the man in charge didn't like me. I mentioned it to my agents, but they shrugged it off. They said that after I renegotiated my contract, I would have more power with the team because of my guaranteed numbers. At that time, those points went over my head. I had yet to understand the business of basketball. I didn't know that coaches faced a constant struggle to keep their jobs and that many had been fired unfairly because of a diva-like star.

I also knew his stance on players, especially rookies making big money. I'm sure there was resentment, because I probably made more my first two years than he made in his whole career. I can understand that frustration, being that generations before me had paved the way, yet we were reaping the benefits. However, that wasn't my fault.

The world was changing, contracts were changing, the way we watched TV was changing, and if Coach wanted to fight the system, he would have to fight that. When it came to business, I was going to be just as competitive as I was on the court. I was a model rookie. I was actually mad that the veterans didn't send me on more embarrassing rookie hazing missions. I wanted to go through every step of the process, because I was excited to be here. I couldn't be inconvenienced, my feelings couldn't be hurt, and I couldn't be intimidated—I was too grateful. I think that made Nellie resent me more. Imagine trying to mess with somebody and bring them down, but every suggestion is accepted without complaint. That's what I did. I just wanted to become a better player. I'm glad I didn't know how serious that talk at the end of practice truly was. I would find out later.

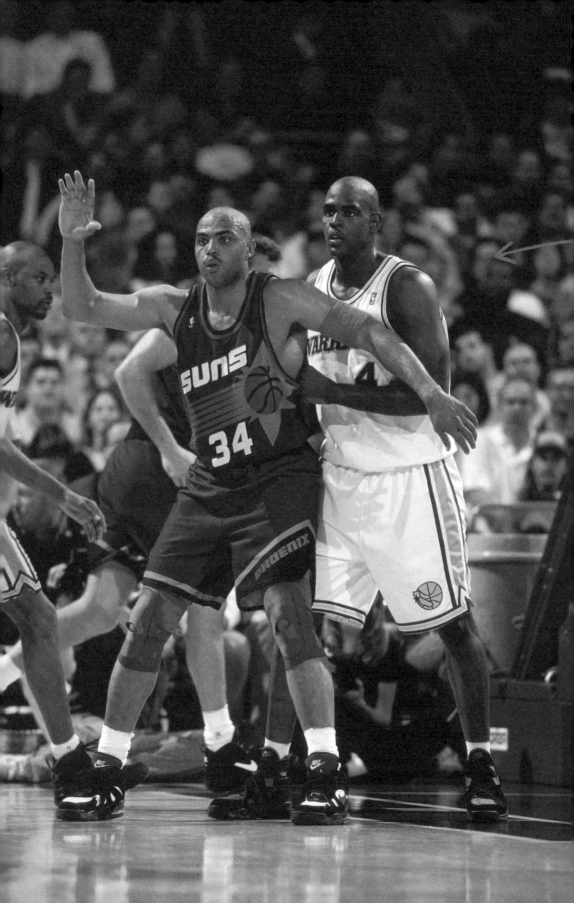

One game set the tone for the rest of my rookie season and provided an opportunity to continue showcasing a game that was honed in Detroit. It was the sixth game of the season. We were playing the Phoenix Suns and my favorite player of all time, Charles Barkley. The cat who visited me in high school with Rick Mahorn and gave me love. I wanted to show him that I got my weight up. My family and friends were in town, and my brothers and boys were talking smack. They knew it was time for the pupil to meet his master. They knew more than anyone that I patterned my game after Chuck. They knew that this was my first game against "the Round Mound of Rebound," and they were just as excited as I was. They expressed it through busting my balls.

I was ready out of the gate. Matched up against A. C. Green, I caught the ball on the right block and spun baseline for a hard right-hand dunk. Charles pump faked me at the free-throw line and went in for the easy two-hand flush. We went back and forth throughout the game. Playing against and watching his greatness was a dream come true. He did everything: run the floor for layups, dominate the offensive boards, hit long jumpers and threes, get others involved, even dimed Oliver Miller for a dunk and one. I played a great game against the man I emulated. Funny how you can do something at the end of a journey that outweighs the memories of anything during the journey, or how you can make a lasting memory while planting your flag.

The Suns' Danny Ainge came off pick-and-roll where the screen was set by A. C. Green. Billy switched, and I jumped out late on Ainge, who changed his jump shot in midair to a pass to a cutting Green. My boy Spree came from the weak side and intercepted the pass. I took off as soon as I saw him get the steal. He took one dribble and lobbed me a perfect three-quarter-court pass. I caught the ball between the free-throw line and sideline, and with all my momentum going forward, I could dribble, power it up off my strong leg, and treat this like the old low-block drill. Charles was dead center at the free-throw line. I didn't think he would foul me or even try to block my shot, but he did. He tried to grab me, wanting to make me earn the two at the line. Bad move. This was a once-in-a-lifetime meeting at the rim. I had to flush it on him. I took it behind my back, planted, and my favorite poster was created. I would have definitely put this on my wall back in my room on Biltmore!

It wasn't until later when I saw the highlight that I realized he fell back, off-balance, out of bounds. Who could believe I had been in college just a couple of months ago? Now I was in the big leagues making memories. *God is great*, I thought, and then looked up to the stands where my brothers and friends were. I raised my hands. I wanted them to see my face and to acknowledge that I had slayed the dragon. I knew I had a long way to go, and I knew that it was just one play, but this was the best feeling ever. We gave the fans a great game. Barkley had five dunks and countless highlights, scoring thirty-six points and thirteen rebounds. I had twenty-one points plus a bunch of rebounds and assists, but the Suns won.

My dunk on the reigning MVP was immortalized in a Nike commercial. I had inked a shoe deal with Nike a few weeks after signing the trading card contract the previous summer, and the way they welcomed me to their campus was the best recruiting effort I'd ever seen. I arrived at a barbershop in Oakland for the shoot. It was in a local neighborhood, and everyone came out and showed us their support. It made me feel like I was back in Detroit. The love, the dude announcing that we had better win the next game because he bets on us.

The commercial took only about an hour and a half to record, with makeup and everything. Anyone who knows how television and movies work knows that for a commercial that iconic, that tight, and that brilliant, it usually doesn't happen that way. But we had a great director. He sat down with me, Spree, and Mully for five minutes. He told us he just wanted us to sit and talk like we do in the barbershop. He let us know that there was no script. In the commercial, the dudes playing customers waiting for their turn in the barber chair were comedians, Joe Torry and Reynaldo Rey. They were throwing rapid-fire jokes about anything and everything.

Spree looked at the cats next in line and asked the comedians, "Did you guys see Chris dunk on Charles Barkley? Catch it like this...went around the back."

I caught an imaginary ball to simulate the posterization. Then, me quoting Chuck: "He's too high; he's too high."

Spree: "Then what did Barkley say?"

Me, after a pause to think: "I don't believe in role models, but you're mine!"

The director: "Cut! Great job, fellas. That's a wrap!"

We freestyled the entire shoot. I bet there are more great takes somewhere in a storeroom that could've been used as commercials too. The new commercials, the money, the notoriety—all that was good. But I was really motivated by Coach Nelson's talk with the little fellas at practice. I had learned how to turn hate into fuel. I knew that I couldn't control anything but my effort, focus, and determination, I was going to control that by giving it all I had. I kept following Mully and his routine. I tried to work on my terrible free-throw shooting. I got back in shape after the appendectomy.

✦ ✦ ✦

I was excited to attend my first All-Star Game in Minnesota. Penny and I headlined the first rookie showcase game and had a blast. Lindsey Hunter, Toni Kukoč, J. R. Rider, and Sam Cassell were on my team. I scored eighteen points and had ten rebounds in the win. Penny scored twenty-two and won MVP. Neither one of us cared. I was like a kid in a candy store. My mother, who'd rather have stayed in her room and watched it on TV, was dragged around Minnesota like the favorite rag doll of an energetic child. My pops was everywhere. By the end of the weekend, players I hadn't had a chance to rap with yet came over and repeatedly said, "Young fella, I met your pops. He's a good man." After the great Karl Malone retired, I did a commercial with him, and he relayed a story about meeting my father and how my pops was a good old country boy. He said that was why he always liked me.

This would be the first of many visits to the All-Star Game for my father, a ritual he enjoyed more than anyone in our family. One of the most special moments I've had with my father came at the 2009 All-Star Game in Phoenix, when I was working as an analyst for TNT. I was doing a special interview with Bill Russell, so I was already on cloud nine. I asked our executive producer, Tim Kiely, if I could bring my father to the interview. Knowing how much it meant to my father, and being a good cat anyway, he said sure.

I learned a lot that day. I was so nervous during the interview that I messed up a lot of footage that we couldn't use on air. I was moving, laughing, not following up with questions—I couldn't concentrate. My father had been telling me about this man my whole life. Mr. Russell wasn't directing his answers toward me; he was looking at my pops. As I was packing up my notebook to leave, I overheard a conversation between my father and Mr. Russell. Then Mr. Russell pulled me into the conversation and said, "Yes Mr. Webber, that's why I'm proud of you—because of this kid here. I know you raised him with values, I watched his journey, and I'm proud that he stayed focused and that he's handled everything with integrity." Then he let out a trademark cackle. "I had a great father, Mr. Webber; I recognize one when I see one."

My father, "El Presidente," was speechless. My father, who never looked for validation, was being honored by his idol. Mr. Russell understood where my father was from, the things he had to overcome, and the tenets of being a man. He was proud of my pops for walking me through the storm. They laughed about the old days, made jokes about me, and said their goodbyes. That is my number-one basketball memory of all-time.

One of the most memorable games of my rookie year came in March against Shaq, Penny, and the Orlando Magic. In the first game in Orlando, I had thirteen points and ten rebounds, but Shaq gave us twenty-eight and Penny had twenty-three. We lost. It was our turn now. Our team was rounding into playoff mode. We were down 101–85 with nine minutes left in the fourth quarter when we went on a run and made a tremendous comeback. With about two minutes to go, I got a rebound and fouled Shaq out on the putback; he went to the bench with twenty-nine points and twelve rebounds. Nellie got kicked out in the first half, and assistant coach Gregg Popovich was now our coach.

With thirty seconds left, I stole the inbound pass. Billy O. scored off a missed Avery jumper and gave us a one-point lead. With seconds left and time running out, we had a foul to give. Dennis Scott drove on Mully, two dribbles to the left then spinning back to his right, and Spree coming over for help almost stole the ball. D. Scott went up for a layup that I swatted, outletting it and securing our victory at the buzzer, 117–116. The Orlando bench went crazy. They wanted to know where the call was. Penny, Shaq, the coaches, and veteran Tree Rollins all stayed out on the floor and yelled at the refs, who they felt missed a game-deciding goaltending call. Pop rushed us back to the locker room.

The end of the year was the culmination of our hard work and focus. I was honored, relieved, and humbled when my agent called and told me that I had won Rookie of the Year. I couldn't believe it. I mean Penny was playing with Shaq, and we were on the West Coast. No one ever watched our games. I was proud to bring Rookie of the Year honors back to Detroit. It was almost a year to the day from my infamous time-out.

I ended up averaging 17.5 points, nine rebounds, 3.5 assists. 2.2 blocks, and 1.2 steals in the 1993–94 season. I became the first NBA rookie ever to register more than one thousand points, five hundred rebounds, 250 assists, 150 blocks, and seventy-five steals. But a funny thing happened at the award presentation. I was so proud that I was being presented with the trophy for Rookie of the Year in our home arena at center court, with my father by my side, that I tried to be a little too cool, holding the trophy up and turning it around so that the crowd could see. Instead, my hard-earned hardware slipped, hit the floor, and broke in half. It was hilarious.

We went 50–32 that season and finished third in the Pacific Division, the largest improvement of any team that year. I'd been waiting a year to get back to a tournament, but the playoffs were more intense than any basketball tournament I'd ever been a part of. I couldn't even imagine that the players, teams, and coaches could turn it up another notch, but they did. Before our series with the Suns, we were given extra-thick notebooks filled with players' tendencies, go-to plays, and situational information.

We had played Phoenix four times that year with no success. Barkley always seemed to have his way with us. I personally had a great series, shooting 55 percent from the field and averaging close to a triple-double—15.7 points 8.7 rebounds, 9 assists, 3 blocks, and 1 steal—but they swept us 3–0. Barkley was out of his mind, averaging thirty-seven points and thirteen rebounds. The Suns were just flat-out better than us. But overall, it was successful year. I had achieved a dream, could now take care of my family, and was having a blast the whole time. I couldn't wait to come back next year and finish what we had started. I loved our team, our style of play, the fans, the chemistry, the weather. There was no place else that I wanted to play.

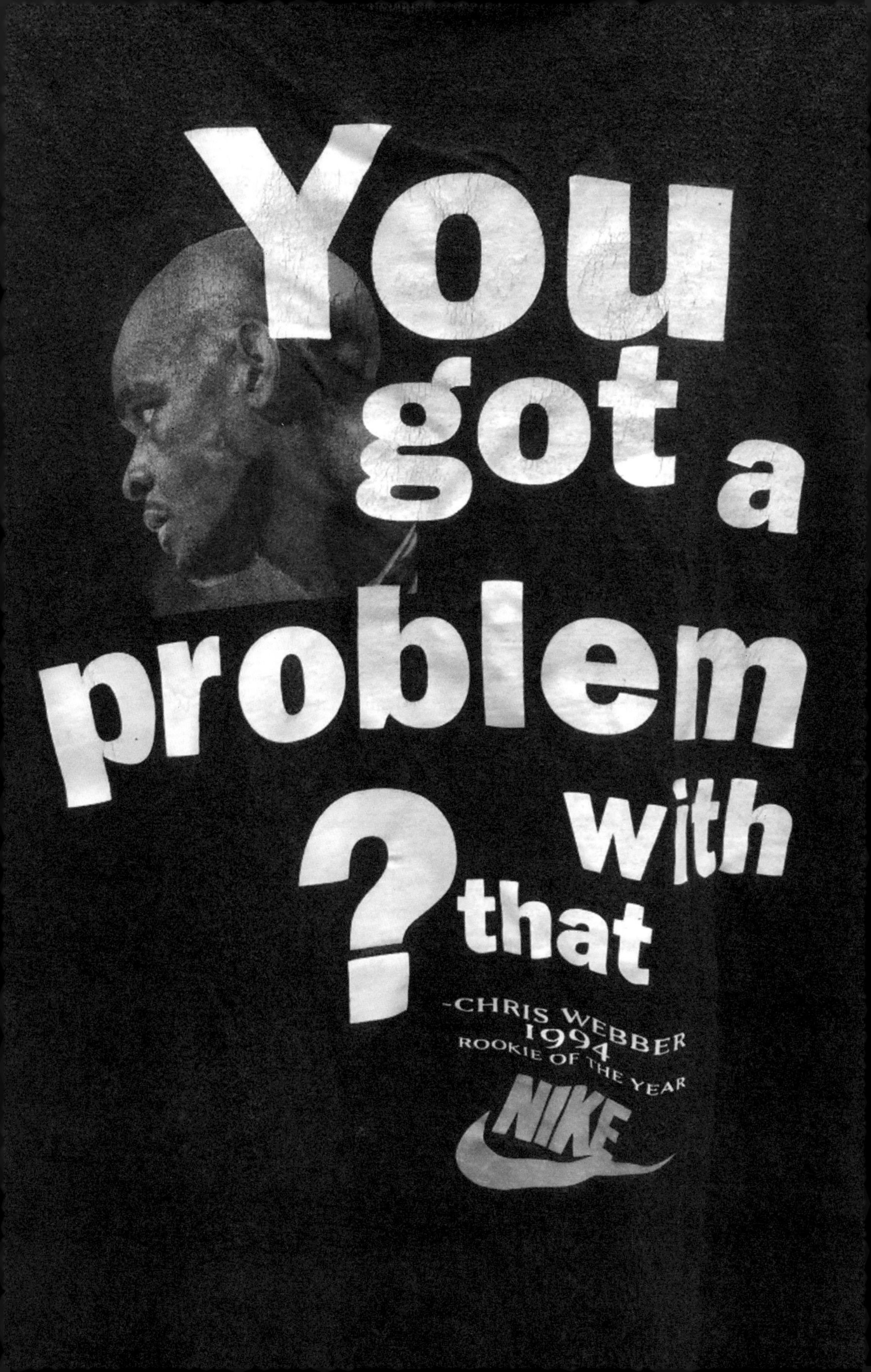

You got a problem with that?

-CHRIS WEBBER
1994
ROOKIE OF THE YEAR

NIKE

Back home in the D, the summer was great. I ran a few games at the St. Cecilia's summer league. I tried to convince my mother to move. No luck. I spent time with my grandfather sitting quietly on his porch and even had a beer or two with him. I spent a lot of time in the gym. I now knew what to expect from opponents, and I also knew my strengths and weaknesses.

Many guys get confused trying to improve during the season. You're supposed to be consistent during the season and help your team, because the margin for error is so small that you can't try things in which you don't have muscle memory and total confidence. The off-season is when you enhance your game. I put the work in every summer. I filmed a few commercials for Logo Athletic and signed a couple of new endorsements. Got a chance to go to my old church and even visited some friends back on campus.

What sucked about making the playoffs that year was that I wasn't able to support the rest of my brothers at home or Michigan. They were in the tournament, and I was praying that they would win it all. But Jimmy, Ray, Juwan, and Jalen lost to the eventual champs, the Arkansas Razorbacks, with President Clinton cheering on his team, in the Elite Eight, 76–68. It was the end of an era as Juwan and Jalen declared for the league.

Irony would peek its head out. Syracuse, the seventh seed, advanced to the second round and had a chance to win in the last seconds of regulation when Arkansas inbounded the ball. Syracuse deflected the inbound pass, and after a scramble, Lawrence Moten got the ball and called a time-out. But Syracuse was out of time-outs. Arkansas tied the game and later won in overtime. My parents immediately got in touch with the kid and his family to support them. I thought that was cool. They didn't even let me know. That's just who they are. I played with Lawrence later on, and he told me how much he appreciated it.

I opted out of my fifteen-year contract. It should not have been a surprise to anyone; it was just business. So, after my successful rookie campaign, I was a free agent. My agents were in constant contact with the Warriors brass, discussing a new contract. I went back to Oakland in late August to start working out with the fellas. Then talks stalled. We were at a standstill. I wasn't in on any conversations, so I can only repeat what my agents told me. But, for the record, I wanted to play for the Golden State Warriors. I wanted to retire in Oakland. I loved the fact that Alvin Attles, the Warriors great, came to practices. I loved our team. I'd only played for a few teams in my life, so I wasn't used to change.

I talked to my agents about working it out, but they told me that it wouldn't be a good decision financially. It would be tough to go back and play for a coach who didn't want me. I guess we were too far gone. I would've gone back and played for almost nothing; that's how green I was. I felt bad. I didn't know what was happening, and I was missing training camp.

✦ ✦ ✦

I did a terrible television interview with Craig Sager. I got upset and felt like I was being persecuted. Dr. Harry Edwards, a Cal professor, civil rights activist, friend, and mentor, gave me support, verbalizing what I couldn't express or hadn't even thought of. The Warriors' owners came to my house and told me personally that they were going to let me leave as a free agent. They had to choose Nellie over me. I didn't know that it had to be one or the other.

Nellie whispered to reporters and others that I was a malcontent. He told them that we didn't get along, that I wouldn't listen. This would backfire, because the players supported me and disagreed with my leaving the team. It would also come to light later, when he coached the New York Knicks and other veteran teams, that Nellie would lie about his players and try to manipulate situations. He played owner against player and wanted total control. The owners told me that they didn't believe a word of the accusations, but they had made a commitment to the coach. I was crushed, but I understood. I thanked them, but I also made it clear that I wanted to stay and that they were going to regret their decision. More fuel for me.

I saw Mully at a gas station and brought him up to speed. He told me to keep my head. I was beside myself. He told me that was part of the business. He said, "Prove them wrong. I'm pulling for you."

I got a chance to speak to Spree and Billy O. as well. They were mad. I could see this becoming a problem for the Warriors in the future. These guys knew me and had raised me that rookie year; they knew my heart and my intentions and were pissed that I had been made out to be the villain. I sensed that the one characteristic that held the team together had been lost with my exit. Trust. Everyone now felt that Nellie's mission statement was a lie. I figured that I was just the first domino to fall.

So I was the reigning Rookie of the Year, in the middle of training camp, with no team. I made a list of teams that I would play for and gave it to my agent. I don't remember all the teams on my list, but one team stuck out: the Washington Bullets. Washington was a notorious league cellar dweller, best known for having the league's tallest player, Manute Bol, and its shortest player, Muggsy Bogues. The previous year they had posted a 24–58 record. Wes Unseld had just stepped down as coach. A guard-heavy team, their leading scorers were Calbert Cheaney, Don MacLean, Rex Chapman, and Tom Gugliotta. There was one reason that I wanted to play for the Bullets: Juwan Howard. My boy, my brother, my dog was drafted fifth overall that summer by DC. He was the only person I knew in the league besides my former teammates in the Bay.

After high school and college, all I wanted to do was be around family, friends, and people I trusted. I also knew Juwan and I would play well together. I knew we would enjoy the experience. I knew I could depend on him. I knew we could turn around any organization. So, after being aggressively recruited by several teams, I chose to go to Chocolate City, Washington, DC. I didn't know if I would like the city, but I fell in love with it right away. In this international urban jungle, I would find the jewel of my life and make lifelong friends.

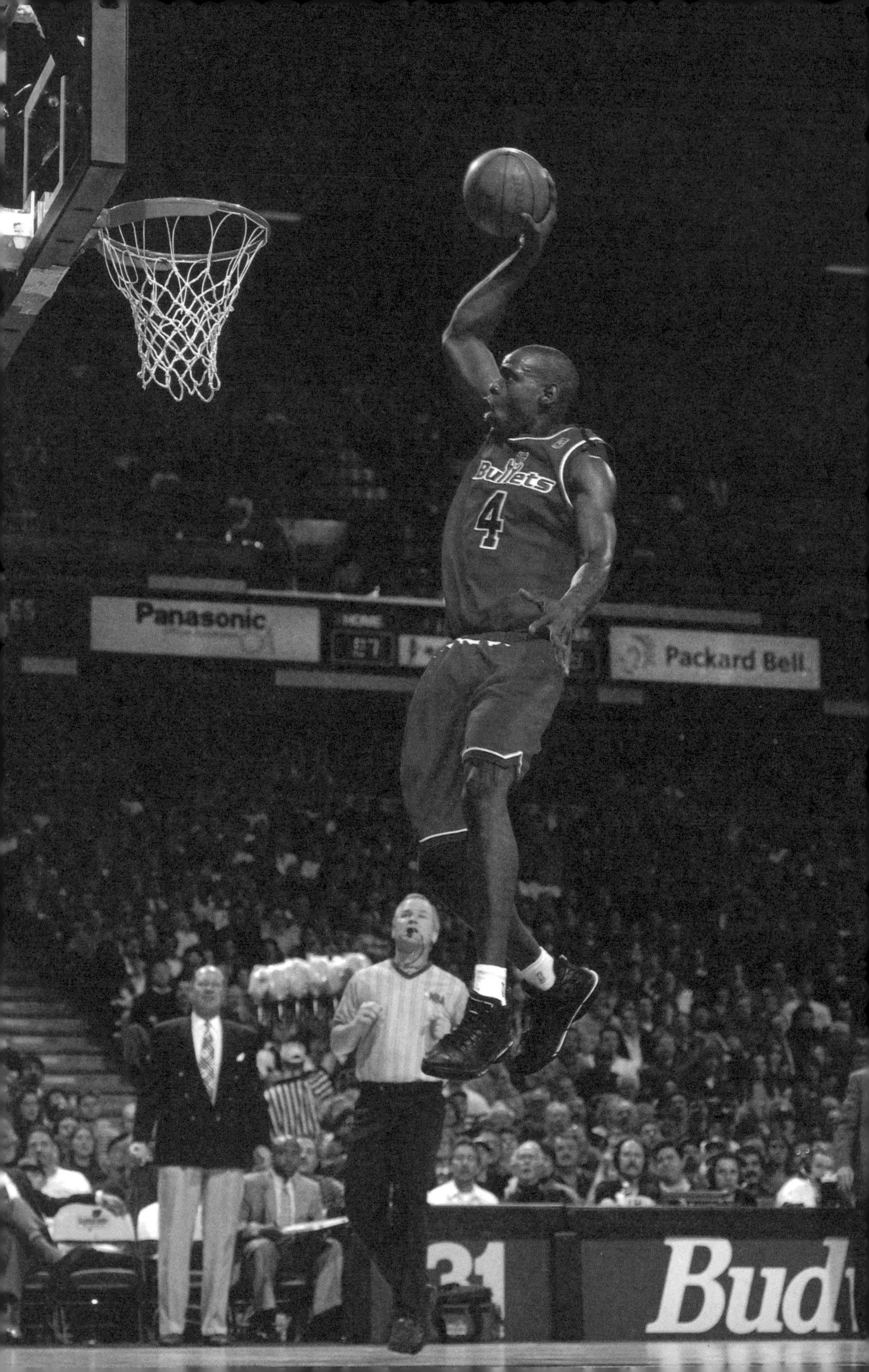
Bullets
4
Panasonic
Packard Bell
Bud

Chapter 61

At Home in DC

I was at a point in my life where I wanted to expand, learn, and experience, and DC was the place for that. I started to curate my African American historical collection in DC. The culture made it easy. I was always attending an auction or visiting a museum or historical site. I loved the culture that DC afforded. From Potomac to Georgetown, the restaurants, the concerts, and the nightlife seemed tailor-made for me. I used to hang out at Blues Alley, a small jazz club where I sat in a dark corner and watched Rachelle Ferrell, Will Downing, Roy Ayers, and other musical greats perform.

Of course, there was a mind-set of political self-awareness in the city that reminded me of home, and I felt my mother's presence encouraging me to embrace the moment. I did the restaurants and museums and even sponsored some political events to encourage awareness of the multiple issues affecting the black community. I also had a chance to increase my business acumen. I became friends with a few local business leaders, who served as mentors. I respect entrepreneurs, businessmen, and businesswomen. I think there are characteristics that transcend sport or business and are shared by people who are successful in any genre: prioritizing, self-discipline, organizational skills, remaining focused during setbacks, managing different personalities, making tough decisions, meeting timelines, showing up early and staying late, thinking of the big picture, thinking on the fly, and being steady, trustworthy, and dependable.

I really matured in Washington as an individual, but I would definitely have some bumps along the way. First, I had to deal with the realization that I would not experience the same health and success on the court that I had in years past. The Washington Bullets left a lot to be desired. I should have probably checked on the little things before I signed with them, but I just wanted to play with Big Nook. I'd take that over the amenities offered by the best teams. Still, Juwan and I had our work cut out for us, but we loved almost every minute. Thank God for our fans. During my time in Washington, we would reach sixth in league attendance.

There was a lot of fanfare upon my arrival in Washington. They flew me to my first practice in a helicopter because they wanted me to have a press conference in DC. I just wanted to go to practice. I don't think it was fair to Juwan. He was the number-five pick in that year's draft, and that alone was cause for celebration. He was a gifted power forward who could score in many different ways, and defensively he was among the best in the game. He was a born professional. He's always been a man of character, a consummate pro. During that year, he became the first NBA player to graduate on time with his class after leaving college early to play in the NBA. He was disciplined like that.

That was one of the reasons why I wanted to play with him. I learned so much from him and enjoyed so much with him. He was someone who understood where I was from and what I had been through and appreciated the moments as much as I did. Those were some of the best times. But it still wasn't fair to him. I didn't call him to tell him I was gonna do it. I just planned it. Looking back, I should have given him the heads up. Let him make the decision as to whether or not it would be good if we played together. I mean, I wanted to go off and forge my own identity; why wouldn't he want to do the same? I took it for granted as a friend that it would be cool. Thank God it worked out for the both of us. We were closer than ever, except now we had money in our pocket and options. Juwan bought a big house in Potomac. I remember the first time I went to see him. I felt so many emotions:

1. *I almost died laughing like, "Hell naw. Who are you to think you can live this nice?"*

2. *"Damn, this place is crazy. Only Juwan would have this style. It's dope."*

3. *"Most people will come over here and think you had it easy. I know your grandmother is in heaven smiling."*

Once I settled in, I borrowed one of his classic Porsches all the time. We went everywhere together—restaurants, clubs, and our favorite comedy spot, Takoma Station. Sometimes, even when we went out separately, we'd end up sitting side by side at different tables with different groups. Our friendship was real. Our friends were friends, our families were family. There was never any jealousy off the court, not with women, material things, agents, gossip, nothing. Nothing petty, no competing for basketball dominance. We were truly brothers. I didn't care about low team expectations, because I thought we could surpass all those together.

He's one of the best, if not the best, passing big men I've ever played with. He used to give me two to three easy buckets a game. He could read a play before it would develop. We had experience and chemistry, having known and played with each other for six years. We would go at it in practice against each other as we tried to change the team culture from accepting losing to embracing growth. We would challenge the other guys to play hard for us, the team. They bought in. We knew the odds were stacked against us; we were a young team in a veteran league. We were used to that. Michael Jordan's Bulls were dominating, and Patrick Ewing and the Knicks were in position to try to challenge for the Eastern Conference title. We wanted to make a name for ourselves as a young, hungry team on the rise. We played hard and were exciting.

I was geeked to get the season started, but because of contract negotiations, I missed the first seven games. Despite that, I got off to a good start. The fans were loud and loyal. We had a nice home court presence, even though we didn't win much. Coach Jim Lynam, a short, energetic, funny man, was our coach. He pissed fire. He'd fight a giant in a second with his short self. He had heart. I liked him. He had the trust of the team, and we played hard for him even with little success. One of the hardest things in coaching is keeping your players believing and respecting you as a coach during a losing season. You start looking for signs that the team has its head and heart in the right place. Is the locker room healthy? Do the guys practice hard and share the ball in games? We did. Small victories.

SUPPLY AND DEMAND

I'm not superstitious, but I was pissed at Scott Skiles, who held my number 4 jersey hostage. The number was special to me. It was a cross between Derrick Coleman, who wore number 44, and my best friend in high school, Kevin, who wore number 4. I wore the number because I wanted to be a big that had the skill set of a small, and a small number represented that. Skiles didn't even want the number. He told me I could have it for $200,000. Supply and demand. I didn't even respond. So number two it was. I think that this is when I solidified my reputation as a bad boy.

◆ ◆ ◆

Three days before Christmas, we were in Oakland for a game with my old squad. A Bay Area radio station held a contest for the best-dressed babies, since I was a baby for leaving the Bay. Get it? Contestants were judged, and the winners received tickets to the Warriors-Bullets game. People came to the arena in diapers sucking on big bottles. They looked ridiculous. When I came out to warm up, I had to laugh at the creativity of these jackoffs.

There had been a lot in the media around this game. Stories had been told over and over about my friendship with the veterans who took me under their wing. I'd been asked over and over if I missed the guys. "What exactly did Mully teach you about basketball?" "Do you miss going to the gym late night with Spree?" "How many times have you spoken with Billy O. this week?" I was tired of the questions, but looking back, I guess it was a pretty big deal. The team had traded for the number-one pick and not only lost that player but also the three draft picks that they traded for the pick. I didn't think about it in those terms. I thought about it in terms of, Why would you let me go? I still didn't know what the problem had been. But that night, it didn't matter. I was going to make them feel regret. I was going to send all those loyal fans home unhappy. I would do my talking on the hardwood. The message was going out loud and clear to Golden State ownership, executives, and coaches.

When I walked onto the court, I was treated to some of the loudest boos I'd ever heard. I expected it. I wished I could explain my side, but that wouldn't have mattered. As I hugged Spree and Billy O., the boos got louder, like they were saying "Don't touch our guy, don't hug him."

I knew this pissed them off. I loved to mess with the crowd. Why not? They messed with me. Unfortunately, the crowd had the last laugh, as I missed a dunk and then dove on the floor for a loose ball and tore ligaments and dislocated my shoulder. As I lay on the floor in pain, I thought, *You've gotta be kidding me!* I'd never been hurt for any serious period of time. As the trainer walked me off the court, the crowd booed. That was low. I'll be back.

It took the doctors twenty minutes to put my shoulder back in place, as the muscles had tightened around the socket. Two guys had to lie on the ground and yank my arm as I lay face down on the training table. I was in a lot of pain, but I went out on the bench and sat with my team. However, that became a distraction for our team, which was getting blown out at this point. Fans were more interested in talking trash to our bench than in watching the game. I was hurting anyway. This would be the first of many injuries I endured over a long career.

The game took place on December 22, and I didn't return until February 3. In my first year with the Bullets, we went 21–61. I played fifty-four games and had a few triple-doubles and averaged twenty points, 9.6 rebounds, and nearly five assists per game. The only thing that kept me halfway going was watching my boy Juwan handle his business on the court. He was going to work.

◆ ◆ ◆

On the home front, my mother finally picked out a beautiful house in Farmington Hills, Michigan. It was worth the wait. It was the perfect hub for our large and ever-expanding family. We'd spend hours playing in the pool, or walking the many acres, or making a pallet and sleeping on the floor. That house gave me a sense of completion. After thirty-five years in the factory and thirty in the Detroit public school system, respectively, Moms and Pops retired. I tried to buy my childhood home from Pops, but he said the house wasn't for sale.

One of the most memorable moments of the next season would come almost exactly a year after my shoulder injury. We traveled back to Oakland to face Golden State. The game was not memorable: I scored twenty-six points, but we lost, 132–117. I finally got my revenge in a game against my former team five days later, in front of my home crowd. Juwan sat in the locker room next to me before the game and whispered, "You know I got you, right?" I just gave him a pound. That was all I needed to hear. He knew I wanted to win against my old team. He knew we weren't as talented as them, but that night we were going to be better. The little things are the biggest things among friends.

Juwan had twenty-four points, ten rebounds, and five assists. He was throwing oops, leading the break, knocking down jump hooks and jumpers. I went H.A.M. I started off the game hitting my first nine shots. I finished with forty points, three of four from three-point range, along with ten rebounds and ten assists. We routed my old team 115–94. It felt great. The small victories allow you to concentrate on the missions ahead. All year, I had tried to avoid Don Nelson and any comments he made or "may have made." The media ran story after story about young, rich athletes, the changing of cultures, and the age of the free agent. Reporters told me how Nellie was blaming me and calling me a malcontent off the record. I hated the idea that he was attacking my character, but what was I going to do? Call a press conference? Troll him through the media?

No. There are certain battles that may appear lost. But they are not. You can't always address everything, such as someone with a lie and a platform. There are only a couple of options. Worry and get thrown off track trying to control what someone is saying about you, or focus on the task at hand, allow time to build a case, and use it as fuel for doing what you need to do. I would not let Nellie throw me off my rhythm or make me change who I was. I was not going to let lies make me bitter. I would not reduce myself by catering to gossip. What would I have gained by doing so? Respect? Honor? From whom, and for what? No, that wasn't me. He knew it.

After we gave the Warriors the business, a ball boy came over to me in the locker room and told me Nellie wanted to see me out in the hall. My first reaction was "Yeah, right!" Then, after grabbing my stuff, I walked toward the tunnel that houses the visiting team's buses. There he was standing in the hall, coming in my direction.

"Webb, I'm sorry, man. It never should have gone that way," he said. "I'm sorry. You know I did a lot to get you. We all miss you; you're a good kid."

"Thanks. No worries, Coach."

"Tell your parents I said hi."

That was it—short and sweet. I never talked about it to the press, even though he said some shady stuff later. Like 'Pac says, "You and I know what's going on." That's my father in me. I'm not one for a bunch of talking or hand holding when we know the situation. I let it go.

I'm glad I had a chance to let that go, because several days later, I dislocated my shoulder again. At the end of the previous season, I knew I should've had surgery, but the team strongly suggested otherwise.

I disagreed, and even went to see an independent doctor for a second opinion. But in the end, I folded and listened, and I paid for it that season. My shoulder kept popping out. Sometimes it would pop out while I was tying a shoe. I had put in so much work over the summer, but by the end of the season, I only got to run in fifteen games, averaging twenty-four points, eight rebounds, and five assists. I was twenty-two years old, and I had missed ninety-five out of a possible 246 regular-season games. More than one full season missed due to injury. I was bummed, bored, and depressed.

However, things weren't all bad in DC that year. The best thing about playing for the Bullets was meeting E. A pretty young teacher in Baltimore, she was at a charity event with a man I assumed was her father. I zeroed my ass right over and introduced myself to him, and then to his daughter, Erika. She was everything. Beautiful, taught in the 'hood, only wanted to help her community, and loved her father, who raised her. She had graduated from Morgan State (an HBCU) and had the self-knowledge to match. She loved music and food and was a true bohemian. We dated for a very short time, but she never left my heart.

I was going through it knowing that my brothers Jeff, Jason, and David were in high school starting their careers and I was missing it. But they weren't missing me on the court. Jeff earned a reputation as a lockdown defender (Rodman was his favorite player) at Bishop Borgess High School. David and Jason were winning their first of three state championships at Country Day. They played with great player and family friend Shane Battier. I was impressed with their group; they were disciplined, God-fearing, and mature beyond their years. Jason was an athletic small forward, and Dave was a big point guard who could lock down and score. I stayed in touch and got the rundown from family. It was killing me not to be there, let alone missing my little ladybug Rachel. I had to stay focused.

Chapter 62

Melancholy is the happiness of being sad.

—Victor Hugo

It seemed like it was one thing after another. After leaving Golden State, it was as if the clouds had opened and poured down a harsh reality. No matter how much you accumulate, you still can't change the outcome in others' lives. Times when you thought that money could make thigs better, you start to experience grown man pain caused by curve balls thrown your way. The events that sobered my every smile would start when Larenda, my close neighbor, first crush, and friend since childhood, was murdered. She was locked inside of her house, which was then set on fire. Only five houses down and across the street from our hut. I went home to the house and saw the charred doors. I imagined her running, screaming, searching for a way out as flames surrounded, then engulfed, her beautiful body. She couldn't have been more than twenty-four or twenty-five. I was devastated. We all were.

Shortly after, word got out that Kubo, my old band leader who'd been arrested for armed robbery, and was coming to the end of his eight-year sentence, had done the unthinkable. He broke out of jail. We all questioned why someone with so little time left would risk getting caught, only to serve more time. Well, allegedly, Kubo escaped, fled, and made it to a busy K-Mart parking lot. He planned on stealing a car. I never asked where he was planning to drive. He went up to the vehicle of an elderly man and yelled something to the effect of "Give me your keys, old man!" The man looked at him with shock and fear, then had a heart attack on the spot. Dropped dead. Kubo was charged with murder. He had a year or two left on his sentence, and now had to spend the rest of his life in prison. I felt sorry for his family and, of course, the family of the elderly man that lost their loved one. I felt awful for Wes, now my brother Jeff's best friend. I didn't know what to do.

Rule #1: Money Can't Buy Peace

I spent the rest of the summer rehabilitating my left shoulder. I did take time out to do a little acting on a popular show called *New York Undercover*. I had a good time filming. I even got to die. It was funny. I got stabbed while in jail taking a murder rap for my younger brother. Something I would definitely do. One fact is that my sister, who was twelve, watched it at home and cried when I died because she thought it was real. Second, I think this show was Taye Diggs's first TV gig. I laugh every time I see him on TV or in the movies because I brought the best out of him and made his career. HA!

But weeks after shooting, my world would be rocked with terrible news. My mother called me and said softly, "Your grandfather passed away." I don't remember much after that except the funeral, and we turned that mutha' out. My siblings and I sobbed in unison. We went on so loud and long that the preacher had to cut his sermon short, saying, "When you die and someone—specifically, your grandkids—don't mourn you like this, you haven't lived. We can tell a lot about this man by how he is loved." Amen.

Losing my grandfather did something to me. The other incidents in my life affected me—disloyal friends, constant calls to bail someone out of debt (I hadn't learned to say no), untimely deaths, the time-out—but the death of my grandfather sent me into a deep depression. I spent time with my mom, who nursed me back to health after my surgery, but besides that, I kept to myself. Even when I had my boys at the crib, I was still alone in the midst of company. I couldn't wait to get back on the court.

◆ ◆ ◆

I went to visit Mike Tyson in prison. I think I did it for myself as much as I did for him. I just wanted to encourage him and let him know that there were people rooting for him on the outside. He was convicted to prison for six years in 1992 for rape. I had to get special permission from the governor to visit him at the Indiana Youth Center, which was a state prison facility. When I went inside, I remember thinking this place was cold and no place for a champ.

Mike was in good spirits, but drastically overweight. We spoke about peace, music, race, meditation, and spirituality. Through all he had been through, it seemed like he was actually in a good place. I had a good time and a great conversation with the champ, and it was worth all the logistical trouble.

I had so much time on my hands. I would come home from shoulder rehabilitation and have nothing to do the rest of the day. Kev moved in with me. He experienced a terrible situation at Florida A&M University. Kev had a good freshman year in the conference and was having a successful college career, but the basketball program was thrown into disarray after crazy allegations were levied against his coach. The school's solution was to replace the coach of the basketball team with the head football coach. Kev's dream of playing professionally was shattered. I suggested he come move to DC, which he did. It was great having my best friend around. He was friends with Juwan's best friend Juice as well. He completed the family. I really can't explain how I was affected by the shoulder injury.

Trying to fill your time with something constructive at age twenty-two was tough. I isolated myself from my family. I'd go months without calling home, got a group of new friends, and stayed to myself. I lived vicariously through all my boys. It helped to keep out of shit, but I lived it through them, so I was in it, too.

The thing about a "crew" is the fact that one man must take on the responsibility of the group from time to time. This assignment can wear you down and exhaust you mentally. I had damn near half of Detroit with me in DC. They never distracted me from basketball, but it's hard to concentrate on self-improvement with five or six guys around all the time. I felt like I was giving them an opportunity to see something different and eat and go places they normally wouldn't be able to experience. They served as a camouflage and distraction as to what I was avoiding. Scared of being hurt, and not being valuable on the court.

I used the downtime in both good and bad ways. On the good side, I opened a gym. I convinced partners of a young upstart (and now very large) gym company to allow me to open a gym in a local mall. I argued that if they would allow me to design the gym for young athletes, I could build something successful. They afforded me the opportunity, and I designed the space to make sure that shoppers would pass by and look through a large glass wall and see our members working out or playing basketball. The idea worked so well the gym was a success, and the mall's revenue increased.

Then one morning, on the way to practice, I was speeding and didn't have my license. When I was pulled over, I told the officer my name and that I had left my wallet in my bag at home. After about an hour, the officer informed me that my truck was stolen. I told him that couldn't be true— I had paid cash for it. He asked me to get out of the car. I refused. I was on the phone with my agent, who was taping the conversation. When I was first pulled over, I called my agent and asked him to call the team and tell them I'd be late. I also asked him to record the conversation.

Not all cops are bad, but the ones that are have power. I knew some of the good ones, and they told me to watch out for the bad ones. They alerted me when I first moved to DC to watch out for the ones who would follow you home from restaurants, games, and events. They told me that a certain number of officers wanted to make a name for themselves in this political city with a big arrest.

The officer sprayed me in the face multiple times with pepper spray, and I couldn't breathe. He then pulled me out of my car and onto the ground with his foot on my face. I could feel the traffic whizzing by. I understood it right away—it was a power thing. After a trial and an admonishment from the judge to the officer for being caught in lies, I was acquitted. But it's still no fun fighting for your good name. Retractions are always in fine print. But all things work together for good. There was only one black lawyer in the courtroom, and that inspired me to make a commitment to empowering more black and brown youth to become lawyers.

I kept active so I wouldn't have time to feel. I was dealing with injury. Death. I was in a place that was attracting all this to me. Not that I was guilty or anything like that, but it reflected my mind state, which was negative, clouded, and unproductive. It seemed to be incident after incident piling up, so I took a step back. I cleared out my personal space, unclogged my mind, and focused on positivity and hoops. I made a decision to only keep positive spirits around me. I changed everything from my diet to my daily rituals, to what time I woke up, to scheduling time for reading. I was focused on the best in life. I had a positive boost of encouragement come from an unlikely source: Mike Tyson.

Later, Mike had been out of jail for some time but was suspended and couldn't fight. One day, I was sitting in my basement, and Kev came downstairs and said, "Mike Tyson is at the door." I told him, "Don't answer it." I then went into my safe room, where I could see the house from all different angles, and I saw Iron Mike sitting on the porch looking into the surveillance camera. I couldn't hear what he said, but it seemed like he was mouthing, "I know you're in there." I really didn't want any company. I didn't want conversation or encouragement. I wanted to be left alone. The champ was persistent. He stayed on the porch for over half an hour.

I felt so bad; I didn't even have an excuse like I didn't know he was at the door. When I opened the door, he just laughed. He said, "I know what you're going through. You can do what you want to do. I'm going through the same thing." He talked to me about how he was still training. Specifically, about this five-mile hill that he had a love-hate relationship with. He loved the hill because he wasn't going to let it beat him. He hated the hill because of what it put him through, and he loved the hill because of the motivation that it offered. We played a couple of games of pool, and I talked boxing with him for a couple hours. I will always remember his sincerity and kindness. I also remember having a sneak peek at his fury. One time when he was talking, he got pumped up and started throwing punches. Six-inch punches in front of my face. It was exhilarating and scary as hell. If one of those punches came an inch closer, I'd need a hospital. Mike is a good man.

I fell in love with reading at an early age. During this hard time, books became my therapy. Paulo Coelho's *The Alchemist*. *The Prophet* by Kahlil Gibran. *The Seven Spiritual Laws of Success* by Deepak Chopra. *The Purpose Driven Life* by Rick Warren, and other books by Coelho. I'd read the work of philosophers, such as Marcus Aurelius, Alain LeRoy Locke, Epicurus, Seneca, and Niccolò Machiavelli. I also read the Bible every night.

I ramped up my charity efforts. Over time, I helped raise millions of dollars for charities around the world. I traveled, studied, and worked with many cultures in various countries. I wanted to help whenever needed, and DC gave me the chance to do that within the hectic professional basketball schedule.

I also started my African American artifact collection in DC. Originally these artifacts were in my home, until friends at one of those charitable dinners encouraged me to let them travel on exhibit. Though my collection has changed and expanded over time, my favorites remain the same:

- *A handwritten postcard from Malcolm X to Alex Haley dated February 19, 1965. This was during the time Malcolm was visiting Mecca on a spiritual journey and Alex Haley was writing Malcolm's autobiography. On the cover of the postcard is a monkey in red shorts blowing a kiss. Malcolm writes on the back, "One hundred years after the Civil War, and these chimpanzees get more recognition, respect, and freedom in America than our people do." I had to laugh when I read it. The reason why I love this card is because of the time that it symbolizes. Malcolm X had just been kicked out of the Nation of Islam. In his biography, Malcolm referred to his time in Mecca as an awakening. An epiphany that involved loving everyone.*

- *Another favorite is from Toussaint L'Ouverture, a passport for the schooner Assistance out of Philadelphia and commanded by Captain Daniel Man, circa 1800. The reason I love this so much is because of who Toussaint was and what he did. He was born into slavery, loved reading (supposedly the writings of Julius Caesar and Alexander the Great), helped defeat British forces as a general, freed the imprisoned French governor general, and helped drive the English from Saint-Dominique. Napoleon Bonaparte hated Toussaint but wrote a note asking the general to come to France and guaranteeing his safety. Unfortunately, the guarantee was a lie, and after being lured to France, Toussaint was kidnapped at a dinner and held on a French warship. He died of cold and starvation on April 7, 1803. One year later, Haiti proclaimed its independence.*

- *My third favorite is from* Phillis Wheatley, Poems on Various Subjects, Religious and Moral, *first edition, London, 1773. I love this book because of its age. It represents not only freedom of mind and expression but also the pursuit of happiness. I use it as a prop when I speak at schools. I start off by saying, "Boys are smarter than girls, right?" All the boys raise their hands and yell in agreement, and the girls boo. I then tell everyone about Phillis Wheatley and what she had to endure.*

Born into slavery in North Africa, transported to North America, and purchased by a family in Boston, she was taught to read and write by her slave masters. At age twelve, she was reading Greek and Latin classics. In 1773, she wrote her first poem at the age of fourteen. At twenty she decided to publish her poetry. No one believed that a black person, let alone a black woman, could write such complex and beautiful passages. John Hancock himself made her recite paragraphs as proof that she was capable of writing such a masterpiece. I then bring the class back to the present, and I compare racism with gender inequality. It seems to make a little more sense to the kids. They understand that everyone is capable of accomplishing great things if given the opportunity matched with hard work.

I have other pieces in my collection. One of the nicest is a suit that James Brown wore in one of his last performances. In my opinion, James Brown and Michael Jackson are the best entertainers who have ever graced the planet. The kids get a kick out of seeing all the glitter and detail on the suit. They also love the videos of the Godfather of Soul dancing, and love listening to his music and interviews with him explaining funk. Sharing all this, I was rediscovering myself and the parts of my childhood that I didn't appreciate at the time. I used to consider going to the museums

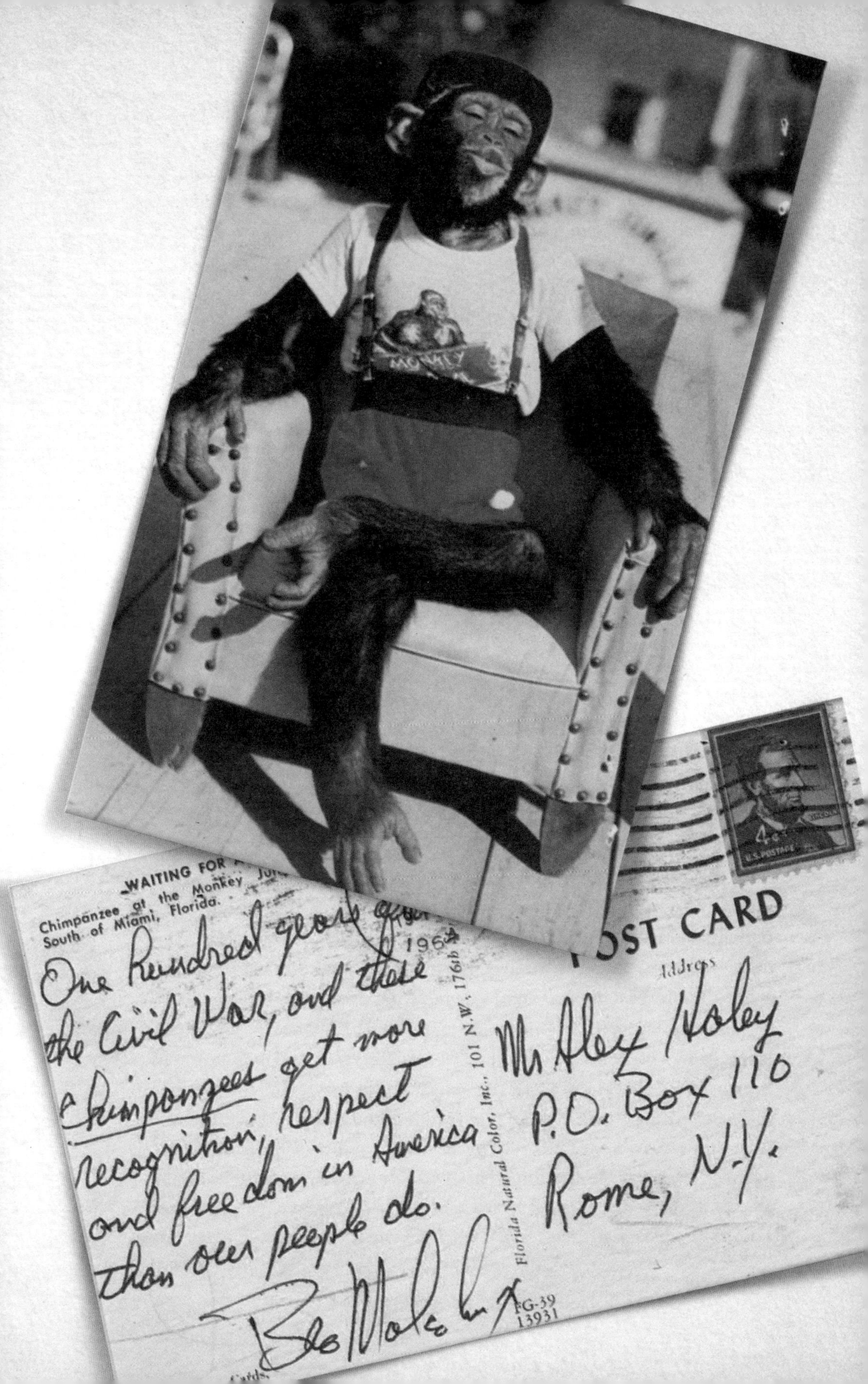
MONKEY
WAITING FOR A
Chimpanzee at the Monkey Jun
South of Miami, Florida.
One hundred years
the Civil War, and these
chimpanzees get more
recognition, respect
and freedom in America
than our people do.
Bro Malcolm X
Florida Natural Color, Inc., 101 N.W. 176th
FG-39
13931
POST CARD
Address
Mr Alex Haley
P.O. Box 110
Rome, N.Y.
U.S. POSTAGE
4c

with my mother a drag. Her conversations on black history felt more like unwanted lessons than an informative conversation. I took for granted all the knowledge and culture that I was receiving daily.

Every day was Black History Month in our family. My mother had us write papers on the great kings and queens, inventors, scientists, and doctors of Africa. She tested us on what was found in King Tut's tomb. She would relate our personal areas of interest to a great black pioneer who came before us. For example, she nicknamed my brother Jeff "Matthew" because he liked to explore. She told him, "You can be a great explorer like Matthew Henson. He sailed around the world and spoke many different languages. He codiscovered the North Pole. Can you imagine how much fun it must've been for him to go to the North Pole and see something that no one had ever described to him? I can see you doing that!" She was wonderful.

The older you get, the more you both appreciate and emulate your parents. I think I will always collect and always share my collection with others. You never know what influence you are having on someone. Thank God for positive people who reinforced the principles that my parents taught me, self-awareness and pride in the past. Things I live by.

I t was an event that I can't wait to tell my son and daughter about. It is infamous, iconic. It was an instant classic and now timeless. It will forever stay dope!

It took place in New York. The year was 1995, and the event was the was second annual Source Awards. I was there to present an award, but I ended up with the perfect view for all the happenings.

The night would be remembered as one of the most identifiable moments in the well-dissected East and West Coast beef, but to me and many others, it was the greatest collection of hip-hop artists and performances ever witnessed. It was a hip-hop head's dream that can never be duplicated.

It was raw. Kev and I couldn't believe all our favorite artists were there in this small venue, just walking around crewed up. There was no visible security, but everyone I gave dap to was obviously strapped. It was a party—everyone was drinking and smoking during this live taping. Wu-Tang had a hundred people in their own section. Death Row had a section. Kev and I sat behind Biggie and Lil' Cease passing bottles and smoke back and forth in their section. We were front and center for a legendary performance by all the Death Row artists.

DJ Quik performed "Dollaz + Sense" (a diss song about MC Eiht) live while he stood in front of MC Eiht, spittin' right to him. He started it off by saying, "I'm going to dedicate this to my fiancé, MC Eiht."

Biggie did a medley of his album, and Lil' Kim stole the show. For me and Kev, this was like going to WWF's WrestleMania.

After they won the "Best New Rap Group," André 3000 of Outcast said, "I'm tired of all these close-minded folk . . . The South got somethin' to say."

It was the energy of the culture at the time. I felt him. Not because I was from the South, but because he was speaking for the frustrated underdog.

Suge Knight, head of Death Row Records, famously, said, "Any artist out there that wants to be an artist and wants to stay a star and don't want the producer to be all in the videos dancin', come to Death Row." A direct shot at Puffy. Snoop asked the crowd if we had any love for Dr. Dre and Snoop Dogg. He was hard. It was him against the world as he said, "You ain't got no love for Snoop Dogg and Death Row? Let it be known, then."

After that moment, I presented the award for "Solo Artist of the Year" with Puffy and Faith Evans . . . to Snoop. I'm on stage thinking, Damn, what the fuck just happened? And what's about to happen? Puff didn't run from any comments. He squashed it and shared love with the West. Snoop was Snoop. He was smooth.

Industry Rule #4,080

I started making beats my sophomore year. Jason, aka Maji, showed me the ropes, and KG, the DJ for Naughty By Nature, would tighten up my skills. Making beats was something that relaxed me. It was therapeutic and something I could do late nights after a long road trip or nights when I couldn't sleep because I couldn't come down, still hyped from a game. I love music, and I would spend hours at record stores or even in someone's garage looking through boxes off of a tip.

Maji was half of the Detroit rap duo Kaos & Mystro. I was a fan of their music, and I met him and would see him at the club during his DJ set. I would freestyle and ask him about beats and etc., and he showed me the ropes. His beats to this day are some of the dopest I've heard. I visited KG in the summers at his home in East Orange, New Jersey. He threw the best barbecues, pool parties, and pickup games. He was close with his family like I was, and going to stay with him was like a fresh retreat. I'd chill in his pool and relax with his fam during the day and at night we'd hit the streets. Him, his brother, group members, and friends. We even went on *The Arsenio Hall Show* together.

I saw some of R&B's best groups come together in K's basement. Jane' and Next would form under his leadership. I'll always have love for K's parents and his brothers, Face, Pookie, and Mook, along with Vin, Treach, and all of 118th Street.

I had a state-of-the-art recording studio in the basement of my place in DC and would let groups record if they would listen to a few of my beats. I wanted to produce, and there was a rap group in Detroit named No Coast. We became friends, and I was pitching this group to different labels and getting a lot of positive feedback. But at the end of meetings, the label reps would always ask me if I was still rapping. Finally, one label exec called and said that I should come out with an album and then introduce No Coast to all my fans. I agreed, and I actually made a dope album, *2 Much Drama*, on my label, Humility Records. I had a song with a sample from Erykah Badu singing, "The world keeps burning." Method Man was in that video. I had a song featuring my man Kurupt called "Gangsta Gangsta." The album was dope for its time. Shaq's album showed us that if you put something dope out, the people will support it.

However, I was supposed to be trying to win a championship, and in the midst of turmoil and injury, the last thing I wanted to do was to put out an album. I didn't want to live in that energy. A month before the release date, I called my lawyers, managers, and agent and told them not to release the album. Days before shipping and release, the project was trashed.

Chapter 65

T he next season we drafted Rasheed Wallace with the fourth overall pick in the draft. I was excited. Rasheed was a seven-footer who could run, shoot, and loved to play D. All I could think about was the potential of 'Sheed, Juwan and me. We could switch everything on defense, pass, post up, or space the floor. I thought we could have a tall starting lineup. I loved his passion too. I was excited I'd have someone to throw alley-oops too.

Then the business of basketball intervened. After only sixty-five games, we ended up trading him to Portland for Rod Strickland. It was tough because I hated losing 'Sheed, but I loved playing with "Strict 9," who led the league in assists with us. Tim Legler, a three-point shooting two-guard, also reached a milestone. The flamethrower led the league in three-point percentage. We embraced the small victories because we damned sure took our lumps in the Jordan era.

I realized in DC that I had to improve my game to sustain and surpass in this league. I was now expected to lead us to victory, I didn't have any vets to rely on, and the Bullets hadn't been to the playoffs since 1987–88. I knew that I could use my quickness and athletic ability against forwards and centers, but I also had the opportunity, playing with Juwan and a seven-foot-seven Gheorghe Mureşan, to space the floor, knock down the jumper, and pass it inside on duck-ins.

I started working with a shooting coach named Buzz Braman. Back then, it wasn't cool for a big man in the NBA to shoot jumpers, let alone threes. Even though I could space the floor and beat my man with my quickness, conventional wisdom said I should get closer to the basket—which gave the less-athletic defender less space to cover, taking away my advantage.

We started with free throws. In order to have lasting impact, I had to be able to hit free throws late in the game. I had to make defenders pay when they used fouls as a last resort. My hard work at the line paid off. I'd have the largest improvement in free-throw percentage in NBA history the following season: from 45.4 percent to 75 percent. I was proud of that because I worked

hard and long to achieve it. We spent hours in the gym and watching video of my moves and other players' moves.

We worked on shooting off the catch, off the dribble, off two then three, off the combo of four or five dribbles. Shooting off of bad passes or good passes. Through it all, I was steadily improving. And the better an offensive player I was, the better passer I could become. You can always use your IQ to gain an advantage, but it makes it easier if your defender goes for every pump fake and jab step because he knows you're capable of scoring at any time. Just as in high school and college, I wanted to make my teammates better by getting them shots in their spots and by building trust. Whenever I had the ball, my teammates could cut hard looking for the pass. Oftentimes it could be unrewarding—making a cut five times and only receiving the pass once—but if you cut, you must cut with integrity.

I was obsessed. I didn't want love, money, or recognition. I wanted to win. I sacrificed a lot of friendships at that time, and I'm blessed that my family lived through those selfish days of me chasing the hoop dragon.

Meanwhile, my father and I did a Nike and Coca-Cola commercial together. I was proud of my pops; he always wanted to be an actor. So I gave him his shot.

Speaking of shot, my father would also bring the house down with a once-in-a-lifetime shot at the MCI Center. The Bullets had changed their name to the Wizards out of respect for the victims of gun violence in DC, and a publicity promotion for one of the national fast-food chains would reward the entire crowd with free food if a guest out of the stands could hit a three. During a time-out Juwan yelled to me, "Don't look now, but your pops is about to take the jumper." I knew what "the jumper" meant, I also knew that if you missed the shot, you hilariously got booed…relentlessly. I didn't know if my father knew that.

Pops came onto the court, acknowledged the cheering crowd with a wave, and turned his old baseball cap to the back. At first, I turned away. Then I turned back around and watched; his form was a mix of Vinnie Johnson and Bill Cartwright. He cocked back and hurled the ball up—off the glass through the net! The crowd went bananas. Juwan ran out on the court and hugged him. My father calmly put up his finger as to say, "I'm number one, I did that for y'all, you're welcome." My mother's face was priceless. It said, Oh my, I'm going to hear about this one forever.

The great part about having so many teammates over time is that you have some really special ones. Players who do some incredible things or have some extraordinary traits. Rod Strickland's finishing ability under the rim was something rare. His ball control and vision and passing awareness were sick. God Shammgod had handles and would show me his bag of tricks after practice. Ben Wallace will always be special to me because he was my rookie. Every day, he battled with me and Juwan in practice, and regardless of who he was guarding, we gave him the business. He was a stand-up dude and a beast on the court and never backed down. He made us better, too, and we respected his heart. I must say that I feel responsible for his signature Afro. It was during the season and I suggested that he, Darvin Ham, and I grow our hair just to infuse some new energy in the season. Looking in the mirror in the locker room of Bowie State's gym, we dapped and agreed. I kept mine for about a year and Darvin kept his for a couple of months, but Ben didn't cut his for eleven years.

We knew as a team that we were going to go out and play hard every night. We were a close unit and had class clowns like our Romanian center, Gheorghe Mureșan. Gheorghe had one of his best games against Shaq, hitting turnarounds, jump hooks, and even a Jordanesque layup. Gheorghe and Manute Bol shared the distinction of being the NBA's tallest players. I'm amazed at how quickly he adapted to our culture and language.

Chapter 66

Somehow, with all that was going on, in the midst of coaching changes (Bernie Bickerstaff was now running the show), injuries, and trades, we made the playoffs in the 1996–97 season and set the city on fire! In a play-in game, we won 85–81 on the road against Cleveland in the last game of the season, and I posted twenty-three points and seventeen rebounds with three threes. I felt personal redemption after the surgery and everything I had gone through. It was great to end our nine-year playoff drought, but our reward was a date with the Chicago Bulls, one of the greatest teams ever assembled with one of the greatest players of all time.

The Bulls were on their run for an unprecedented second three-peat. Juwan and I felt that we honestly had a chance to win one or maybe even two games in the five-game series. We had played them well in the regular season and knew that we had a chance to make things interesting. Our first game was in Chicago at the old, loud, raggedy home of the Bulls. I got in foul trouble early and fouled out with only eight points. Juwan tried to hold us down and hit 'em with twenty-one, but we lost 98–86. Jordan had twenty-nine and Scottie Pippen fourteen.

In the second game, I witnessed an epic game by one of the greatest players of all-time, Mike himself. Our team bus pulled into the tunnel at the stadium. As players unloaded, we see Michael Jordan sitting on the closed door of his car (the only car parked inside) smoking a cigar. As we got off, he looked at Juwan and me and asked, "Who's gonna check me tonight?" Calbert Cheaney was conveniently getting off after me, and we both tried not to look back at Cal, who was looking like a sacrificial lamb. Well, it took a legendary MJ performance for Chicago to come out on top. We lost 109–104 in a hard-fought game. We gave them everything they wanted. I played my type of game—hitting threes, posting up, dunking, and ending up with 21–12 and six assists. Juwan had eighteen, but it wasn't enough. Mike scored fifty-five points.

I remember yelling to Juwan during the game, "This muuug sold his soul to the devil. These shots he's hitting are impossible."

Jordan smiled. I think he was smirking because I was telling the truth, and he knew it. We lost the third game at home in the Landover Arena. That place was loud as shit, and the fans were the realest. We came up short in front of our locals on a Pippen buzzer beater and lost by 96–95. But we were the team that played the Bulls the toughest throughout the playoffs that year. We left an impression with the champs, who sang our praises, saying that we were the team of the future. We agreed. We were next. Things seemed to be finally coming together.

ALL-STARS

That year, I also got the chance to go to the All-Star Game. All-Star Games are always special. Each one has a theme, feel, and tempo of its own. I never tried to get MVP, and I wasn't obsessed with scoring. I wanted a chip, nothing else. I did want to throw oops, dunk a few, and have fun. I always took that weekend as time to be grateful, reflect, and celebrate!

That year, Cleveland was hosting the event, and the NBA was also celebrating the fifty greatest players of all time. I watched while the pillars of the game stood and rehearsed while receiving their commemorative leather jackets. Then I went by and shook everyone's hand and introduced myself. I remember thinking how great Wilt Chamberlain looked at sixty. I watched Wilt and Jordan meet for the first time and Magic and Bird joke together. I saw Russell and his trademark cackle pat Wilt on the back. I stared at the Big O, Oscar Robertson, and George Gervin and wondered what they were rapping about. I shook George Mikan's hand. It was by far the best basketball moment of my life from a fan's perspective.

The weekend and game would not disappoint. A young Kobe Bryant won the dunk contest, Glen Rice broke Wilt's record for points in a quarter and a half with Wilt right there watching, and Jordan recorded the first triple-double in NBA all-star history. I have a picture signed by all forty-nine players, minus Pete Maravich, who had passed away. It's without a doubt one of my favorite pieces.

With the season over, I wanted to be around family more. I was missing my brothers' and sister's lives. They were growing up without me. Jeff was playing for Aquinas College, missing his big bro, and I was nowhere around. Thank God he had his high school sweetheart, Laisha, there. Jason had the opportunity to play for Tom Izzo and Michigan State. I was over the moon but wasn't surprised when I was told of Tom's offer; he is who I know him to be, a stand-up guy. Jason's leadership, game, and athletic ability would do the rest. As far as the times, I can't explain, but I felt something coming. I didn't know what, but over the summer it came.

Juwan and I talked about how we were ready to take the team to the next level. We had laid it all out on the floor that season and missed out on the playoffs by one game. We had been predicted to win forty-three games. We had won forty-two. Then, in the mix of getting it all together and working on my life and my game, I was blindsided. I knew this could be the blow to totally take me out. I was at a store with my man Kevin when the dude behind the bulletproof glass said, "Hey, Webb, you've just been traded!"

I'd never seen this guy before, so I didn't know whether to take him seriously. But something about this man's face told me that he wasn't playing. Traded where?

I called my agent. I asked him had he heard, and he responded, "Those mothers! They didn't even have the courtesy to call me. I had to hear it off the wire!"

Still in shock, I asked, "Where'd they trade me?"

He paused and, exhausted, exhaled. "Sacramento."

I couldn't believe it. We both just sat on the phone, speechless. Once I came to, so to speak, I wouldn't accept it. I immediately asked my agent to make calls and told him I was open to anything or anywhere...just not Sacramento.

Chapter 67

Mama: Oh, God has something extraordinary planned for you…

Me: Come on, Ma. This is hoop. This is not good.

I knew it was real. I can't exaggerate the fact that I knew this was it. What it was, I didn't know, but this was it, and it didn't feel good. We sat in my truck in front of my house, quiet and stoic. Kev had tears in his eyes. I laughed. It wasn't funny, but it was. I chose DC and anticipated how challenging growth would be for our squad. We were on our way. Mike was retiring, the East would be open, we were young and had gone against the best and learned from it. We just needed a couple of moves from the front office. But I didn't choose Sac. I was traded for perennial All-Star and future Hall of Famer Mitch Richmond, along with Otis Thorpe, who was much more than solid.

It wasn't just me. Players looked at Sacramento as basketball purgatory. The graveyard filled with vestiges of "could've been" and rumored "potential." Past ownership wasn't known for being hoop savants or keeping up with the rest of the NBA. The arena, though filled with avid fans, was one of the oldest in the league and had the scars to prove it. No one could remember a time they were on TV, won, were popular, or when a Kings jersey was coveted. Players also hated the lack of a big city or normal amenities. You were hard pressed to find a restaurant open past 9:00 p.m., and even the best hotels didn't have twenty-four-hour room service. This place just seemed slow.

The team won twenty-seven games the year before my arrival and hadn't had a winning season since the 1982–83 season. There was a generation of hoop fans who had never seen the Kings in the postseason. They were known for being bad and dry with no flavor. I knew what I was getting into. I made players and teams better. I knew that it would take a lot of energy for the task at hand. With the rest of their roster after trading Mitch, it was only Corliss Williamson left. It was going to be more than leading a franchise to some wins but the changing of a culture. The work, attention to detail, dedication, commitment, would be tough—but to believe, really believe, would be the most difficult of them all. But if I believed, the rest would follow. I love to believe in what I'm doing. I know the commitment and loyalty I possess, so I want my devotion to be for a solid get down. I didn't think Sac was worth believing in. I didn't think Jordan himself could turn it around. It would have to be the perfect storm.

I hit the gym the next day with Kev and Buzz. I don't know how much work I got done, but my body was there. There was no time for decompression or being lazy and pouting; I had to be prepared for whatever. I found out later that summer that one of the reasons I was traded was that the Wizards understood that they were going to have to pay me and didn't want to. I was officially traded after the 1997–98 regular season, but the playoffs were still rolling. As a result, they wouldn't have to negotiate with me with the collective bargaining agreement deal expiring. Also, pulling the trigger on the move when they did meant it would be lost in playoff news. Great distraction.

My lawyer called me back a day or so later and told me that there was a lot of interest from teams around the league. The catch was that the looming negotiations for the new CBA between the players' union and the NBA would hamper a quick resolution. It felt like forever. I immersed myself in hoops, and I also isolated myself. Isolation is not always the correct answer to situations, many times it's just symptomatic of larger issues, but for me it was like a boxer going away to prepare for a title fight. All normal activities, routines, and plans are interrupted, and everyone around usually understands the importance of the moment and offers encouragement. I didn't communicate at all that I needed space, but I damn sure assumed that if you really knew me, you knew it was time for me to work. I could chill, laugh, and whatever else later.

I called my mom depressed and got off the phone with her even more down than I had started. She was too encouraging, nonchalant, and confident in me and the situation. I told her how I couldn't believe this was happening, and I asked why God would do this to me. "Do what to you? Open a door for you? Bless you? God has something extraordinary planned for you!" she said. "Mama, this is hoop. This is not good."

The team hired Rick Adelman, former head coach of the Portland Trail Blazers, who took that team to the finals. As for the league, negotiations stood at a standstill, and for the first time in NBA history, there would be a lockout. From July 1, 1998, to January 20, 1999, teams were barred from making player transactions or holding workouts and meetings. So I couldn't work on another trade, and players did what players do. We hooped. We had an unsanctioned televised game in Vegas that was entertaining, but every player was out of shape. I worked out at different gyms, and I hadn't moved yet because I wasn't planning on actually going to Sac. One day I was hoopin' in DC and actually played on Mitch's team. We killed it. Then when we were getting our stuff ready to leave, we talked about our situations. He was somewhat excited; he may have been the only one who understood how I felt. After January 20 and the new collective bargaining agreement hit, we were hoping it would be a madhouse for player movement. The agreement's timing affected the flow of the regular season. Only fifty games would be played as opposed to eighty-two, and there would be no All-Star Game.

One of the teams that made it known that they wanted me to rock their jersey was the Los Angeles Lakers. I had a call with Jerry West that I will remember for a lifetime. We talked about my career, life in general, and commitment. We discussed how the great thing about sports is the rush of the chase. Most people don't understand that. The fulfillment of the pain from battle and the energy you get from winning and losing. Though very different currents, energy nonetheless. Mr. West told me he was considered a loser by the media, and he didn't get the name "Mr. Clutch" until after his career. Instead, they had other names for him that were unflattering. He lost nine times in the NBA Finals. He told me that when he was a player they put the details of his personal life (divorce) in the paper and how much he resented that. He told me he also understood what I was going through, and he wanted to harness my passion with Shaq's. Jerry thought I could take pressure off of Shaq in the paint, and I was one of the best passing big men he'd seen.

I was floored and honored that he would share his wisdom with me. We spoke a couple more times, and then he made it official. Jerry and the Lakers proposed a trade: Elden Campbell, Nick Van Exel, and Eddie Jones in exchange for me and another player whose name doesn't come to mind. I was convinced this move was in destiny's notepad under my name. My agent set up a call with Geoff Petrie, GM for the Kings, who was not budging. Geoff was a cool, calm personality and was an ex-hooper for the Portland Trail Blazers. He was Rookie of the Year in 1970–71, averaging 24.5 points, but his career was cut short by injury.

My agent spoke to him several times, and Geoff made it known he had no interest in moving me for anyone. I thought he was bluffing. I got on the phone with Geoff and in no uncertain terms I made it known that I was not coming.

"Chris, I believe that we can build something special together here!" he said. "You know we hired Rick Adelman, I'm going to try to sign Vlade Divac, and we have a rookie guard that I think you'll love playing with. His name is Jason Williams. We also have a kid from Croatia named Peja. We feel you have the game to lead us. Wouldn't that be special? After some time, I think you'll love it here."

"Geoff, thanks, but I'm not going to play for the Kings. I'm not coming. As you know, there is a trade on the table, and I think that with those guys you could do something pretty special. I really want to win a championship. There is nothing I'd rather have; I think this will allow both sides to get something good out of this. You don't want a guy who doesn't want to be there."

"I understand how much you want to win, and that's why we want you, Chris. We don't want them; we want you."

That's about all I remember, because after a little more back and forth, I absolutely lost it. I did not want to be there, and he and he alone had the means to help me win a championship. I hung up on everyone on our conference call and went to the gym with Buzz and Kevin. I was dead set on not reporting for training camp, scheduled for January 21, let alone for the first game on February 20. That wasn't happanan, Captaaan!

My father was on my neck. He hated all the reports of me promising not to report to Sacramento. He said he was offended that someone could be paid that much money to play a game and not report. I understood his perspective considering I knew his story, but I was adamant that I wasn't going—until time kept ticking down and the only option I had was to report to camp. Geoff dug his heels in; there was nothing I could do.

Billy Owens lived in Sacramento, having played there the past couple of years. Funny thing about that was, coming out of the draft, Billy was selected third overall by Sacramento. When he left his home to go meet with the organization, he fell asleep at takeoff and when he woke up, he was landing in Sac, and all he saw was farmland and a big building in the middle. His agent told him that that building was where the Kings played, and Billy told his agent right then that he wasn't going to ever put on a Kings jersey. Ironically, he was traded to Golden State for Mitch Richmond and famously broke up the gun-slangin' threesome known as Run TMC. So when I called to tell him I wasn't coming, he actually was telling me how he liked it there and the people were cool. I wasn't trying to hear it, but again, I had no other options.

Well, as irony would have it, I left the Detroit airport headed for Sacramento and fell asleep before we even took off. I woke up to the sound of the pilot telling the flight attendants to prepare for landing, looked out the window, and saw nothing but farmland. My eyes filled with liquid anger. I hid out at Billy's house while he was signing with the Sonics. While in Sac, I would not communicate with the team. I was working out at a local gym until Rob Pimental, the Kings' equipment manager, surprised me at the gym.

"Hey, dude, we are excited to have you here!" he said. "Just wanted to come get your sizes and make sure you have everything you need."

"No disrespect, home boy, but I'm not going to be playing here, and I don't want to waste your time. Thank you."

"Well, let me know if you need anything."

I'd be seeing him a lot sooner than expected, as my agent confirmed that I'd either have to play or sit out the season. I called my brother Jeff to vent one last time before my imposed sentencing, and he just started raving about the team. "I heard you guys are going to sign Vlade," he said.

"Yeah."

"Well, have you ever seen Jason Williams play?"

"Who?"

"Jason Williams, the seventh pick of the Kings. He's so cold. Hoooo, you're going to love playing with him! According to my sources—"

"Jeff, you don't have any sources."

"According to my sources, Peja can shoot the lights out. Y'all are going to be good. Mark my words."

"You and Mama. Boy, y'all believe anything."

I watched January 21 pass by, hoping for a miracle, a Hail Mary, a magic trick, crime—I didn't care. I was just waiting for anything. Funny, I was praying and saying all the right things, but I thought I knew what God wanted for me. I'd pray, "Keep me in your will, for I know you have what's best in mind for me, Lord. Please work this out the way you see fit." But I didn't think the answer could be in Sac. (How are you going to ask and tell God at the same time?)

January 22 was a big day for the Kings. They signed Vlade Divac to a six-year deal. That would be evidence of their commitment to winning. I also reported to the Kings' facility for the first time. I was so conflicted.

Everyone in the front office was so nice, and it seemed to be a great environment. I just didn't want to be there, but it didn't matter. I saw Rob as I walked into the locker room, and he gave me a sincere "Hey buddy." I shot him the middle finger, and he smiled and shot one back.

Coach Adelman had me come to his office while the team warmed up. I sat down, and he grabbed my attention right away. "Hey, Chris, I know you're excited and can't wait to get started." I didn't want to laugh, but I did. "I just want you to know that with me you have a clean slate. I can't wait to work with you." Much more was said, but I don't remember much else, because that statement meant so much to me. That one statement of course had to be followed through with action, but damn how could I not ride with someone who put it out on the table? I needed that. That five-minute conversation, along with Geoff's adamant belief in what he assembled, would be the building blocks of what was to come. The mortar, the glue, however, would be the team.

I walked onto the court of the old gym all taped up and not ready to go. I sought out Corliss because he was the only player I somewhat knew off the court, and I wanted to give him his respect. I needed him to know that I knew this was his team, and though it's not anymore, we were all going to get off so we could win. We needed the big dogs to lead. I also thanked him for giving up the number four, which he'd been wearing since he got into the league. I went over and talked to Vlade, and he introduced me to a young, shy Peja Stojaković. I heard this loud mouth voice with a southern drawl joking and talking junk. I went over and said what's up with a big smile, and he said, "Yessiiiiir, tha Faaaab Fiiive!" Coach came over, had us huddle up, and explained the philosophy of the team.

Rick wanted fast-paced ball movement, and he gave us a playbook that we could interpret and modify on the fly. He said we would all need to be patient because he was going to ask us to play in a way that we may never have or that may not make sense at first. Offensive freedom means a lot of responsibility for every player. He assembled a great coaching staff: former players John Wetzel and a "Showtime" teammate of Magic's, Byron Scott. A leading voice in the locker room thanks to Coach Adelman's style was offensive wizard and basketball Yoda, Pete Carril. I loved our discussions. He's a wise teacher. I already had the mind-set in workouts to get prepared for running, playing faster, and pushing the rock. I knew that West Coast play was more open. But I didn't know that I'd be playing with a young globetrotter, a wizard with the ball. But in the first ten minutes of practice,

I'd find out that I was playing with a light of energy. He dazzled fans, coaches, and peers alike.

The 'hood fell in love with him and called him "White Chocolate." To me, he was "J. Will," but he was special on and off the court. Coach put us in three-on-two drills, where two defenders are on the far end of the court and three offensive players attack. After a shot attempt, make, miss, or steal, the two defenders pushed the ball back at one offensive player (usually the offensive man in the middle), who now played D in a two-on-one situation. Well, I was on the wing with J. Will, and he pushed the ball, faked a defender with a right hands-up cross with a left hands-up shot fake, hesitated, and hit Corliss in stride on the right side as the defense anticipated me receiving the ball.

The next play down, he hit me, I whipped it back to him, he no-look zipped it right back to me, and I was wide open. Then he screamed, "Hoooo!" like Ric Flair. I was familiar with the magic. I'd seen it before with less than a handful of players. I loved playing with guys who had it, because they were sincere, unselfish, and good for everyone. They were who they were. No faking it. Laughing, I screamed, "This cat is crazy!" That quick, the ice was starting to melt. That quick, Vlade's game and personality would hammer through any ice that was left and needed to be broken.

In drills we started off with great chemistry. If I lifted my eyebrows, J. Will knew I was spinning for an oop, and he would place it right on target. Or he would have an open shot, and if you had rebound position and your defender had his head turned, he would pass it by the defender's ear hitting you. Offensively he was smart and quick and knew how to make the team better, but he also knew that he could get his at any moment. He had game. Vlade wore his spirit on his sleeves. He was easygoing and easy to talk to. He didn't have to say much; his eyes and actions said it all.

Coach Adelman was the first pick in the seventh round of the 1968 draft and played point guard for nine seasons in the NBA. He was an assistant coach for six years and head coach for eight. He guided Portland to the championship twice, losing to the Bad Boy Pistons and Jordan's Bulls. The best way to describe his system is "Play hard, together, and let it fly...responsibly." Our practices were, in one word, *efficient*. Coach was the most organized and prepared coach I'd ever seen in my pro career. It was the most prepared team I'd been on as well. Offensively and defensively. You could work on your game on your own time, but practices were for his system.

We'd shoot a million shots, skeleton drill our offenses, and do a million back cuts and back-cut-related drills and some three-on-three and fast-break drills. His system, if followed, would be the basis for chemistry and exciting, unselfish play. Our first year we spent what seemed like an endless amount of time on philosophy. Coach Carril would stop a live scrimmage (right as it was getting good) to interject a thought, explain what you did wrong, or give you praise and explain another option. Every play seemed to have four or five different options, all with the same philosophy and thought process. If you understood and gave in to marching orders, you could have a consistent impact and freak your game on the fly; there wasn't much guessing. The impact of Wetzel and especially B. Scott was welcomed. We could get old stories about the NBA, Showtime, Magic, and Kareem. Byron was fresh out of the league and could hold guys accountable and understood the get down.

After implementing a system, you have to be consistent in the evaluation of talent for the role in the system, not necessarily talent overall. Geoff would prove he had an eye for evaluating talent. He knew that we wanted as many open shots as possible with free flow. So he had me and Vlade, who could score on the post and garner a double-team; we were great passers so the flow would be potent, double-team or not. We could also get our own shot in one-on-one situations. We had to have guys who could shoot and dribble. Every player, if his talent level fit the situation, was allowed to push the rock or take his man on his own. You also had to be able to cut and finish, as Vlade and myself loved to hit the cutter to relieve pressure or whether we were playing the ball in the post or out of our corner action, which was an offensive staple. I was asked by Coach Carril to "consider with an open mind" facilitating from the high post, which, at the time, was a basketball sin. I would accept the challenge early but embrace the role later.

Practices were fun but very ugly in the beginning, as you must learn and understand players' strengths and weaknesses and how to use them in play. You had to test their limits and boundaries, the ebb and flow. This wasn't just "pass to your man and watch" or "dribble a bunch of times." This was team hoop. Trust doesn't happen overnight but you trust someone based on their habits and interactions with you. I learned through our practices that we had a talented squad, and by the end of training camp, I'd started to gain respect for management and my teammates. Vernon Maxwell is an NBA champion and vet who brought a toughness to practices and games that our team needed. He showed the young fellas how to work consistently. If someone got the big head in practice, he'd bring you back to reality by busting your ass in a shooting drill or practice. I've also seen him beat multiple players in a street race, in which he would take off his shoes and race barefoot.

With talented shooters like Peja, Terry Dehere, and J. Will, the floor was spaced, which added a continuity to our style that I loved relying on. Tariq Abdul-Wahad was our athletic slasher and helped speed up the pace of play. My old nemesis, Lawrence Funderburke; Corliss; and I rounded out the big fellas.

Before our first game against San Antonio, Vlade and I had a conversation, and together, we ran the team in the locker room based on our understanding of roles. We had to communicate. That we were changing a culture, rewriting all the failure that this organization was used to. It was going to take work, and it would start with us, so let's lead together. I was preaching to the choir; he was with it. We both wanted a positive, hardworking, and unselfish environment where every man was held—and more important—and held himself accountable.

Our first chance to kick the tires and see what this group of new Kings could do would be on the road against the Spurs. Fans and players alike would get to see glimpses of what we could become through spectacular individual and collective play. I scored the first two points of the new era. I knocked down a jumper over Tim Duncan at the top of the key off a pass from Vlade. J. Will introduced himself to the league as only few have, hitting twenty-one points. He put on a show, and though he didn't create his style of play, he mastered it. He was a true showman. His crossovers, pull-up threes, and exciting passes had teammates and opponents saying, "Damn." He would shoot from the deepest range I've seen, regularly! Vlade showed off his passing skills, and I had a solid game dueling against the "Twin Towers," Duncan and David Robinson. We scored eighty-three in a losing effort but knew we could play much better. Scoring was not something that we'd ever have to worry about; we would flow like water.

Two nights later in ARCO Arena, a place opponents jokingly called "the Barn," we had our first home game, as the new-look Kings went up against the Vancouver Grizzlies. The excitement of the crowd was unique, sincere, and crazy loud. It was loud like the fans at Golden State's Oracle Arena with a passionate, collegiate, fanatic feel—the perfect combo. We'd give our home crowd a dose of something they ain't never had before and would turn them out! We beat the Grizzlies 109–87. We played fast and deadly. Vlade and I showed our potential of what we could do. I had twenty-five points, fifteen rebounds, eight assists, nine blocks, and three steals in my Sacramento home debut. Being pissed, I guess, whatever gets it done. Vlade grabbed sixteen boards and had ten assists, Peja lit up the two spot, and J. Will was…J. Will. I'm surprised his moves didn't have the crowd at ARCO passing out like members of some churches 'cause he was showing them the truth.

No one expected us to accomplish anything. Not a winning season, not the playoffs, not to be anything special—and I think that brought us together. We'd go up and down with wins and positive play as a unit. But we consistently grew our chemistry. The team came through for me on February 25 when we played my old team, the Wizards. I loved giving my former teams the business. My team wanted this for me, just as Washington had wanted it for me against G. State. Juwan and I battled, and Mitch would try against his old squad; however, we came out on top with a 115–105 victory. I had seventeen-ten-ten, another triple-double against a former team. Vlade went to work and had twenty-two and seventeen dimes. Damn, he could pass. Juwan had seventeen and eight rebounds. We were so familiar with each other's game it was always tough playing against each other.

One situation that brought me closer to my boy Vlade was on March 24. We were hosting the New York Knicks. I knew—or should I say that I thought I knew—what Vlade was going through. In actuality, none of us had a clue. In the first year of knowing him, I'd come to learn that he was one of the toughest and kind-hearted people I'd met in my life. I let him know that if there was anything I could do for him to just let me know, and he knew I was there. But what can you do for a man who needs the ear of God and a miracle? Vlade was known for coming to practice with bed head, always looking sleepy and having a word of encouragement or joke for everybody. What we couldn't see was that he was staying up all night, sometimes for twenty-four hours, trying to contact his family to see if they were safe. Vlade's parents lived in a small town south of Belgrade, Serbia. He wanted to get them—his brother, nieces, nephews, and other family members—out of the war zone to safety. Vlade and his family's lives had been disrupted since February 1998 because of the Kosovo War.

On March 24, before the game, Vlade did an interview with Larry King on CNN. Vlade wept for the innocent civilians hurt by politicians and said that NATO was wrong. Only Coach and Geoff knew how much Vlade's heart was aching. He was there for the team in any way he could be and was still encouraging others. You'd never know that his every thought was on the safety of his friends and family. My job was to make sure that being at the arena and games was a getaway, a safe haven, so we could have fun just being brothers. During this difficult time, I came to love and respect my friend and his beautiful wife, Ana. When the pressure was on and the world was unfair, he was still a good, kind man.

J. Will and I grew closer. We had the same interests, but most of all, he was just a cool, humble cat. He was the type of dude you'd hear coming before you saw him, whether he was walking down the hall or you were standing outside hearing his ride bumping down the block. Jason was quick-witted and hilarious. He also loved doing magic tricks. On the road, I'd go to a mall or go eat with him, and we'd usually stop by a magic store. He ate, slept, and drank hoops. Team chemistry fell into a groove.

We finished the season winning ten out of eleven to make the playoffs as a seventh seed in the West. In the strike-shortened season, we finished 27–23, matching the victory total of the previous year. It was the first winning season for the Kings in Sacramento.

With no training camp and a newly comprised team, we'd finished the season first in scoring, first in pace, fourth in assists, second in rebounds, first in three-point attempts, third in three-point makes, first in field goal makes, and second in field goal attempts. Five guys averaged double figures, and three more guys averaged at least eight points per game. We shared the rock and loved playing with each other. I made second team All-NBA, the best honor since my rookie year. I averaged twenty points, but I was more excited about leading the league in rebounds, at thirteen a clip.

We entered the playoffs as the seventh seed, against Utah, the heavily favored two seed. Sacramento was excited for their first playoff series in forever. Businesses closed early to let their employees watch the game, and buildings were covered with wrappings saying "Go Kings." There were purple lights throughout the city. It was a special moment for everyone. I'd never seen anything like it. Although we were expected to get swept, we had other plans. We knew how much this meant to the fans; Jason and I were pumped and wanted to share that excitement with the people of Sacramento. Fans were camping out for tickets around ARCO Arena, and we heard about it, so we took them some pizzas and sat out there and rapped with them for a while. No newspapers, no media, just us and them. That was cool.

Karl Malone and John Stockton were the pioneers of the modern-day pick-and-roll, maybe the deadliest guard-forward combo the game has seen, and they were in their prime. Unlike most teams, their offense was built inside out, and unlike most teams, they gave you a heavy dose of a play, the pick-and-roll, that caused havoc with its catch-22 scenario. Either you lived with a Stockton jumper or got hit in the head with a Karl Malone finish.

I knew the temperature of our team and what the league thought of us, and I knew that there was a risk that some guys could become content with just making it to the playoffs and then mailing it in. I also knew that other teams thought that we played soft because we knew we could outscore everybody at any time. But I felt that this series with Utah would be about more than just the score but how we would be defined. I had a conversation with Coach Adelman in the locker room before Game One. I said, "Coach, I think this game is more about setting the tone than winning. We are not going to get the respect of the refs in this game, so let's set the tone." He didn't agree with the tone I wanted to set, but I ended up getting a technical for my trouble.

Utah ran a play called "flex." It was a staple in high school and college, especially for John Wooden and UCLA and Bobby Knight and Indiana, but the Jazz executed it with such precision that everyone copied it. The play called for Stockton to pass the ball to the wing from the center of the court, cut off a screen set at the corner of the free-throw line, and then go across and either set or receive a screen and come back up to the spot he had vacated. On the first play of the game, Stockton passed the ball from the center of the court and cut—but as soon as he cut, I met his ass with a screen that would make most point guards say nighty night. Nine seconds into the game. I dropped him; he went down, popped up immediately, and patted me on the butt. The ref signaled the scorer's table indicating a technical foul on yours truly.

Stockton was tough as hell. He was a true warrior. My move didn't faze him physically or mentally, but I knew that my plan had worked. Now the Jazz understood that we meant business. We lost the first game and then won the next two, winning our home debut in the playoffs in front of a hysterical crowd. It took a last-second shot and a legendary performance from Stockton to beat us in the pivotal Game Four. We were eliminated in Game Five in Utah, but we knew that we were building something special. Malone was voted league MVP, and Utah would go on to lose to Portland in six. But in Sacramento, as far as hoops, things would never be the same again.

Back on the home front, my brother David signed with Central Michigan University, and I was crazy proud. He won three state championships in high school and had a decorated career. He was even invited to play in Magic's Roundball Classic all-star game with a young Kobe Bryant. He proved to be the player, leader, and man I thought he

would, and even more. J. Will and I watched his games whenever possible. One game was against Purdue when he went off and the Chippewas won. J and I were running around my house like little kids screaming for joy as David and his team came out on top. He made the Big Ten pay for not respecting his game, almost like the all-stars for me. Resilience was a Webber trait. David had a legendary record-setting career at Central Michigan. Even though it was rough not being there in person because the seasons coincided, it gave me usable pain. That was how I looked at it. David was killing on the court, surprising everyone. I was planning on doing the same.

Chapter 69

The next season seemed to be a validation of our fighting spirit. We wanted it with whoever. Our chemistry was A1, and we fully trusted ourselves and our system.

The five-game series didn't start off as a rivalry. There was no history to make the games infect fans with hatred. Sac didn't have any rivals. They were always the whipping boy, so bully's bullied. But just as we let Utah know that we weren't an easy out, we were planning on the same against the odds-on favorite to win the chip. The fans at Staples Center were hyped. They could feel that their dominance was at hand and we were just a formality. The stars were out. Denzel, Steven Spielberg, Garry Shandling, all came to watch their team. We came out in Game One firing. J. Will was doing his thing, at times giving Kobe the blues; I dominated my matchup with A. C. Green; and Vlade played well against his old team; but we lost Game One, 117–107. Shaq dominated with forty-six and seventeen. Kobe and Glen Rice were hot as well. My twenty-eight, five, and five were not enough.

Game Two was not even close, 113–89. Kobe hit us with thirty-two, and Shaq added nineteen rebounds. I had twenty-two points, twelve rebounds, and six assists. The City of Sac couldn't wait for us to get home. We needed their energy.

I believe the rivalry between the Sacramento Kings and Los Angeles Lakers started in Game Three of that series. The way we played against them at home, and the fact that we didn't bow down to them had a hatred brewing. In Game Three, then Four, then Five, a special, passionate, beautiful David and Goliath feud began. A rivalry needs two willing competitors, but more important, the competitors must have a history of vitriol. Since the Kings never had a history of winning, we were never thought of in their universe of dominance. We were like Switzerland to them, but now we were a new regime—an honest threat. The fact that we weren't given a chance from anyone except Sac fans, we embraced the underdog role and doing so brought the best out of their young stars and future champs.

"The fans did it!" was what I would tell anyone who asked me how the rivalry started. Vlade encouraged it, and we poured gasoline on the situation. The let it burn, game. It was hype from the jump, or should I say before, our fans were outside tailgating like a college football game day Saturday. It was standing room only, and we had a whiteout, meaning everyone had on white T-shirts. The fans sensed that they were going to witness something special and were on the edge of their seats with anticipation. They knew we were undefeated at home in the playoffs, and the national media didn't know what was going to hit them.

We knew at home we could neutralize Shaq's dominance with space and speed. Before the series I had a talk with Coach Carril, who begged me to play at the midpost and free-throw line. "They're going to criticize you, these so-called experts. Don't listen. We have a plan."

I'm glad I trusted him. I dominated in the series, averaging twenty-four points, ten rebounds, and seven assists. By series end, starting with these events at home, I'd become a King. The game started off with neither team hitting any shots, and I could sense this young Laker team was cocky. They had an air of invincibility unaccompanied by discipline. Ron Harper had been yelling at guys, telling them to trust each other. We got Brian Shaw in early foul trouble by speeding up the pace. We were down as many as ten. They led at the half.

It started to heat up in the third quarter when Shaq bulldozed his way through the paint and Scot Pollard was called for a foul. Now, everyone knew that Shaq was beating the hell out of Scot, and the fans were calling bullshit. Literally. When Shaq got to the foul line, the fans started chanting "Bullshit!" in unison. They were ready. They messed with him every time he stepped to the line. He had to take it personal, any true warrior would. We played well and got back into the game and trailed 71–66 at the end of the third. This was when I learned about the heart of our team.

The fourth quarter was the loudest I'd ever heard the arena. I could not hear Vlade call a play when he was yelling within arm's length. I hit Peja to give us the lead by three, and I felt the court shake. It got even louder when I hit a jump hook in the paint with just over three minutes remaining. I had twenty-nine points, fourteen rebounds, and eight assists, and we won our third game when facing elimination, 99–91. Kobe followed up and had a crazy night; his thirty-five points were a playoff career high. He was still coming into his own. The very first steps of his legendary career.

Game Four. The so-called experts considered Game Three to be a fluke. They didn't understand our mission and the power of the home crowd. In a game we never trailed against the Lakers, we showed our ass. At the 9:07 mark in the second quarter, I was called for a flagrant foul on Robert Horry as he came down the lane. I didn't think it warranted a technical, and neither did the crowd. They went bonkers. A couple of minutes later, as I drove down the lane, my boy Glen Rice knocked the hell out of me and was assessed a tech. I thought it was a clean block, but the refs took his aggression as retaliation for my foul a few plays earlier. The game got chippie. We fought through bad shot selection as a team by playing defense as one. Coming down with time running out, I called my own play and hit a shot at the halftime buzzer. Again, for the tenth time that night, it was louder than any arena I played in before this evening.

In the third, the shit hit the fan. Kobe stole the ball from Tony Delk, and Vlade tried to foul him as the ref was calling foul on Kobe. Kobe pushed Vlade off of him as Vlade tussled with him and hit the floor. Was it a flop? Hell yeah! Vlade was known for flopping and chose the right time. The ref called a double tech, and you could see Kobe's frustration and anger. The next play, Glen fouled Corliss, and the crowd continued to annoy the Lakers as they screamed "Kobe sucks!" in unison. That was the first time I'd heard any crowd get on him. A true sign of greatness, they were the league's darlings. We made him better. We made him a legend. How? Because his answer to the crowd and opponents was legendary… buckets. He had thirty-two. His third game in the thirties, legendary shit.

We were doing some legendary shit as well. The only time a number-eight seed came back from 2–0 to beat a number-one seed was Denver over Seattle in 1994. We wanted to be the second. I made a behind-the-back pass to Vlade, who dunked over Kobe to put us up 94–83, and I looked over and saw our new team owners, the Maloof family, going crazy. Their investment had been repaid right there with that game, something that the city and organization thought they would never see. Our back cuts were precise, as we were executing for Coach Carril, who was at home recovering from a heart attack. This execution, which is beautiful when done according to plan, can embarrass opponents if they don't communicate with each other on defense. The Lakers did not communicate.

The last minute of the game seemed like it took thirty, and the crowd and players enjoyed every second. The crowd went crazy. We won. Ran away with it, 101–88. They tried like hell to win. Kobe and Shaq each played forty-six minutes. Kobe had thirty-two, and Shaq had twenty-two and sixteen. Glen Rice added seventeen. Vlade had a double-double. Nick Anderson played some great D and hit some buckets. I had twenty-three points, thirteen rebounds, eight assists, seven blocks, and four steals. As we players hugged and started to leave the court, already beginning to think about the upset in Game Five, one of my favorite moments in Sac occurred. As I left the court, Vlade pulled me over and said, "You're a KING now!" He was right.

Game Five. I saw the fear in their eyes. I couldn't tell you whether it was us or the thought of losing with the expectations they openly expressed at the beginning of the season. But you could tell. We were headed back to LA, and Ron Harper got on a couple of radio stations asking the crowd to get to the game early and be as enthusiastic as possible. Our crowd was in

their heads. Now, if we were a veteran team and I was a better leader at the time, we would have made sure to change some things up and keep them guessing. They came out tentative. Phil brilliantly changed his scheme to make us adjust defensively. Our defense had the Lakers confused, especially in Games Three and Four after we were able to study them. I zoned up on D on every play. I basically begged Horry and A. C. Green to shoot the ball. A shot from either of them, no matter how many they made, was a success,

CHRIS WEBBER

as we wanted to keep the ball out of the hands of Shaq and young Kobe. Me zoning up would also help deter penetration, encouraging a jump shot.

We were assessed a technical foul early in the game for illegal defense, and I saw Kobe and Shaq celebrating. I knew Phil gave them something to hold onto and distract from this ass whooping that could be. We embraced the challenge as a team. Jason and I especially, we were talking to the crowd, laughing and having fun, no matter the score. We fought all game, dazzling the crowd with crazy oops, penetrations, and passing. Back in Sacramento, over seventeen thousand fans poured into ARCO Arena to watch the game on the Jumbotron, and many were turned away. The rivalry was cemented when Rick Fox and Nick Anderson got into a dustup. Both were assessed a technical foul.

We lost the game 113–86 and the series 3–2. I only scored twenty and was the only King to score in double figures. Shaq proved why he was the dominant player with thirty-two. Kobe inserted himself as a name in future barbershop arguments about "top five ever." They finished the season as champions. I was happy for them. They were magnificent. A duo unlike any ever witnessed. Who knew that the series with the Lakers would seal my fate as a King? I wanted to be a Laker. I wanted to win a chip and play with the best players and coaches and live in the City of Angels, but as it turned out, that series made me want to be a King for life.

I was a free agent going into the 2000–2001 season. It seemed as if the team was getting better with every game. Geoff's plan and the Coach's leadership were a perfect combination. We had a great locker room atmosphere, and going to practice every day was something I looked forward to. However, I kept my options open. I was the most sought-after free agent of the summer, and I was bombarded with questions regarding where I would play next season. My body was feeling great, and I felt the most athletic I ever had in my life.

The owners of our team, the Maloofs, put up billboards around town that said something to the effect of "If you stay, we'll mow your lawn." I never really got that, but as I was being recruited by my own team, I was having the best statistical season of my career. My work was continuing to produce positive results, and I finally came to grips with being in an offense that asked me to play at the high post and with more pick-and-roll play.

Our team led the league in points per game for a third straight season. I was named First Team All-NBA and an MVP candidate averaging twenty-seven, eleven, and four. I was an All-Star starter for the second year in a row, and the fact that this year's game was in DC was more sweet validation. We ended the season tied for the league's third-best record at 55–27 (an eleven-game improvement) and finished second in the Pacific Division. The Lakers won the Pacific with a 56–26 record, beating us out by one win.

We were still the lil' brother in this scenario, but we were getting our weight up. We were now experienced, and with the addition of Doug Christie, Hedo Türkoğlu, and Bobby Jackson, our confidence grew by leaps and bounds. Our starting lineup graced the cover of *Sports Illustrated* with the headline "The Greatest Show on Court." We were becoming the darlings of people who loved underdogs. With the international popularity of Vlade, Peja, and Hedo, we had fans all over the world staying up late or waking up early to watch our games. We even played on national TV. I laughed at commentators who hated on us the whole telecast. We knew we would be criticized for our style of play, but we also knew that our system was the only way we could succeed, and it was working for me.

That year, in the playoffs, we had different expectations. We expected to get out of the first round no matter who our opponent was. It was the Phoenix Suns, featuring Jason Kidd and Shawn Marion and coached by my old DC point guard, Scott Skiles. I didn't play well, but we won the series 3–1. Our improved defense (thanks in large part to Assistant Coach Elston Turner) held them under a hundred in every game.

Our reward was to play the Lakers again. In Game One, Peja and I had a nice rhythm. He could hit a shot from anywhere and only needed a millisecond and a half inch of space. As Kevin Harlan said of Peja, "He's a flamethrower!" We had our own play called "Four-Special," which NBA coaches ask me to teach or explain to this day. Vlade and I were the first teammates in Kings history to make an All-Star Game together. We were a true threat, and the Lakers knew it. With the addition of Doug Christie, we had a lockdown defender, and Bobby Jackson could hurt you on both ends of the floor.

Both players were warriors with unquestionable heart, but the Lakers were trying to do something special: win back-to-back titles. We lost Game One 108–105, but it took legendary games from two legendary players to defeat us. Shaq had forty-four and twenty-one, while Kobe had twenty-nine. Peja had twenty and I scored thirty-four on the road. In Game Two, I was hampered by a high ankle sprain and couldn't run or jump with any force. I managed twenty-two points and eighteen rebounds, and Peja had twenty; but Shaq had forty-three points and twenty rebounds, and Kobe went for twenty-seven and nine. We lost 96–90.

Now we were down 0–2, hoping that our home court advantage would kick in. The fans were ready. The city lit up in support. Again, businesses shut down early, pastors were praying for us in local churches, schools were having pep rallies for us, everyone was all in, and it was a great feeling. The fans were at a fever pitch for Game Three. They had thoughts of us getting the first win of the series, but it was not to be. I had twenty-eight and fourteen rebounds, but Kobe led all scorers with thirty-six, and Shaq had twenty-one and eighteen. We lost Game Four after a crazy performance by Kobe. He put up forty-eight and sixteen while his Big Buddy added twenty-five and ten. I dropped twenty-one points, eleven rebounds, and eight assists in the losing effort. I also noticed that J. Will only played nineteen minutes. His playoff minutes, and especially his crunch-time minutes, had taken a dramatic hit, and he wasn't happy about it.

The Lakers went on to repeat as NBA champions, defeating Allen Iverson and the Philadelphia 76ers in one of greatest playoff runs in the history of the game. They only lost one game the entire postseason.

While all this was happening, my little brother David, the kid Harv would bring into our team huddles at five years old to ask his advice, the kid who wore number 11 after Isiah Thomas, the hardest working athlete I'd ever seen, graduated from Central Michigan University. His team, once sorry as hell, went on to win the Mid-American Conference title, and he became the 2000–01 MAC Player of the Year. He even eclipsed

Dan Majerle's single-game scoring record. His teammate Chris Kaman was eventually drafted into the NBA. We both finished the best seasons of our careers. Dave went home to work on his game, which had pro potential. I went on vacation by myself to clear my head and think about free agency.

When I got back home, I worked out with Dave and Buzz. Dave also worked with me on my shot and was a big part of my improved shooting. I also fielded offers from many teams, though not from the Lakers. Having one of the most potent one-two punches in league history lessened the need for an All-Star power forward. Joe Dumars and the Pistons recruited me with passion and made it a tough decision. I was a fan of Joe D, and he was so candid on our visit, acknowledging the challenges of playing in your home city and promising a championship in years to come. He also had Martin Lawrence dressed as his popular character Jerome do a recruiting video asking me to play for the Pistons. I was humbled, and it was funny. San Antonio came in a close second, being that I had a great relationship with Coach Popovich. They promised me I'd start alongside Tim Duncan because the Admiral, David Robinson, was experiencing back problems. I was a fan of Tim's, but I felt like it was his hand against mine in a card game, and I wasn't throwing mine in.

I wanted to win a championship in the place where I had helped change the culture, that had changed my outlook, that was a family that I experienced pain and joy with. I was a King, period. I resigned with the Kings, and they held a big parade for me downtown. I had never seen anything like it. It was like a championship parade with thousands of people gathered. I remember how proud my father looked when he stood on the stage with all his children. I thought, "Man, what's going to happen when we finally win one?"

Geoff Petrie made a speech, and the owners pumped up the crowd and thanked me. It was a wonderful moment, one I'll never forget. I told the Maloofs that I was signing with the team for life. Though we couldn't make that type of a deal, I told the Maloof family that I wanted to stay in Sacramento when my playing days were done and run the team. I went from not wanting to be there to never wanting to leave. I loved being a King. I wanted the pressure; I knew the choice I was making. Sacramento let me know this was home. They welcomed me, and I loved them.

Before the season, I left for New York to hang out with some friends and see Michael Jackson perform at the Garden. I canceled plans to go to the concert after hanging out too long in the city the night before and was going to attend one a day later, September 11. I woke up, turned on the TV, and watched in shock as the Twin Towers, only a few blocks away, fell. I walked around the city just blocks from where the Towers had stood, and it was a ghost town. No cabs, and most restaurants and businesses were closed. A cloud seemed to be raining ashes from the heavens; it was eerie. People were frantically calling and trying to find loved ones.

Chapter 71

One for the Ages

Before the 2001–2002 season, we traded J. Will for Mike Bibby, an old-school point guard from the Vancouver Grizzlies. I hated to see Jason go; he was my partner in crime. I also knew he was hurt. He was one of the true basketball junkies. Hell, he'll probably die on the court. He made us the most exciting team in the league. I thought he got blamed a lot for his style of play, with long threes and sick passes, but looking back, he was just ahead of his time.

Mike Bibby came in and earned his paycheck from day one. A workaholic, gym rat, basketball junkie just like Jay. Our pick-n-roll play would start off where J's and mine ended. We were on the same page from day one. He was a knockdown shooter who could finish at the rack as well. Smart and competitive.

For Sacramento fans, players, and the organization, the 2001–02 basketball season was one for the ages. We were the best and most consistent team in Sacramento history. A lot had been accomplished in my four seasons, but we had so much more potential, and we all knew it. We won a franchise record and league-best sixty-one games, five more than the previous season. For the first time in franchise history, we were Pacific Division champs. But we were always striving for "greater greatness." A memorable conversation with Coach Carril set the tone for my play and outlook. He wanted me to take a couple less shots a game and create for others on the team. He said I was one of the best passers the game had seen, regardless of position. He wanted me to make players better, get them easy shots and instill confidence. Our strength as a team was putting constant pressure on the defense no matter the unit in the game, and I had to breed that confidence in a short amount of time. He wanted me to be "patient and transfer some of my shit to the young kids." If I didn't, they wouldn't grow and be ready. I had to make the team better. I got it.

We had seven players averaging in double figures. We were number one in the league in shot attempts, second in field goal percentage, first in pace, fourth in assists, third in steals, first in total rebounds and defensive rebounds. Our defense was ranked

sixth overall. We were a balanced team. I shot 49 percent, averaged 24.5 points, 10 rebounds, and 4.8 assists along with 1.7 steals and 1.4 blocks. I only played fifty-four games after injuring my ankle on my man Juwan's foot in the preseason, and Peja, the human flamethrower, missed eleven games. We could have won more. We came out every night and sliced and diced our opponents while enjoying every second of it. Vlade and I would compete to see who could throw the nicest dime. Peja would laugh when I would yell at him to shoot it when he'd catch the rock thirty feet away. Our IQ was special. We trusted each other, which allowed for patience as a team. We ignored a side of the court all game until taking advantage of it later on in the contest. Using a team's strength against them and executing before they could make any adjustments.

I was falling more in love with the city. I was active in the Sacramento community and many local programs and charities. I saw the impact of the team's play. We inspired. No longer were the residents of Sacramento looked at as the little brother. They had the team everyone wanted, and they weren't the butt of sports fan jokes any longer. Things changed. A sign that things had changed or how they came back around again showed in our first playoff opponent, the Utah Jazz. We had dominated the Jazz during the regular season. Now we were playing them in the playoffs as the number one seed, and they were the eighth. Funny how quickly things can flip. Our first ever playoff series was against them. They were the favorites, and we were the lower seed. We had championship aspirations, and payback wasn't even on my mind. That was too small of a goal. We beat them 4–1, dominating the series. On April 29, 2002, in our closeout game, we defeated the Jazz 91–86. Peja had thirty. I had twenty-three points, nine rebounds, and four steals. Karl Malone had just fourteen points and three assists, and John Stockton added twelve points and nine assists.

Our game was clicking on all cylinders, and that was a good thing, because up next we had the Dallas Mavericks. At the time, Dallas was led by the dynamic trio of Dirk Nowitzki, Steve Nash, and Michael Finley. Don Nelson was the coach, so they played fast and let it fly, averaging 109 points per game in the postseason and leading all teams. But they couldn't hold us. Nash averaged 18 points and 8.6 assists, and Finley averaged 24.6. This is one of my favorite series of all time. The pace, the back and forth, the talent on both sides. Mike Bibby averaged 21.8 and 6.8 assists, while Vlade averaged 15.6 and 9.8 rebounds. Dirk and I went at it. He averaged 25, 11.6, and 3.2 assists. I averaged 25, 10.6, 3.4 assists, and two blocks. This was the fastest-paced series I've ever played. Every play seemed like a fast break. No matter what position you played, you had to get back on defense because everyone could score. But again, we were on a mission and won the series 4–1. Sactown!

On to play the Lakers. We knew the series would be hard fought, but we knew it was our time and no one could deny us what destiny had declared as ours. We didn't know, however, that this would be an epic series for the basketball ages!

IT WAS THE LOVE

It was the love, but it was the journey. We didn't just blink our eyes and become the number-one seed. Passion is everything—bonding, brotherhood. When you share a common background, belief system, goals, route, and understanding, that energy can be something else. Something that will sear your souls together forever. To understand anything further, we must understand moments, the true time of quiet love...

When I started to do research for this book, I went back to Sacramento and talked to Vlade, Bobby Jackson, Doug, and Peja about one of those moments. Bobby had been away from the team for a while because he broke his knuckle in a game on Christmas Day. That actually turned out to be a blessing because he spent time with his mother, Sarah, who was battling cancer. We were about to head out on an East Coast trip when we got the news that she had died. I don't remember specifics or talking much about it among teammates; I don't even think I spoke about it to Vlade. But vibes were tangible. We were going to make it up to his home in Salisbury, North Carolina, to support our brother—period.

Coach called the team together, and before he could get a sentence out, we started raising our hands in anticipation of who was going. We were prepared to forfeit our next game if it conflicted with the funeral schedule. After speaking to Bobby's cousin Scott, I asked the organization not to let Bobby know. No big deal, no press. They agreed. I remember us walking into the small church in the country thinking, *I know Vlade, Peja, Hedo and a couple of others ain't never seen nothin' like this*. It was an old-school church, hootin' and hollerin' fire and brimstone. The reverend tore the house down as he praised Sarah "for her dedicated life of service" and warned the mourners to "get your soul right, for He's coming soon."

I sat in the designated area in the choir section behind the pulpit, crying my eyes out for—but never looking at—Bobby. He knew I was there. He was a momma's boy like me. Scot told me, "When you guys entered and walked past Bobby, he immediately broke down. Up until that point, we were worried because he was not showing any emotion. He had to be strong for so many people. But you guys came and was strong for him, and that allowed him to finally grieve."

Wow. I never would've thought it meant so much. But just as it is one of mine, Bobby says that's one of his favorite sports memories. For me, it was the love. Here's some of the transcript from my sit-down with the guys talking about that moment:

Chris: You know, Bobby, I don't wanna look at anything in a negative way, and I know how special your family is. I know it was one of the worst moments in your life when your mother passed. And I remember how the rest of us felt. I could never understand what you felt. But when the team flew into your town, and your family—I don't want this to sound crazy, but to me that was one of the...

Vlade: I was so proud of our team.

Chris: That was I hate to say one of the best moments in sports, 'cause that doesn't sound right.

Vlade: Yeah. It's crazy. I did ask you today—

Bobby: Yeah, he asked how old was my mom when she passed away. She was fifty-nine.

Vlade: She was so young. And you know, it was very emotional for the whole team, you know, going there to support not just Bobby. You know, it was like no basketball, no nothing. That's a life there. We got to step it up and give him and his family support that they need for that moment. I was so proud of us.

Bobby: I think the biggest thing for me was when you lose a loved one, and somebody who's always been the backbone of your family. I think I was having the best season of my career in the NBA and I actually ended up getting hurt, and my mom was diagnosed with breast cancer. And that year, I was actually having the best year of my life. And then I end up breaking my knuckle in three places on Christmas Day. By the grace of God, I had the ability to stay with her for the last three weeks on her deathbed.

So I always think things happen for a reason, and I think that was regardless of how great I was doing on the basketball court. I think if I didn't get hurt, I think I wouldn't have had that time to spend with her those last three weeks. Outside of that, you guys coming out and being there, especially after that long East Coast road trip, it meant a lot to me because number one, I missed the team. I missed the camaraderie. I missed the brotherhood. But you only get one mom, and so you guys coming, and when Coach asked you guys, do you wanna go to support Bob? And you guys said, without a doubt. And you guys changed the plans. For me, that will always stick with me because... of the way you thought of me, as a brother. I think that will always stick with me.

And to this day, my family still talks about it. And you know, and to grace your presence and come into small Salisbury, North Carolina, it was tremendous not just for me, but it was tremendous for the city, and it was tremendous for my mom, even though she was laid to rest. I think that was probably one of the best highlights of my career. You guys having my back on probably one of the saddest days of my life. And I'm gonna be indebted to you guys. Especially the organization for making that move and allowing you guys to come out there and support your brother. 'Cause I think if it was somebody else... we were just that type, and we would've done it for anybody. That was just the type of bond and brotherhood that we had when we played together.

When you play for the love, it's not just about points or assists or who looks good. It's about a plan together, doing the extra things, the little things, the commitment, the integrity of dedication in all areas. Individual journeys and God's grace collectively brought us all here.

Even with Peja not being 100 percent, we were ready. Our history with the Lakers was well-documented: technicals, fights, close games, flops, fouls, battles, and defeat at every turn. However, the Lakers chemistry was starting to deteriorate, and since we as a team needed every advantage to combat two all-time greats in Kobe and Shaq, we didn't feel sorry for them. The only problem was, one of the two could be all that a team needed to win on any given night.

I had more fun in this series against the Lakers than I would ever have in basketball. In this epic seven-game series, we scored 692 total points, and the Lakers scored 695. Shaq played 41 minutes per game, shot 53 percent from the field, and averaged 30 points, 13 rebounds, and 2.4 blocks. Kobe averaged 44 minutes, shot 41 percent from the floor, and averaged 27 points, 11 rebounds, and 6 assists. Mike Bibby averaged 23 points on 44 percent from the field. I played 45 minutes per game, shot 51 percent from the field, and averaged 24 points, 11 rebounds, and 6 assists with a block and a steal. The second units on both teams played smart, hard-nosed ball and embodied team spirit. Both coaches were true wizards.

But in Game One, I don't know what happened. We flat-out got beat in our home arena. We were stunned. The Lakers came out and showed us emphatically that the champs were in the building, 106–99. Shaq had twenty-six points and nine boards. Kobe scored thirty. Peja wasn't able to go. I put up twenty-eight and fourteen. I do know that after the loss, when we were in the locker room, there was a feeling of "We know that's the best they can play, and we haven't begun to fight." The hardest part of the loss was waiting until the next game. We knew we were going to dominate.

Game Two was more like Kings basketball: dunking, passing, moving, everyone getting involved. We got a big game from

Bobby Jackson, who came off the bench with seventeen points. Vlade had fifteen points and fourteen rebounds. I had twenty-one points and thirteen rebounds and was sure to involve others. Kobe "only" had twenty-two (great job by Doug), while Shaq got his with thirty-five and twelve, but we won 96–90. The series was tied 1–1.

Going into Game Three, we were confident as ever. We knew their plays, were confident in our strategy, and were all on the same page. We knew we had taken their best shot and were still standing. We wanted Game Three and to take control of the series. After player intros, I took off my shooting shirt at the scorer's table and gave it to Rob, our equipment manager. I looked into the crowd of Lakers fans and got my expected "Booooo!" I loved that. I was smiling. As I started to take off my sweats, I looked to my left and saw Jack Nicholson. We had always smiled, or I'd give him a pound, but this time he whispered to me, "You are the calm before the storm." I don't know why he said that shit, 'cause he had me pumped.

Man, we went out and dominated from the beginning. The Lakers only put up fifteen points in the first quarter, while we scored thirty-two. We held them to twelve third-quarter points. Again, it was our style of play with beautiful continuity. When the dust settled, we had won 103–90. Bibby was a stone-cold killer, dominating with twenty-four points and five assists. I added twenty-six and nine boards. Doug dropped a double-double with seventeen and twelve and played his ass off on D as usual. Everybody played well. Kobe shot eight for twenty-four from the field and scored twenty-two points. Shaq still had twenty-two and nineteen. Though it was a seven-game series, our historic matchup will forever be defined by a few plays in two games.

"Damn. Damn. Damn…"

Game Four

My family was already going to the games between Sacramento and LA. I had a feeling that this could be it. That I had a legitimate chance to go to the championship. I called every head coach that I played for and flew them and their spouse out to the series. I didn't want them to miss it, and I also wanted to say thanks.

Game Four was one for the ages. A win would put us up 3–1, handing us full control of the series. We'd have two more games remaining at home, needing one win in the final three games overall. You need that type of odds going up against these cats. We started off strong—the same as Games Two and Three. Dominating, moving the ball, hitting shots, cutting, and playing great D. At the end of the first quarter, the crowd was actually booing their team! The champions. We held a sizable twenty-point advantage (40–20). We weren't playing around. There had been a lot of talking in the media about the chemistry, or lack thereof, between Shaq and Kobe. We were hoping that the end was playing out right in front of our eyes. In the second quarter we increased our lead to twenty-four, but it was hard to sustain without our best three-point shooter in Peja, plus the simple fact that the Lakers had two all-time greats in Kobe and Shaq.

Shaq went to work in the first, and Kobe woke up in the second. We were outscored 31–25 in the second quarter. Hedo took over, and we went into halftime up 65–51. It should've been 65–48. At the end of the half, the refs counted a three-point shot by Samaki Walker that left his hands after the buzzer. I couldn't believe it. Because of that play, today we have replay and a light that illuminates on the backboard when the clock hits 00.0 for a shot clock violation.

The second half was all about Shaq. The Lakers came out of the locker room playing stifling D. They pressured three-quarters court, and it slowed down our offense. Since we had to double-team Shaq, they were getting great looks from three, especially in the corners.

The final seconds of the game would be some of the most memorable in NBA history. Up two with 11.8 seconds left, we needed a stop to seal the victory. The Lakers inbounded the ball, and Kobe came to the top of the key to receive it. He drove to his right smothered by Doug, took and missed a right-hand floater that ricocheted off the rim into Shaq's hands. Shaq flopped the ball up quick, trying to avoid getting fouled and beating the clock. He missed. Our team was in the paint trying to get the ball. One rebound would seal the deal. One stop was all we needed. As time was running out, Vlade tapped the ball out of the paint in the direction of the top of the key. The rest was in slow motion.

Standing in rebound position, squarely in the center of the paint, I looked back, and the ball was headed right for Robert Horry, aka "Big Shot Bob." I ran and stretched out; I wasn't worried about fouling. I didn't know if I could even get that close to him to challenge the shot. I immediately sprinted a couple of steps and stretched out with all my might toward Horry, who was in full follow-through. He let it fly. I looked back at the basket, and my heart fell in my stomach as the crowd roared, signaling victory. It was only the second time that their team had the lead all night. They had made the first and last shot of the game. I guess sometimes that's all it takes. We lost, 100–99.

Got to, got to payback
(The big payback)
Revenge, I'm mad
(The big payback)
Got to get back, I need some get-back
Payback, payback
(The big payback)
That's it, payback, revenge
I'm mad!

You get down with my girlfriend, that ain't right
You hollering and cussing, you want to fight
Payback is a thing you gotta see
Hell, brother, do any damn thing to me
You sold me out for chicken change
(Yes you did)
You told me that they, they had it all arranged
You had me down, and that's a fact
And now you punk, you gotta get ready
For the big payback
(The big payback)
That's where I land, on the big payback
(The big payback)

"The Payback"
James Brown

We were stunned, but we weren't deflated by the loss. We'd come too far. We felt like we could've swept them, but we'd expected this. In a game like that, no matter how hard at the time, we did what a good team does. A good team looks and self-analyzes and keeps it to, "What could we have done better?" That's what we did.

Game Five

I had our entertainment department at the arena play James Brown's "The Payback" in the arena during warm-ups. I know at first they didn't understand, but man, that barn was rockin'! The sopranos singing *ooooooh*, the horns, guitar riff, the heavy drums, the funk. The words reverberated through the arena into the locker room: "I might not know karate, but I know ka-raaazy!"

Mike Bibby and I had a special relationship. We worked out together with his crazy shooting drills. I'd fly to Phoenix, and his mom would cook for me. I'd spend time with him and his family. We became close very quickly. Earlier in the season we were in Boston, trailing 90–92 at the end of the game. Coach called a time-out and called a play. As we left the huddle, I told Mike, "What he talkin' 'bout; let's go home. Give me the ball. I'ma bout to win this." He laughed. We took the ball out with ten seconds left. Mike changed the play and ran a pick-n-roll on the left side, giving us options, and if I was denied, he could go to work on the drive or step back. He trusted me. He knew what it was. He went left, drew two defenders, and passed it back to me at the top of the key for three. All net. For the win. I walked back to the huddle screaming, "I told you. I told you!" The best part about it was that he loved it.

Now, back to Game Five. The crowd was louder than ever. They were waiting for something to pop. Phil Jackson and his coaching staff wore ear plugs. It seemed as if everyone in the lower bowl of the arena had a cowbell and rang it like they were trying to pop anyone's eardrum in listening distance. The game started off close and kept going back and forth. Early on, Coach got a technical, and rightfully so. There were terrible calls made. Shaq was committing offensive fouls like a muuufug. In the first quarter I noticed that defensively the Lakers were going over every dribble handoff between me and Bibby, so I started to fake the handoff and keep it. It worked for me and ultimately our team at the end. With a minute or so in the first quarter, I faked a dribble handoff with Bibby and drew a foul on Shaq, his second. And that was big. He had twelve in the first. I had ten points, and the Lakers led 33–27. LA had an impressive record, winning twelve out of thirteen postseason games on the road dating a year back. That's tough.

Peja made his series debut in the second quarter. We were asking a lot of him, being that he was injured, and we had no practice time available. The game was intense. Shaq was throwing everybody around like rag dolls. Doug fouled out, Shaq fouled out, and LA held a one-point lead with 25 seconds left in the game. Lakers ball. Kobe received the rock off the inbounds. He drove with 25 seconds left. Vlade came over on help side D and blocked his shot. Our ball. Time-out. 8.2 remaining on the clock, 92–91 Lakers. Coach Adelman called my play option: I was to catch it, with Mike coming around. In other words, our dribble handoff. I had been faking it all game. We left the huddle. Mike looked at me and said, "Pass me the ball … I'ma knock it down." I didn't respond; I just laughed.

Vlade set the screen. I caught the inbound pass and dribbled toward the baseline where Mike was starting to come off the baseline with Derek Fisher trailing him. I knew he was going to stay with Mike or flop. Mike, coming to his left, took the handoff. I set a screen on Fisher, and Samaki Walker, who was guarding me, stayed with me. Perfect. Fisher flopped as Mike went up with a picture-perfect jumper. Wet—all net. He went back to the bench yelling, "I told you! I told you!"

Now time for one last play. Kobe caught the inbounds with Bobby Jackson draped all over him. I came over for the double-team and got a clean block. Game over. 92–91. We took a commanding 3–2 lead after everything. We were up and ready to get one more so that we could represent the West in the NBA Championship. Shaq finished with twenty-eight and seven rebounds, and Kobe had thirty, five, and five; but Bibby had twenty-three, and I had twenty-nine and thirteen. This was surreal. I was closer than I've ever been to winning a chip in the league. It was on.

Game Six

Forget an intro, set-up, or transition. We were cheated. Anyone who saw the game knows that. I don't care if anyone agrees or disagrees, I know that we were cheated, and no one can tell me different. It was a helpless feeling. It was the first time I felt I was cheated throughout an entire game in my life. The loss in Game Six hurt more than any loss I've ever been a part of. Any! The mental preparation, the focus, the reward was at our fingertips.

Who could have? Forget all the yap, here are the facts. I had twenty-six points, thirteen rebounds, and eight assists. Mike Bibby twenty-three. Shaq had forty-one and seventeen, and Kobe had thirty-one and eleven.

We were dominating early. Scoring at will. Then we started to notice terrible, timely calls. Meaning calls that stopped runs and ended droughts or started scoring barrages for them. In the fourth quarter alone, the Lakers shot twenty-seven free throws. Twenty-seven. That means an early bonus, leading to more free-throw opportunities. It also means we had to play tentatively all game because we were in foul trouble. Vlade fouled out; Scot Pollard fouled out in eleven minutes. They did him wrong.

One time as our team was running back on defense, I screamed, "Don't play no D." We laughed and put our hands down, and a foul was called. We still fought back, and the final three minutes of the game says it all. I was called for an offensive foul on a made jump hook. That was my fourth. That basket would have increased our lead to four with a free throw coming. Next play, on the other end, Robert Horry grabbed Vlade's arm, and Vlade was called for the foul. The referee who made the call wouldn't even look at me; he didn't have the balls. He knew what was going on. Vlade now had to go to the bench. Lawrence Funderburke (who replaced Vlade) drove to the hole on a play and was fouled by Shaq. It should've been a flagrant. It was a horrible foul.

The very next play, right in front of a referee, I went and blocked Kobe's shot as he was driving on the baseline. The refs called a foul on me. Kobe was surprised they made the call. I then went to my jump hook that Horry couldn't stop. He fouled me, not just that he fouled me, but I saw the ref turn away as my shot totally missed the rim... from seven feet out. It was a helpless feeling. One I've never experienced. The final straw came—we were trailing by one and the Lakers were inbounding the ball with twelve seconds on the clock. We were in a full-court press. Mike was denying an entry pass to Kobe, who then elbowed the shit out of him and almost knocked him out. Mike was shook up. He had cartoon birds swirling around his head. He was bleeding from his mouth and laying on the floor, trying to get his thang together. Kobe shot two free throws because the refs called a foul on Bibby.

The refs again couldn't even look at us. They were terrible. I don't care about the score. We lost; we were downright cheated. I don't care about could've, should've. I was there. I know. I went into the locker room crushed. As a team, we were going over how they cheated us. I even said to the cameras from TV stations around the world that this was not a fair contest tonight. They knew. Everyone knew: the commentators, the garbage-ass refs, the reporters—but so what? Play on...

Game Seven

"The Payback" by James Brown was rockin' through the stadium yet again. Reverberating through our locker room. Hedo got the start for Peja, who wasn't 100 percent healthy. The guys were loose and confident as usual, but we knew what we were up against: Goliath.

Vlade won the tip, and we came out hitting first, getting our crowd in the game. It allowed us to play a tad tentatively (good or bad) on the defensive end because we didn't want to get into foul trouble. We'd rather have a track race. The game stayed close throughout, despite our fast start. The Lakers fought back and took the lead 22–21 at the end of the first. The Lakers switched defensive strategies for Game Seven. They double-teamed me, consistently. I was used to it from other teams but was surprised against LA. Offensively, I was effective through penetrating and passing. As a team, we managed to regain the lead at half, 54–52.

Shaq was a beast. He was so dominant that we had to collapse around him. Offensively, I started to drive more with the intent to score, but as the defense closed in, I'd facilitate finding the open man. With nine minutes left in the fourth, there had already been thirteen lead changes and ten ties. Vlade fouled out on a bad call, but we couldn't complain. Up to that point we had let scoring opportunities go, shooting ten of twenty-two from the free-throw line. And now I had to check Shaq the rest of the way. I'd have to use my length to be any kind of deterrent on his shot and do the work early, keeping him from establishing post position too low. Easy to say, harder to do.

It's 5.3 seconds left, last play of regulation, and all tied at 100. Game, championship, and season on the line. I'm checking Shaq on the right block. I had to pick my poison. So I want him to go middle over his right shoulder. I knew they were going to come to him. I pushed him out as far as I could and forced the shot over his right shoulder. He shoots for the game. Misses, and it's overtime. To this point, it's been an epic series and overtime seems like the only way it should end.

I scored the first bucket of OT, hitting a jumper over Diesel, but his presence on the floor caused so many problems. His duck-ins, choosing which direction from which to double-team, his passing, his game. We had the lead with two minutes left, 106–104. But we'd miss Vlade down the stretch. Peja wasn't himself, and I didn't do enough. Meanwhile, the Lakers played championship ball. Shaq had thirty-five and thirteen, Kobe had thirty and ten. Bibby had twenty-nine, and I finished with twenty, eight, and eleven. Not enough. I gave dap to Shaq and Kobe, sincerely wishing them the best. Those were some bad boys! At the end of the day, we couldn't blame anyone but ourselves. We lost the game. We lost the series. Period.

YOU TRIPPIN'

I just knew that we were going to win the title. I knew our work ethic and talent, and I felt that it was time. I had a close relationship with my teammates, and I felt that as the leader and most desperate to win a chip that I would offer a little more incentive. A Benz. I ordered thirteen drop-top Mercedes Benzes that would be delivered to my teammates the first of July. Though the incentive didn't guarantee a championship, our efforts made me want to show my appreciation. After we lost the series, the guys were hurt. They knew the plan. So appreciative I adjusted. I sent every teammate and a plus-one to Jamaica, my favorite place. But there was a catch. I placed them at a resort of my choice. The resort was called Hedonism, and it was a nudist establishment. Everyone of all ages was naked at all times. They got a kick out of it, except Lawrence Funderburke. He wanted to kill me, but I didn't care. He had gone to Ohio State. Some enjoyed it a little too much, but that's neither here nor there.

The world keeps moving and no one cares, so I had to stay ready. Any night in the NBA, you can get it. At that time the Western Conference was a power forwards league, and to separate yourself, you had to do it all. Rebound, pass, shoot, dribble, post up, play D. The league was changing, and I was happy about that, but I was numb over the summer. I just went through the motions to stay busy, and because I knew I had to do the work, my heart wasn't in it. I was hurt over the loss.

About a month later, my agent called and told me that
I had been subpoenaed by the federal government to
testify about my relationship with Ed Martin before
a grand jury. When I asked why, he said that Ed was running
a numbers racket at the plant, and his house was raided by
federal agents. He was being charged with a number of crimes,
including tax fraud. He said they found some pieces of paper
listing basketball players' names, and my name was on his list. He
told me that many players had already gone in to testify and that
it was no big deal. They weren't out to get me, just tell the truth.

I testified in front of the grand jury, but I really didn't have
much to offer. The prosecutor must've thought I did, because
he kept coming at me. At one point our back-and-forth got so
contentious that I asked to speak with my lawyer. I knew I had
the biggest name on the list, but I was there testifying about a
man's tax fraud, and I was being badgered as if I was on trial.
I know what it's like to have someone in power use celebrity as
a way to hurt, harm, or climb a political work ladder, but with
this, I also assumed that it was well known and documented that
I didn't get paid to go to college. I embraced my plight and that of
many people who come from where I came from. I spoke about
it, there were stories done and written, and people and coaches
knew the integrity of my family. But something didn't feel right.

Basketball was running on an all-time high. I followed in the
footsteps of Isiah Thomas and bought the Great Lake Storm,
a CBA team in Flint, Michigan. At the same time, my brother
David got a tryout with the Kings. He came to training camp and
did more than hold his own. He went to work, but that's not just
my opinion. Mike, Bobby, and Doug all felt he could've made the
squad. After a preseason game against the Jazz, John Stockton
himself came over and said, "Damn. Your brother can play."
He didn't make the team, but he really did his thing. I was so
proud of him.

I came a long way, the average years played by an NBA player
was about three and half to four years. I was entering my tenth
season. I was excited, and though we were still hungover from

405

disappointment from the season before, we shook it off in time to get it popping again. Right away we got back to the great play we'd become known for. We won fifty-nine games, were crowned Pacific Division champs, and secured the second-best record in the NBA. We were second in a defensive rating. As always, Coach Carril's offensive style had us first in pace. I averaged 23 points, 10.5 rebounds, 5.4 assists, 1.6 steals, and a block. The Lakers chemistry and dynasty was coming to an end, and our aspirations to win a championship remained. Defeating the Lakers was second on our list of our priorities. We had a great rhythm, and our chemistry was stronger than ever. I was selected as an All-Star for the fifth time, but I did not attend. Something wasn't right.

We visited the Lakers on Christmas Day. It was one of our classic backdoor, open-jump-shot, dunk-on-you, smile-and-win games. I had twenty-five and fifteen. Peja split their heads open with twenty-six. Kobe had twenty-seven and fifteen rebounds, and Shaq had twenty-seven and seventeen rebounds. We loved playing on Christmas, while kids were opening their presents and hanging with family. We loved showing the world what the greatest show on the court looked like, but we really weren't crazy happy with the win. We had bigger fish to fry. Nothing other than a trophy would work. The next morning, I went to work out and shoot free throws with Buzz, and my basketball life would change forever.

I was talking with Buzz, laughing and shooting free throws, when in the middle of taking a shot I felt a sting-like pain on the side of my left knee. It felt like your tongue touching a battery. It was really uncomfortable. It was a sharp, long, unrelenting, dull pain that increased when I tried to move laterally or stop and run backwards. I thought nothing of it and tried to shake it off, but I couldn't. Over time it got worse, and there was so much pain that I had to hop up and down the stairs after some games. I even had a pair of crutches that I'd use on occasion. I had to ice my knee before games because of swelling and intense pain. I remember leaving a movie because I couldn't sit due to the pain.

The pills prescribed made me sick, and the pain at times was nasty. The best pain reliever was the promise of holding the Larry O'Brien Trophy. That's what got me through—until I got a call from my agent telling me that Ed was lying to the feds about our relationship. I knew that they were squeezing him, but at first, I thought nothing of it. Then, my agent said, "He has to give them something, and you're the biggest name he knows. The media is going to be at practice today. He used you, and you should let everyone know. You should tell him how he preyed on kids."

I knew Ed was full of shit, but I should've stayed silent. It was out of my control. Sending shots through the media was the last thing I should have done. I should've never let his emotional response affect me. But I did. In a press conference after a workout, I told the media that Ed was an old man who preyed on kids. I was pissed that he lied. Later some people reached out to me saying Ed wanted me to know that his feelings were hurt, but he apologized. He said he didn't know what else to do and that the feds were putting words in his mouth. He also needed money and asked if I could help (ain't that a bitch). Who knew what the truth was, but I didn't want nothing to do with nothing.

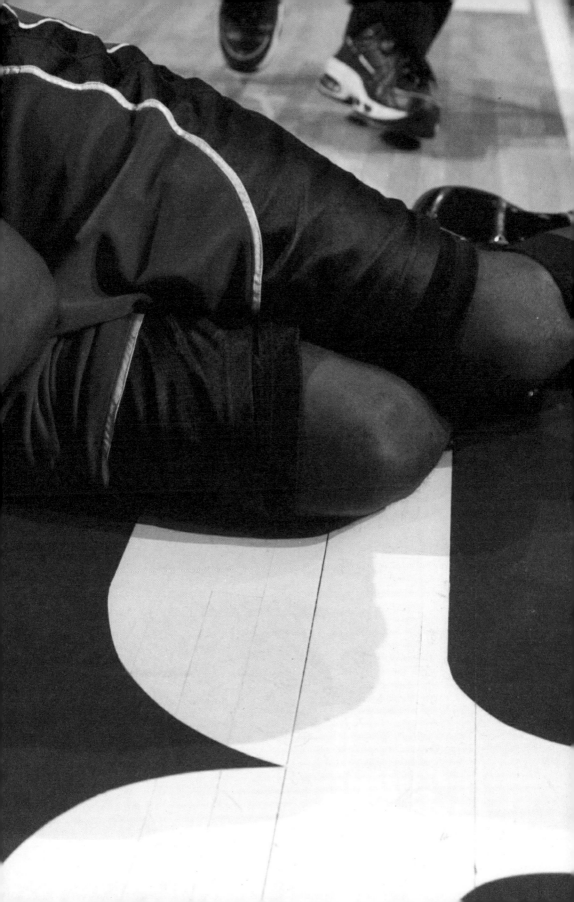

We headed into the playoffs as first in the Pacific, and the only team that played as well as we did was our "little brother," the Dallas Mavericks. They won sixty games. The Mavs were up and coming, but they even knew we were better. First things first. Utah Jazz. We ran through Utah in five games, losing one where it would only be right, in Utah. We lost to Stockton and Malone in a game that would serve as the duo's last home win. I'll give them that, but I had the honor of sending the great guard out the right way, with a win and a blowout large enough to get him an early standing ovation that was due. I had twenty-six and eleven in his final game. He had eight points and seven assists in what would be the last time this legendary duo suited up together.

John Stockton announced his retirement after the game. I sat on the plane with a beer reminiscing with my rookie, Gerald Wallace, about Stockton and Malone stories. I told him that it was an honor to be on the court with him for his last game and that one day we would tell our kids about the legend of John Stockton.

The time for nostalgia was over. We were going up against a team full of flamethrowers, future Hall of Famers, and transcendent game changers. We had beat them the year before in five games, and we knew we were the better team, but we didn't underestimate their growth. We started the series off in Dallas. Game One. My knee was burning, and I had to get treatment and ice prior to the game to get my leg to function. But I was a go, and our team came out and showed that this was our time. If not now, then when? That was my mental state. We won Game One 108–91 in a sold-out American Airlines Center. Mark Cuban put his foot in the new arena. It was, by far, one of the best arenas I'd ever played in. Peja came out throwing darts, giving them twenty-six. I had twenty-four and nine assists. We moved the rock, executed on O, and played locked-down, focused D. We also won Game Two, 124–113. Dirk was held to eighteen and eleven, but three more players—Van Exel, Nash, and Finley—had twenty, so even in a loss, they scored in droves.

I remember smacking the floor in pain and frustration. I had been injured many times, but this time something wasn't right. I was killing whomever was trying to check me. The ice and stem had me feeling great before and after our halftime break. We were down double digits.

I asked Coach to stay in. We felt like we could make a comeback at any moment. I was hot. I had my defenders up all game, hitting jump shots, so in the third quarter, I made a cut in an attempt to go for an oop, and I felt something in my knee pop. Without anyone pushing me or tripping me, without any contact at all, I fell to the floor. I immediately knew it was over. I also knew my game would never be the same.

My worst fear appeared. I couldn't believe that after all that had transpired over my time in Sac, let alone the growth of our team and heading for a championship, this happens. I was still feeling the pain of losing to the Lakers. I wanted redemption. Shit ain't supposed to happen this way! I was helped off the court by Mateen Cleaves and G. Wallace. My young boys. I saw it in their eyes. We were all disappointed. In seconds the truth settled in. Individually and collectively, we were done. I sat in the locker room quietly, in disbelief. Mentally, I was exhausted.

I went straight to surgery, which was performed by Dr. James Allen, a world-renowned surgeon. When it comes to sports medicine, he's worked on everyone. He's funny, calming, and thorough. He allowed my mom to watch the surgery, and I thought that was sick but nice of him. I had a torn medial collateral ligament, but what was different was that I also had to have a procedure called microfracture. This procedure is to repair cartilage by creating tiny fractures in the underlying bone. This allows the bone marrow, which contains stem cells, to seep out of the fractures, creating a blood clot that helps build cells. This surgical technique was rather new, and all my knowledge was limited to the fact that it helped end Penny's and Jamal Mashburn's careers. For me, the outlook was bleak. There wasn't enough info.

The worst part about the surgery is that you can't put any pressure on your leg or knee for six months. So your muscle in that area really weakens and atrophies. I couldn't do anything after surgery but lay down. I would close my eyes and practice in my head. I didn't want to lose anything. The last few years I hadn't felt all that athletic. I suffered ankle injuries that constantly took their toll on me. I felt that this injury could be it. No one my size came back from this. I knew that the chips were stacked against me. I was still dealing with the pain of losing to the Lakers two years prior and the letdown of not getting to go after a championship after being seriously injured.

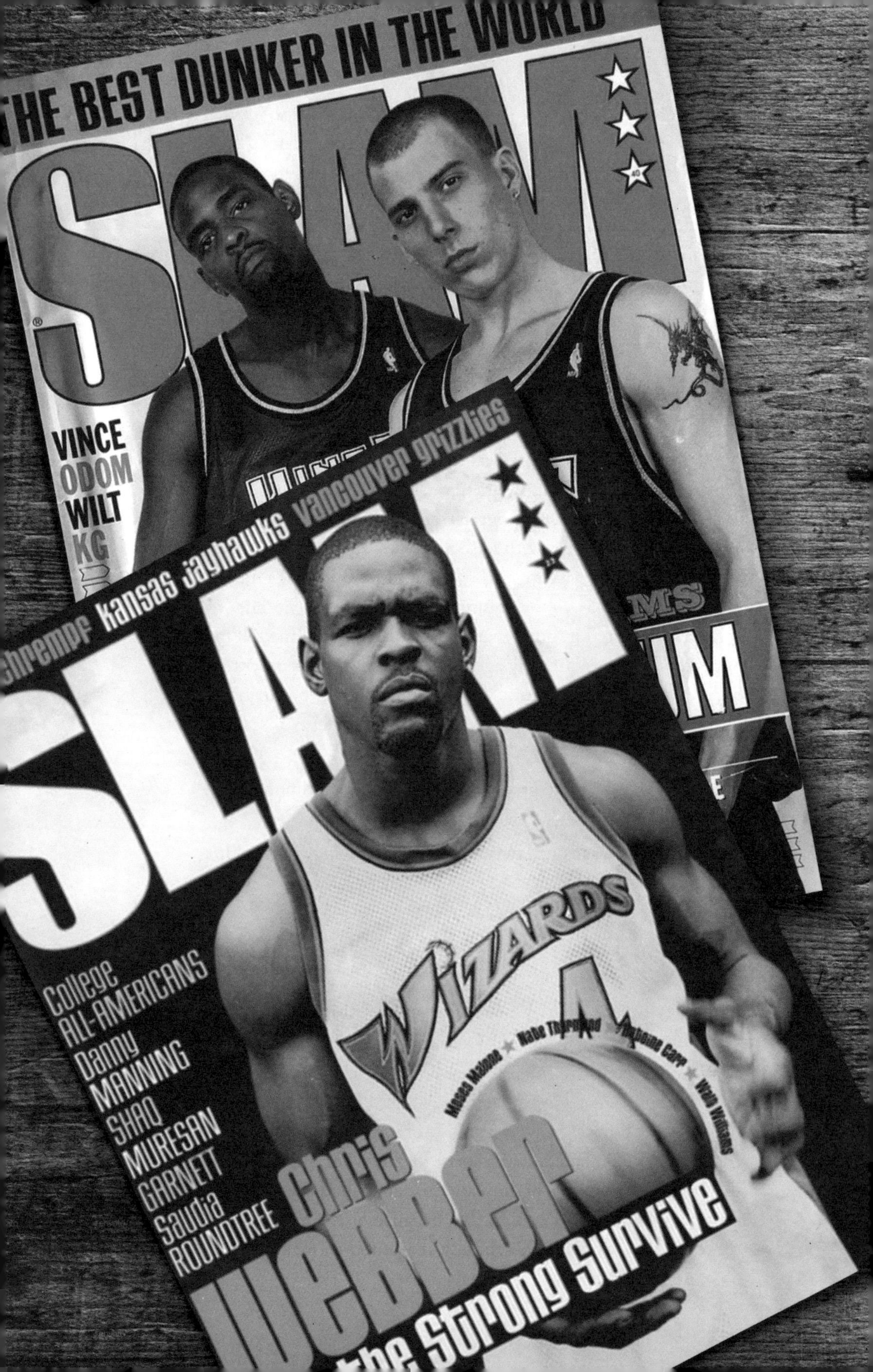

THE BEST DUNKER IN THE WORLD

SLAM

VINCE
ODOM
WILT
KG

chrempf kansas jayhawks vancouver grizzlies

SLAM

College
ALL-AMERICANS
Danny
MANNING
SHAQ
MURESAN
GARNETT
Saudia
ROUNDTREE

WIZARDS

Chris
WEBBER
the Strong Survive

I had paperwork from Zeke's loan to my pops, and he could testify for the rest. The fact that Ed was mad at me for not being close to him like the other cats helped prove our point. My lawyer couldn't wait to put him on the stand. We even had film from the Final Four and pictures from the weekend of my brothers' and sister's outfits. My brother wore a Miami hat because we couldn't afford a new Michigan one. We found out that the total of the truck that I didn't own or drive was $9,000 but was quoted as being a value of $20,000 and something. "He was a numbers man. You don't think he's going to put a hundred on ten?" I agreed, so he filed a motion talking about a scrap of papers with false numbers, and the judge made a ruling that there was no such thing as $280,000. The number was false. That was victory number one. Of course, no one (to this day) reported it, but I was confident. You couldn't tell me nothing until days later my agent told me that the prosecutors decided to charge my aunt and my father with perjury and obstruction of justice. It was a gut punch.

"Why?"

"Well, you asked to go outside during your testimony."

"Yeah."

"Well, she was your lawyer, and they're saying you couldn't speak with her."

"What?"

"You weren't allowed to speak to her."

"What?"

"They want to put pressure on you, so they're going after your family."

I asked what the consequences of their charges were, and he said that with felonies, jail time should be expected. Tou-fucking-ché. Ed passed away a couple of months before the trial. I felt terribly conflicted. I was sorry for his wife, and I felt that the pressure of the feds on him and his family had been wearing on him. But I knew I was in this because of his bravado. He represented a whole high school but wanted to make sure to

413

young hoopers he was "The Godfather" because he had a relationship with my family. Now that my family was added to the indictment, I had some thinking to do.

After contemplating, I went over to my lawyer, Steve Fishman's, house, and his lovely wife made some burgers while I played with the kids in the kitchen. I asked Steve to give me the skinny on everything. Where we were and headed. He told me that there had been significant movements in our trial. He said, "The government don't play, and they hate to be embarrassed. If this goes to trial, they will schedule it during the season and make you miss a significant number of games, probably around playoff time. They must not be as confident in their case, because they have offered a plea."

"Why?"

"Because they hate to lose. They've offered a dismissal of all charges against your father and aunt."

"Do they have anything on my father and aunt?"

"Not from anything we see."

"What else? What about me?"

"Well, they are offering to drop three of four counts and are offering you a plea deal that could be a misdemeanor."

"Was it good?"

"The government rarely goes this far. You'd have to plead guilty to contempt of court."

"If they don't believe me and think I'm lying, isn't that perjury? Contempt means you were disobedient to or disrespectful toward a court of law or its officers."

He reiterated that the judge would not be easy on me and there was no guarantee it would be a misdemeanor. She would also adjourn court for two years, and I would have to bring my charitable educational program and run it in the D. I would be assessed a fine of $100,000 and court costs. I would also be placed on probation for two years. Then after all my obligations were met, I would come back and see whether or not the judge would approve, and if I'd have a felony or misdemeanor.

I was pissed there were no guarantees, and I could win my case. As far as risk went, it was a no-brainer. Without blinking, I agreed to the deal. They had me when they started messing with my pops, plain and simple. My aunt had lost about thirty pounds throughout the ordeal. Her name was maligned in the papers. Her peers threw shots at her. It was affecting my father as well. Not to the extent of weight loss or anything, but to accuse us of taking money is like taking his character and saying he isn't who he is. Being viewed differently by his fellow worshippers, the people on his job, his family. It was in the paper every day and on talk radio, and I didn't want my father going through that crazy circus. If you've ever been to trial, you understand the crazy shit they can ask you or try to embarrass you with. They make sure that even if you're innocent, that you come out worse for the wear. I did not want my father going through that with the pressure of jail time. I couldn't risk it. "Go ahead and tell them I'll take the deal," I said.

I was thankful that the judge was fair and that I could try to move on. There were rumors that the lead prosecutor was making my case a live audition for the NCAA. He wanted to work for the NCAA and let it be known to the appropriate people. What could be better than having me on his résumé?

I got to work quickly with my family and head of my foundation, Erika Bjork. Bjork was my right-hand lady and moved with knowledge and surgical precision. We set up a summer school program in one of the worst neighborhoods in Detroit. I was there every day from 8:00 a.m. to 4:00 p.m. I became close with the staff, students, and parents. We had a curriculum for reading, art, and math, but reading was the main focus. Kids were rewarded with surprises like trips to the movies to see the book that we read come to life, or other good stuff to keep them excited, interested, and on their toes. Of course, we included field trips and gym time. The classes were as fun as they were challenging. This experience with the kids was one of the best experiences of my life. They gave me true love and sincere company, and the time with my mom, pop, and aunt was special as well. Talk about love.

My parole officer was impressed with our efforts and wrote a dope recommendation. I became close to him, and he helped immensely with my program. At the end of our time together, I found out that he was familiar with Ed through the court system and interviews. He told me that Ed was disappointed that I didn't stay in touch and keep him in my circle after I went pro.

I went to court, and the judge was pleased with me for taking her orders seriously. Damn right I took them seriously. I went downstairs, pulled out a blank check, wrote "One hundred thousand dollars and zero cents" on the line that said amount, signed my name, and then, with the support of my crutches, walked out of the courthouse and stood on the steps of the federal building. I gave an apology to anyone who was hurt by the events that took place or something like that; I was so pissed I don't really remember what I said.

Kev pulled up in front of the building behind the reporters, and I slid off into the wind. I was hurt, pissed, and relieved that it was over... but it wasn't. Country Day fought off the MHSSA's attempt to remove me from the Michigan men's high school basketball record books (even though I can't find my high school stats anywhere in the record books). They also fought the NCAA and whoever else wanted to remove my name or trophies that we won. They had proof that I didn't take money to go to Michigan. Led by the Honorable Dennis Archer Jr., they made a compelling case and defeated both the NCAA and MHSSA.

I did not know this then, but at the same time, the University of Michigan was taking down our Final Four banners at Crisler Center. I couldn't believe it. Why were they jumping the gun? They knew there was no such thing as the $280,000. They knew Ed before me. Many years before me. They knew Ed and didn't even tell me they knew Ed. So, you as a university have been dealing with Ed for over thirty years and dozens of players, and you blame me?

My anger grew. We believed the president of the university at the time was using me to be a distraction from what only they knew. I got calls from school officials apologizing to me for how I was being treated. They told me it was unfair, but they never said why. They'd say we know what happened and that your family would never do those things, but they would never say why the school conceded and the banners were coming down. The school announced that I was banned for ten years. Not one person from the University of Michigan spoke up for me—no teammates, no coaches, no one. I was now the bad guy, and the discussion of college athletes and pay versus education again had a villain. Pawns, I tell you. I was the bad guy. The poster boy for all that was wrong with college. Me. The one whose mom spoke to me about how "We Webbers don't sell our souls." Now it looked like we'd had a family fire sale of souls for $30,000 to Ed Martin Racketeers Inc.

At that point I had to just take it. Running around crazy trying to prove the impossible will smother your peace. I started to peep game. My grandfather used to say, "All you gotta do is sit still and watch."

I was speaking with Bill Russell once, just rapping about basketball. I asked him, "Who was better between Shaq and Wilt?" He replied, "They'll never play. I don't compare ghosts." He was speaking of all the careers that can't be compared. Point taken. So instead of a list of all-time greats, here's my list of the all-time great NBA ballers I played with and against:

Best HOPS

1. Gerald Wallace
2. Ben Wallace
3. Keon Clark
4. Kenny "Sky" Walker
5. Andre Iguodala

Best Passers

1. Rod Strickland
2. Jason Williams
3. Vlade Divac
4. Juwan Howard
5. Billy Owens

Best Handles

1. Jason Williams
2. Rod Strickland
3. Allen Iverson
4. God Shammgod
5. Ronald Dupree

Best Shooters

1. Peja Stojakovic
2. Chris Mullin
3. Kyle Korver
4. Rip Hamilton
5. Tim Legler

Best Defenders of the Throne

They'd swat your shit. I looked forward to dunking on them.

1. Dikembe Mutombo
2. Hakeem Olajuwon
3. Alonzo Mourning
4. Shawn Bradley
5. Ben Wallace

Best Nicknames

Gotta open it up to all sports for this one...

1. The Great One (Wayne Gretzky)
2. Magic Johnson (Earvin Johnson Jr.)
3. The Hitman (Thomas Hearns)
4. The Black Mamba (Kobe Bryant)
5. The Mailman (Karl Malone)

I was a scratch the first fifty-three games of the season. It was difficult sitting out with an injury for most of the season. I was suspended the first ten games of the season for violating the league's substance policy. I now was into holistic medicine. Everything from acupuncture, THC oil, CBD, and cannabis, because the medicine they were giving me was constantly making me sick, and my stomach felt like it was growing a hole. It was embarrassing, but I knew the world would catch up on natural medicine later. My job was to heal. I'd miss the first game of the season against Cleveland, and some new kid named LeBron James made his introduction to basketball greatness. He was nice! I made sure I lived in the gym and got in great shape. I could only think of getting back to the playoffs and trying to win a championship. Nothing else felt worth it. My thought was that you only get so many chances, and I wanted a championship. I was advised that waiting a full year might be in my best interest, but I couldn't do that. No siiir! I played in my first game on the day after my thirty-first birthday, eleven months after my injury and nine months after surgery. Our team was 44–15, and I was on a mission to come out and not miss a beat. I wanted to come out and defy any negativity. I did. In only thirty minutes, I shot twelve for eighteen and had twenty-six points, twelve rebounds, and four assists —the most by any player in NBA history who had sat out fifty or more games in a season. We beat the Clippers 113–106 in my return. The small victories. I worked my ass off and stayed the course over the summer and season, patiently waiting, and it paid off.

Although I played well, my knee experienced some fatigue and extreme pain from time to time. I played in twenty-three games, averaging eighteen points and nine rebounds, my lowest total since my rookie season. We made it to the playoffs with fifty-five wins. We had a rematch in the first round against the Mavs. It was eerie playing in that arena where I had suffered my injury, but I had to jump back on that horse. Juwan had joined the Mavs, and I knew they got him just to guard me because he could do it better than anyone. But I averaged nineteen points and nine rebounds, and we won the series 4–1, with Mike leading the team in scoring at twenty-four a game. He was coming into his own as a leader.

Trouble was, my knee was absolutely killing me. I was laboring when trying to run or stop on a dime. My muscles had atrophied, and fatigue was setting in. With Kevin Garnett and crew up next, I would be in for it even if I was completely healthy or in prime condition, and I definitely was not.

Both teams knew that it would be a tough series. The Timberwolves had acquired some new players, including my boy Spree and Sam Cassell. I knew how good both of these cats were, but I had confidence in our guards. I couldn't move laterally, and I was in so much pain that my after-practice routine was cut. But so what? The series went back and forth, and on off days I would not leave the hotel or house, only walking to use the bathroom or shower. I had to stay off my leg and wear a knee brace that was crazy uncomfortable. Meanwhile, KG was playing his best ball ever. He was the league MVP that year and proved it every night. Spree and Sam Cassell wanted to make the most of what could be their last go-round. On our end, Peja was hitting some of the toughest threes and layups you'd ever seen, and Doug was playing his ass off on the defensive end. Vlade was not playing like a thirty-six-year-old who'd had three different pro careers.

Game Seven in Minnesota went down to the wire. We were trailing the Wolves 83–80. Off the inbound pass, I stepped back behind the line, dribbled, and pump faked KG in the air for the open three. I knew it

was good. It went in and out. Game over. I knelt on the court after that miss. I knew the end was near. I got up, wished K. Boogie the best, and embraced my OG Spree and made sure he knew I was pulling for him. I took my time leaving the court, taking it all in. I knew this could be my last hurrah. I decided in the locker room that I would retire. I couldn't move, and it was frustrating. My leg hurt like hell, and I didn't want to be remembered as a "Fred Sanford" runner. My midseason return was one for the books. But I was in pain, and if it was going to get worse, and if

I couldn't be successful, it wouldn't be worth it. I didn't tell anyone my decision.

The Timberwolves eventually lost to the Lakers in six, and the Lakers lost in the Finals to the Pistons in five. Funny, Joe D. predicted this.

✦ ✦ ✦

BLUNT ASHES

I met Nas during my playing days, and we quickly became lifelong friends. I've traveled the world to watch him perform and witnessed him write classics in the studio, and he's come to games. We've raced Rolls Royces and traded books on Africa. We have a mutual respect for each other's profession and for what it takes to be great. As a hip-hop fan, I realize that he's one of, if not the best to ever, to do it. Back then, I never would have thought that I would produce beats for hip-hop's Michael Jordan.

The first beat I made for him was for his album *Hip Hop Is Dead*. We were in the studio, and he was spitting out song after song. Early one morning around three o'clock, he told me to put in a CD of beats I'd been playing earlier that day. I did. After listening about four or five times, he casually told the engineer to load one of them up. I didn't pay any mind to it; why would I?

About a week prior, we were at my house sipping, listening to some old music, and philosophizing with my father about the world: old days, old music, stars, fads, etc. After my pops went to sleep, we sat there and talked about our fathers, friends, stardom, the block, the setups, and life in general. Now we were in the studio, and he said, "Let me hear what I just did." Out of the speakers I heard Nas talk:

"Yo, I wonder if Langston Hughes and Alex Haley got blazed before they told stories. Well I'ma get blazed before I tell y'all stories. I saw this man on TV today; he lost his son, his son died, and so he had him cremated, took his ashes and made it into a diamond ring. Now he watch his son shine every day. I just thought about that while I'm sitting here ashin' in this ashtray."

Then the rap started:

"The making of a mad band, intricate stories of DeVante Swing, Ava Gardner, the crashin' of James Dean..."

I jumped up and ran out of the room. I couldn't take it. I could not sit and listen to the next word. The second one I did for him was another song that I could definitely relate to. Salaam Remi was in the studio with Nas cooking up crack as they do when they get together. I just so happened to mention to Salaam that it was a sample that I'd been wanting to chop up for the longest time, and I would as soon as I got home. I said, "Remember Nipsey Russell in *The Wiz*? When he was in the junkyard? I want the words in the beginning and backup singers singin'."

Nas had already recorded "Surviving the Times" but wasn't 100 on the beat. Salaam gave me the a cappella, and I made the beat around the vocal. The subject matter of his rhymes and the sample went perfect. I also think I wanted to use that because I heard my basketball career through his words of the song.

The song starts off with Nipsey singing:

> But that's the whole tragic point, my friends.
> What would I do...
> If I could suddenly feel
> And to know once again
> That what I feel is real.
> I could cry, I could smile
> I might lay back for a while
> Tell me what would I do
> if I could feel?

Of course, Nas murdered it. "Surviving the Times" was featured on his greatest hits album.

Peace-Son-Salaam Remi-Jungle.

I knew my game would have to adapt, once again, after injuries. Not to mention this one was serious, significant. I couldn't shake it, but I felt good. The Lakers weren't the same. Shaq was in Miami, and we always beat Dallas. I felt like we had a legitimate chance to get to the championship. I knew that I would never be the same physically, my knee wouldn't let me be. I had to readjust my game. More than physical, something else wasn't right—our team chemistry. I mean, it was good. There was nothing you could see on the surface, but Vlade left for LA, where it all began for him. I think even in the players' hearts, we knew that if we won one it wouldn't feel as good without the big fella. I let my chaplain, Pastor Carthen, know my concerns. I tried to understand why I felt so uneasy. Well, change was coming. I could feel it.

We started off the season 0–3, the worst start since our core came together. We managed to recover and posted a 15–6 record after the slow start. We were still ballin', and as a team we felt that we could still win a championship, but ownership felt different. This is where things go left. February 22, 2005, in ARCO Arena, we hosted the Atlanta Hawks. I had thirty points and seven assists in a 114–104 victory. The win brought our record to 34–20. I was thirty-one years old averaging 21.3 points, 9.7 rebounds, and 5.5 assists. Pretty good for damaged goods. After the game, we jumped on our team plane and headed to Dallas, one of my favorite cities to hang out in.

The night before the game against Dallas, while I was getting ready to go out with some high school friends, I received a call. It was our GM, Geoff Petrie.

"Hey, Chris. Wanted to give you a call."

"Hey, Geoff. What's going on? What's good?"

"We were calling because we just got an offer for you."

"An offer? For me?"

"Yeah, the 76ers called and said they wanted to make an offer for you. What do ya think?"

"What do I think? What do you mean, what do I think? I think if you don't want me here anymore, I don't want to be here. After everything we've been through, Geoff, that's fucked up."

That's all I remember of our conversation. We got off the phone, and I couldn't believe it. I was in shock. This hurt far more than Golden State or Washington. I never saw this day coming. I thought I'd retire with the team after a championship and then come back and run it like Joe D. did in Detroit. That's why I stayed. I stayed for forever, not just a contract. That was why Geoff knew to call me. I had a no-trade clause, and an agent might have had a cooler head and said don't accept it. I was pissed, hurt, and emotional. That's why I agreed to the deal. I could've blocked it. I was happy to play with AI.

Within five minutes of getting off the phone with Geoff, I received a call from "Chuck" letting me know how pumped he was to have me join him. I was honored. I spoke with his mom, who told me she'd cook whatever I wanted, and I felt welcomed. I was looking forward to playing with the great Allen Iverson in a legendary city like Philadelphia, but the trade came at a terrible time. Speaking of irony, speaking of a slap in the face, my first game in Philadelphia was against the Kings! It was two days later; I hadn't even adjusted to the thought of not being a King. I mean, I had to let everything go in three days.

I called and asked my mom to head to Sac and pack my things up and put them in storage. I never came home. Never said goodbye to Sac. I knew I had to move immediately. Thank God for my man Matt Barnes, my teammate who was traded to Philly with me. This was a crazy situation, but he helped me get through the year. In Philly, I didn't have a place to stay, so I stayed in the same hotel as the Kings, the Four Seasons. I actually went out with Mike Bibby and Bobby Jackson the night before the game.

I headed out of the hotel at the same time as the team but in different transportation. It was devastatingly surreal. We lost by two, but that didn't faze me. I was numb. As the rest of the season went on, I saw how great Philly fans were. There was only one problem: I wasn't the same player. I needed a system of movement rather than one-on-one play to be at my best. That wasn't our system. Funny how life can play out sometimes. I would've given my right arm to play with a guy like AI in my prime. I would've destroyed. We would've destroyed. We would've won. He was the best player I'd ever played with, a miracle of heart and a small assassin. But he was older, and I was older with a bad wheel. We had a new coach and a team that was young and inexperienced. Our coaches didn't trust our young guys who were proving every day that they were ready in practice. Lou Williams, Kyle Korver, and Andre Iguodala later proved that they were leaders, but as for now we needed more to help.

We made the playoffs and had a +10 win column from the year before. We were eliminated by the Pistons (3–1) in the opening round of the playoffs. It was cool to go home and have my mother's cooking during the playoffs and see everyone, but that was fifteen to twenty-five tickets a game. Crazy. I averaged nineteen, the most an Iverson teammate averaged in the playoffs during his tenure in Philly. It was difficult scoring in the current system. Players had to wing it constantly. The organization hired Mo Cheeks over the summer, and I couldn't have been more excited. But I missed playing in Sac. Suck it up, and move on.

Allen Iverson could do it all. He was six feet, maybe 135 of pure pit bull. Plus, if you've seen him throw a football or any of his football videos, you know he could have played in the NFL. I was amazed at his athletic ability. Specifically, his quickness, stamina, and toughness when attacking guys who weighed up to 100–125 pounds more than him. I watched him drop sixty effortlessly in a game. Everyone makes fun of the fact that he famously questioned the importance of practice at a press conference. I agree with the philosophy that for Allen Iverson, practice was not important. He dominated practices just like games. He paralyzed drills by scoring whenever he wanted to. He disrupted offensive drills by getting steals at will. It wasn't an exercise. He treated everything like a game, he was always ready. He only had one speed. He only knows one way—H.A.M.

We became close friends. He showed me around the city, and I purchased a crib a couple of blocks from his. The Philadelphia 76ers organization is top notch. However, at the time, they were going through a transition, and the team chemistry did not reflect the professionalism of the organization. Every player was in his own bunker. At first it was not fun playing as a team, and definitely nothing like I had in Sac.

The young guys felt like no one supported them. Offense was not one that flowed and let everyone touch the ball. There was a sense of frustration, individually and collectively. One day, I tried to change that. The locker room was, at times, more than toxic, and during a losing streak, when tensions were at their highest, I asked Coach to give us the day off, and I rented out a paintball experience. I had all the fellas participate. We were outside with acres to strategize, and we split our roster into two teams. I wanted everyone to release all the bad energy. It was the worst I'd seen. It worked and brought us a little closer together.

Another experience that brought the team closer was our trip to Spain. Anytime you travel and explore a new country as foreigners, it brings you closer together. You go through things for the first time as a unit. In the opening game against Milwaukee, AI scored thirty-five and had nine assists. I had thirty-two and fourteen rebounds, with five assists and two blocks, but we lost in overtime. We knew then it was going to be rough year. I averaged 20 points and 9.9 rebounds, the most points by any of Allen's teammates over his illustrious career. He gave 'em 33 a night, and we were the league's top-scoring duo. We missed the playoffs the next season.

Knowing that our shot at winning was coming to a close, AI and I got together at his house before the 2006–07 preseason to discuss how we were going to lead the upcoming season. He told me how much he wanted to win and in Philly. He explained what he could do to be a better leader and how we could both help the team. We laid out our plan of attack. It was cool vibing with him like that. Our plans and optimism were short lived. Allen was traded to Denver in early December, just fifteen games into the season. I wasn't shocked by the trade; I could sense disconnect between Iverson and the team. You also felt the organization making a shift to the younger play-

ers. I understood the pain of putting all your energy into a team, only to be asked to leave after you gave them your loyalty. Cold game. I also raided his locker of everything after the legend left. I'm no fool. He was an all-time great. I took shoes, jerseys, you name it. He didn't want them. Plus, I knew that I would soon follow. I appreciated the city and experience. I then asked for a buyout for the chance of a lifetime—to play in my city for my team, the Detroit Pistons.

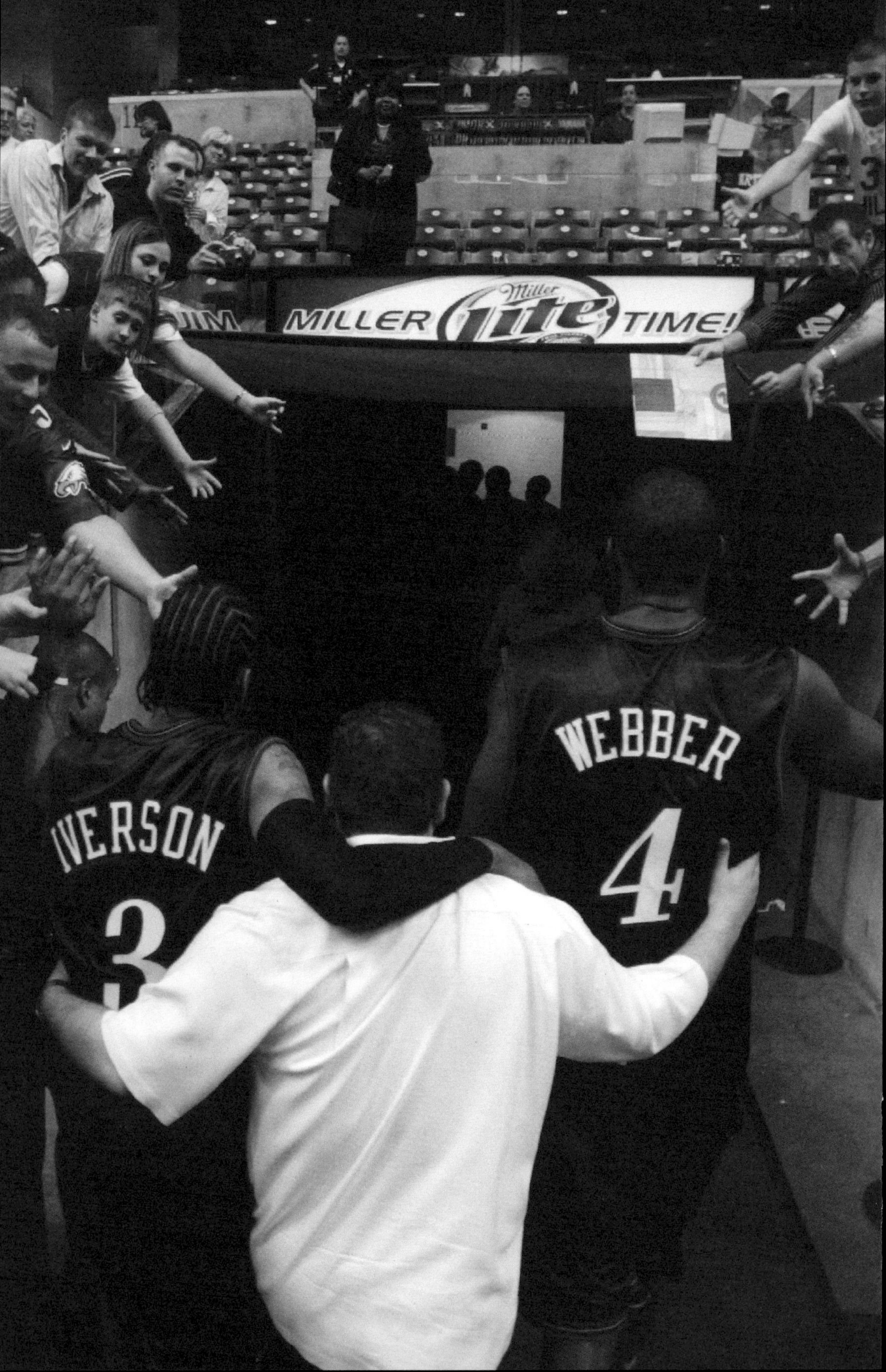

Miller Lite
MILLER
TIME!
WEBBER
4
IVERSON
3

The Detroit Pistons, my favorite team of all time, with two of my favorite players in Joe D. and Isiah Thomas. Philadelphia accepted my request, and just two days after the request, with moms, pops, my brother and sister, Mr. Mont, Harv, and Iyapo, I was having a live press conference on ESPN in Detroit.

Joe: "First of all, thank you, everyone, for coming out this afternoon. It's a very good day for all of us here. You know, usually you come, and you just introduce players that you acquire, and you talk about what they do on the basketball court to help your team win, and of course we're going to do that today. If he couldn't play basketball, he wouldn't be sitting here right now. Chris brings a lot more to the table than just another basketball player coming here to play for the Detroit Pistons. I think he embodies everything we try to stand for as a basketball team and an organization. I think he is what we want to be about as a team. People of his character, of his background, of his upbringing—those are the type of people I want to bring to the Detroit Pistons. So he's more than just another basketball player sitting here. I feel like he's a pretty special guy from a special family from a special background. There's an obvious connection here to Detroit, and I'm proud to say today that that not only is Chris Webber back home, but he's back home as a Detroit Piston, and we could not be happier."

I was blown away.

After a few questions, a local writer, with microphone in hand, would speak his piece. It's always something. Trolling before the internet.

Reporter: "Welcome back. Do you want me to take this opportunity—I'll deal with the elephant in the room. The Ed Martin situation you talked a lot about—'When it's all said and done, I'll tell everybody what's really going on.' You have a great forum, a chance to address that. What do you want to say about that and to the people of Michigan?"

Pissed off, but with a smile I replied. "Well, today I'm talking about being a Detroit Piston, and I don't think this is the forum

to talk about something that happened fifteen years ago right now. I'm here, and I'm excited to be a part of the organization, and I'm just really happy. So, to talk about anything that's not about that would be a waste of my time." Hater acknowledged and addressed.

After the press conference, Bobby Knight called and left a message for me. It read, "Ask that little fucker! when he's going to stop lying and writing fake articles." (That's something the reporter was accused of.) You have to love Bobby.

I couldn't wear the number 4, because it was in the rafters with Joe D's name on it. I called my nephew Colton and told him I would be coming home to play for the Pistons; he was eight years old at the time and told me that he'd had a dream where I won a championship and had the number 84 on. His mother, Heather, got on the phone and said, "Oh my God, he's been talking about this number 84 for about two weeks." That was all I needed. I told Joe I wanted the number 84. Out of the mouths of babes, right?

My first game was against Utah. I was told I'd be coming off the bench the first game and then start for the rest of the season. The Pistons had been successful for the entire time under Joe's leadership, and I was proud to be part of his system and ready to follow. I got to the arena, and the marquee read "Chris Comes Home." I came off the bench to a standing ovation. It was overwhelming.

But one of the best things about being a Piston was the locker room vibe on and off the court. The vibe was the best I'd ever seen, maybe because we were one of the oldest teams in the league and settled. Before my first start in Detroit, I was sitting at my locker with Tupac's "Me Against the World" blasting, watching 'Sheed bop up and down like we were at a concert. I thought, *Thank you, Lord.* I was ready. I was nervous like it was high school, and that's always a wonderful sign for me. I paced back and forth by the bench trying to control my emotions while Mason, the famous DJ I had grown up listening to on WJLB-FM 98 and who was now a Pistons announcer, was introducing me to my hometown crowd:

"Former Country Day and Michigan Wolverine, a six-ten forward wearing Pistons jersey number 84...C. Webb...Chris Webber!"

The Palace went berserk. It was the hometown welcome any kid from 6 Mile would dream of. I thought it was crazy that five years earlier, I was standing on the steps of the federal courthouse surrounded by vultures. In a place where I wasn't sure I felt accepted, I was being welcomed with open arms.

Country Day retired my jersey, and that made me proud. My family, along with Joe Dumars and other Pistons, came to the ceremony. We went on to win fifty-three games and captured the Central Division title. We had the most potent starting five in the league, with all players averaging double figures. Chauncey Billups proved to be one of the best leaders I'd come to know. Rip Hamilton the best mid-range player I'd seen and was one of the best-conditioned athletes I'd play with. Tayshaun Prince had one of the highest basketball IQs of any player I'd ever seen, and Rasheed Wallace, well, he was Sheed. And I loved playing with him. I enjoyed every minute of being a Piston. They were a close group and had already built a championship bond through work and sacrifice, but they welcomed me into the group as one of the brothers seamlessly.

In the postseason, we swept Orlando in the first round. In the second round we defeated Chicago 4–2, advancing to the Eastern Conference Finals to face LeBron and the Cavs. We lost in six games. I played pretty well, but in the locker room with beer in hand, licking my wounds after the loss, sitting next to Rip Hamilton talking, I realized that the end of my career was near. That was painful to acknowledge. But it was satisfying knowing that I would retire as a Piston.

I spoke to Joe Dumars after the season, and I felt like I was going to be back the next year. But halfway through the next season, I was still waiting on a call from Joe, so I went to Sacramento to work at my restaurant and hit the gym. Chris Mullin, my old teammate, came up for a few days to hang out. He talked to me about reuniting as a Warrior with him and Nellie. Mully was now GM and made a pretty good pitch: full circle, redemption—all that good stuff. The truth is he didn't have to recruit me; I just wanted to play.

Instead, I played ten games with the Warriors and officially retired on March 25, 2008. I was ready to walk away. Funny thing, I thought I would be more emotional. I thought I would shed some tears while sipping on some whiskey late at night reminiscing, but that never happened. I just knew it was my time. I was exhausted emotionally and physically. It takes so much energy to dream and believe every season. My knee wouldn't let me be the player that I had once been, and I wasn't willing to accept being any other type of player or have a much lesser role. It hurt to limp up and down the court. I was forced to hop up the stairs on my right leg because I couldn't put any weight on my left.

When you add it all up, I played 831 games in my career, averaging 37 minutes a night. I scored just under 21 points per game while shooting

48 percent from the field. I scored 17,182 points, grabbed 8,124 rebounds, dished out 3,526 assists, and blocked exactly 1,200 shots. I was a five-time All-Star and made the All-NBA Team five times. I knew that I had had a great career, one most guys could only dream of. But the league had become all about the best players leading a team to win the championship. So reluctantly, I joined the club of great players, including Charles Barkley, Karl Malone, Patrick Ewing, and Dominique Wilkins, who never won a ring. Still, I'd have it no other way. As the great Isiah Thomas said, "There are bus drivers and people who ride the bus." I was a bus driver. I'd rather be a bus driver with a great career and no championship than to ride the bus and let someone else drive. I was a leader. I was proud of that.

FULL-TIME ALL-STAR.
PART-TIME WISHMAKER.

MAKE ★ (A-WISH.)

TWENTY YEARS
2,400 WISHES

Chris Webber
2003 Wishmaker of the Year

Time wounds all heels.

—John Lennon

I've talked about my time at Michigan and how much I loved it—the fellas, dorm life, friends, time-outs, and all, but I've never spoken openly on the controversy or my disappointment in the university. Many people want to know what happened, so I'll tell this story. Then I'll get back to the good.

First and most important, I've never spoken about this because I couldn't. One of the conditions of my plea deal was that I couldn't speak about it for ten years. After ten years, who do you talk to? The people who made those decisions are long gone.

There were other reasons too. I figured that time would absolve me. I've also had school officials agree that I didn't take anything to attend college. It's also been proven in court. The university was simply scared of the backlash that might come from other players' relationships with Ed, and they were afraid that people would connect the dots. So they threw me under the bus. Also, I figured that no matter what I said or wrote, there would always be people who believe I was guilty.

So why open that old wound at this stage of my life and at this point in this book? It's because of the most important reason: I'm not mad. I have a wonderful life. I love the University of

Chapter 79

Time Wounds All Heels

Michigan, the alumni, the students, and the faculty, and it was over thirty years ago. I'd rather let things heal and move forward.

Our past experiences either make us bitter or better. We become bitter when we replay past misfortunes in our mind over and over as though the next time, the outcome will be different. But it never is. That's when we start blaming ourselves or others, questioning ourselves, or questioning God. We become better when we use the lessons of the past to fortify us, to learn and grow. But make no mistake, some people in the media and at the University of Michigan tried to erase my very existence, and that betrayal hurts to this day.

Taking the Final Four banners down, erasing my personal records, banning me from the program and campus, making false accusations—life is all about relationships and perceptions. Everything I worked for and achieved in college was questioned.

I went on a speaking tour where I examined how we come out of the worst moments in our lives—about how success is a journey. Fortune 500 companies, families, prisons, entrepreneurs, churches, cancer patients all used the story of my pain to remind them of their own strength and what was in them. I encouraged them to just get through the day and to worry about the next day after they made it through this one. To embrace pain so it wouldn't manifest through anger or unhealthy emotions and behaviors. It was surreal to be speaking to large crowds, because at times I was talking to myself, encouraging myself to let the anger go.

*In the end, we will remember not the words of
our enemies, but the silence of our friends.*

—Martin Luther King Jr.

After the ten-year ban was over, I hopped on the horn and
reached out to my childhood friend Mike Jack. I told him I'd be
in town for a game, and I had tickets for him and his son, and that
we should break bread. We had dinner at his house, and after a
long discussion about old times with him and his wife, Amira,
I told him, "It might be time." I told him that the reason I called
is because I'd been contacted by representatives of the University
of Michigan, and it always felt like it was on the sneak tip. Like
they were trying to feel me out or check my temperature—to see
where I stood or how I felt about the university. It never seemed to
be in an official capacity, but it was always on some official school
business (if that makes sense). I anticipated future conversations
and didn't want any lawyers in the upcoming discussions because
that would prolong, if not halt, any progress, and I knew that
Mike was in a unique position.

I trusted Mike, and he had history with the school. Growing
up, he was one of my closest friends. As kids, we worked out,
played, and dreamed of making it to college and the pros. His
house was draped with Michigan gear. My ex–Super Friend
teammate was the ultimate Wolverine fan growing up. I knew
his character, and that's all I needed. He is trustworthy. The
university would have comfort in his presence as well. He had
been an assistant men's basketball coach under Coach Beilein at
Michigan. He was a Michigan man. It was crazy because while
Mike was living his dream coaching at my alma mater, our timing
was terrible. I couldn't help him in any way because I was banned
from the program at that time.

Anyway, I gave him the rundown and told him that all
I wanted out of the conversation of reconciliation was to

clear things up. Straighten out a few things and start a new relationship moving forward. I did not want the reconciliation to be a PR stunt, a gimmick, moneymaking scheme, or for a recruiting boost. I felt like I had been left on an island, and that if we were going to do something, then let's do something positive and set an example. Mike was all for it and suggested that he call Greg Harden, a longtime athletic department employee and trusted mentor.

Mike went to Ann Arbor, and the meeting went better than he expected. So well that they called me from Greg's office in July 2016, and we spoke briefly. They both wanted me to meet with Warde Manuel, the athletic director of the university. I was game, and to show good faith, I flew myself up to Michigan for a secret meeting in Livonia. It was impossible for me to walk through the lobby of the hotel to a room designated as the meeting place without being recognized. The parking lot and elevators were crowded with Michigan fans who were preparing for a day of football. The Wolverines were going up against Wisconsin. I was optimistic about the meeting, being that Manuel went to the university. I assumed he would be able to understand and see through the smoke and mirrors of misinformation. Mike Jack, Warde Manuel, G. Harden, and I sat in the small room and got acquainted with small talk, and then got to business. Warde asked, and I told him how I felt.

I explained my recruiting process and court proceedings. I told him that I didn't take money to attend the university. I told him I was disappointed in the school for using me as a scapegoat when they and every other school and coach knew we weren't up for sale. That was never the word on the Webbers. I told him that it was hard for me to forgive considering all that my family, especially my parents, had to endure. I was most disappointed with the stain and untrue stigma. He listened, started to speak, and then paused for a beat. Then he said that he was very familiar with my situation. That he had done some research into the investigation, and he and others familiar with the information felt that I had been "left behind"—and that the school needed to "apologize to the eighteen-to-twenty-year-old Webber because we didn't protect you. We overreacted. You were low-hanging fruit."

Well ain't that a bitch... I looked at Mike and laughed inside. I knew they knew the truth, but I never thought I'd hear the words from one of them. He said he understood my thoughts and would "circle back after some more recognizance."

I guess talks stalled because two years passed, and they never followed up on the meeting. Mike reached out, and we received no return call.

That felt like a kick in the nuts after all the phone calls, flights, and secret meeting places. But it's not about man, it never is.

My time at Michigan helped make me who I am today. And even though I experienced betrayal and humiliation, I wouldn't trade any of it. God's grace saw me through, and I choose to focus on the positive. I did return to Michigan again a couple years later, but we'll get to that.

11 NATIONAL CHAMPIONSHIPS
42 BIG TEN CHAMPIONSHIPS
3 HEISMAN TROPHIES

M M M M M

#WINNINGEST

CHRIS
WEBBER

MICHIGAN
4

JIM
HARBAUGH

There are rewards. February 6, 2009, will be a day that I will always remember. One year after retiring, the Sacramento Kings retired my jersey, making me the eighth King with that honor. It was a wonderful time for me and my family. I was able to reminisce about the great times there. Geoff Petrie, Doug Christie, Mateen Cleaves, Vlade, Scot Pollard, and the Maloof brothers, Gavin and Joe, were all in attendance. I never truly had a chance to look back at my career. I knew my accomplishments, I knew the road I took, but as an athlete you're taught to never celebrate the win too long. Get ready for the next game. Well, there is no next game.

As I was introduced the tears wanted to flow. It took everything in me not to let them. The crowd. The crowd felt like family. They are family. They made me feel loved with their ovations, signs, and number 4 jerseys. They remembered as I did. The intangible vibes were damn near visible in that arena. Accompanied by my family—parents, brothers, sister, nephews, my fiancé, Erika, and in-laws to be—I was on cloud nine.

Geoff spoke first. I never got to thank him for trading for me against my will and believing in me. I never got to thank Coach Adelman for putting me in a position to succeed and to help the team succeed. Their moves were legendary. Mateen was up next to speak. Though he was a Spartan (nobody's perfect), he had become one of my best friends over time. He's a true warrior, and I respect his mentality. He's a real one. I was happy he was there. Doug Christie, my homeboy, said, "Julius Caesar once said, 'Veni, vidi, vici'—'I came, I saw, I conquered.' Well, you came, you saw, you conquered." I had to look at the floor as I listened because I knew what he was capable of inspiring, having me crying like a baby. Doug is a true warrior.

I watched my white number 4 Kings jersey be hoisted into the rafters. My mind was racing with the essence of memories past. Not total memory but almost the quick summary of relationships and highlights. I thought about my boys: Kev, Yop, Harv, Mr. Mont, the Super Friends, and our road on the daily grind. I thought about Coach Keener and Coach Fisher and the impact their presence had on my career. I thought to myself how my brothers and sister, who were feet away, would never know how important they are to me. They never let this game shit get in the way of our relationship. They always supported me. I thought about my dad and his draft-day hug and what he went through, and my mom's sacrifices, example, and prayers, and I just apologized to God.

I thanked him for his wisdom and mercy. I was standing in the arena where he had blessed me against my will. He gave me something that I wanted, and my stubborn ass tried to be in control. That's why no one can never tell me that there isn't a God. Sure, one has to work and try to earn it, but I know what God did for me. I know how he lifted me, gave me a table in the presence of my enemies, and I know he kept me. I know how he truly loves me. When I submitted and accepted, this ended up being one of the best rides I've taken, on the team I'd play for the longest.

It is not the critic who counts; not the man who points out how the strong man stumbles, or where the doer of deeds could have done them better. The credit belongs to the man who is actually in the arena, whose face is marred by dust and sweat and blood; who strives valiantly; who errs, who comes up short again and again, because there is no effort without error and shortcoming; but who does actually strive to do the deeds; who knows great enthusiasms, the great devotions; who spends himself in a worthy cause; who at the best knows in the end the triumph of high achievement, and who at the worst, if he fails, at least fails while daring greatly, so that his place shall never be with those cold and timid souls who neither know victory nor defeat.

—Theodore Roosevelt

SLM

CHRIS WEBBER

AMERICA WA

MATE

20
ALL
A

JUWAN
HOWARD

JASON KIDD'S NEW

SLM

JERSEY D

2003 PLAYOFFS

Chris WEBBER
KING OF KINGS

MICHAEL JORDAN

LEBRON & THE
HS ALL-STARS

PEE WEE
KIRKLAND

AL HARRINGTON

SCOTTIE PIPPEN

STEPHEN JACKSON

KEITH VAN HORN

Comcast
WEBBER
4
FEB. 6, '09
4ever our KING of
Than
LOV
an
CHRIS WEBBER OUR TRIPLE DOUBLE
amento
SSION
4
BBER
CHRI
#1 IN
#1 IN
KINGS

LIGHT
HOME
GUEST
ARCOArena.com
Budweiser
4 ever
will be
THE KING
of my
KINGS,
Y2K
SECURE
TOTAL
100%
Support
and
WEBBER
RANKINGS
ACRAMENTO
ANS
C·WEB
#4
WELL
worth
waiting
4

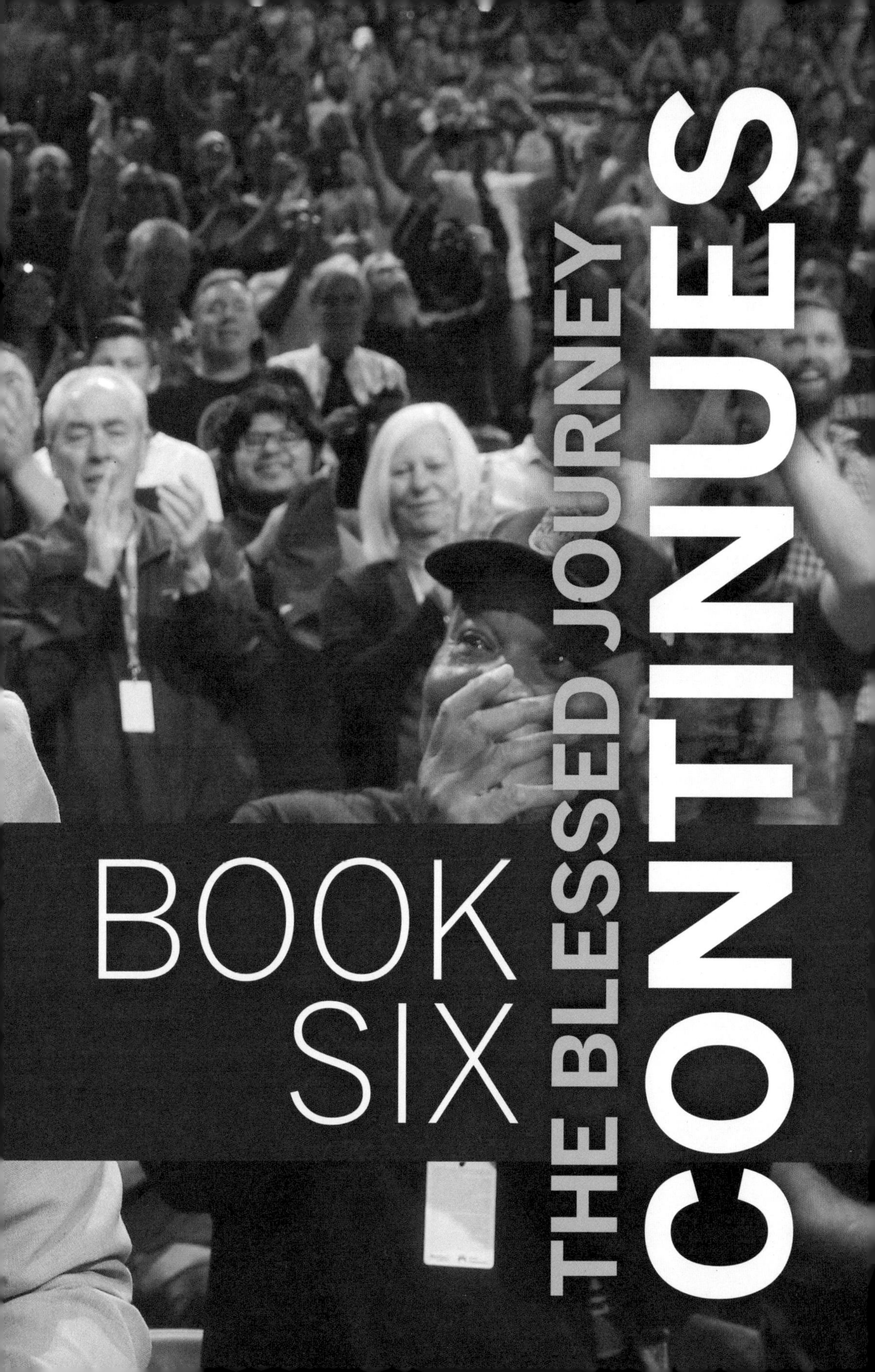

BOOK SIX

THE BLESSED JOURNEY CONTINUES

I've been blessed to start and partner in many successful business ventures. That's my true sport today—business. But I've never truly retired from basketball. Immediately after retiring from the Golden State Warriors, I was blessed with an opportunity to work for TNT and NBA TV as an analyst, color commentator, and host.

Charles Barkley, Kenny Smith, and Shaquille O'Neal, along with Ernie Johnson, made up the crew on *Inside the NBA*, one of the best sports shows ever. I called games alongside Marv Albert. Who would've thought in a hundred years that I'd partner with Marv Albert, the voice of the NBA, one of the most iconic voices of sports, and have fun doing so? We were a pretty good

team, if I do say so myself. He taught me a lot, and I soaked up his game.

Dick Stockton and Kevin Harlan were integral in my career improvement as a commentator. Reggie Miller and Steve Kerr helped usher me into my gig, unselfishly sharing their knowledge. Commentating ensured that I didn't miss the locker room aspect of professional sports, and most guys who are retired will tell you that they miss the locker room.

Commentating was my way of staying close to the game for a while longer. I wanted to act as a conduit and express the emotions that come with basketball, along with the Xs and Os of play. Because when it comes down to it, I'm a fan.

Jeff was cracking jokes. Jason was on the ladies. Rachel's poetry had everyone in tears, and David sang "So High" by John Legend. My mother smiled like I've never seen her smile. My pop's posture was proud and presidential. I was gazing across the lake, Pastor London was reading a passage from the Bible, and in front of about a hundred family members and friends, on a cloudless, hot, and humid day, I said "I do" and married the girl of my dreams, Erika, in our backyard. My soul was settled.

✦ ✦ ✦

I sat in the hospital playing with my wife's hair and looking out the window, and a flood of memories flowed through my mind. I thought about our marriage, honeymooning in Egypt, and walking to the top of Mount Sinai to pray for a family that we wanted to start. Then we sat there at the top, speechless, and watched the sunrise. We swam in the Red Sea. We descended through the great pyramids and visited our ancestors in the museums. We dreamed out loud under the stars that lit up the Nile and ate lamb, rice, and vegetables until we couldn't move.

I reflected on how we had to put our passions on hold. My wife was writing a cookbook and going to culinary school while designing furniture and remodeling our home. I was building a school in Detroit and working in basketball as an analyst. I was part of an ownership group bidding on an NBA team. Everything seemed great for us two young lovers, and...none of that mattered.

We tried everything but could not conceive. It was heartbreaking, full of expectations and close calls. It drained me. During this five-year journey, I lived in depression, full of guilt. Having all the money in the world doesn't matter. It was stressful for both, and the torment switches: one feels helpless while the other feels guilty, the feelings ping-ponging back and forth. My wife went through several tests and painful surgeries. I was giving her shots daily. Shit, I don't know how she did it. Her healthy ass. She was taking hormones, steroids. I don't know. She won't even drink cough syrup.

More than a few times we were in the "pregnancy safe zone" and announced with excitement to family and friends...before later informing them of the disappointing news that we were no longer expecting. For me, a few times specifically come to mind.

One Thanksgiving was one of those somber times at a big family holiday dinner that included my parents, her parents, my brothers, their wives and girlfriends, and her friends and family. We had previously told them all the wonderful news that we were finally pregnant and were planning to celebrate together in our home with prayer, laughter, tears, and wine on one of our favorite family days. But during our tradition of going around the table and saying what we were thankful for, when it got to my wife, she broke down: "I'm thankful for God and my family... I love you all. And I'm sorry to tell you that I do not understand...umm...I'm sorry...we lost our...we are no longer pregnant..."

Everyone at the table started to fall apart, but Erika said, "No, no. I don't understand, but I do believe that everything happens for a reason, and we are not giving up!"

My father asked everyone to hold hands, and he prayed, asking God to give her strength and for us to have a baby. We cried our eyes out.

However, my fearless wife wouldn't let us feel sorry for ourselves, and she made us try and try again, until finally our wildest dreams came true...we were pregnant! After being deep into the safe zone, we decided to take a short flight to the Dominican Republic to celebrate. I asked the doc, and he thought it was a great idea and would serve to keep our stress levels down. We landed, and our plans were to immediately hit the beach, read, walk, eat, make love, and pray, but our joy was interrupted—crushed, really. One day my wife came out of the bathroom, and she didn't have to say a word. Our eyes met, and we both knew. It was over, again.

We sat on the beach quietly, sometimes crying, sometimes laughing at someone on the beach or in the water. I had a few more than a few drinks as we sat silently. I remember looking up at the night sky and stars, mad at God. Hurt that something so important to us both seemed so unattainable.

The next day we ate lunch on the beach and were getting ready to hit the spa. We noticed paparazzi taking pictures but didn't think much of it, and I wasn't in the mood to be fucked with. We went to the spa, cried, and drank champagne. We abruptly made plans to leave. We weren't much in the mood for relaxation and celebration. When we got home the next night, we were in the kitchen, and I saw a crazy unflattering picture of us in a tabloid, with my wife's body blown up out of proportion to make her look fat. I couldn't believe it! The headline talked shit about her and us. It was on the beach and taken the same day we lost our baby.

That was the lowest I'd ever been because it was my life affecting her negatively and such an unfair moment. A true low point. But just when you think you've hit rock bottom, life enlists a more powerful machine to excavate even deeper.

The other time that comes to mind when "my world" would relentlessly pound our hope came in 2013—at the Final Four in Atlanta. Michigan was playing somebody. I don't even care to remember the specifics. Leading up to the game, I was called out on TV by my ex-teammates, TV hosts, and analysts, all of whom were begging, berating, and examining fake scenarios of why I should come to the game to support Michigan. Now, mind you, Michigan was in control—they banned me. Anyway, there were two massive problems with me going to the Final Four and sitting with my Fab Five teammates as many suggested.

First was the fact that the court system told me I could not be associated with Michigan for ten years, nor could I speak about what happened at Michigan. I was still in that ten-year window at this time. Of course, not once did reporters report this. That's a whole other story.

Second, I wasn't in the mood. My wife and I were approximately four and half months in the baby basting process. It was the night before the big game, and I'm watching ESPN and listening to all the hubbub about the Game of Games (Go Blue). During the commercial break, I go in the back to hit the bathroom and walk in to find my wife sitting on the floor crying. It happened again. We lost another sweet soul.

Later that night, while watching the talking heads on TV, my relationship with Michigan came up again. Foul shit was being said. My wife decided then, still in pain, that we would go to the game and support Michigan the next day. She thought it was something we should do. She knows how much I love Michigan, and she knew how much I hated Michigan at that time. We fought and argued. I didn't want to go. My job is to protect her. How could I have her out at some game after this just happened? A game?

We arrived at the stadium to be greeted by cameras and reporters. I was bombarded with questions about how it felt to be back at a Michigan game after all these years, our chances, and so on. All I remember is getting out of the car with my wife, feeling so guilty that I couldn't protect her from my world. Being so hurt by what we just lost. I played it off, posting pictures and smiling, but I remember absolutely nothing about that game.

After consulting our physicians, we were told that we would never conceive. It wasn't in the cards, and they suggested that we look at some other options, like adoption. But my baby still believed. It was a lonely process because we would go years without sharing our disappointments with anyone. We didn't want to get everyone's hopes up, and we didn't want to be pitied either. We felt like we were just being a drag, always having bad news. But after seven long years of prayer, faith, confusion, stress, love, doubt, and whatever other emotions you can name, we finally conceived!

✦ ✦ ✦

Sometimes, you can't truly appreciate a moment until it becomes a memory. Other times, the close misses, failed attempts, stacked odds, and difficult journey have you crying, laughing, and shouting for joy when you see the finish line.

In the midst of the commotion in the delivery room, I felt thankful, elated, and exhausted. I plopped down in the middle of the room on a wobbly, uncomfortable blue plastic chair. I was having an out of body experience. My face sported an ugly, nervous smile that I couldn't replicate if I tried. I exhaled as if I had been holding my breath for years. I was overwhelmed. The levy in my tear ducts failed, spawning a mass exodus of memories that warmed my cheeks. I sniffed and smiled. We had tried so many times and lost. They had told us this would never happen. It felt as if I caught a glimpse of that mythical god "impossible," and for a quick second, caught his eye and mouthed the words, "Ha! You lied, you lied."

But suddenly, I was smacked back to reality when the doctor in the delivery room whisper-yelled, "Okay, Mr. Webber, we need you back here! Please give your daughter to the nurse—we don't want you to miss baby B's entrance." Or exit, depending on how you look at it. "Here comes your boy!" Twins… beautiful twins.

I played with my wife's hair while she rested. My mind began to race as the noise, traffic, and craziness of the hospital left with the sun. I was over the moon. Then, I started experiencing the second stage that many parents before me also grasped. *But what now? I'm somebody's daddy—life just got real! What am I supposed to do?* I began to think about their future, all the wonderful possibilities, their dreams. *Who are my children? Who will they become? What will make them smile?*

I knew that I would love, provide for, protect, educate, discipline, and inspire these two beautiful lil aliens posing as earthlings. I then thought about how unfair life can be, with its ups and downs and disappointments. I looked at my daughter and thought about the day when a lil punk might break her heart or how her ideas and efforts could be marginalized by her boss simply because she's a woman. My thoughts then shifted to my lil man. How it's tough to be a true man and how because of the color of his skin, he'll always be guilty until proven innocent to some people. I thought about how I would teach them to love God and their family. To embrace their uniqueness, listen to music, and enjoy the outdoors, books, and the arts.

To be curious, inquisitive, defiant, appreciative, and focused on the good days while being thankful, balanced, and strong on the tough ones. I then thought back on my life and got lost in the midst of a sea of a thousand thoughts.

Then, my breathing slowed. I felt a familiar sense of peace come back over me. It was God. "Look at what I did for your mother and father and those who came before you. Remember what your parents taught you? Look back at your life. I've never left you. Just teach your children that I am God and that my Grace is sufficient."

In 2018, Mike Jack called me and said he wanted to see if I would call in to an Ann Arbor radio station on Michigan's campus. I was reluctant at first until he told me that it was to bring awareness to a charity that I used to be very familiar with. Michigan From the Heart arranges visits to the C. S. Mott Children's Hospital for student athletes who offer a welcome distraction by spending time with pediatric patients and their families. When we were Fab Fivin', we made a friend, a sixth member, so to speak. His name was Randy. Randy Kyle was diagnosed with cancer at age eleven or twelve. He would also inspire me. The foundation meant a lot to me. It reinforced that there was something bigger than us all, that we don't have control over life. Principles of perseverance, being grateful, and toughness, these kids were so inspiring. Their heart was uplifting, and their humility was moving.

I called in to the show, hosted by former Michigan running back Jamie Morris. We talked about old times, the foundation, and then I surprised them with an auction package to attend an NBA game and visit Turner studios to watch me, Chuck, Shaq, and Kenny live. The proceeds benefited the foundation. They loved it. Then they surprised me. Jamie had told Coach Harbaugh, the Michigan head football coach, that I was calling in, and before you knew it, we were having a conversation of a lifetime.

Now, I had spoken with Coach many times. I was a big fan of his before I signed with Michigan as a teenager, and long ago I wanted him to get the job (he went on to coach at Stanford). For the last couple of years, he had asked me to attend a football game or come up to campus, and I would always decline. I felt like he didn't know what he was getting himself into. That there were people who could react negatively to our relationship, adding another bullseye to his back. I didn't want that, but Coach wasn't deterred. On this call, he asked me if I would come up and be an honorary captain for the football team for an upcoming game. His sincerity, I was honored. I couldn't turn him down again. He wanted to bring me back to the university. He wanted to help heal

wounds and hurt feelings. I appreciated him for that. He put his rep on the line, and my loyalty is what he will have forever. I was excited about going to the game, but I did have a real concern.

We were playing Penn State at home, and again, I did not want to be a distraction. I wanted them to keep their focus. They were playing some of the best football I'd seen in the Harbaugh era, and I didn't want the controversy of my return to hurt the team in any way. I even stayed away from some of the normal activities that captains were afforded because I wanted it to be about the team and team only.

I drove up with Mike to Ann Arbor the Friday before the game. I had not been back in twenty-five years, and the campus brought back so many memories. We pulled up to Schembechler Hall, where we were given a tour of the training facility, weight room, training, and recuperation area. They were second to none. We watched them practice, and then Coach asked me to speak to the team after.

I freestyled the speech, but my notes embody the gist:

"No one loved you three weeks ago...they were calling for heads. Everybody wanted Coach fired. Now we are sitting pretty. You've proved them wrong so far, but so what? Don't be lulled to sleep by the new passengers on the bandwagon. This will happen all throughout life. People leave when you're trying and come around when you're flying. The only way to win and stay sane is consistent work ethic, consistent passion, attention to detail, and discipline. It's about you, gentlemen, and you only. We are just riding your wave."

I stayed around after and took some pictures with coaches and players. I hung out with the equipment managers and threw the football around with Mike Jack. Even though my old home, the Crisler Center, stood yards away, and I hadn't been allowed to step inside. Banished. With hopes to be forgotten. Standing among pictures of the greats to play at Michigan. I felt at home. I was content.

My father and Jason traveled up with me to the game on Saturday. We all loved Michigan. I did understand that this would be one of those special moments, one that you never forget. We arrived at the parking lot of the Michigan football stadium filled with thousands of tailgating fans.

I wanted to enjoy the day and say "What's up?" to every person I could. There were number 4 basketball jerseys everywhere. It felt as if I had never left.

Standing on the fifty-yard line, in front of one hundred thousand screaming fans, I was introduced with my father by my side. I ran off the field, and Coach Harbaugh called me over and said, "Tom Brady got the same reaction." It was a moment of redemption. A moment that honored my time there. A moment that acknowledged God's mercy. Though some tried, they couldn't erase the kid. I went up to a suite and watched them kick Penn State's ass, and headed back to Detroit.

Later, we were having a family get-together for the twins' second birthday. In the middle of enjoying cake, ice cream, and daddy juice, my brother Jeff yelled at someone to turn on the TV. Juwan was introduced as head men's basketball coach of the University of Michigan. He came out smooth with his blue suit and maize tie. His tears told the story. He couldn't get a full sentence out. His love for Michigan was evident. I was happy for him. I had lobbied for his hiring publicly. To me it was a no-brainer. He was asked about his coaching philosophy, his lack of experience, how he'd recruit, and, of course, about the Fab Five and the removed banners. I laughed. He called me after saying, "We did it. Thanks for the love and support." I smiled.

You prepare a table before me in
the presence of my enemies!

Psalms 23:5

"Scars are a sign of healing."

Kintsugi (also known as Kintsukuroi) is a Japanese art form in which the history and imperfections of an object are showcased and celebrated. In this practice, broken pottery is mended back together with platinum, silver, or gold. This philosophy honors fragility, breakage, and repair as part of the beauty and history of an object. Embracing flaws, uniqueness, character, brokenness, and restoration rather than being shameful or ignoring imperfections, misfortunes, or flat-out screw-ups. I've come to appreciate that.

I believe that's what God does to us. He loves us. He wants us to depend on him and to have a personal relationship with him. He knows that we are imperfect even at our best. His love, grace, and mercy are the platinum, gold, and silver that mend our broken pieces. Just like pottery, we are fragile. But he strengthens us when we are weak.

Chapter 86

God's Grace

I want to first thank God for His grace and mercy, for allowing me to be here tonight. It is truly an honor. I would like to thank the Naismith Hall of Fame. I'd like to thank Jerry Colangelo and basketball fans over the world for this wonderful honor. This award for me is not just about a game, a series, or a season. This represents to me the culmination of perseverance, excellence, and consistency. That's why I want to take time and thank those that God put in my life to help me get here.

First, my parents. Mom and Daddy, I love you so much. I'm just going to keep it short. You showed me how to love. You prepared and protected me. Dad, I watched you come home every day from the factory—GM—never crying about the what-ifs, never crying about anything, taking care of our family. You showed me how to be a man, and I thank you and I love you. Mom, as the oldest of your five children, I remember at a young age you explaining to me what teamwork and responsibility meant, because my responsibility was a big one at the time. As the oldest of five, I had to watch the kids and explain to them that, even if it was just cooking, they had to shut up and be quiet because Mommy, even though you had two jobs, was working on another job—something called a master's. And I remember you being at home babysitting, typing, because you didn't have enough to pay. And I remember you getting it done. That's work ethic. I love you.

To my brothers Jeff, Jason, David; my sister, Rachel, I love you guys. My nieces and nephew, Noble, Jordan, Colton, Casey, Leisha. To Detroit, what up doe? What up doe…

Ashley, I love you. Charlene, your nephew thanks you for everything that you've done for him. Pastor London Wood, Dinella Damon, Uncle Leroy Paul, Auntie Maddie Rochelle, your sweet Mickey, thank you. And to my lady, my baby, Erika. My twins, I love you. Thank you for being a wonderful mother to our children.

I'd like to tell all of you a story about a lady named Mrs. Stearnes. Some may know that I have an African American history collection, and sometimes I take them to schools and I speak about the stories behind the faces. Well, Mrs. Stearnes, for me, was a catalyst for my love for history. The first time I fell in love with sports was in her history class. She sparked my love for the history, hypocrisy, the reverence, the absolute power of sport. As class would wind down, before class and recess, Mrs. Stearnes would wow us with stories from the past. We would beg her to tell us more about the greatest players to ever play. And looking back, she took advantage of it by putting that information that we shared upon tests, and we would even celebrate during Black History Month. She spoke of traveling all-star teams and music and food. She told me that we were blessed, that there was a time when, even if we had the obvious talent to compete, there was a gentleman's agreement among the owners that effectively banned blacks from the NBA, NFL, or MLB. She would whisper nightmares about the Klan chasing teams from city to city or recount how it tore at men from the inside not being able to do what they loved. She encouraged us to know our history. She wanted us to familiarize ourselves with some man named Jackie Robinson. She was proud of this man. She spoke [about] him with certainty and conviction.

One day after class, she asked me to stay after. I was worried. I thought I was in trouble, and, thankfully, that wasn't the case. She spoke kindly and softly and said, "I know you get teased a lot, but I see something in you. Everyone does. You have to be like Jackie. You have to be strong. You have to pray, and don't let people get to you. They're going to try to get to you. He was special, and you are too." I didn't know why she told me all this. I didn't even play sports at the time. Then later, at the end of our discussion that day, Mrs. Stearnes pulled out a small picture box and opened it. And she showed me a picture inside and explained to me that the man wearing a baseball hat in the photo, his name was Turkey Stearnes. Turkey Stearnes was her late husband. He started playing baseball professionally in 1920, retiring in 1942. He played for the Detroit Stars and ended up with the Kansas City Monarchs. He's considered one of the greatest baseball players of all time. He batted over .400 three times and led the Negro leagues in home runs seven times. He has fifty more home runs as the number-one hitter than whoever's in second place. To supplement his income, he worked summers in a factory owned by Walter Briggs, owner of the Detroit Tigers—a team that didn't employ blacks.

Now, I know this seems like a down or a baseball story, but to me, this is an existing example of God's grace in my life. You see I was being filled with the energy of those that have been in the struggle. Not just from family and friends but those in my village. Mrs. Stearnes saw something in me before I saw it in myself. Her presence and expectation of my life's potential have stayed with me since our conversation in class that day— not as a burden, but as validation, holding me to a standard. So how can I move forward after having people like that in my life and hearing first-hand accounts of dreams deferred to the past? How can I not think that I must pay it forward or honor those that have paved the way?

And so tonight, just a few miles from Boston, how could I not thank the great Bill Russell, Red Auerbach? How could I not thank others... Yes, please clap for them. How could I not thank Spencer Haywood or Dr. Harry Edwards, Dr. John Carlos, or the Big O and the many other trailblazers that gave themselves or gave up themselves for us and the next generation.

I'd like to thank Temple Christian, my coaches, my teammates there. I'd also like to thank Curtis Hervey, my AAU Coach. Harv, the way I approached the game with preparation and toughness, that was you. Mr. Mont, you know I love you. Iyapo, Kevin, Josh Koby, Antonio Ragland, Mike Jackson, Omar Wedlow, love you guys as well. To the greatest high school coach in Michigan history, my coach, Coach Keener, thank you for being such a great coach. Nedra, I thank you for having his back and having our back with all the food and the barbeques and the honey buns. To the Honorable Dennis Archer and Trudy Archer, thank you for your support and your love and kindness. You helped my transition in high school.

I'd like to tell you a story about Isiah Thomas. He was my guardian angel. Only a few family and friends knew this, but my brothers and I were big fans of Isiah. We would do everything that Isiah did. I would even, after I got to the league, say "Hi, Mom," after every interview because he did it. Now you have to flashback, I'm sixteen years old, and Zeke calls our house to speak to my parents and ask if he could come over and speak with us. He came over to our little shack on Biltmore, shout out to Six Mile, Evergreen, Fenkell, Puritan. He came to the 'hood because I told him he was comin' through. Everyone came out and bothered him. He was just cool, patient, and gracious. After speaking to my parents, Isiah took me aside. You talked, you were kind, you said you understood what I was going through. You told me don't worry. You explained that if

I needed anything you would be there—financially, mentally, spiritually. You're explaining this about the long run and I have to stay focused. Told me don't start believing the press. You told me keep doing my thing because we are more than hoopers.

Zeke, I remember like it was yesterday. You said "we." You gave me confidence, you validated my game through setting your expectation, and finally, you protected me from the vultures. You protected me from the vultures. That's why I never had to take a penny from anyone. You found me. You took time out of your life. You took pressure off of me, and you planted a seed, and I've helped so many kids, only because of your generosity and what you've shown me. Thank you, Isiah. I love you.

To the student body, the alumni, and the faculty and the staff at the University of Michigan, I flat out love you. It was my pleasure to don the number 4 jersey, the maize and blue. I loved every moment at the University of Michigan with my teammates, my brothers. First, I'd like to thank Coach Steve Fisher and his wife, Angie. Coach, your calm approach, focus, and deliberate ways and intense practices allowed us to be ourselves. We could stick to instructions and just let it all hang out. Juwan Howard, Ray Jackson, Jalen Rose, Jimmy King, I love you. All of my former teammates at Michigan, I love you. I can't believe what we accomplished. I'm proud.

I'm always asked what do I think of the Fab Five and, very honestly, I know it was a wild ride, but I stole an email from a friend of mine, Peter Gilbert. I snuck an email, and I would just like to read to the fellas what he wrote, and I can't believe he got it. "The Fab Five is one of the iconic stories of modern day sports history. Five young black men that changed the fabric and culture of sport in American society. Five men that changed the game of basketball. The Fab Five had a brash audacity in everything they did. They played basketball like a house on fire. It was joyful. The Fab Five were not puppets of the system. They played their game. They played as though they knew deep inside that they represented a new day ahead. Basketball was not just a game but a statement. When we played ball, you saw our lives played out on the court. Each one of them represented their families, mentors, and community. Basketball was a culmination of their unique, individual upbringing. They were a movement whether they knew it or not. There were love letters and death threats. They were embraced by many, vilified and hated by more. They played as though they knew deep inside that they are representing a new day ahead." Guys, I still see vestiges of our game, and I'm just so proud of what we've done.

I thank the University of Michigan, I thank the fans, I thank the students, and I love being part of this family.

When I got to the NBA, it was just a great community and, as a rookie, I had so many people to help me. I'd like to thank the late David Stern for all he's done for the game. I'd like to thank commissioner Adam Silver. Anyone who knows the NBA intimately knows that we are a league of men, but we have some boss women running things around here. So, I really like to thank Leah Wilcox and Chrysa Chin. I love me some Leah Wilcox and Chrysa Chin. I'd also like to thank Fallasha Erwin, Bill Strickland, and Reverend Earl Smith. I'd like to thank the fans of Golden State, Mully, Spree, and Billy O. I'd like to thank the city of DC, Chocolate City. You see, I played for a lot of teams. My teammates Ben Wallace, Strickland, Strict Nine, Juwan, Legs, T-Murray, Mureșan, Whit, Cheney, and D. Ham. Buzz Braman, I thank you for helping me get that jumper nice. It's because of you that I can stand here.

Now, to the best fans in the world, to the Sacramento Kings. I just wanted to talk a little bit about God's grace. I want to talk about the fact that God has to lead you, and you're not always supposed to know where you're going or how good it's going to be when you come out on the other side. It's just about trusting him, trusting God, trusting the process. Sacramento, my faith will forever be strong because God gave me you. J. Will, what's up baby? Vlade, Peja, Bibby, Bobby Jack, Doug Christie, Sign Lady, Geoff Petrie, Coach Adelman, thank you for just bringing that style to our game. Erika Bjork, thank you for allowing my charities to do so well and to work with the communities. Thank you for keeping me connected to the Sacramento community.

Thank [you to] the Philadelphia 76ers. AI, you were the best player I ever played with and then it was an honor to rock with you every day on the court. I'll just skip and say finally, the Pistons, Joe D. Chauncey, Rip, it was an honor to be able to play in my city with you guys. Thank you.

To my man Charles Barkley, I'm honored to have you welcome me into the Hall of Fame. You changed the way the game was played from a powerful position. Personally, you have shown me the way in life more than once. The first time was high school. Rick Mahorn brought you by, and I got a chance to meet you. I studied your game, I knew your truth. I knew your attitude. You complimented me and encouraged me and, for the first time after seeing you, I thought, "Hey, maybe I could do this if my favorite player says I can." The second time, I just want to thank you on behalf of all athletes for what you've done with life after basketball.

I've never left basketball, and I've been a part of the NBA for close to thirty years between playing and commentating. The reason I've had such longevity is because of you. You wrote the playbook: be honest, be yourself, and whatever happens happens. Charles, I know others open the door for you as far as athletes and commentators but personally, Charles, everything changed with you. So, on behalf of any athlete on TV today that gets to share their opinion based on their experience, I want to give you your flowers and say thank you. You've made millions for many. Thank you.

I'll be quick, and speaking of commentating, the journey after life, I'd like to thank Marv Albert, my partner on air for the last several years. You were a joy to work with. I learned so much from you. Our discussions on basketball were some of the best. Dick Stockton, Reggie Miller, thank you for showing me how to prepare for games. Steve Kerr, Kevin Harlan, and the many producers, directors, and PAs that work with me, thank you very much.

I'd like to thank my business partners, Lavetta Willis and Jason Wild. You guys, we've done some big things and to follow in the footsteps of those like Magic Johnson and Dave Bing, Isiah, Vinnie Johnson, and Junior Bridgeman is an aspiration. Thank you guys for setting the bar and taking your game out of the league but excelling in business as well.

And lastly, it would be unfair if I didn't talk, or it wouldn't be right, I'd be remiss if I didn't get to talk about moments that raised you. I talked about all the wonderful people that helped put into my life and, again Kevin, Iyapo, Adrian, Vince. If I missed anyone else in high school, I'm sorry. But there are moments, moments that raise you as well. Moments when you have to stand alone. Moments when you can't cop out. Moments when all you can do is stand. Moments when you question everything. There's no guarantee in winning. Sports is the most fair platform because it's unfair to everyone. I know a little about that, but it's all about the commitment. It's all about the moments when people doubt you. Wins aren't guaranteed, the losses are. And I'm just here to tell you: no matter who you are—a champion like Kevin Garnett or Isiah or Paul Pierce, Ben Wallace—or a guy like myself that just went through the league and did my thing, you're gonna have to bounce back. And I would hope for many athletes that you do take mental health very seriously and you get help, but also I would like to tell others... [clapping] thank you. But also I'd like to tell others that hopefully you can embrace sport, embrace the fact that there's no guarantee, and face the fact that that's why we get to work early and leave late. Embrace the fact that I'm still the same dude that had to go up against KG, Tim, Shaq, Keem, all these guys in a week. Just embrace the journey. Embrace it, embrace it, embrace it. Do not run from it. And if anybody ever wants to know how I feel, there's a song by Marvin Sapp. It goes, "I never should have made it. I never would have made it without you. I would have lost it all, but now I see you were there for me. I can say I'm stronger, I'm wiser, I'm better, I'm so much better. When I look back at all you've brought me through, I can see now that you were the one I held on to." Thank you, very much.

Chapter 87

Never could have made it, without you
I would have lost it all
But now I see how you were there for me
And I can say
Never would have made it
Never could have made it without you
I would have lost it all
But now I see how you were there for me and I can say
I'm stronger, I'm wiser
I'm better, much better
When I look back over all you brought me through
I can see that you were the one I held on to
And I never, never would have made it
Oh I never could have made it,
never could have made it without you
Oh I would have lost it all
Oh but now I see how you were there for me
I never, never would have made it
No, I never, never could have made it without you
I would have lost my mind a long time ago
If it had not been for you
I am stronger, I am stronger
I am wiser, now I'm better
So much better
I made it through my storm
And my test because you were there
To carry me through my mess
I am stronger, I am stronger
I am wiser, I am wiser
I am better, I am better

"Never Would Have Made It"
Marvin Sapp

Never Would Have Made It

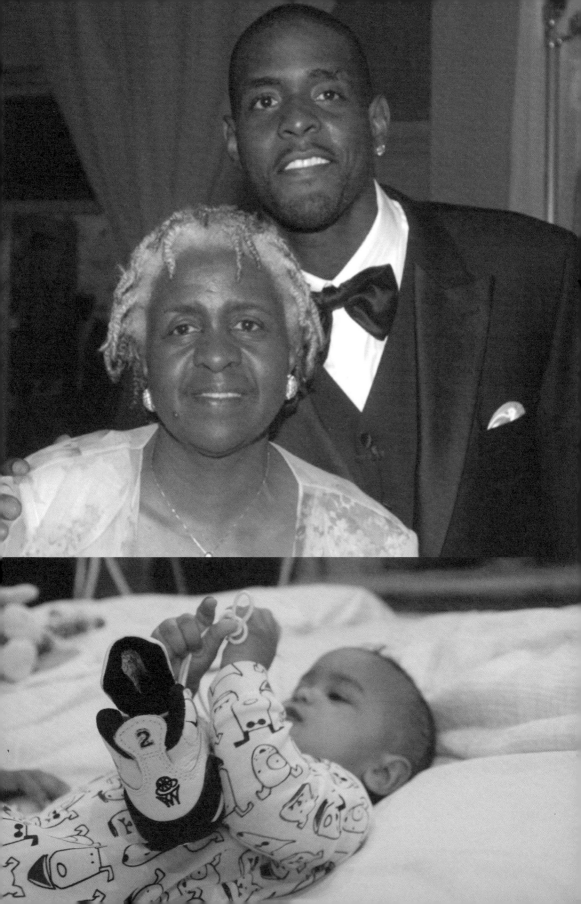

Acknowledgments

To my teammates, Naren Aryal, Steven Beer, Kevin Cottrell, Danny Moore, Kristin Perry, and Lavetta Willis.

Thank you for your many contributions to this work of love. I appreciate you. You help make this a reality. I'm forever grateful.

Index

Italicized entries denote page numbers for select photos

Photo Credits

Unless otherwise noted in the book or below, all photos in *By God's Grace* are courtesy of the Webber Family.

Page 88:	James Drake/*Sports Illustrated* via Getty Images
Page 131:	Courtesy of Adrian Tonnon
Page 142:	Courtesy of Peter Gibbons
Page 152:	Courtesy of Trudy Archer
Page 165:	Courtesy of V. Archer
Page 166:	Courtesy of V. Archer
Page 218:	"Fab Five," University of Michigan Basketball, 1992/93, BL0072352, Robert Kalmbach, Athletic Department (University of Michigan) records, Bentley Historical Library, University of Michigan.
Page 220–221:	USA TODAY Sports
Page 230:	"Fab Five," University of Michigan Basketball, 1993, BL007350, Robert Kalmbach, Athletic Department (University of Michigan) records, Bentley Historical Library, University of Michigan.
Page 234:	"1993 Basketball Media," 1993, BL010114, Unknown, Athletic Department (University of Michigan) records, Bentley Historical Library, University of Michigan.
Page 236:	Courtesy of Charlene Johnson
Page 240–241:	"Fab Five and Steve Fisher, UM Men's Basketball, 1992," 1992, BL010131, Unknown, Athletic Department (University of Michigan) records, Bentley Historical Library, University of Michigan.
Page 248–249:	Andrew D. Bernstein/NBAE via Getty Images
Page 258:	David E. Klutho/*Sports Illustrated* via Getty Images
Page 264:	John W. McDonough/*Sports Illustrated* via Getty Images
Page 268:	"Penny Hardaway, John Wooden, Chris Webber, at 1993 Wooden Award Ceremony," 1993, BL012775, Unknown, Athletic Department (University of Michigan) records, Bentley Historical Library, University of Michigan.
Pages 294–295:	Courtesy of the Coleman A. Young Foundation
Pages 296–297:	Lou Capozzola/NBAE via Getty Images
Pages 298–299:	Martha Jane Stanton/NBAE via Getty Images
Page 300:	Allen Einstein/NBAE via Getty Images
Page 308:	Nathaniel S. Butler/NBAE via Getty Images
Pages 314–315:	Sam Forencich/NBAE via Getty Images
Page 318:	Sam Forencich/NBAE via Getty Images
Page 328:	Rocky Widner/NBAE via Getty Images
Pages 358–359:	Brian Bahr via Getty Images
Pages 368–369:	Rocky Widner/NBAE via Getty Images
Page 380:	Bryan Patrick/ZUMA Press via Alamy
Page 382:	Rocky Widner/NBAE via Getty Images
Pages 388–389:	Kevin Winter/ImageDirect via Getty Images
Page 394:	John G. Mabanglo/AFP via Getty Images
Pages 408–409:	Glenn James/NBAE via Getty Images
Page 418:	Greg Nelson /*Sports Illustrated* via Getty Images
Page 420:	Rocky Widner/NBAE via Getty Images
Page 429:	Fernando Medina/NBAE via Getty Images
Page 430:	*Sporting News* via Getty Images.
Pages 432–433:	D. Lippitt/Einstein/NBAE via Getty Images
Pages 434–435:	Allen Einstein/NBAE via Getty Images
Pages 450–451:	Rocky Widner/NBAE via Getty Images
Pages 452–453:	Rocky Widner/NBAE via Getty Images
Pages 454–455:	Rocky Widner/NBAE via Getty Images
Page 515:	Courtesy of Erika Bjork
Back Cover:	Rocky Widner/ NBAE via Getty Images

Webber Publishing Group

By God's Grace

Page 283: "Pick Yourself Up" written by Dorothy Fields and Jerome Kern

Pages 262–263: North Carolina vs. Michigan (Men), April 5, 1993, Box Score courtesy of Sports-Reference.com

Page 509: Photo credits

For more information, please visit:
webberpublishinggroup.com

Cover and interior design by Danny Moore

Library of Congress Control Number: 2019916334
CPSIA Code: PRFRE0124A
ISBN-13: 978-1-64543-277-7

Printed in Canada